HB
171
.M5569   Modern economic
1988   classics--
         evaluations
         through time

$57.00

DATE			

MODERN ECONOMIC CLASSICS—
EVALUATIONS THROUGH TIME

GARLAND REFERENCE LIBRARY
OF SOCIAL SCIENCE
(Vol. 424)

MODERN ECONOMIC CLASSICS—
EVALUATIONS THROUGH TIME

Bernard S. Katz
and
Ronald E. Robbins

GARLAND PUBLISHING, INC. • NEW YORK & LONDON
1988

Library of Congress Cataloging-in-Publication Data

Modern economic classics—evaluations through time/[edited by]
Bernard S. Katz and Ronald E. Robbins.
p.cm.—(Garland reference library of social science; vol.
424)
Includes bibliographies and index.
ISBN 0–8240–7793–8 (alk. paper)
1. Economics. 2. Economics literature. I. Katz, Bernard, 1932– .
II. Robbins, Ronald E., 1942– . III. Series: Garland reference
library of social science; v. 424.

HB171.M5569 1988 330—dc19 87–32785 CIP

Printed on acid-free, 250-year-life paper
Manufactured in the United States of America

Dedicated to our parents

CONTENTS

PREFACE   xiii

ACKNOWLEDGEMENTS   xv

                PART ONE: ECONOMIC THEORY

Progress and Poverty, by Henry George

  1. REVIEW   1
      Quarterly Review, 1883

  2. "The Forgotten Man: Henry George,"   5
      George R. Geiger, 1941

  3. "Progress and Poverty's Continuing Challenge,"   14
      James M. Roberts, 1971

The Theory of the Leisure Class, by Thorstein Veblen

  4. REVIEW   25
      D. Collin Wells, 1899

  5. *Prejudices*,   30
      Henry L. Mencken, 1919

  6. "A New Theory of Thorstein Veblen,"   43
      John Kenneth Galbraith, 1973

  7. REVIEW   59
      Raymond Vernon, 1974

The Theory of Monopolistic Competition, by Edward Chamberlin

8. REVIEW   65
    Morris A. Copeland, 1934

9. "On Maximizing Profits: A Distinction Between
        Chamberlin and Robertson,"   70
    Stephen Enke, 1951

10. "The Impact on Industrial Organization,"   82
    Joe S. Bain, 1963

11. "Chamberlin's Monopolistic Competition:
        Neoclassical or Institutional?,"   86
    R.D. Peterson, 1979

The General Theory of Employment, Interest and Money,
    by John Maynard Keynes

12. REVIEW   108
    G. D. H. Cole, 1936

13. REVIEW   112
    Horace Taylor, 1936

14. "Keynes and the General Theory,"   115
    Alvin H. Hansen, 1946

15. "After Twenty Years: The General Theory,"   125
    James R. Schlesinger, 1956

16. "Keynes Today,"   137
    Joan Robinson and Francis Cripps, 1979

17. "Keynes' Politics in Theory and Practice,"   143
    James Tobin, 1983

Social Choice and Individual Values, by Kenneth J. Arrow

18. REVIEW   154
    Harold M. Somers, 1952

19. REVIEW   155
    Irving M. Copi, 1952

20. "Arrow and the 'New Welfare' Economics --
    A Restatement,"   158
    E. J. Mishan, 1958

21. "Kenneth Arrow's Contribution to Economics,"   161
    Carl Christian von Weizsäcker, 1971

22. REVIEW   163
    John Broome, 1984

PART TWO: POLITICAL ECONOMY

Imperialism: A Study, by J. A. Hobson, and *Imperialism: The
  Highest Stage of Capitalism*, by V. I. Lenin

23. REVIEW   166
    Paul S. Reinsch, 1908

24. REVIEW   169
    The *Economist*, 1939

25. "The Meaning of Economic Imperialism,"   171
    James O'Conner, 1970

26. "Lindsey's Lenin and the Problem of Imperialism," 183
    Mark Obrinsky, 1984

27. "Hobson, Wilshire, and the Capitalist Theory
    of Capitalist Imperialism,"   195
    Peter J. Cain, 1985

The Modern Corporation and Private Property,
  by A. A. Berle, Jr. and Gardiner C. Means

28. REVIEW   203
    I. Maurice Wormser, 1932

29. REVIEW   206
    Stuart Chase, 1933

30. REVIEW   211
    Charles A. Beard, 1933

31. "The Corporation Gap,"   214
    Robert Lekachman, 1968

32. "The Literature of Economics: The Case of
        Berle and Means,"   220
    George J. Stigler and Claire Friedland, 1983

Capitalism, Socialism and Democracy, by Joseph A. Schumpeter

33. REVIEW   241
    Charles R. Walker, 1943

34. REVIEW   242
    Ralph H. Blodgett, 1943

35. "Schumpeter as a Teacher and Economic Theorist,"   245
    Paul A. Samuelson, 1951

36. "Address to the Entering Class at Harvard
        College 1972,"   256
    D.P. Moynihan, 1973

37. "Schumpeter,"   263
    Peter F. Drucker, 1983

The Road to Serfdom, by Friederich A. Hayek

38. REVIEW   270
    Charles E. Merriam, 1944

39. REVIEW   273
    Henry Hazlitt, 1944

40. "Freedom, Planning, and Totalitarianism:
        The Reception of F. A. Hayek's *The Road
        to Serfdom*,"   277
    Theodore Rosenof, 1974

The Affluent Society, by John Kenneth Galbraith

41. REVIEW   298
    David M. Potter, 1958

42. REVIEW   300
    Time Magazine, 1958

43. "The Affluent Society After Twenty-Five Years,"   301
    J.R. Stanfield, 1983

PART THREE: EMPERICAL ECONOMIC STUDIES

Business Cycles, by Wesley Clair Mitchell

44. REVIEW   321
    O. M. W. Sprague, 1913

45. "Mitchell's Business Cycles,"   324
    Joseph Schumpeter, 1930

46. "Wesley Mitchell in Retrospect,"   329
    Geoffrey H. Moore, 1978

A Monetary History of the United States, 1867-1960,
    by Milton Friedman and Anna Jacobson Schwartz

47. REVIEW   339
    Robert M. Solow, 1964

48. REVIEW   347
    Harry G. Johnson, 1965

49. "The New Economic Faith,"   358
    Robert B. Zevin, 1981

PART FOUR: MANAGEMENT

The Principles of Scientific Management,
    by Frederick Winslow Taylor

50. REVIEW   367
    Engineering Record, 1911

51. "Frederick Winslow Taylor Revisted,"   368
    J. Boddewyn, 1961

52. "Frederick Winslow Taylor, The Messiah of
        Time and Motion,"   380
    Spencer Klaw, 1979

The Practice of Management, by Peter F. Drucker

53. REVIEW   395
    Leo Teplow, 1955

54. REVIEW   400
    Asa Briggs, 1955

55. "An Evaluation of the Practice of Management,"   402
    Ronald Ritchie, 1970

56. "The Other Half of the Message,"   414
    Tom Peters, 1985

NAME INDEX   421

PREFACE

It may appear axiomatic that great books have survived
the ravages of critical review. Students of economics and
business, however, may tend to forget that these works begin
and live their lives embroiled in controversy. The editors
of this volume believe that readers should be made aware of
the trial of these treatises: that different generations of
critics may well set standards that differ from the preceding
assuring reevaluations of great works.

In this book we have included the reviews of thirteen
classics, some of which have survived, relatively unscathed,
the critical review of time, while others, of varying vintage,
are still wrapped in the ribbons of debate. In order to relate the critical journeys that are taken by great books we
have chosen a simple route - the words of its reviewers. Each
major work chosen is commented on by important critics in
different eras. We have chosen early, middle and late period
reviews to obtain the sense of how the classic has been viewed
through its years. Our choices of the specific reviews and
reviewers are, indeed, biased. On the one hand we have sought
dissident views, and on the other, complimentary ones. We did
not actively seek polarization among reviewers, we sought only
other perspectives. Whenever possible, in order to give flesh
to these worldly authors, we have introduced those commentaries
that have also given the profile of the person and of their
times. We sought the readable reviews, those lacking jargon
and excessive technical technical detail as we have aimed the
tone of the book to the college trained, but non-professional
reader. We are secure, however, that the reviews cross professional and non-professional lines.

The specific works chosen are but a selection of a broader
landscape. All those works of greater, or lesser, impact will
be reserved for another day. However, each of our choices
have significantly contributed in shaping our current knowledge
and perspectives. In one instance we have taken two books
and treated them as a single entry, Hobson's and Lenin's works
on imperialism, as in many ways they treat the same concept
with a similar analysis.

The reviewed books are grouped into four major categories: economic theory, empirical economic studies, political economy, and management. Within each of the general classifications the books and reviews are presented in chronological order. The broad categories chosen fill a need for economics and business students as they become introduced to the great books. On one hand, those undergraduate students interested in economic thought may well find the points of view expressed as alternative interpretations from their own understanding and perspective. They may also find a reinforcement. For those who may desire but a summary of the classics and an insight to the writers will also find this volume rewarding. It is suggested that this book be perceived as an in-depth, but truncated, annotated bibliography for each of the classics.

Our ambition in compiling this volume is to provide the reader with the recognition that great works of economics are always lively areas of controversy.

ACKNOWLEDGEMENTS

The preparation of a volume such as this required the involvement of many individuals, some known, more unknown. To the general resources of Lafayette College and to those who are distinctly recognizable, Carol Riffert, Elaine Molchan, Carmela Karns, and Carolyn Lee, we offer our gratitude. To our families, we offer an apology for the stolen time.

This volume has completely relied on the words and efforts of others. If this book is of value it is they to whom credit should be given. Permission to reproduce the reviews and essays have been granted by Management Review, "The Modern Corporation and Private Property," Nov., 1932, © 1932, "The Practice of Management," February, 1955, © 1955, American Management Association, New York, all rights reserved; "An Economist's View of Planning," copyright © 1944, "The Corporation Gap," copyright © 1968, by the New York Times Company; "Between Two Worlds," © 1958 Saturday Review magazine; "Keynes Today," M.E. Sharpe, Inc., Armonk, New York 10504; "Twentieth-Century Classics Revisited," Vol. 102, No. 1, Winter, 1974, Daedalus, Journal of the American Academy of Arts and Sciences, Boston, MA; "The Forgotten Man: Henry George," copyright © 1941, by the Antioch Review; "Principles of Scientific Management," reprinted from ENR, August 5, 1911, copyright © McGraw-Hill, Inc., all rights reserved; the reviews by C. R. Walker, and D. Collin Wells, The Yale Review, copyright © Yale University Press; "The Affluent Society," copyright © 1958 Time, Inc., all rights reserved; "The Meaning of Economic Imperialism," copyright © 1970 by Monthly Review Press, Monthly Review Foundation; New Management, "The Other Half of the Message" by Tom Peters, copyright © 1985; "After Twenty Years: The General Theory," by James R. Schlesinger, Quarterly Journal of Economics, copyright © 1956, reprinted by permission of John Wiley & Sons, Inc.; and the review by Charles A. Beard in the New York Tribune, copyright © 1933, reprinted by permission of I.H.T. Corp. We would also like to thank Peter Drucker, John Murray, J. Boddewyn, Spencer Klaw, J.K. Galbraith, Basil Blackwell Ltd., The Economist, The Banker, Robert B. Zevin, the Progressive Labor Party, Paul Samuelson, George Stigler and Claire Friedland, the Cambridge Univ. Press, and the New Statesman and Nation for their permissions.

Modern Economic Classics—
Evaluations Through Time

Progress and Poverty
by
Henry George

REVIEW: Editorial Staff (1883)*

There has been a strong disposition among certain English
critics to regard Mr. George as though he were nothing more than
a charlatan, and to think, upon that ground, that a passing
sneer will dispose of him. In both these views we consider them
wholly wrong; but even were the first of them never so well
founded, we should fail to see in it the least support for the
second. Were Mr. George's subject mathematics or Biblical
prophecy, then no doubt the case would be widely different. An
ingenious writer, not many years ago, maintained that the earth
was shaped like a Bath bun; and another, that Mr. Gladstone was
the real beast of the Revelation; but had Dr. Tyndall lectured
against the first theory in Albermarle Street, or had Canon
Farrar denounced the second at Westminster, we should have
thought the distinguished critics about as wise as the men they
criticized. We do not find a 'Janus' crossing swords with the
Jumpers, nor the Astronomer Royal refuting Zadkiel's Almanac.
But though the Zadkiels and the Jumpers of abstract science and
theology are for ever safe from any serious notice, and reach
their highest honour when we sometimes condescend to smile at
them, the moment they enter the domain of politics they become
amenable to a new kind of tribunal.

Our meaning is not recondite. False theories, when they
bear directly upon action, do not claim our attention in proportion to the talent they are supported by, but in proportion to
the extent to which action is likely to be influenced by them;
and since action in modern politics so largely depends on the
people, the wildest errors are grave, if they are only sufficiently popular. How they strike the wise is a matter of small
moment; the great question is, how they will strike the ignorant; and the modern politician, who disdains to discuss a doctrine merely because none but the very ignorant could be duped
by it, acts much like a man who lets himself be knocked down by
a burglar, because his honour will not permit him to fight any
one but a gentleman. Thus it is easy to call Mr. George's

1

proposals ridiculous, and to say that his fallacies have been again and again refuted; but nothing is gained by these facile and futile sarcasms. For practical purposes no proposals are ridiculous unless they are ridiculous to the mass of those who may act upon them; in any question in which the people are powerful, no fallacy is refuted if the people still believe in it; and were Mr. George's book even a lower class of production than it has ever been said to be by its most supercilious critics, we should not, for that reason, in the present condition of things, esteem it one jot less worthy of a full and candid analysis.

Let those who disagree with us consider the following facts. 'Progress and Poverty,' whatever its merits or its demerits, is remarkable first and foremost as containing one special proposal. This is a proposal, urged with the utmost plainness, for the wholesale and indiscriminate plunder of all landed proprietors. We say *plunder*, and we use the word advisedly; that, and that alone, will express Mr. George's meaning. Other writers have again and again suggested that it would be well if the class in question could be bought out by the State; but Mr. George's point is, that there shall be no buying in the matter. Let us not buy them out; let us simply use force and turn them out. 'That,' he says, 'is a much more direct and easy way; nor is it right,' he adds, 'that there should be any concern about them.' Now without pausing at present to comment on this teaching, let us ask simply what success it has met with. 'Progress and Poverty' has been published but for three years--for 'three years in America, and in England' only one. In America its sale was so large and rapid, that it had already gone through a hundred editions there, before it was known by so much as its name here; and here, though its circulation has been most probably smaller, its reception in some ways has been even more significant. In America the author, so far as we have been able to learn, has failed hitherto to make any practical converts. He has been more fortunate on this side of the Atlantic. One of the chiefs of the Irish Land League has become his enthusiastic disciple; and what was yesterday the mere aspiration of the thinker will probably tomorrow be the actual demand of the agitator. Nor is this all, or nearly all. Mr. George's London publishers have lately reissued his book in an ultra-popular form. It is at this moment selling by thousands in the alleys and back streets of England, and is being audibly welcomed there as a glorious gospel of justice. If we may credit a leading Radical journal, it is fast forming a new public opinion. The opinion we here allude to is no doubt that of the half-educated; but this makes the matter in some ways more serious. No classes are so dangerous, at once to themselves and to others, as those which have learnt to reason, but not to reason

rightly. They are able to recognize the full importance of
argument, but not to distinguish a false argument from a true
one. Thus any theory that serves to flatter their passions will,
if only put plausibly, find their minds at its mercy. They will
fall victims to it, as though to an intellectual pestilence. Mr.
George's book is full of this kind of contagion. A ploughman
might snore, or a country gentleman smile over it, but it is well
calculated to turn the head of an artizan.

This alone would suffice to give it a grave importance; but
half of the story yet remains to be told. It is not the poor,
it is not the seditious only, who have been thus affected by Mr.
George's doctrines. They have received a welcome, which is even
more singular, amongst certain sections of the really instructed
classes. They have been gravely listened to by a conclave of
English clergymen. Scotch ministers and Nonconformist professors have done more than listen--they have received them with
marked approval; they have even held meetings, and given lectures to disseminate them. Finally, certain trained economic
thinkers, or men who pass for such in at least one of our Universities are reported to have said that they see no means of
refuting them, and that they probably mark the beginning of a
new political epoch.

It is easy to think too much of the importance of facts
like these; it is equally easy to think far too little of them.
It is to this latter extreme, we fear, that the Conservative
party inclines; we have therefore no hesitation in putting our
case strongly. We say once more, and with even greater emphasis, that were Mr. George's arguments intrinsically never so
worthless, were his knowledge never so slight, his character
never so contemptible, his book has acquired an importance, from
the special success it has met with, which would make it our
duty to examine its widest falsehoods with the same attention we
should give to the gravest truths.

We have other reasons, however, for taking Mr. George seriously. Our arguments thus far have supposed him to be a charlatan pure and simple; but we have supposed that for argument's
sake only. Our own judgment of him is something widely different. It is true, as we purpose presently to show in detail,
that in all his main positions, he is as false to fact as the
most cracked-brained astrologer, and as hostile to society in
his proposals as the most malignant criminal; but in spite of
this, he himself is neither criminal nor crack-brained. In tone
and in moral method he betrays many faults and weaknesses. His
self-conceit is inordinate, his temper is often petulant, his
finer feelings are so tainted with self-consciousness, that he

can rarely express them without striking an attitude; and his
practical programme, as we have seen, is monstrous. None the
less we believe that, in spite of all these defects, the intention he has started with is thoroughly pure and honest; and
that, however his character may change for the worse hereafter,
he is at present an unselfish philanthropist. He is the friend
of the poor, he is not the enemy of the rich. He seeks to save,
not to ruin civilization; and he almost equals a Czar or an
English Tory in his hatred and horror of our modern proletarian
anarchists. Morally, therefore, he fully deserves a hearing;
and our condemnation of his doctrines, though it will certainly
not be softened, will at least be accompanied by a certain respect for himself. What we have said of his character applies
with equal force to his intellect. Grave as his errors are,
they are the errors of a vigorous thinker; and he falls into delusions which most men would escape from, from perceiving arguments that most men would be blind to. It is indeed no exaggeration to say, that he uses more logical strength in flounder-
ing in the quicksands of falsehood, than has sufficed to carry
others far up the rocks of truth. Should any reader, out of
prejudice, be inclined to question this, let him turn aside from
Mr. George's main thesis, to the remarks he makes by the way,
and to his handling of subsidiary subjects. We shall there find
not only casual sentences which have all the terseness, and more
than the truth of Hobbes; we shall find chapters also in which
certain of the most cherished delusions of Radicalism are sub-
mitted to a keener and far more merciless criticism than they
have ever met with since they began their wretched existence.
Mr. George's power will thus be at once apparent. In the
strength with which he attacks one order of falsehoods, we shall
learn the strength with which he supports another; and if the
delusions to which he is himself a victim are greater and more
dangerous than those over which he triumphs, this will only form
the weightiest reason possible why we ourselves should try to
dispel the former. The difficulty of the task is, we think, not
equal to its importance. It has required greater skill on Mr.
George's part to see his way into his errors, than it will require on ours to see the way out of them.

If this be the case, however, it is but fair to Mr. George
to acknowledge that, in some measure, we have his own talent to
thank for it. His book is a model of logical and lucid arrangement. He shows us exactly what he wants to prove, and the exact
steps by which he means to prove it. The track of his thought
is thus so distinctly marked, that we can at once see where he
stumbles or goes astray, or where he jumps instead of bridging a
chasm. Half the ease we find in proving his meaning false is
due to the clearness with which he shows what his meaning is.

The great problem which he attempts to solve is as follows: He starts with reminding us that the present century has been, so far as material progress goes, the most astonishing period in all of human history. Wealth has increased beyond the dreams of the alchemists. Science and industry have performed greater miracles than any foreseen by Bacon in his visions of the new Atlantis. Nor do the wonders show any signs of ceasing. Scarcely a week passes without some new achievement--some new invention which will minister to our comfort, or help us to escape from some immemorial evil. But there is an evil which, amidst all this progress, nothing touches, nothing seems to alleviate. On the contrary, it is growing daily greater; and, having long been a disgrace, it will soon be a menace to our civilization. That evil is the poverty of the industrial classes. It is true that, in some sense, the poor have been always with us; but never before were their numbers or their misery so great and so portentous as they are, or are fast becoming. 'Material progress,' says Mr. George, 'does not merely fail to relieve poverty; it actually produces it': and it can be seen to do so, he adds, under such varieties of local circumstance, that the fact in question is plainly no mere accident, but is bound up in some way with material progress itself. Here, he exclaims (we are quoting his own words), 'is the great enigma of our times. It is the central fact from which spring the industrial, social, and political difficulties that perplex the world, and with which statesmanship and philanthropy and education grapple in vain. From it come the clouds that overhang the future of the most self-reliant nations. It is the riddle which the Sphinx of Fate puts to our civilization, and which not to answer is to be destroyed.' Mr. George in his present volume undertakes to answer it. He engages to show us, not only why poverty is connected with progress, but further, that the connection is not in any way necessary; that the evil is artificial, not natural; and that it is in our power almost at once to cure it. . .

*Quarterly Review, Vol. 155, (January 1883):19-21

"The Forgotten Man: Henry George": George R. Geiger (1941)*

One of the most curious anomalies of the entire literature of social reform has been the almost total neglect, even ignorance, in liberal and progressive circles of the work of Henry George. He is indeed the forgotten man, apparently the unmentionable. Try to find a reference to him in, say, the New Republic or the Nation. (Even the New Masses and the Daily Worker are a little more generous. Once in a while they remem-

ber his anniversaries and have some unaccountably charitable
things to say about him.) This ignorance occasionally has ludi-
crous results. Not that George is confused by the allegedly literate with Lloyd George, but it's almost as bad as that when Mr.
George Catlin (certainly an alleged literate) writes in his rather recent *Story of the Political Philosophers* that the George
Junior Republic in New York State--a colony for the young--was
established as an outgrowth of Henry George's work! Which is
about the same as suggesting that Karl is one of those funny Marx
Brothers, or that he helps run a men's clothing chain with a cou-
ple of other fellows. A trivial point surely--possibly even a
typographical error. ....Although, as some wag has put it, they
can't *all* be typographical errors. The omissions of George are
not all inadvertent. There are reasons, then. What are they?
The following catalogue is perhaps not complete, and it is certainly uneven, containing both good and bad reasons--and all of
them insufficient ground for the neglectful contempt that our
present-day intelligentsia professes towards George's philosophy:
He is connected with "the land question," and that is out
of date.
He believed in a "single tax" which was to be a utopian
panacea.
He believed in classical economics.
He believed in God.
He has no standing in academic circles: it is not sophisticated to refer to Henry George as it is to mention Thorstein
Veblen.

Look at the single taxers! They are all crackpots--vege-
tarians, theosophists, spiritualists, Esperantists, believers in
chiropractic and anarchism.

He was perhaps a pioneer in American political economy, the
economically literate might acknowledge, but no more important
than Daniel Raymond or Thomas Cooper.

And so on. To be sure, arguments such as these, whether or
not they are caricatures or straw men, are seldom explicit.
They don't have to be, since for most individuals it is unnecessary to give reasons for not paying attention to Henry George:
he is simply outside their universe of discourse.

This may be a very negative approach to the American economist and philosopher, but negative is the word to use in referring to his reception today. Now, the purpose here is certainly
not to refute all the arguments which have been used to ration-
alize this inattention. In fact, some of them are irrefutable,
e.g., the one about single taxers. Admittedly they are the chief

trouble with the "single tax" (whatever might be implied by that
very inaccurate phrase); and all that could be essayed in this
area would be the usual *tu quoque* argument, viz., look at all
the other brethren of social reform! Would Marx be a Marxist
(and of which variety) were he alive today? Try the same with
all rebels and their followers--including Jesus. There will always be the lunatic fringe. To judge social theory in terms of
it is to confuse economics and politics with psychiatry. But
even if all the arguments cannot be examined, an attempt will be
made to look at a few of the more significant of the reasons for
disregarding the work of George.

Possibly the most serious of these is the misconception
which lingers about the phrase "the land question." George's
reputation stands or falls in direct proportion to the attention
given to land as an economic factor. But apparently land has
become old-fashioned, something bucolic which may affect a few
Southern novelists with a wistful nostalgia. At most it refers
to the need for preventing erosion and for conserving natural
resources (as if land itself were not *the* natural resource).
That "land" might have a more elemental referent than fertile
prairies and grassy plains and virgin forests seems as implausi-
ble as the opening of another frontier. Indeed, as Gilbert
Chesterton complained, "our urban populations have virtually
forgotten that we all live on land." Our contemporary economic
architects have been equally forgetful. To be sure, there have
recently been a few sporting admissions that "Henry George may
have been right after all," or that in town and regional planning more attention must be paid to increased land value taxation. But certainly there have been indications of serious
blindness in the drawing of social patterns and the planning of
political structures. There are programs and there are plans,
all of them seemingly founded on the proposition that industry
and capital and finance are ethereal essences, floating about
balloon-like, quite aloof from the ground.

Henry George had a very different approach to "the land
question." It was for him a concept as much metaphysical as
economic. Land was Nature. It was our own Earth. It was all
that was unmade by man, the physical world which provided the
foundation for each of his efforts. Without land man was as
rootless as a pulled flower. But metaphysics is unpopular now.
So is classical economics. Therefore the sweep of meaning which
George gave to land seems dated and irrelevant, too bound up
with the rationalism of the traditional land-labor-capital distinctions. It's a profound pity, however, that the fallacy of
association has to operate here so crudely, causing the obloquy
which has been attached to metaphysics and classical political

economy to fall upon the idea of land itself. For "the land
question" can stand upon its own feet, quite independent of the
benefits (or the handicaps) of classicism.

First of all, whatever it is called—by the standard term
of "land" or by something more modern—there is a physical base
for the economic process. It does not have to be celebrated by
metaphysics or rhetoric: it is literal not poetic. Men labor
and produce goods; the goods are distributed and consumed, directly or in a roundabout fashion. This is the *physical* process
which economics studies (although economists are often more fas-
cinated by the psychological processes involved in demand and
motivation). Now, to confine discussion of this process to the
worker, or to his tools, or to the esoteric manipulation of the
fiscal means by which the worker is able (rather, unable) to buy
back the goods he produces, without casting even the most fur-
tive of glances at the geographical site which the worker uses,
or at the raw materials which he transforms into commodities, or
at the avenues of transportation which distribute the goods, is
certainly a symptom of some kind of allergy. To be sure, the
phrase "raw materials" does have a familiar ring these days!
The war and national defense have had some disintoxicating effects upon our economic smugness.

But what magic has "raw materials" which "land" does not
have? Certainly it is not simply Henry George who would insist
that natural resources are but one element of "land," more spectacular but just as earth-bound as the familiar Illinois-prairie,
barn-yard connotation of the word. It should be superfluous—at
least for those who have taken the trouble to read George—to
point out that the most sedentary of accountants, working in
some lofty aerie of a New York skyscraper, is using land—in
fact, using perhaps the most precious land on earth. (The absurd paradox of the matter seems to be that the more valuable
land is, the more it tends to be ignored—at least by many who
consider themselves to be both progressive and economically literate.) It should be equally gratuitous to indicate the crushing economic power that resides in franchises, rights-of-way,
control of industrial sites, and all the myriad aspects of what
in economics is so harmlessly designated as "land."

Whether this is a problem for semantics raises a nice issue.
In one sense that problem has already been raised by those not
exactly liberal archcritics of George, Messrs. Ely and Seligman.
They have asserted again and again, in their most graciously pa-
tronizing style, that "land," as used by George and his followers, is much too broad an economic term. There are many kinds
of land, and therefore one must be more specific and talk about

this kind of land or that. (Had they been writing at present they would have undoubtedly made much use of the semantical subscript.) Thus, there is no "land question." There are specific problems of adjustment here and there. Now, this approach has a realistic and plausible, even pragmatic, tone; it becomes specious, however, when we remember that Henry George was a social reformer, perhaps an unsung revolutionary. For he used "land" as Marx used "labor" and "capital." That is to say, beyond the economic analysis, which both men elaborated rigorously, there was the cry for action. The Ely-Seligman argument could show that similarly there is no problem of "labor," or of "capital," or of class conflict because there is no referent for labor or capital or even for class consciousness. And that argument might be sound if all that language did was to communicate information. But language is hortatory and persuasive; it arouses emotion and directs action.

The denial that there is any "land" is of a piece with the psuedosophisticated denial that there are "natural rights," or that "all men are created equal," or that "labor creates value." Denials like these have a sophomoric illumination which give a sense of superiority, the superiority of finding out that there isn't any Santa Claus. But, as has been pointed out many times, these admittedly abstract, sometimes even unreal, concepts of economics and politics are to be understood as strong weapons for social change. They are presumptive fictions, "as-if" hypotheses, moral ideas, which are not to be taken as representing any tangible "referent," but rather as indicating goals to be achieved, programs of action that must be inspired by great words. What would a Mexican mural be without the motto of "land and liberty"? This argument must not be misunderstood. "Land," in George's philosophy, is by no means a purely emotional term, although it is certainly surrounded by poetic, even religious, haloes. Its economic aureole is much more brilliant. The present paragraphs are simply suggesting that an abstract, metaphysical, even sentimental, interpretation of "land" has a quite definite place, at least in helping to stir the apathy which the word ordinarily encourages.

Only one major economic aspect of the land question can be introduced here. Yet it will be the largest and the most provocative of controversy; it should at least indicate that George's point of view was not a piddling one. Whether he was right or wrong, he had a depth and perspective that seem comparatively unfamiliar to those--they really ought to know better, too--who still think of "the land question" as something rural, rustic, at most, suburban. To put it bluntly, George argued that since land was the physical foundation of the economic process, its control was the basic control. Something more than a figure of speech is intended by foundation; land provides the materials which are to be transformed into commodities, it affords the location for the transforming, it supports the worker who from it *pro-duces* goods. Therefore, to dominate land, argued George, means to dominate the entire economic structure. The monopoly of land is the parent of all monopolies; the private ownership of land is the most dangerous form of economic power, for all privilege is related to it, directly or indirectly. To be "radical," then, to seek for the roots of exploitation means to investigate first the land question. And in this connection, it is strange that the words of Marx seem to be unknown or ignored by those who claim the name of progressive:

> We have seen that the expropriation of the mass of the people from the soil forms the basis of the capitalist mode of production. . . . The only thing that interests us is the secret discovered in the new world by the political economy of the old world, and proclaimed on the house-tops: that the capitalist mode of production and accumulation, and therefore, capitalist private property, have for their fundamental condition the annihilation of self-earned private property; in other words, the expropriation of the labourer.[1]

And again:

> The expropriation of the agricultural producer, the peasant, from the soil, is the basis of the whole process. . . . The monopoly of landed property is an historical premise, and remains the basis of the capitalist mode of production, just as it does of all other modes of production, which rest on the exploitation of the masses in one form or another.[2]

George indeed agreed with Marx that there was a class struggle, but it was between those who owned the earth and the others who sought their permission to work on it. Marx seems to bear witness to that possibility.

Now, the point here is not to avoid argument, much less to pontificate. It is well realized that the focus of George's type of generic exposition can be shifted so as to throw into illumination other sources of economic exploitation, notably "capital." The force of the George-did-not-go-far-enough contention is equally understood (although very often that complaint indicates the entire logic of George's position has been missed). Whether his concentration on land was myopic or the

exaggeration needed to get a good idea a hearing need not be
fought out again. But what should become clearer is some awareness of the expanded range of meaning which George gave to "the
land question." A sensitivity to such an expansion of meaning
and to the series of implications which flow from it seems to be
at the same time the most difficult and the most unavoidable orientation that has to be made in coming to grips with George's
proposals. Especially does it appear difficult to disintoxicate
our ultramoderns from the confortable notion: Well, maybe George
had someting to say at the time he wrote. There was still some
free land. But the last frontier has been long since reached,
there is no more land, the whole subject is of antiquarian
interest.

George had the shrewdness, however, to realize that free
land did not necessarily mean the untrod ranges of newly discovered continents, or the virgin territory that once gave opportunity to the colonist and the pioneer. He saw that "free land,"
in this literal sense, was simply poetic. The focus of his badly misnamed "single tax" was to *make* land free, even if it were
under a skyscraper in downtown Manhattan--and owned by the Astor
family. How could this bit of magic be done? "We may safely
leave them the shell," he wrote, "if we take the kernel." The
shell is the land itself; the kernel is land value. Land is
free, according to George, only when the owner has no power of
exploitation. That power rests in (1) the withholding of land
from use by means of its high price, and (2) the private appropriation of land rent, which is definitely a social product.
Thus, for land to be free, it must be forced into use--when and
where socially necessary; and its rent must be directed into
public instead of private channels. These aims he proposed to
accomplish by a tax on land values, a tax which would gradually
rise so that all (or nearly all) of land's economic rent would
be absorbed.

"Single tax," like "the land question" itself, is another
nominalistic bogy. The phrase, more than the idea, is the hur-
dle. For whether a tax on land value be single or one of many
has nothing whatever to do with its merits. It is even questionable whether George himself would have boggled at the problem. (There is only one casual reference to "single tax" in his
entire *Progress and Poverty;* furthermore, when the words became
current later, he expressed his strong disapproval of them.) Be
that as it may, it is certainly true today that George's taxation schemes can be appreciated no matter what one's reaction to
a "single tax" might be. Yet that appreciation has been very
meager on the part of the "progressives" to whom this entire
essay is largely being directed. Even the most orthodox of

economists do not scruple to pay their wholehearted respect to
the soundness of high taxes on land values and correspondingly
low taxes on land improvements. Not so the fiscal experts who
write taxation schemes for the liberal weeklies. They do not
seem able to look beyond the rather obvious criterion of ability
to pay and the belligerent one of taxes-as-clubs. These criteria, of course, have both strength and plausibility, and, as
transitional devices, they are imperative. But few of our left-
wing fiscal experts appear to have bothered much about an explicit theory or philosophy of taxation. Taxes for them are so ofte:
purely *ad hoc*. Perhaps these writers do have an implicit logic,
i.e., that *unearned* incomes ought to be the first and neatest
subject for the taxation ax. If that is so (and it would be a
good idea to make such an assumption--or any other--an avowed
one), then the imbalance of talking only about excess capital
profits and never about the unearned increment of land is
glaring.

The land value is peculiarly social value and therefore
superbly adapted for social uses via taxation is so elementary
an observation that no economic literate can be ignorant of it.
Maybe it's too elementary to be impressive, just as it is apparently too athletically simple to suggest that society should
collect the value which society creates. Now, that there are
"other values which society creates" is absolutely correct, and
that there are other antisocial incomes besides that of the traditional unearned increment of rent is equally clear. But (1)
a tax upon any unearned income in no way precludes taxes upon
other unearned or antisocial income; and (2) the argument that
of any economic return, land rent is par excellence social in
nature and least justified as a fund for private exploitation
seems just as effective today as in its original labor-theory
dress. In any case, the complaint here is directed at the complete neglect--and that is not an exaggeration--with which our
present-day liberal greets the notion of high land-value taxation. As a possible evidence that this neglect is primarily the
result of a fashionable ultra-sophisticatedness, the following
contention, recently offered to the writer, may be introduced:
Everyone knows that population is no longer increasing. (This
was before the draft!) Therefore, no more land booms are possible. George's proposals were the product of an era of speculative land bubbles. (Has Florida, 1929, been so quickly forgotten? And are we not reading today about the speculative
high jinks at the power dam sites, notably Muscle Shoals?)
They have little relevance now when population is becoming static and land values frozen.

This approach has the specious competence which follows a reading of the census reports; it is being mentioned here, not for the sake of refutation, but because it seems somewhat of an entire attitude, the why-ain't-you-heard-where've-you-been-everyone-knows attitude. It's simply *de trop* to be familiar with George. (In passing, it may simply be noted that this argument makes some interesting assumptions: (a) that increase of population alone causes increase in land value; (b) that existing land values--if they do not increase, even if they decrease--do not have to be considered as a problem; (c) that ideas which become spectacularly clear at a given stage in economic development have little relevance at other periods--which, for example, would make any ideas stemming from the paleotechnic phase of the industrial revolution, even those of Marx, *ipso facto* inapplicable for neotechnics.)

This is not an essay on fiscal problems. For there is much more to George than single tax or even the land question. But his name has been made so parochial, so bound up with a special economic technique, that some exposition of his direct proposals is always necessary. George's chief criticism of the phrase "single tax" was precisely that it connoted only a fiscal program, whereas his interest was always a moral one. Until only yesterday this was still another reason why he could be so confidently ignored. Because economics had nothing to do with ethics. Depending upon one's school, economics could be regarded as a calm, objective study of historical phenomena which informed us how our institutions came to be what they were; or as an acute psychological analysis of why people wanted things; or as an intricate mathematical manipulation of a price calculus. Whether our institutions were any good or not; whether people's desires had any relevance; whether price had an ethical dimension; what economics was for anyway--these queries were impudent, sophomoric, at best meaningless. That is, they were until the last few desperate years have made them the most screamingly pressing of all questions. "Knowledge for what?" has become menacingly real. . . .

[1]*Capital* (Chicago, Kerr ed.,), Vol. I, pp. 841, 848.

[2]*Ibid.*, p. 787; and Vol. III, p. 723.

The Antioch Review, Vol. I, (September 1941): 291-307

"Progress and Poverty's Continuing Challenge": James M. Roberts (1971)*

Henry George is considered one of the most influential of American economists. In his book *Progress and Poverty* (1879), he demonstrated that monopoly and privilege are at the roots of the economic and social problems that persist in spite of the advanced technology of our day, as they have been in every society in which they appeared.[1]

During his life he lectured extensively in the United States and Great Britain and wrote numerous articles, pamphlets and books concerning his social and economic principles and their application. George's influence may also be traced to Australia, China, Canada, Denmark and Germany. His first and most important book, *Progress and Poverty*, has been translated and is currently available in at least nine foreign languages. Theodore Roosevelt and Woodrow Wilson were among many who expressed high regard for Henry George and his work. Leo Tolstoy is quoted as saying that

> People do not argue with the teaching of George; they simply do not know it. And it is impossible to do otherwise with his teaching, for he who becomes acquainted with it cannot but agree.[2]

Henry George was born in Philadelphia on September 2, 1839, the son of middle-class, first generation Americans of Scottish and English descent. George's informal education ended early in his life and his thought and its logic were developed almost exclusively through his own observations and experiences--on a voyage around the world, in mining camps and print shops, and in such cities as San Francisco, New York and Philadelphia. And it was only after he had formulated his ideas and that he turned to the work of others to complete and fortify his argument.[3]

It might be noted, although there are those who would deny it, that the problem of *individual existence* for the majority has not changed much from the time of George's work. Further, since George drew largely from the circumstances of life as he knew and observed them, *Progress and Poverty* is as relevant today as the day it was written.

The thought of *Progress and Poverty* is of sufficient scope to qualify as an economic philosophy and some instances of ready acceptance of George's philosophy, particularly in the United States can be shown (as in the adoption of the anti-trust laws). However, his work and its most specific proposals stir great resistance and controversy. Even those who consider his proposals

must finally reject them on some illogical ground or forfeit
their standing as economists. There is nothing so implacable
as ideological enmities which breed impatience even with logic.
George was himself aware of this and recognized the possibility
that the political economics of *Progress and Poverty* would not
find ready acceptance and he clearly showed his lack of optimism
when he wrote:

The truth that I have tried to make clear will not find easy
acceptance. If that could be, it would have been accepted long
ago. . . .

Will it at length prevail? Ultimately, yes. But in our
own times, or in times of which any memory of us remains, who
shall say?[4]

If Henry George exposed to view the truth of political
economics in 1879, we should expect that at least ninety years
later it would be generally accepted. Particularly we should
expect this acceptance by a society supposedly dedicated in all
things to truth and justice. Since such is not the case it must
be concluded that either George did not discover the truth he
thought he had or else the arguments and those forces that are
able to keep that truth obscured have been powerful indeed!

I

The Philosophy of *Progress and Poverty*

The major thesis of *Progress and Poverty* begins in the
introduction with Henry George's paradox which he had already
presented in articles, editorials and speeches:

This association of poverty with progress is the great enigma of
our times. It is the central fact from which spring industrial,
social, and political difficulties that perplex the world, and
with which statesmanship and philanthropy and education grapple
in vain . . . not to answer is to be destroyed. So long as all
the increased wealth which modern progress brings goes to build
up great fortunes, to increase luxury and make sharper the contrast between the House of Have and the House of Want, progress
is not real and cannot be permanent. The reaction must come.[5]

The study of political economics has failed to yield the
answer to the problem of man's failure to deal justly with one
another. This problem leads to poverty, depressions, and insecurity. And political economics has failed to resolve the problem because it is based on a series of dogmas rather than on
scientific findings. George presents his first principles as

scientifically deductible and empirically observable truths of the highest sanction (natural law), fundamental and recognizable to all.[6]

The economic structure of the book is largely based on the much-used Benthamite pleasure-pain doctrine; ". . .the law that is to political economy what the law of gravitation is to physics --that men seek to gratify their desires with the least exertion."[7] The reform reasoning has its basis in George's own religious, moral and democratic ideas which, because he is a reformer as well as an economist, creates a serious conflict between his two principles concerning the nature of man.[8] It is here that Henry George meets and, in the final analysis, refuses to accept an either/or position where freedom and equality are concerned, but instead proposes his own resolution of the antithesis. It is also here that George may be placed in juxtaposition with Thomas Jefferson who, in affirming the best government to be that which governs least, proclaimed himself an individualist and accepted the economic theory of *laissez faire*. But George also held that the welfare of the whole is the proper purpose of the State with government authority curtailing the activities of the individual for the common good. Jefferson had no solution to the antithesis, but believed that a people "enlightened" by education could be entrusted with the full powers of democracy.[9]

The arrangement of *Progress and Poverty* accommodates this duality in two separable chains of thought which are interdependent. Charles Albro Barker labels these two sides of George's argument his "economic syllogism" and "moral sequence" each of which is divisible into three parts. The economic syllogism consists of these propositions: (1) that rent--an increment of monopoly not earned by individuals--always and everywhere opposes and reduces wages and interest, the returns which the economy makes for labor's toil and for capital's postponement of consumption and investment risks. Labor, with or without the assistance of capital, combines with land--including site and resources, but excluding improvements--to create wealth; and capital is that portion of man-made wealth returned to production to procure more wealth. The benefit of site or natural resources conveys an advantage monopolistic by definition to one producer above another and should be understood as rent rather than as wage. And, as George asserted, "Increase in land values does not represent increase in the common wealth, for what land owners gain by higher prices, the tenants or purchasers who must pay them will lose."[10] (2) The forces of the industrial economy operate observably to enlarge the take of land ownership, and that creates unbalance, poverty, and depression. (3) It is thus

necessary to do away with private property in land, but George
suggested the preferable alternative of taking by taxation the
economic rent of land for the public benefit.

Finally, *Progress and Poverty* depends upon a moral sequence
which Henry George put forth as follows: (1) the first premise
is the plain fact of social injustice; (2) the second premise is
theory and democratic idea (expression in equality is the law of
progress with equal opportunity for all men being the universal
moral law);[11] (3) the antithesis between social fact and social
theory is the tragic contradiction. (He is not sure that mankind will solve the question of poverty, progress, equality and
individual life, but is sure only that we must try).[12]

George largely rejected prevailing economic theory, but he
accepted David Ricardo's law of rent[13] to which he added the
theory of marginalism. He also included urban-site values along
with natural resources as creating different land values. In
his rejection of the theory that wages are paid from capital
George quoted Adam Smith to the effect that:

*The produce of labor constitutes the natural recompense or wages
of labor.* In that original state of things which precedes both
the appropriation of land and the accumulation of stock, the
whole produce of labor belongs to the laborer. He has neither
landlord nor master to share with him.[14]

Although he approved of interest as a proper return to capital, George's commitment to labor is clearly shown in the above
quotation. George may be classed as a capitalist in economic
philosophy, but he devoted one chapter of his book to the problem "Of Spurious Capital and of Profits Often Mistaken for
Interest."[15] Here he expressed his dislike of private monopoly
or monopoly gains of whatever kind. He compared the tactics of
the monopolists to those of highwaymen. Monopolies created by
technology, such as the telegraph and railroads, George held
should be owned and operated by the government.

In the last section of *Progress and Poverty*, George returned to his central problem and the reason as he saw it that civilization flourish only to decline. The reason is that

. . .as a social development goes on, inequality tends to establish itself. . . .The unequal distribution of the power and
wealth gained by the integration of men in society tends to
check, and finally to counterbalance, the force by which improvements are made and society advances.[16]

This then completes Henry George's analysis and system of political economics: the problem which his solution attacked was the ever-increasing centralization of wealth which he found was caused by the private ownership of land (and other monopolies) from which flowed an unearned increment destroying the equality and freedom necessary to continued progress. The solution proposed was the expropriation for public benefit of the unearned increment of land (unimproved value) and its natural resources. His proposal became popularly known as the "Single Tax" which meant obtaining tax revenue from a levy on the value of land and other natural resources and abolishing all other taxes.

The so-called single tax movement found many loyal followers in America and England. More copies of *Progress and Poverty* have been circulated--several million--than perhaps of any other economic work, and sales of his many other books and articles on economics have also been substantial.[17] Actually, Henry George's taxing proposal, which he first set forth as editor of a San Francisco newspaper in 1873, was that, "There should be three taxes. . . (1) a tax on the value of land, not counting improvements, above a minimum exemption; (2) a tax on the estates of deceased persons and; (3) license taxes on such businesses as require regulation, liquor and gambling houses for instance."[18]

II

The Politics of Economics

Henry George encountered resistance to his economic philosophy on all fronts following the publication of *Progress and Poverty*. The socialists rejected the philosophy of land value taxation since they believed capital to be the locus of economic privilege. They saw land ownership as being only one form of capital exploitation. George's individualism also reacted strongly against the collectivism of socialism. George insisted that the economy functioned automatically through individual activity in free competition and this worked for the benefit of both the individual and the society. Legitimate *laissez faire* for Henry George would include freedom, equality and real competition which could not be had until private land ownership and other forms of monopolization and privilege grounded in social custom had been eliminated.

Laissez faire capitalists have not supported George because like the socialists they view land as merely a form of capital. Private property, including private ownership of land, is fundamental to their philosophy. The proposal to remove the benefit of private ownership of land through taxation is, as they see it, abhorrent. They generally, although mistakenly, classify George as merely "another socialist."

Among university professors, Henry George's economic philosophy has found active support from only a few, principally from John Dewey of Columbia and Harry Gunnison Brown of the University of Missouri. Economics professors have either largely ignored the writing of Henry George or accepted the work of his two principal antagonists; Edwin R.A. Seligman of Columbia and Francis A. Walker of Massachusetts Institute of Technology. The lack of interest in his work by university professors surprised George as his friend Louis F. Post indicates in his biographical work: "To his amazement economics professors ignored his demonstrations. They went on with their economic bubbling and boiling. . . ."[19]

Generally, the arguments against the proposal of land value taxation have been as follows: (1) the Ricardian theory, worked out to its logical conclusion, reveals that there are as many kinds of rents as there are different situations in the economy of a society; (2) land is no longer acquired by mere occupation, but rather by purchase, and thus to deprive these owners of advantages acquired by their labor is unjust; (3) economic rent may not be so accurately measured that only it would be appropriated; (4) land value taxation disregards the principle of ability to pay; (5) the confiscation of the "unearned increment" by appropriation of the economic rent should be reimbursed by a payment of the "unearned decrement" which the land may suffer.[20]

Most economists regard the critical point in the land value tax, as far as its impact is concerned, as being the nature of rent. The main point of this argument is that rent is a residual accruing to the owner of a scarce good after the *market* rates for his other factors, including wages and interest, are deducted. Land is asserted to be the only one example of a scarce good. The residual is determined by the market price for the good being produced with the aid of the scarce factor and may be either positive or negative.[21]

The obvious answer to this objection is that land is the *only* item that is present and necessary to the production of all goods and services. Indeed, the earth is the cradle of man and, although he can not remain in the cradle forever, it is still necessary even to his very existence. Essentially, this is the reply offered by John Stuart Mill in showing that none of the other rents has either the persistence or the generality of the rent of land. Economists Charles Gide and Charles Rist believed that this reply was sufficient to justify at least a partial application of the land value tax program despite the other asserted objections.[22]

Finally, in a free market society economic reward supposedl goes to those who supply some needed good or service to society through their own productive effort. Capital is similarly entitled to an economic return since it represents a saving of one's productive effort to facilitate future production. Land, however, cannot be considered as merely another form of capital since, whatever its advantages may be, they are not due to any effort of the owner. This remains true even though the land is purchased by a second owner at a price determined by capitalization of the anticipated income from the land. Society and those who pay to use the bare land gain nothing from a mere change of ownership. Land, therefore, being the one item necessary to all production, becomes a distortive factor in the market which in a sense, though it may vary as to degree, is never positive, but always negative.

Fundamental to the land value tax is the fact that it cannot be shifted by the landowner to the user. This is not obviously clear without explanation. But it has never been seriously disputed. It was first recognized by the French Physiocrats in the middle of the 18th century; they favored a land value tax for this reason. Professor Paul A. Samuelson illustrates this in the most recent edition of his economics textbook with the comment that this is true where the owners hold a factor such as land which is in inelastic supply.[23]

A particularly clear demonstration of the non-shiftable nature of the land value tax by using it in a comparison with a tax on sugar, a commodity with an elastic supply, was given by Louis F. Post nearly 40 years ago.[24] His reasoning is as follows: With regard to sugar, higher costs of production and delivery tend to reduce the market supply of sugar, and actually will reduce it unless the ultimate buyer pays the added cost. However, a tax on land, whether improved or not and regardless of its improvements, will have no tendency to reduce the supply of land. On the contrary, it will increase the supply! Why will it make land plentiful? In Post's own words:

Because a tax on sugar would increase the cost of producing sugar, but a tax on land could add nothing to the cost of producing land. Land is unproducible. But it would add to the cost of holding land out of use, which would increase the market supply.[25]

Economics Professor Harry Gunnison Brown of the University
of Missouri points out that the taxation of bare land values
would eliminate the inequity of the present system which penal-
izes a man for building or painting a house or for planting a
tree. In answer to the complaint that there is a confiscation
of a vested right, he asserts that this is no more so than when
the government decides to regulate a monopoly in which innocent
persons in good faith have purchased stock. The government has
given no promise that bare land values will not be subjected to
either full or partial taxation.[26]

In answer to the objections relative to the accurate assessment and collection of a land value tax, the experience with
such taxation in other countries might be considered. It has
been adopted in varying forms in Denmark, South Africa, New
Zealand and Australia. Most recently adopted in South Melbourne
by vote of the property owners, land value taxation is credited
with raising the value of new building permits issued by 2.4
times the previous rate.[27] The tax has also been used in Pitts-
burgh and Scranton, Pennsylvania, but the results, though seemingly favorable, are not conclusive due to the limited form of
the land value tax adopted by those communities. The limited
experience does, however, show that the land value tax is at
least workable.

Henry George based his theory of land value taxation upon
the fundamental difference between land and capital. Such a
tax would apply the unearned increment of land to the general
use of the community while retaining the advantages that are
inherent in private ownership of land. Holding land for speculation would become unprofitable, thus making land more available for productive enterprise. Or, as Professor Samuelson asserts in his textbook, the land value tax will lead to a more
efficient use of land.[28] Further, income derived from socially
beneficial productive effort could be partially relieved of the
burdens of taxation which would reinforce the free market system
by making a fairer distribution of the economic benefits generated by that system.

Henry George envisaged all of these benefits and more in
Progress and Poverty. This is an incomplete list and only a
partial presentation of the economic philosophy of his book,
but even this should have been sufficient to bring a gradual
adoption of the system of land value taxation by at least one
legislature. As has been shown above, land value taxation is
certainly fair and just and in conformity with the free market
system of the United States. Why has its reception been so
hostile?

As has already been noted, Henry George's political economics has been rarely accepted in any degree by economics professors,[29] has been rejected by socialists, and has been dismissed by nearly every capitalist. However, the insurmountable opposition to George's economic philosophy has not come from these sources alone, but also from Christian religious philosophy and thought on economics.

[1]Nicholas Murray Butler has pointed out that this teaching has passed into economic theory everywhere. Commencement address, Columbia University, June 2, 1931 (New York: Columbia University, Office of the Secretary, 1931).

[2]Harry G. Brown, editor, *Significant Paragraphs From Henry George's Progress and Poverty* (New York: Schalkenbach Foundation, 1931), p. 81.

[3]See, V. Webster Johnson and Raleigh Barlowe, *Land Problems and Policies* (New York: McGraw-Hill Publishing Co., 1954), p. 317.
    The basic ideas of Henry George were contained in the thought of John Locke in his treatment of the doctrine of natural rights and the idea that the right of property is justified only by personal labor; by the physiocrats of France, who proposed the *impot unique* to appropriate a substantial part of the net product of land; and by a number of pamphleteers of the 18th and 19th centuries, including Thomas Spence in a 1793 pamphlet, *The Real Right of Man*, William Ogilvie in *Essay on the Right of Property in Land* (1782), Thomas Paine in *Agrarian Justice* (1797), Patrick Dove in the *Theory of Human Progression* (1850), and some land reformers in America from 1840 to 1860.

[4]Henry George, *Progress and Poverty* (New York: The Schalkenbach Foundation, 1929), p. 556.

[5]*Ibid.*, p. 10.

[6]*Ibid.*, p. 11-12.

[7]*Ibid.*, p. 204.

[8]Charles Albro Barker, *Henry George* (New York: Oxford University Press, 1955), p. 268.

[9] Max Beloff, *Thomas Jefferson and American Democracy* (London: Macmillan & Co., Ltd., 1949), p. 255.

[10] George, *op. cit.*, p. 40. n. 3.

[11] *Ibid.*, p. 475-526.

[12] *Ibid.*, p. 268-71, n. 7.

[13] *Ibid.*, p. 169, n. 3.

[14] *Ibid.*, p. 51.

[15] *Ibid.*, p. 189.

[16] *Ibid.*, p. 517-19.

[17] Edwin R.A. Seligman and Alvin Johnson, eds., *Encyclopedia of the Social Sciences* (London: Macmillan & Co., Ltd., 1937), Vol. VII, p. 65.

[18] Barker, *op. cit.*, p. 184, n. 7.

[19] Louis F. Post, *The Prophet of San Francisco* (New York: Vanguard Press, 1930), p. 317.

[20] Charles Gide and Charles Rist, (R. Richards, trans.), *A History of Economic Doctrines* (London: G.G. Harrap & Co., 1915), p. 548-53.

[21] See generally, Alfred Marshall, *Principles of Economics*, 8th ed., (London: Macmillan & Co., Ltd., 1920), Book IV, chaps. 2-3; Book V, chaps. 9-11; George J. Stigler, *The Theory of Price*, 3rd ed., (New York: Macmillan Co., 1966), chap. 15.

[22] Gide and Rist, *op. cit.*, p. 569, n. 19.

[23] Paul A. Samuelson, *Economics*, 7th ed., (New York: McGraw-Hill Book Co., 1967), p. 535-38.

[24] Post, *op. cit.*, p. 34-6, n. 18.

[25] *Ibid.*, p. 36.

[26] Harry Gunnison Brown, "Should Bare-Land Values Be Taxed More Heavily," *Journal of Land Economics*, 4 (1928), pp. 375-90.

[27] Harry G. Brown and Elizabeth R. Brown, "Incentive Taxation in Australia," *American Journal of Economics & Sociology*, 26 (1967), p. 416.

[28] Samuelson, *op. cit.*, p. 538, n. 22.

[29] Elizabeth Read Brown, "How College Textbooks Treat Land Value Taxation," *American Journal of Economics & Sociology*, 20 (1961), pp. 147-67; Harry Gunnison Brown, "Academic Freedom and the Defense of Capitalism," *American Journal of Economics & Sociology*, 15 (1956), pp. 173-82.

The American Journal of Economics and Sociology, Vol. 30, (July 1971): 301-309

The Theory of the Leisure Class
by
Thorstein Veblen

REVIEW: D. Collin Wells (1899)*

The title of this work is pretentious. It is not a theory of the leisure class, but the theory. The subtitle is
promising but deceptive. An economic study is supposed to be
based upon economic data and involve reasoning to economic
conclusions. Of this there is nothing in the book, and the
few references of an economic nature are ill-considered and
vicious. We look for some definition of the "Leisure Class,"
but this is nowhere given. The term is made to cover such
unlike phenomena as the ruling class of barbarian times, like
the Homeric heroes, the mediaeval feudal aristocracy, the English nobility, and the rich of our modern industrial society. Similarly the term status is at times used legitimately
to describe a hereditary condition, such as we find under the
caste system of India, but most commonly as a term for the
individual economic relation which the rich man sustains in a
modern community, which is not properly a relation of status
at all. Such terms as "barbarian," "upper and lower stages
of barbarism," and "savagry," about which there is so much
uncertainty, should have been carefully defined. A most serious defect is the failure to give any authority for statements made. The reasons assigned for this in the preface are
not satisfactory. From beginning to end the work is crowded
with ex cathedra propositions, often of a revolutionary and
startling nature. One seldom meets with such a collection of
"things that are not so." If this is Sociology it is the
kind that brings the subject into disrepute among careful and
scientific thinkers. These faults are so serious and so
characteristic as to make the reviewer's task far from agreeable.

It is difficult to express the leading ideas of such a
book. These are some of them. The leisure class lives by
"exploiting" the rest of the community, either directly, as
under barbarism, or indirectly, as in modern times, through
the control of industry. Leisure class exploit is the utili-

25

zation of human beings, industry proper is the utilization of
non-human nature! This process began when woman was made a
drudge. This the author wrongly supposes to have been first
the case under lower barbarism, "The tribes belonging to this
economic level have carried the economic differentiation to a
point at which a marked distinction is made between the occupations of men and women, and this distinction is of an invidious character." In fact it obtains even in the lowest
savagery. The author postulates a "peacable stage of primitive culture," on grounds "drawn from psychology rather than
from ethnology"! and holds that the predatory disposition
does not become strong "until industrial methods have become
developed to such a degree of efficiency as to leave a margin
worth fighting for, above the subsistence of those engaged in
getting a living"! As if the human struggle were not a
struggle for subsistence and women, from the beginning! The
author's psychology would seem to be at fault in the proposition, apparently based on Mucke, that "The original reason
for the seizure and appropriation of women seems to have been
their usefulness as trophies." From the ownership of women
men advanced to the ownership of things, urged on by the "invidious distinction attaching to wealth" since "the possession of property becomes the basis of popular esteem"! Now
the "life of leisure is the readiest and most conclusive evidence of pecuniary strength," hence "conspicuous leisure, a
non-productive consumption of time," is the usual characteristic of the wealthy.

"The prevading principle and abiding test of good breeding is the requirement of a substantial and patent waste of
time." Around the leisure class (thus baptised) there gath-
ers "a subsidiary of derived leisure class whose office is
the performance of a vicarious leisure for the behoof of the
reputability of the primary or legitimate leisure class."
The "chief use of servants is the evidence they afford of the
master's ability to pay." "Domestic servants of any kind
would now scarcely be employed by anybody except on the
ground of a canon of reputability carried over by tradition
from earlier usage"! Apparently they are employed to smash
crockery "the apparatus of living has grown so elaborate--
in the way of dwellings, furniture, bric-a-brac, wardrobe and
meals, that the consumer of these things cannot make way with
them without help"!

This brings us to "conspicuous consumption," as the second trait of the leisure class. "The general principle is
that the base industrial class should consume only what may
be necessary to their subsistence. Therefore the base

classes, primarily the women, practice an enforced continence with respect to these stimulants (intoxicating beverages and narcotics)"! Women are chattels and "should consume only for the benefit of their masters," since consumption like leisure is chiefly vicarious. The modern man applies himself to "work with the utmost assiduity in order that his wife may in due form render for him that degree of vicarious leisure which the common sense of the time demands." The household is thus based upon a subtle male egoism! Conspicuous consumption must be a "wasteful expenditure of time and substance." "If beauty or comfort is achieved they must be achieved by means and methods that commend themselves to the great economic law (?) of wasted effort." In order to be reputable it must be wasteful." [sic] It is "waste," "Because this expenditure does not serve human life or human well-being on the whole." This seems to assume a mysterious collective enjoyment apart from the enjoyment of any particular human being, or that all consumption above the subsistence minimum is wasteful and objectionable. The fog bank of this kind of sociology is finally reached in the dictum, "Any economic fact must approve itself under the test of impersonal usefulness as seen from the point of view of the generally human."

The treatment of "The Pecuniary Standard of Living" is interesting, but it is surely to interpret a fact too narrowly to say, "The ultimate ground of decency among civilized peoples is serviceability for the purpose of an invidious comparison in pecuniary success." It is true that a "propensity for emulation--for invidious (!) comparison is of ancient growth and is a pervading trait of human nature," and that "in an industrial community this propensity expresses itself in pecuniary emulation" (among other forms which the author entirely neglects), but it is not true that this "is virtually equivalent to saying that it expresses itself in some form of conspicuous waste," unless one is to adopt the potato basis of society. Furthermore, emulation is so largely in acquiring and controlling, i.e., in economic production, as to threaten us with an excess of savings rather than waste.

The same principle of conspicuous waste is used to explain, on the one hand, ornate temples and churches and worship (which is vicarious service of a heavenly master!) and on the other hand devout austerity, which is "wasteful (!) discomfort." It is also said to mould the canons of art, identifying beauty with reputability and therefore with costliness.

The dolicho-blonds of Ammon and Lapouge inherit from
their remote pastoral ancestry a fondness for closely cropped
grazing land. But "a herd of cattle so pointedly suggest
thrift and usefulness that their presence in the public pleasure ground would be intolerably cheap. This method of keeping grounds is comparatively inexpensive, therefore it is in-
decorous." Hence the lawn mower! There is a ray of hope in
the fact that the leisure class has become so large that "exemption from thrift is a matter so commonplace as to have
lost much of its utility as a basis of pecuniary decency."
Since the love of nature is an inexpensive taste to gratify,
it is difficult to understand how the author derives this too
from the "higher class code of taste."

The thesis that dogs are kept because they are useless
and expensive we leave to facts--and dog lovers. The author
similarly accounts for horse-breeding, but surely the history
of agriculture demonstrates the high utility of stock-breeding
and the economic motive of breeders. The truth is that things
that are rare and of fine workmanship are expensive. They are
purchased by the wealthy because they alone can afford to pay
for them though all would like to possess them. The waste is
incidental; probably there is, proportionally, quite as much
outside the leisure class as within it.

How account for fashion? Skirts are worn because they
are expensive and "incapacitate for all useful exertion."
Of course the corset is a most flagrant example of conspicuous waste! All dress is expensive and most of it wasteful,
but "all men abhor futility,"--a sense of economic fitness
which every fashion offends. In an uneasy attempt to placate
this sense the fashion is changed. But "the new style must
conform to the requirement of reputable wastefulness and futility; then we take refuge in a new style, etc." No wonder
the author adds, "having so explained the phenomenon of shifting fashions, the next thing is to make the explanation tally
with everyday facts."

Some interesting analysis, in the chapter on "Industrial
Exemption and Conservatism," is spoiled by the main thesis,
which is, "a leisure class acts to make the lower classes
conservative by withdrawing from them as much as it may of
the means of sustenance, and so reducing their consumption
and consequently their available energy to such a point as to
make them incapable of the effort required for the learning
and adoption of new habits of thought. The accumulation of
wealth at the upper end of the pecuniary scale implies privation at the lower end of the scale." The leisure class are

charged with retarding social progress although progress is
said to be due to surplus energy and theirs is the only class
which can accumulate energy! They are "parasitic"; their office is "exploitation! [sic] We are not surprised that the
chapter closes with the economic maxim: "As fast as pecuniary
transactions are reduced to a routine the captain of industry
can be dispensed with," like the "great leisure class function
of ownership"!

The account of the Veddas of Ceylon, given by the Sarasin
brothers, and Haeckel's enthusiastic comment on the same,
have not established the existence of a period of "peaceable
savagry," the traces of which the author admits to be "faint
and doubtful." Yet from this hypothetical condition of culture the author derives all admirable qualities, such as hon-
esty, sympathy, truthfulness and justice, by way of reversion!
These are "archaic traits," and not the difficult and late
products of human culture, as we have been led to suppose.
Thus is Eden reintroduced, or rather a "protoanthropoid cultural stage of peaceable, relatively undifferentiated economic (!) life carried on in contact with a relatively simple
and invariable material environment." With the predatory
stage came the "régime of status and ferocity, self-seeking,
clannishness and disingenuousness—a free resort to force and
fraud," "qualities to which the dolicho-blond type of European
man seems to owe much of its dominating influence and its
masterful position." The author needs to be reminded that it
was these same dolicho-blonds who abolished slavery, who have
accorded to women the highest honor and whose charity is most
abundant. What of the ferocity of the dolicho-brunette Ro-
mans, of the brachycephalous Mongols of Genghis Kahn and
Timour? These qualities may especially characterise inter-
tribal competition, but within the group or tribe the milder
qualities must have prevailed from the beginning, on penalty
of destruction. It is out of this strife of the larger units
that peace and civilization have come by the gradual enlargement of the field within which these domestic virtues obtain.

Perhaps the most vicious distinction made in the book is
that between pecuniary and industrial economic institutions,
the former having to do with ownership or acquisition, the
latter with workmanship or production. "The pecuniary employments give proficiency in the general line of practices
comprised under fraud rather than in those that belong under
the more archaic method of forcible seizure." The climax is
capped by an elaborate comparison of the ideal pecuniary man
to the ideal delinquent, i.e., criminal; especially in de-
voutness!

"Sports of all kind, including athletics, shooting, an-
gling, yachting and games of skill," are evidence of an "archaic spiritual constitution, the possession of the predatory
emulative propensity in a relatively high potency," and "an
arrested spiritual development." Emulation is the fundamental vice of the leisure class man; "so far as regards the
serviceability of the individual for the purposes of the collective life, emulative efficiency is of use indirectly, if
at all." The author thus stands the evolutionary process on
its head and we will refrain from following the further tor-
ture of the subject. The volume ends with the discovery that
the English language is classic because it satisfies all the
canons of conspicuous waste; It is "futile, archaic and cum-
berous"; this is certainly true of the author's use of it;
the style at times becomes a scientific (?) jargon from which
no clear meaning can be extracted.

Scientific sociology may perhaps be permitted ultimately
to generalize, but only with the utmost humility and caution.
The understanding of human society is not an afternoon's diversion, nor is its reconstruction the pastime of a morning.

Yale Review, Volume 8, (1899-1900): 213-218

Prejudices: Henry L. Mencken (1919)*

Ten or twelve years ago, being engaged in a bombastic
discussion with what was then known as an intellectual Socialist (like the rest of the *intelligentsia*, he succumbed to
the first fife-corps of the war, pulled down the red flag,
damned Marx as a German spy, and began whooping for Elihu
Root, Otto Kahn and Abraham Lincoln), I was greatly belabored
and incommoded by his long quotations from a certain Prof.
Dr. Thorstein Veblen, then quite unknown to me. My antago-
nist manifestly attached a great deal of importance to these
borrowed sagacities, for he often heaved them at me in lengths
of a column or two, and urged me to read every word of them.
I tried hard enough, but found it impossible going. The more
I read them, in fact, the less I could make of them, and so
in the end, growing impatient and impolite, I denounced this
Prof. Veblen as a geyser of pishposh, refused to waste any
more time upon his incomprehensible syllogisms, and applied
myself to the other Socialist witnesses in the case, seeking
to set fire to their shirts.

That old debate, which took place by mail (for the

Socialist lived like a munitions patriot on his country estate and I was a wage-slave attached to a city newspaper),
was afterward embalmed in a dull book, and made the mild
pother of a day. The book, by name, "Men vs. the Man," is
now as completely forgotten as Baxter's "Saint's Rest" or the
Constitution of the United States. I myself, perhaps the
only man who remembers it at all, have not looked into it for
six or eight years, and all I can recall of my opponent's argument (beyond the fact that it not only failed to convert me
to the nascent Bolshevism of the time, but left me a bitter
and incurable scoffer at democracy in all its forms) is his
curious respect for the aforesaid Prof. Dr. Thorstein Veblen,
and his delight in the learned gentleman's long, tortuous and
(to me, at least) intolerably flapdoodlish phrases.

There was, indeed, a time when I forgot even this--when
my mind was empty of the professor's very name. That was,
say, from 1909 or thereabout to the middle of 1917. During
those years, having lost all my old superior interest in Socialism, even as an amateur psychiatrist, I ceased to read
his literature, and thus lost track of its Great Thinkers.
The periodicals that I then gave an eye to, setting aside
newspapers, were chiefly the familiar American imitations of
the English weeklies of opinion, and in these the dominant
Great Thinker was, first, the late Prof. Dr. William James,
and, after his decease, Prof. Dr. John Dewey. The reign of
James, as the illuminated will recall, was long and glorious.
For three or four years running he was mentioned in every one
of those American *Spectators* and *Saturday Reviews* at least
once a week, and often a dozen times. Among the less somber
gazettes of the republic, to be sure, there were other heroes:
Maeterlinck, Rabindranath Tagore, Judge Ben B. Lindsey, the
late Major-General Roosevelt, Tom Lawson and so on. Still
further down the literary and intellectual scale there were
yet others: Hall Caine, Brieux and Jack Johnson among them,
with paper-bag cookery and the twilight sleep to dispute their
popularity. But on the majestic level of the old *Nation*,
among the white and lavender peaks of professorial ratiocination, there was scarcely a serious rival to James. Now and
then, perhaps, Jane Addams had a month of vogue, and during
one winter there was a rage for Bergson, and for a short space
the unspeakable Bernstorff tried to set up Eucken (now damned
with Wagner, Nietzsche and Ludendorff), but taking one day
with another James held his own against the field. His ideas,
immediately they were stated, became the ideas of every pedagogue from Harvard to Leland Stanford, and the pedagogues,
laboring furiously at space rates, rammed them into the skulls
of the lesser *cerebelli*. To have called James an ass, during

the year 1909, would have been as fatal as to have written a
sentence like this one without having used so many *haves*. He
died a bit later, but his ghost went marching on: it took
three or four years to interpret and pigeonhole his philosophical remains and to take down and redact his messages
(via Sir Oliver Lodge, Little Brighteyes, Wah-Wah the Indian
Chief, and other gifted psychics) from the spirit world. But
then, gradually, he achieved the ultimate, stupendous and ir-
revocable act of death, and there was a vacancy. To it Prof.
Dr. Dewey was elected by the acclamation of all right-thinking
and forward-looking men. He was an expert in pedagogics,
metaphysics, metaphysical psychology, psychological ethics,
ethical logic, logical politics and political pedagogics. He
was *Artium Magister, Philosophioe Doctor* and twice *Legum Doctor*. He had written a book called "How to Think." He sat in
a professor's chair and caned sophomores for blowing spit-
balls. *Ergo*, he was the ideal candidate, and so he was nomi-
nated, elected and inaugurated, and for three years, more or
less, he enjoyed a peaceful reign in the groves of sapience,
and the inferior *umbilicarii* venerated him as they had once
venerated James.

   I myself greatly enjoyed and profited by the discourses
of this Prof. Dewey and was in hopes that he would last. Born
so recently as 1859 and a man of the highest bearable sobri-
ety, he seemed likely to peg along until 1935 or 1940, a gentle and charming volcano of correct thought. But it was not,
alas, to be. Under cover of pragmatism, that serpent's meta-
physic, there was unrest beneath the surface. Young professors in remote and obscure universities, apparently as harm-
less as so many convicts in the death-house, were secretly
flirting with new and red-hot ideas. Whole regiments and bri-
gades of them yielded in stealthy privacy to rebellious and
often incomprehensible yearnings. Now and then, as if to reveal what was brewing, a hell fire blazed and a Prof. Dr.
Scott Nearing went sky-hooting through its smoke. One heard
whispers of strange heresies--economic, sociological, even
political. Gossip had it that pedagogy was hatching vipers,
nay, was already brought to bed. But not much of this got
into the home-made *Saturday Reviews* and Yankee *Athenoeums*--a
hint or two maybe, but no more. In the main they kept to
their old resolute demands for a pure civil-service, the budget system in Congress, the abolition of hazing at the Naval
Academy, an honest primary and justice to the Filipinos, with
extermination of the Prussian serpent added after August,
1914. And Dr. Dewey, on his remote Socratic Alp, pursued the
calm reënforcement of the philosophical principles underlying
these and all other lofty and indignant causes. . . .

Then, of a sudden, Siss! Boom! Ah! Then, overnight, the upspringing of the intellectual soviets, the headlong assault upon all the old axioms of pedagogical speculation, the nihilistic dethronement of Prof. Dewey--and rah, rah, rah for Prof. Dr. Thorstein Veblen! Veblen? Could it be--? Aye, it was! My old acquaintance! The *Doctor obscurus* of my half-forgotten bout with the so-called intellectual Socialist! The Great Thinker *redivivus*! Here, indeed, he was again, and in a few months--almost it seemed a few days--he was all over the *Nation*, the *Dial*, the *New Republic* and the rest of them, and his books and pamphlets began to pour from the presses, and the newspapers reported his every wink and whisper, and everybody who was anybody began gabbling about him. The spectacle, I do not hesitate to say, somewhat disconcerted me and even distressed me. On the one hand, I was sorry to see so learned and interesting a man as Dr. Dewey sent back to the unsufferable dungeons of Columbia, there to lecture in imperfect Yiddish to classes of Grand Street Platos. And on the other hand, I shrunk supinely from the appalling job, newly rearing itself before me, of re-reading the whole canon of the singularly laborious and muggy, the incomparably tangled and unintelligible works of Prof. Dr. Thorstein Veblen. . . .

But if a sense of duty tortures a man, it also enables him to achieve prodigies, and so I managed to get through the whole infernal job. I read "The Theory of the Leisure Class," I read "The Theory of Business Enterprise," and then I read "The Instinct of Workmanship." An hiatus followed; I was racked by a severe neuralgia, with delusions of persecution. On recovering I tackled "Imperial Germany and the Industrial Revolution." Malaria for a month, and then "The Nature of Peace and the Terms of Its Perpetuation." What ensued was never diagnosed; probably it was some low infection of the mesentery or spleen. When it passed off, leaving only an asthamatic cough, I read "The Higher Learning in America," and then went to Mt. Clemens to drink the Glauber's salts. Eureka! the business was done! It had strained me, but now it was over. Alas, a good part of the agony had been needless. What I found myself aware of, coming to the end, was that practically the whole system of Prof. Dr. Veblen was in his first book and his last--that is, in "The Theory of the Leisure Class," and "The Higher Learning in America." I pass on the good news. Read these two, and you won't have to read the others. And if even two daunt you, then read the first. Once through it, though you will have missed many a pearl and many a pain, you will have a fairly good general acquaintance with the gifted metaphysician's ideas.

For those ideas, in the main, are quite simple, and often
anything but revolutionary in essence. What is genuinely remarkable about them is not their novelty, or their complexity,
nor even the fact that a professor should harbor them; it is
the astoundingly grandiose and rococo manner of their statement, the almost unbelievable tediousness and flatulence of
the gifted headmaster's prose, his unprecedented talent for
saying nothing in an august and heroic manner. There are
tales of an actress of the last generation, probably Sarah
Bernhardt, who could put pathos and even terror into a reci-
tation of the multiplication table. The late Louis James did
something of the sort; he introduced limericks into "Peer
Gynt" and still held the yokelry agape. The same talent,
raised to a high power, is in this Prof. Dr. Veblen. Tunnel
under his great moraines and stalagmites of words, dig down
into his vast kitchen-midden of discordant and raucous poly-
syllables, blow up the hard, thick shell of his almost theo-
logical manner, and what you will find in his discourse is
chiefly a mass of platitudes--the self-evident made horrify-
ing, the obvious in terms of the staggering. Marx, I daresay, said a good deal of it, and what Marx overlooked has been
said over and over again by his heirs and assigns. But Marx,
at this business, labored under a technical handicap: he wrote
in German, a language he actually understood. Prof. Dr. Veblen submits himself to no such disadvantage. Though born, I
believe, in These States, and resident here all his life, he
achieves the effect, perhaps without employing the means, of
thinking in some unearthly foreign language--say Swahili, Su-
merian or Old Bulgarian--and then painfully clawing his
thoughts into a copious but uncertain and book-learned English.
The result is a style that affects the higher cerebral centers like a constant roll of subway expresses. The second
result is a sort of bewildered numbness of the senses, as before some fabulous and unearthly marvel. And the third result, if I make no mistake, is the celebrity of the professor
as a Great Thinker. In brief, he states his hollow nothings
in such high, astounding terms that they must inevitably ar-
rest and blister the right-thinking mind. He makes them mysterious. He makes them shocking. He makes them portentous.
And so, flinging them at naïve and believing minds, he makes
them stick and burn.

No doubt you think that I exaggerate--perhaps even that
I lie. If so, then consider this specimen--the first paragraph of Chapter XIII of "The Theory of the Leisure Class":

*In an increasing proportion as time goes on, the anthro-
pomorphic cult, with its code of devout observances, suffers*

*a progressive disintegration through the stress of economic
exigencies and the decay of the system of status. As this
disintegration proceeds, there come to be associated and
blended with the devout attitude certain other motives and
impulses that are not always of an anthropomorphic origin,
nor traceable to the habit of personal subservience. Not all
of these subsidiary impulses that blend with the bait of de-
voutness in the later devotional life are altogether congru-
ous with the devout attitude or with the anthropomorphic
apprehension of sequence of phenomena. Their origin being
not the same, their action upon the scheme of devout life is
also not in the same direction. In many ways they traverse
the underlying norm of subservience or vicarious life to
which the code of devout observances and the ecclesiastical
and sacerdotal institutions are to be traced as their substantial basis. Through the presence of these alien motives
the social and industrial régime of status gradually disin-
tegrates, and the canon of personal subserviences loses the
support derived from an unbroken tradition. Extraneous habits and proclivities encroach upon the field of action occupied by this canon, and it presently comes about that the
ecclesiastical and sacerdotal structures are partially converted to other uses, in some measure alien to the purposes
of the scheme of devout life as it stood in the days of the
most vigorous and characteristic development of the priest-
hood.*

Well, what have we here? What does this appalling salvo
of rhetorical artillery signify? What is the sweating professor trying to say? What is his Message now? Simply that
in the course of time, the worship of God is commonly cor-
rupted by other enterprises, and that the church, ceasing to
be a mere temple of adoration, becomes the headquarters of
these other enterprises. More simply still, that men sometimes vary serving God by serving other men, which means, of
course, serving themselves. This bald platitude, which must
be obvious to any child who has ever been to a church bazaar
or a parish house, is here tortured, worried and run through
rollers until it is spread out to 241 words, of which fully
200 are unnecessary. The next paragraph is even worse. In
it the master undertakes to explain in this peculiar dialect
the meaning of "that non-reverent sense of aesthetic congruity with the environment which is left as a residue of the
latter-day act of worship after elimination of its anthropomorphic content." Just what does he mean by this "non-
reverent sense of aesthetic congruity?" I have studied the
whole paragraph for three days, halting only for prayer and
sleep, and I have come to certain conclusions. I may be

wrong, but nevertheless it is the best that I can do. What
I conclude is this: he is trying to say that many people go
to church, not because they are afraid of the devil but because they enjoy the music, and like to look at the stained
glass, the potted lilies and the rev. pastor. To get this
profound and highly original observation upon paper, he
wastes, not merely 241, but more than 300 words! To say what
might be said on a postage stamp he takes more than a page in
his book! . . .

     And so it goes, alas, alas, in all his other volumes--a
cent's worth of information wrapped in a bale of polysylla-
bles. In "The Higher Learning in America" the thing perhaps
reaches its damndest and worst. It is as if the practice of
that incredibly obscure and malodorous style were a relent-
less disease, a sort of progressive intellectual diabetes, a
leprosy of the horse sense. Words are flung upon words until
all recollection that there must be a meaning in them, a
ground and excuse for them, is lost. One wanders in a laby-
rinth of nouns, adjectives, verbs, pronouns, adverbs, prepo-
sitions, conjunctions and participles, most of them swollen
and nearly all of them unable to walk. It is difficult to
imagine worse English, within the limits of intelligible
grammar. It is clumsy, affected, opaque, bombastic, windy,
empty. It is without grace or distinction and it is often
without the most elementary order. The learned professor
gets himself enmeshed in his gnarled sentences like a bull
trapped by barbed wire, and his efforts to extricate himself
are quite as furious and quite as spectacular. He heaves, he
leaps, he writhes; at times he seems to be at the point of
yelling for the police. It is a picture to bemuse the vulgar
and to give the judicious grief.

     Worse, there is nothing at the bottom of all this stri-
dent wind-music--the ideas it is designed to set forth are,
in the overwhelming main, poor ideas, and often they are
ideas that are almost idiotic. One never gets the thrill of
sharp and original thinking, dexterously put into phases.
The concepts underlying, say, "The Theory of the Leisure
Class" are simply Socialism and water; the concepts underlying "The Higher Learning in America" are so childishly obvious that even the poor drudges who write editorials for newspapers have often voiced them. When, now and then, the professor tires of this emission of stale bosh and attempts
flights of a more original character, he straightway comes
tumbling down into absurdity. What the reader then has to
struggle with is not only intolerably bad writing, but also
loose, flabby, cocksure and preposterous thinking . . . Again

I take refuge in an example. It is from Chapter IV of "The
Theory of the Leisure Class." The problem before the author
here has to do with the social convention which frowns upon
the consumption of alcohol by women--at least to the extent
to which men may consume it decorously. Well, then, what is
his explanation of this convention? Here, in brief, is his
process of reasoning:

1. *The leisure class, which is the predatory class of
feudal times, reserves all luxuries for itself, and disap-
proves their use by members of the lower classes, for this
use takes away their charm by taking away their exclusive
possession.*
2. *Women are chattels in the possession of the leisure
class, and hence subject to the rules made for inferiors.
"The patriarchal tradition . . . says that the woman, being
a chattel, should consume only what is necessary to her sustenance, except so far as her further consumption contributes
to the comfort or the good repute of her master."*
3. *The consumption of alcohol contributes nothing to
the comfort or good repute of the woman's master, but "detracts sensibly from the comfort or pleasure" of her master.
Ergo, she is forbidden to drink.*

This, I believe, is a fair specimen of the Veblenian
ratiocination. Observe it well, for it is typical. That is
to say, it starts off with a gratuitous and highly dubious
assumption, proceeds to an equally dubious deduction, and
then ends with a platitude which begs the whole question.
What sound reason is there for believing that exclusive possession is the hall-mark of luxury? There is none that I can
see. It may be true of a few luxuries, but it is certainly
not true of the most familiar ones. Do I enjoy a decent bath
because I know that John Smith cannot afford one--or because
I delight in being clean? Do I admire Beethoven's Fifth Sym-
phony because it is incomprehensible to Congressmen and
Methodists--or because I genuinely love music? Do I prefer
terrapin à la Maryland to fried liver because plowhands must
put up with the liver--or because the terrapin in intrinsically a more charming dose? Do I prefer kissing a pretty
girl to kissing a charwoman because even a janitor may kiss
a charwoman--or because the pretty girl looks better, smells
better and kisses better? Now and then, to be sure, the idea
of exclusive possession enters into the concept of luxury. I
may, if I am a bibliophile, esteem a book because it is a
unique first edition. I may, if I am fond, esteem a woman
because she smiles on no one else. But even here, save in a
very small minority of cases, other attractions plainly enter

into the matter. It pleases me to have a unique first edition, but I wouldn't care anything for a unique first edition of Robert W. Chambers or Elinor Glyn; the author must have my respect, the book must be intrinsically valuable, there must be much more to it than its mere uniqueness. And if, being fond, I glory in the exclusive smiles of a certain Miss _____ or Mrs. _____, then surely my satisfaction depends chiefly upon the lady herself, and not upon my mere monopoly. Would I delight in the fidelity of the charwoman? Would it give me any joy to learn that, through a sense of duty to me, she had ceased to kiss the janitor?

Confronted by such considerations, it seems to me that there is little truth left in Prof. Dr. Veblen's theory of conspicuous consumption and conspicuous waste--that what remains of it, after it is practically applied a few times, is no more than a wraith of balderdash. In so far as it is true it is obvious. All the professor accomplishes with it is to take what every one knows and pump it up to such proportions that every one begins to doubt it. What could be plainer than his failure in the case just cited? He starts off with a platitude, and ends in absurdity. No one denies, I take it, that in a clearly limited sense, women occupy a place in the world--or, more accurately, aspire to a place in the world--that is a good deal like that of a chattel. Marriage, the goal of their only honest and permanent hopes, invades their individuality; a married woman becomes the function of another individuality. Thus the appearance she presents to the world is often the mirror of her husband's egoism. A rich man hangs his wife with expensive clothes and jewels for the same reason, among others, that he adorns his own head with a plug hat: to notify everybody that he can afford it-- in brief, to excite the envy of Socialists. But he also does it, let us hope, for another and far better and more powerful reason, to wit, that she intrigues him, that he delights in her, that he loves her--and so wants to make her gaudy and happy. This reason may not appeal to Socialist sociologists. In Russia, according to an old scandal (officially endorsed by the British bureau for pulling Yankee noses) the Bolsheviki actually repudiated it as insane. Nevertheless, it continues to appeal very forcibly to the majority of normal husbands in the nations of the West, and I am convinced that it is a hundred times as potent as any other reason. The American husband, in particular, dresses his wife like a circus horse, not primarily because he wants to display his wealth upon her person, but because he is a soft and moony fellow and ever ready to yield to her desires, however preposterous. If any conception of her as a chattel were actively in him, even un-

consciously, he would be a good deal less her slave. As it
is, her vicarious practice of conspicuous waste commonly
reaches such a development that her master himself is forced
into renunciations--which brings Prof. Dr. Veblen's theory
to self-destruction.

His final conclusion is as unsound as his premisses.
All it comes to is a plain begging of the question. Why does
a man forbid his wife to drink all the alcohol she can hold?
Because, he says, it "detracts sensibly from his comfort or
pleasure." In other words, it detracts from his comfort and
pleasure because it detracts from his comfort and pleasure.
Meanwhile, the real answer is so plain that even a professor
should know it. A man forbids his wife to drink too much
because, deep in his secret archives, he has records of the
behavior of other women who drank too much, and is eager to
safeguard his wife's self-respect and his own dignity against
what he knows to be certain invasion. In brief, it is a commonplace of observation, familiar to all males beyond the age
of twenty-one, that once a woman is drunk the rest is a mere
matter of time and place: the girl is already there. A husband, viewing this prospect, perhaps shrinks from having his
chattel damaged. But let us be soft enough to think that he
may also shrink from seeing humiliation, ridicule and bitter
regret inflicted upon one who is under his protection, and
one whose dignity and happiness are precious to him, and one
whom he regards with deep and (I surely hope) lasting affec-
tion. A man's grandfather is surely not his chattel, even by
the terms of the Veblen theory, and yet I am sure that no
sane man would let the old gentleman go beyond a discreet
cocktail or two if a bout of genuine bibbing were certain to
be followed by the complete destruction of his dignity, his
chastity and (if a Presbyterian) his immortal soul. . . .

One more example of the Veblenian logic and I must pass
on: I have other fish to fry. On page 135 of "The Theory of
the Leisure Class" he turns his garish and buzzing search-
light upon another problem of the domestic hearth, this time
a double one. First, why do we have lawns around our country
houses? Secondly, why don't we employ cows to keep them
clipped, instead of importing Italians, Croatians and blacka-
moors? The first question is answered by an appeal to ethnology: we delight in lawns because we are the descendants
of "a pastoral people inhabiting a region with a humid climate." True enough, there is in a well-kept lawn "an element of sensuous beauty," but that is secondary: the main
thing is that our dolicho-blond ancestors had flocks, and
thus took a keep professional interest in grass. (The Marx

motif! The economic interpretation of history in E flat.)
But why don't *we* keep flocks? Why do we renounce cows and
hire Jugo-Slavs? Because "to the average popular apprehension a herd of cattle so pointedly suggests thrift and usefulness that their presence . . . would be intolerably cheap."
With the highest veneration, Bosh! Plowing through a bad
book from end to end, I can find nothing sillier than this.
Here, indeed, the whole "theory of conspicuous waste" is exposed for precisely what it is: one per cent platitude and
ninety-nine per cent nonsense. Has the genial professor,
pondering his great problems, ever taken a walk in the country? And has he, in the course of that walk, ever crossed a
pasture inhabited by a cow (*Bos taurus*)? And has he, making
that crossing, ever passed astern of the cow herself? And
has he, thus passing astern, ever stepped carelessly, and--

But this is not a medical work, and so I had better haul
up. The cow, to me, symbolizes the whole speculation of this
laborious and humorless pedagogue. From end to end you will
find the same tedious torturing of plain facts, the same re-
lentless piling up of thin and over-labored theory, the same
flatulent bombast, the same intellectual strabismus. And always with an air of vast importance, always in vexed and formidable sentences, always in the longest words possible, always in the most cacophonous English that even a professor
ever wrote. One visualizes him with his head thrown back,
searching for cryptic answers in the firmament and not seeing
the overt and disconcerting cow, not watching his step. One
sees him as the pundit *par excellence*, infinitely earnest and
diligent, infinitely honest and patient, but also infinitely
humorless, futile and hollow. . . .

So much, at least for the present, for this Prof. Dr.
Thorstein Veblen, head Great Thinker to the parlor radicals,
Socrates of the intellectual Greenwich Village, chief star
(at least transiently) of the American *Athanoeums*. I am
tempted to crown in mention of some of his other astounding
theories--for example, the theory that the presence of pupils, the labor of teaching, a concern with pedagogy, is necessary to the highest functioning of a scientific investiga-
tor--a notion magnificently supported by the examples of
Flexner, Ehrlich, Metchnikoff, Loeb and Carrel! I am tempted,
too, to devote a thirdly to the astounding materialism, almost the downright hoggishness, of his whole system--its absolute exclusion of everything approaching an aesthetic motive. But I must leave all these fallacies and absurdities
to your own inquiry. More important than any of them, more
important as a phenomenon that the professor himself and all

his works, is the gravity with which his muddled and highly
dubious ideas have been received. At the moment, I daresay,
he is in decline; such Great Thinkers have a way of going out
as quickly as they come in. But a year or so ago he dominated
the American scene. All the reviews were full of his ideas.
A hundred lesser sages reflected them. Every one of intellectual pretentions read his books. Veblenism was shining in
full brilliance. There were Veblenists, Veblen clubs, Veblen
remedies for all the sorrows of the world. There were even,
in Chicago, Veblen Girls--perhaps Gibson girls grown middle-
aged and despairing.

The spectacle, unluckily, was not novel. Go back through
the history of America since the early nineties, and you will
find a long succession of just such violent and uncritical
enthusiasms. James had his day; Dewey had his day; Ibsen had
his day; Maeterlinck had his day. Almost every year sees
another intellectual Munyon arise, with his infallible peruna
for all the current malaises. Sometimes this Great Thinker
is imported. Once he was Pastor Wagner; once he was Bergson;
once he was Eucken; once he was Tolstoi; once he was a lady,
by name Ellen Kay; again he was another lady, Signorina
Montessori. But more often he is of native growth, and full
of the pervasive cocksureness and superficiality of the land.
I do not rank Dr. Veblen among the worst of these haruspices,
save perhaps as a stylist; I am actually convinced that he
belongs among the best of them. But that best is surely depressing enough. What lies behind it is the besetting intellectual sin of the United States--the habit of turning intellectual concepts into emotional concepts, the vice of or-
giastic and inflammatory thinking. There is, in America, no
orderly and thorough working out of the fundamental problems
of our society; there is only, as one Englishman has said,
an eternal combat of crazes. The things of capital importance
are habitually discussed, not by men soberly trying to get at
the truth about them, but by brummagem Great Thinkers trying
only to get *kudos* out of them. We are beset endlessly by
quacks--and they are not the less quacks when they happen to
be quite honest. In all fields, from politics to pedagogics
and from theology to public hygiene, there is a constant emotional obscuration of the true issues, a violent combat of
credulities, and inane debasement of scientific curiosity to
the level of mob gaping.

The thing to blame, of course, is our lack of an intellectual aristocracy--sound in its information, skeptical in
its habit of mind, and, above all, secure in its position and
authority. Every other civilized country has such an aristo-

cracy. It is the natural corrective of enthusiasms from below. It is hospitable to ideas, but as adamant against crazes. It stands against the pollution of logic by emotion, the
sophistication of evidence to the glory of God. But in America there is nothing of the sort. On the one hand there is
the populace--perhaps more powerful here, more capable of putting its idiotic ideas into execution, than anywhere else--
and surely more eager to follow platitudinous messiahs. On
the other hand there is the ruling plutocracy--ignorant, hostile to inquiry, tyrannical in the exercise of its power, sus-
picious of ideas of whatever sort. In the middle ground there
is little save an indistinct herd of intellectual enuchs,
chiefly professors--often quite as stupid as the plutocracy
and always in great fear of it. When it produces a stray rebel he goes over to the mob; there is no place for him within
his own order. This feeble and vacillating class, unorganized
and without authority, is responsible for what passes as the
well-informed opinion of the country--for the sort of opinion
that one encounters in the serious periodicals--for what later
on leaks down, much diluted, into the few newspapers that are
not frankly imbecile. Dr. Veblen has himself described it in
"The Higher Learning in America"; he is one of its characteristic products, and he proves that he is thoroughly of it by
the timorousness he shows in that book. It is, in the main,
only half-educated. It lacks experience of the world, assurance, the consciousness of class solidarity and security. Of
no definite position in our national life, exposed alike to
the clamors of the mob and the discipline of the plutocracy,
it gets no public respect and is deficient in self-respect.
Thus the better sort of men are not tempted to enter it. It
recruits only men of feeble courage, men of small originality.
Its sublimest flower is the American college president, well
described by Dr. Veblen--a perambulating sycophant and plati-
tudinarian, a gaudy mendicant and bounder, engaged all his
life, not in the battle of ideas, the pursuit and dissemina-
tion of knowledge, but in the courting of rich donkeys and
the entertainment of mobs. . . .

Nay, Veblen is not the worst. Veblen is almost the best.
The worst is--but I begin to grow indignant, and indignation,
as old Friedrich used to say, is foreign to my nature.

*Alfred A. Knopf, Prejudices: First Series, (1919): 59-83

"A New Theory of Thorstein Veblen": John Kenneth Galbraith
(1973)*

The nearest thing in the United States to an academic
legend--equivalent to that of Scott Fitzgerald in fiction or
the Barrymores in the theatre--is the legend of Thorstein
Veblen. The nature of such a legend, one assumes, is that the
reality is enlarged by imagination and that, eventually, the
image has an existence of its own. This is so of Veblen. He
was a man of great and fertile mind and a marvelously resourceful exponent of its product. His life, beginning on the frontier of the upper Middle West in 1857 and continuing, mostly
at one university or another, until his death in 1929, was not
without adventure of a kind. Certainly, by the standards of
academic life at the time, it was nonconformist. There was
ample material both in his work and in his life on which to
build the legend, and the builders have not failed.

There is, in fact, a tradition in American social thought
that traces all contemporary comment on and criticism of
American institutions to Veblen. As with Marx to a devout
Marxist, everything is there. The Marxist, however, is somewhat more likely to know his subject. It is possible, indeed,
that nothing more clearly marks an intellectual fraud in our
time than a penchant for glib references to Veblen, particularly for assured and lofty reminders, whenever something of
seeming interest is said, that Veblen said it better and
first.

The legend deriving from Veblen's life owes even more to
imagination. What is believed--about his grim, dark boyhood
in a poor immigrant Norwegian family in Minnesota; his reaction to these oppressive surroundings; his harried life in
the American academic world of the closing decades of the
last century and the first two of this; the fatal way he attracted women and vice versa and its consequences in his
tightly corseted surroundings; the indifference of all right-
thinking men to his work--has only a limited foundation in
fact.

Perhaps one who writes prefaces should perpetuate any
available myth. Economics is a dull enough business and sociology is sometimes worse, and so, sometimes, are those who
profess these subjects. When, as with Veblen, the man is enlarged by a nimbus, the latter should be brightened, not dis-
solved. One reason that economics and sociology are dull is
the belief that everything associated with human personality
should be made as humdrum as possible. This is science.
Still, there is a certain case for truth, and in regard to

Veblen the truth is also far from tedious. His life was
richly interesting; his boyhood, if much less grim than commonly imagined, had a deep and lasting effect on his later
writing. Veblen is not a universal source of insight on
American society. He did not see what had not yet happened.
Also, on some things he was wrong, and faced with a choice
between accuracy and a formulation that he felt would fill
his audience with outrage, he rarely hesitated. He opted for
the outrage. But no man of his time or since has looked with
such a cool and penetrating eye, not so much at pecuniary gain
as at the way its pursuit makes men and women behave.

This cool and penetrating view is the substance behind
the Veblen legend. It is a view that still astonishes the
reader with what it reveals. While there may be other deserving candidates, only two books by American economists of
the nineteenth century are still read. One of these is Henry
George's *Progress and Poverty*; the other is Veblen's *Theory
of the Leisure Class*. Neither of these books, it is interesting to note, came from the sophisticated and derivative world
of the eastern seaboard. Both were products of the frontier--
reactions of frontiersmen, in one case to speculative alienation of land, in the other to the pompous social ordinances
of the affluent. But the comparison cannot be carried too
far. Henry George was the exponent of a notably compelling
idea; his book remains important for that idea--for the notion of the terrible price that society pays for private ownership and the pursuit of profit in land. Veblen's great work
is a wide-ranging and timeless comment on the behavior of people who possess or are in pursuit of wealth and who, looking
beyond their wealth, want the eminence that, or so they believe, wealth was meant to buy. No one has really read very
much if he hasn't read *The Theory of the Leisure Class* at
least once. Not many of more than minimal education get
through life without referring at some time or another to
"conspicuous consumption," "pecuniary emulation," or "conspicuous waste" even though they may not be quite certain
whence these phrases came.

At first glance the Veblen origins are the American
cliché. His parents, Thomas Anderson and Kari Bunde Veblen,
emigrated from Norway to a farm in rural Wisconsin in 1847,
ten years before Thorstein's birth. There were the usual
problems in raising the money for the passage, the inevitable
and quite terrible hardships on the voyage. In all, the
Veblens had twelve children, of whom Thorstein was the sixth.
The first farm in Wisconsin was barren or, more likely, seen
as inferior to what, on the basis of better intelligence, was

known to be available farther west. They moved, and in 1865
they moved a second time. The new and final holding was on
the prairie and now about an hour's drive south from Minne-
apolis. It is to this farm that the legend of Veblen's dark
and deprived boyhood belongs. No one who visits this countryside will believe it. There can be no farming country anywhere in the world with a more generous aspect of opulence.
The soil is black and deep, the barns are huge, the silos numerous as also the special bins for sealing surplus corn, and
the houses big, square, comfortable, if without architectural
pretense. A picture of the Veblen house survives--an ample,
pleasant white frame structure bespeaking not merely comfort
but affluence. Since this countryside was originally open,
well-vegetated prairie, it must have looked rewarding a hundred years ago. Thomas Veblen acquired 290 acres of this
wealth; it is hard to imagine that he, his wife, or any of
the children could have thought of themselves as deprived.
Not a thousand, perhaps not even a hundred, farm proprietors--
families working their own land--were so handsomely endowed
in the Norway they had left. Nor, in fact, did the Veblens
think themselves poor. Thorstein's brothers and sisters were
later to comment, sometimes with amusement, on occasion with
disgust, on the myth of their early poverty.

There were other things that separated the family from
the general run of Scandinavian immigrants and made Thorstein
less of an accident. Thomas Veblen, who had been a skilled
carpenter and cabinetmaker, soon proved himself a much more
than normally intelligent and progressive farmer. And it
seems certain that however he viewed the farm for himself, he
regarded it as a stepping-stone for his children. Even more
exceptional perhaps was Kari, his wife. She was a notably
alert, imaginative, self-confident, and intelligent woman who
identified, protected, and encouraged the family genius from
an early age. In later years, in a family and community where
more hands were always needed and virtue was associated, accordingly, with efficient toil--effectiveness as a worker was
what distinguished a *good* boy or girl from the rest--Thorstein
Veblen seems to have been treated with some tolerance. Under
the cover of a weak constitution he was given leisure that he
used for reading. This released time could only have been
provided by remarkably perceptive parents. One of Veblen's
brothers later wrote that it was from his mother that "Thorstein got his personality and his brains," although others
thought them his own decidedly original property.

Thorstein, like his brothers and sisters, went to the
local schools, and on finishing with these he was dispatched

to Carleton College (then styled Carleton College Academy) in
the nearby town of Northfield, Minnesota. His sister Emily
was in attendance at the same time; other members of the family went also to Carleton. In an engaging and characteristic
exercise of imagination, their father acted to keep down college expenses. He bought a plot of land on the edge of town
for the nominal amount charged for such real estate in that
time and put up a house to shelter his offspring while they
were being educated. The legend has always held or implied
that the winning of an education involved for Thorstein Veblen
a major and even heroic hardship. This should be laid finally
to rest. A letter in the archives of the Minnesota Historical
Society from Andrew Veblen, Thorstein's brother, notes that
"Father gave him strictly necessary assistance through his
schooling. Thorstein, like the rest of the family, kept his
expenses down to the minimum . . . all in line with the close
economy that the whole family practiced." A sister-in-law,
Florence (Mrs. Orson) Veblen, wrote more indignantly, "There
is not the slightest reason for depriving my father-in-law of
the credit of having paid for the education of his children--
all of them--he was well able to do so; he had two good farms
in the richest farming district in America."

    It was, nevertheless, an exception to the general com-
munity practice that the Veblen children should be sent to
college rather than put to useful work, as Norwegian farmers
would then have called it, on the farm. They were also sent
to a Congregational college--Carleton--rather than to one of
the Lutheran institutions that responded to the language,
culture, and religion of the Scandinavians. The Veblen myth
(as the Veblen family has also insisted) has exaggerated the
alienation of the Norwegians in general and the Veblens in
particular. It is part of the legend that Veblen's father
spoke no English and that his son had difficulty with the
language. This is nonsense. Still, in the local class structure, the Anglo-Saxons were the dominant town and merchant
class; the Scandinavians were the hard-working peasantry.
But the Veblen children were not educated to remain peasants.

    Carleton was one of the denominational colleges that were
established as the frontier moved westward, and unquestionably
it was fairly bad. But like so many small liberal-arts colleges of the time, it was the haven for a few learned men and
devoted teachers--the saving remnant who seemed always to show
up when such a school was established. One of these men in
Veblen's time was John Bates Clark, who later taught at Columbia University, where he was recognized as the dean of American economists of his day. Veblen became a student of Clark's;

Clark thought well of Veblen.

This approval may have required imagination and tolerance, for in various class exercises Veblen was already giving ample indication of his later style and method. He prepared a solemn and ostentatiously sincere classification of men according to their noses; one of his exercises in public rhetoric defended the drunkard's view of his own likely death; another argued the case for cannibalism. Clark, who was presiding when Veblen appeared to favor intoxication, felt obliged to demur. In a denominational college in the Midwest at this time it seems possible that cannibalism had a somewhat higher canonical sanction. Veblen resorted to the defense that he was to employ with the utmost consistency for the rest of his life: no value judgment was involved; he was not being partial to the drunk; his argument was purely scientific.

Veblen finished his last two years at the college in one and graduated brilliantly. His graduation oration was "Mill's Examination of Hamilton's Philosophy of the Conditioned." It was described by contemporaries as a triumph, but it does not survive. While at Carleton Veblen had formed a close friendship with Ellen Rolfe; she was the daughter of a prominent and affluent Midwestern family and, like Veblen, was independent and introspective--very much apart from the crown--and also highly intelligent. They were not married for another eight years, although this absence of haste did not mean that either had any less reason to regret it in later leisure. The legend has always pictured Veblen as an indifferent and unfaithful husband who was singularly incapable of resisting the advances of the women whom, however improbably, he continued to infatuate. But the Veblen family considered the fault to be at least partly Ellen's. She had a nervous breakdown following an effort at teaching; in a far from reticent and not necessarily accurate letter Florence Veblen concludes, "There is not the least doubt she is insane." It was, in any case, an unsuccessful marriage.

After teaching for a year at a local academy following his graduation from Carleton, Veblen departed for Johns Hopkins University in Baltimore to study philosophy. At this time, 1881, Johns Hopkins was being advertised as the first American university with a specialized graduate school on the European model. The billing, as Veblen was later to point out, was considerably in advance of the fact. Money and hence professors were very scarce; the atmosphere was that of a conservative southern town. Veblen was unhappy, did not complete the term, and began what was to be a lifetime of wandering over the American academic landscape.

His next stop was Yale. It was a time of considerable controversy at Yale--of what scholars with a gift for metaphors from the brewing industry call intellectual ferment. The principal focus of contention was between one Noah Porter, a pretentious divine then believed to be an outstanding philosopher and metaphysician, and William Graham Sumner, the American exponent of the British philosopher and sociologist Herbert Spencer. The practical thrust of Porter's effort was to prevent Sumner from assigning Spencer's *Principles of Sociology* to his classes. In this he succeeded; Spencer was righteously suppressed. Porter's success, one imagines, proceeded less from the force of his argument against Spencer's acceptance of evolution as a social as well as biological axiom than from the fact that he (Porter) was also then the president of the university. In Veblen's later writing there is a strong suggestion of Spencer. Natural selection is not the foundation of a system for Veblen, but it serves him as an infinitely handy explanation of how some survive and prosper and others do not. In Veblen's scheme cupidity is more often the basis for such selection than moral worth.

There has been solemn discussion of the effect of this philosophical disputation at Yale, and of his own dissertation on Kant, on Veblen's later writing. My instinct is to think it was remarkably slight. This is affirmed in a general way by the other Veblens. In later years his brother Andrew (a physicist and mathematician) responded repeatedly and stubbornly to efforts to identify the sources of Thorstein Veblen's thought. He did not think anyone could be singled out: "I do not believe that anyone much influenced the formation of his views or opinions." It must be sufficient that after two and a half years at Yale--underwritten by a brother and the Minnesota family and farm--Veblen emerged with a Ph.D. He wanted to teach; he had also, on the whole, rather favorable recommendations. But he could not find a job, and so he went back to the Minnesota homestead. There, endlessly reading and doing occasional writing, he remained for seven years. He professed ill health for a part of this time; Andrew Veblen, later letters show, thought the illness genuine; other members of his family diagnosed his ailment as partly an allergy to manual toil. He married, and Ellen brought with her a little money. From time to time he was asked to apply for teaching positions; tentative offers were righteously withdrawn when it was discovered that he was not a subscribing Christian. In 1891 he resumed his academic wandering: he became a graduate student at Cornell.

The senior professor of economics at Cornell at the time was J. Laurence Laughlin, a stalwart exponent of the English classical school who, until then, had declined to become a member of the American Economic Association in the belief that it was socialistically inclined. Joseph Dorfman of Columbia University, the eminent student of American economic thought and the pre-eminent authority on Veblen, tells Laughlin's story of his meeting with Veblen in his massive and important *Thorstein Veblen and His America* (Viking, 1934), a book to which everyone who speaks or writes on Veblen is indebted. Laughlin "was sitting in his study in Ithaca when an anemic-looking person, wearing a coonskin cap and corduroy trousers, entered and in the mildest possible tone announced: 'I am Thorstein Veblen.' He told Laughlin of his academic history, his enforced idleness and his desire to go on with his studies. The fellowships had all been filled, but Laughlin was so impressed with the quality of the man that he went to the president and other powers of the university and secured a special grant."

Apart from the impression of Veblen's manner and dress so conveyed, the account is important for another reason. Always in Veblen's life there were individuals--a minute but vital few--who sensed and were captured by his genius. Often, as in the case of Laughlin, they were conservatives--men who in ideas and habits were a world apart from Veblen. And repeatedly these men rescued their prodigious and highly inconvenient friend.

Veblen was at Cornell rather less than two years--although long enough to begin advancing his career with uncharacteristic orthodoxy by getting articles into the scholarly journals. Then Laughlin was invited to be head of the department of economics at the new University of Chicago. He took Veblen with him; Veblen was awarded a fellowship of $520 a year, for which he was to prepare a course on the history of socialism and assist in editing the newly founded *Journal of Political Economy*. He was now thirty-five years old. In the next several years he advanced to the rank of tutor and instructor, continued to teach and to edit the *Journal*, wrote a great many reviews and numerous articles--among others, pieces on the theory of women's dress, on the barbarian status of women, and on the instinct of workmanship and the irksomeness of labor-- all work that foreshadowed later books. In these years he also developed his teaching style, if such it could be called. He sat at a table and spoke in a low monotone to the handful of students who were interested and could get close enough to hear. He also discovered, if he had not previously learned, that something--mind, manner, dress, his sardonic and challenging indifference to approval or disapproval--made him extremely attractive to women. His wife found that she had more and more competition for his attention. This competition was something to which neither she nor the academic communities in which Veblen resided ever reconciled themselves. In 1899, while still at Chicago and while Laughlin was still having trouble getting him small increases in pay or even, on occasion, getting his appointment renewed, he published his first and greatest book. It was *The Theory of the Leisure Class*.

There is little that anyone can be told about *The Theory of the Leisure Class* that he cannot learn better by reading the book himself. It is a marvelous book; it is also, in its particular way, a masterpiece of English prose. But the qualification is important. Veblen's writing cannot be read like that of any other author. Wesley C. Mitchell--regarded, though not with entire accuracy, as Veblen's leading intellectual legatee--once said that "one must be highly sophisticated to enjoy his [Veblen's] books." All who cherish Veblen would wish to believe this. The truth is simpler than that. One needs only to realize that if Veblen is to be enjoyed, he must be read very carefully and slowly. He enlightens, amuses, and delights but only if he is given a good deal of time.

It is hard to divorce Veblen's language from the ideas it conveys. The ideas are pungent, incisive, and insulting. But the writing itself is also a weapon. Mitchell noted that Veblen normally wrote "with one eye on the scientific merits of his analysis, and his other eye fixed on the squirming reader." Veblen also startles his reader with an exceedingly perverse use of words. Their meaning rarely varies from that sanctioned by the most precise and demanding usage. But in the context they are often, to say the least, unexpected. This Veblen attributes to scientific necessity. Thus, in his immortal discussion of conspicuous consumption, he notes that expenditure, if it is to contribute efficiently to the individual's "good fame," must generally be on "superfluities." "In order to be reputable it [the expenditure] must be wasteful." All of this is quite exact. The rich do want fame; the dress, housing, equipage that serve this purpose and are not essential for existence are superfluous. Nonessential expenditure is wasteful. But only Veblen would have used the words "fame," "superfluity," "reputable," and "waste" in such a way. In the case of "waste" he does decide that a word of explanation is necessary. This is characteristically both airy and matter-of-fact. In everyday speech, he says, "the word carries an undertone of deprecation. It is here used for want of a better term . . . and it is not to be taken in an odious sense. . . ."

And so he continues. The wives of the rich forswear useful employment because "abstention from labor is not only an honorific or meritorious act, but is presently becomes a requisite of decency." "Honor," "merit," and "decency" are all used with exactness, although these words are not often associated with idleness. A robber baron, Veblen says, has a better chance of escaping the law than a small crook because "a well-bred expenditure of his booty especially appeals . . . to persons of a cultivated sense of the proprieties, and goes far to mitigate the sense of moral turpitude with which his dereliction is viewed by them." One does not ordinarily associate the disposal of ill-gotten wealth with good breeding.

Thus the way *The Theory of the Leisure Class*—or anything by Veblen—must be read. If one goes rapidly, words will be given their ordinary contextual meaning—not the precise and perverse sense that Veblen intended. Waste will be wicked and not a source of esteem; the association of idleness with merit, honor, and decency will somehow be missed as well as that between the crook and his expenditure. The book yields its meaning, and therewith its full enjoyment, only to those who too have leisure.

When Veblen had finished the manuscript of *The Leisure Class*, he sent it to the publisher, Macmillan, and it came back several times for revision. Eventually, it is believed, Veblen was required to put up a guarantee before Macmillan would agree to publish the book. It is tempting to speculate as to the reason for this reluctance. The book could not have been badly written in any technical or grammatical sense. Veblen, after all, was by then an experienced editor. Nor was he any novice as a writer. One imagines that the perverse and startling use of words, combined no doubt with the irony and the attack on the icons, was more than any publisher could readily manage. But someone must also have seen how much was there.

The thesis of *The Theory of the Leisure Class* can be quickly given. It is a tract, the most comprehensive ever written, on snobbery and social pretense. Some of it has application to American society at the end of the last century— at the height of the gilded age of American capitalism—but more is wonderfully relevant to modern affluence.

The rich have often been attacked by the less rich for enjoying a superior social position that is based on assets and not moral or intellectual worth, for using their wealth and position to sustain a profligate consumption of resources

of which others are in greater need, and for defending the
social structure that accords them their privileged position.
And they have been attacked for the base and wicked behavior
that wealth sustains and that their social position sanctions.
In all this the attackers, in effect, concede the rich their
superior power and position; they deny them their right to
that position or to behave as they do therein. Usually the
denial involves a good deal of righteous anger or indignation.
The rich have been thought worth the anger and indignation.

Here is Veblen's supreme literary and polemical achievement. He concedes the rich and the well-to-do nothing, and
he would not dream of suggesting that his personal attitudes
or passions are in any way involved. The rich are merely an-
thropological specimans whose behavior the possession of money
and property has made more interesting and more visibly ridiculous. The effort to establish precedence for oneself and the
yearning for the resulting esteem and applause are the most
nearly universal of human tendencies. Nothing in this respect
differentiates a Whitney, Vanderbilt, or Astor from a Papuan
chieftain or what one encounters in "for instance, the tribes
of the Andamans." The dress, festivals, or rituals and arti-
facts of the Vanderbilts and Whitneys are more complex; that
does not mean their motivation is in any way different from
that of their barbarian counterparts.

Indeed, it is inconceivable that the affluent should be
viewed with indignation. The scientist does not become angry
with the primitive tribesman because of the extravagance of
his sexual orgies or the sophistication of his self-mutilation. Similarly with the social observances of the American
rich. Their banquets are equated in commonplace fashion with
the orgies; the self-mutilation of the savage is of a piece
with the painfully constricting dress in which (at that time)
the well-to-do bound up their women or their women corseted
themselves.

It is well to remember that Veblen wrote in the last years
of the last century--before the established order suffered the
disintegrating onslaught of World War I, Lenin, and the lev-
elling oratory of modern democratic politics. It was a time
when gentlemen still believed they were gentlemen and--in the
United States at least--that it was wealth that made the difference. And, by and large, the rest of the population still
agreed. Veblen calmly identified the manners and behavior of
these so-called gentlemen with the manners and behavior of the
people of the bush. Speaking of the utility of different observances for the purpose of affirming or enhancing the indi-

vidual's repute, Veblen notes that "presents and feasts had probably another origin than that of naive ostentation, but they acquired their utility for this purpose very early, and they have retained that character to the present. . . . Costly entertainments, such as *the potlatch or the ball*, are peculiarly adapted to serve this end." The italics equating the potlatch and the ball are mine; Veblen would never have dreamed of emphasizing so obvious a point.

The book is a truly devastating put-down, as would now be said. But much more was involved. *The Theory of the Leisure Class* brilliantly and truthfully illuminates the effect of wealth on behavior. No one who has read this book ever again sees the consumption of goods in the same light. Above a certain level of affluence the enjoyment of goods--of dress, houses, automobiles, entertainment--can never again be thought intrinsic, as in a naive way established or neoclassical economics still holds it to be. Possession and consumption are the banner that advertises achievement--that proclaims, by the accepted standards of the community, that the possessor is a success. In this sense--in revealing what had not hitherto been seen--*The Leisure Class* is a major scientific achievement.

It is also true, alas, that much of the process by which this truth is revealed--by which Veblen's insights are vouchsafed--is scientifically something of a contrivance. There is no doubt that before writing *The Leisure Class* he had read widely on anthropology. He has a great many primitive communities and customs at his fingertips, and he refers to them with an insouciance that suggests--and was probably meant to suggest--he had much more knowledge in reserve. But the book is wholly devoid of sources; no footnote or reference tells on what Veblen relied for information. On an early page he explains that the book is based on everyday observation and not pedantically on the scholarship of others. This is adequate as far as Fifth Avenue and Newport are concerned. Accurate secondhand knowledge can be assumed. But Veblen had no similar opportunity for knowing about the Papuans.

In fact, Veblen's anthropology and sociology are weapon and armor rather than science. He uses them to illuminate (and to make ridiculous) the behavior of the most powerful class--the all-powerful class--of his time. And since he does it in the name of science and with the weapons of science-- and since no overt trace of animus or anger is allowed to appear--he does it with nearly perfect safety. The butterfly does not attack the zoologist for saying that it is more dec-

orative than useful. That Marx was an enemy whose venom was
to be returned in kind, capitalists did not doubt. But Veblen's venom went undetected. The American rich never quite
understood what he was about--or what he was doing to them.
The scientific pretense, the irony, and the careful explanations that the most pejorative words were being used in a
strictly nonpejorative sense put him beyond their comprehension.

This protection was necessary at the time. And there is
a wealth of evidence that Veblen was fully conscious of it.
During the years when he was working on *The Leisure Class*,
liberal professors at the University of Chicago were under
frequent attack from the adjacent plutocracy. The latter expected economics and the other social sciences to provide the
doctrine that graced its privileges. In the mid nineties
Chauncey Depew, the notable political windbag, told the Chicago
students that "this institution, which owes its existence to
the beneficence of Rockefeller, is in itself a monument of the
proper use of wealth accumulated by a man of genius. So is
Cornell, so is Vanderbilt, and so are the older colleges, as
they have received the benefactions of generous, appreciative
and patriotic wealth." In 1895 one Edward W. Bemis, an associate professor of political economy in the extension, i.e.,
outpatient, department of the university, attacked the traction monopoly in Chicago, which, assisted by wholesale bribery,
had fastened itself on the backs of Chicago streetcar patrons.
His appointment was not renewed. The university authorities,
like many godly men, especially in universities, believed
that they had a special license to lie. So they compounded
their crime in dismissing Bemis be denying that their action
was an overture to the traction monopoly or reflected the
slightest abridgment of academic greedom. The local press was
not misled; it saw this as a concession to sound business interest and applauded. In a fine sentence on scholarly responsibility, the Chicago *Journal* said: "The duty of a professor
who accepts the money of a university for his work is to teach
the established truth, not to engage in the 'pursuit of truth.'"
A forthright sentiment.

The last chapter of *The Leisure Class* is "The Higher
Learning as an Expression of the Pecuniary Culture." It an-
ticipates a later, much longer, and much more pungent dis-
quisition by Veblen on the influence of the pecuniary civilization on the university (*The Higher Learning in America: A
Memorandum on the Conduct of Universities by Businessmen*,
published in 1918). In this chapter Veblen--though also concerned with other matters--stresses the conservative and pro-

tective role of the universities in relation to the pecuniary culture: "New views, new departures in scientific theory, especially new departures which touch the theory of human relations at any point, have found a place in the scheme of the university tardily and by a reluctant tolerance, rather than by cordial welcome; and the men who have occupied themselves with such efforts to widen the scope of human knowledge have not commonly been well received by their learned contemporaries." No one will be in doubt as to whom, in the last clause, Veblen had in mind. Elsewhere he notes that "as further evidence of the close relation between the educational system and the cultural standards of the community, it may be remarked that there is some tendency latterly to substitute the captain of industry in place of the priest, as head of seminaries of the higher learning."

Given such an enviornment and given also his subject, Veblen, it will be evident, needed the protection of his art. On the whole it served him well. In the course of his academic career he was often in trouble with academic administrators-- but mostly on personal and idiosyncratic rather than political or ideological grounds. He was not understood or appreciated by his more pedestrian, if often more fashionable, academic colleagues. A man like Veblen creates problems for such people. They accept the established view, rejoice in the favor of the Establishment. Anyone who does not share their values is a threat to their position and self-esteem, for he makes them seem sycophantic and pedestrian, as indeed they are. Veblen was such a threat. But the rich, to whom ultimately he addressed himself, never penetrated his defenses.

Veblen also enjoyed a measure of political immunity in a hostile world because he was not a reformer. His heart did not beat for the proletariat or even for the downtrodden and poor. He was a man of animus and not of revolution.

The source of Veblen's animus has regularly been related to his origin. He was the son of immigrant parents; he had experienced the harsh life of the frontier; he did so at a time when the Scandinavians were, by any social standard, second-class citizens. They were saved, if at all, only because they could not be readily distinguished by their color. What was more natural than that someone from such a background should turn on his oppressors? *The Theory of the Leisure Class* is Veblen's revenge for the abuse to which he and his parents were subjected.

This, I am persuaded, misunderstands Veblen. His animus

was based not on anger and resentment but on derision. I must
here cite an experience of my own. Some ten years ago, to fill
in the idle moments of one of the more idle occupations, that
of the modern ambassador, I wrote a small book about the clansmen among whom I was reared on the north shore of Lake Erie in
Canada. The Scotch (as with exceptional etymological correct-
ness we call ourselves), like the Scandinavians, inhabited the
farms; the people of the towns were English. From Toronto in
the nineteenth century other Englishmen, in conjunction with
the Church of England as a kind of holding company for political and economic interest, dominated the economic, political,
religious, and social life of Upper Canada to their own unquestioned advantage.

In writing the book I found it agreeable to recapture the
mood of my youth--of my parents, neighbors, the more prestigious members of the other clans. We felt ourselves superior
to the storekeepers, implement dealers, poolroom operators,
grain dealers, and other entrepreneurs of the adjacent towns.
We worked harder, spent less, but usually had more. The more
prestigious clans and clansmen took education seriously and,
as a matter of course, monopolized the political life of the
community. Yet the people of the towns were invariably under
the impression that social prestige resided with them. They
were English not Scotch, Anglicans not Presbyterians, and
identified, however vicariously, with the old ruling class.
Their work, if such it could be called, did not soil the
hands. We were taught to think that claims to social prestige
based on such vacuous criteria were silly. We regarded the
people of the towns not with envy but amiable contempt. On
the whole we enjoyed letting them know.

When I published the book, by far the largest number of
letters I received were from people who had grown up in German
and Scandinavian communities in the Midwest, who told me that
it was really the mood of their childhood that I had described.
"That was how we felt. You could have been writing about our
community." I am sure it was Veblen's mood. The Veblens regarded themselves, not without reason, as the representatives
of a superior culture. The posturing of the local Anglo-
Saxon elite they also regarded with contempt. *The Theory of
the Leisure Class* is this contempt extended to a class structure with class distinctions that were an enlargement of the
posturing Veblen observed as a youth.

The reception of *The Theory of the Leisure Class* divided
the men of reputable and orthodox position from those who were
capable of thought. On the whole, however, it could not have

disappointed Veblen. One Establishment reviewer said that it was such books by dilettantes that brought sociology into disrepute among "careful and scientific thinkers," science being here used in the still customary sense as a cover and defense for orthodoxy. With wonderful solemnity he advised that it was illegitimate to classify within the leisure class such unrelated groups as the barbarians and the modern rich. Another equally predictable scholar avowed that the rich were rich because they earned the money—the gargantuan reward of the captain of industry and the miserly one of the man with a spade were the valuation of their contribution to society as measured by their economic efficiency. But other and more imaginative men were delighted, a point on which again I am indebted to Dorfman. Lester Ward, the first American sociologist of major repute, said that "the book abounds in terse expressions, sharp antithesis, and quaint, but happy phrases. Some of these have been interpreted as irony and satire, but . . . the language is plain and unmistakable . . . the style is farthest removed possible from either advocacy or vituperation." Ward was admiring but a bit too trusting. William Dean Howells, also at the time at the peak of his reputation, was enthusiastic as well. He was also taken in by Veblen. "In the passionless calm with which the author pursues his investigation, there is apparently no animus for or against a leisure class. It is his affair to find out how and why and what it is." The sales of *The Leisure Class* were modest, although few could have guessed how durably they would continue. Veblen was promoted in 1900 to the rank of assistant professor. His pay remained negligible.

Veblen's writing continued and so, in 1906, did his academic peregrinations. Although still ill-paid and in subordinate rank, he was, in a manner of speaking, famous. His married life had become tenuous; he did little to resist the aggression of other women. His classes were small, and orthodox scholars and those of his victims who could understand his argument were either adverse or outraged. But he had become a possible academic adornment. Harvard, urged by Frank W. Taussig, considered inviting him to join its department of economics but quickly had second thoughts. David Starr Jordan, then creating a new university south of San Francisco, could not afford to be so cautious and invited Veblen to Leland Stanford as an associate professor. Veblen survived there for three years. But his domestic arrangements—sometimes Ellen, sometimes others—were by now, for the time and community, an open scandal. Once he responded wearily to a complaint with a query: "What is one to do if the woman moves in on you?" What, indeed? Jordan concluded that there were adornments

that Stanford could not afford. Veblen was invited to move
on. By the students, at least, he was not greatly missed.
Dozens were attracted by his reputation to his classes; only
a handful--once only three--survived to the end of the term.

After leaving Stanford he had difficulty getting another
post, but again an established scholar with an instinct for
the dissenter came to his rescue. H. J. Davenport, then one
of the major figures in the American economic pantheon, took
him to the University of Missouri. There he encountered some
of the students on whom he had the most lasting effect, including Isador Lubin, who was later to be a close aide of
F.D.R. and Harry Hopkins and a protector of Veblen in the
latter's many moments of need. Veblen divorced Ellen and in
1914 married Anne Fessenden Bradley, a gentle, admiring woman
who, however, survived only a few hours. (In 1918 she suffered severe mental illness, and in 1920 she died.)

From Missouri Veblen's wanderings were again resumed.
He went to Washington during World War I--as one of the less
likely participants in the wartime administration. From Washington he went to New York to experiment with life as an editor and then to teach at The New School for Social Research.
His writings continued; as with the early ones, they are sar-
donic, laconic, and filled with brilliant insights. Nearly
all of his nine subsequent books on economics and related
subjects develop points of which there is a hint--or, in the
case of *The Higher Learning in America*, a chapter--in *The
Leisure Class*. None of these books achieved the eminence of
his first one. But the men of established reputation continued
to be appalled. In a review of *The Higher Learning in America*
in the *New York Times Review of Books* in 1919, Brander Matthews
said of Veblen, "His vocabulary is limited and he indulges in
a fatiguing repetition of a dozen or a score of adjectives.
His grammer is woefully defective. . . ." The book is, in
fact, one of Veblen's most effective and compelling tracts.
Other critics were wiser. Gradually, step by step, it came
to be known that Veblen was a genius, the most penetrating,
original, and uninhibited--indeed the greatest--source of
social thought in the time.

This did not mean that he was much honored or rewarded.
The honors and rewards were reserved, as all good practice
requires, for the reputable as distinct from the intelligent.
Veblen's students had frequently to come to his support. Work
became harder to find than ever. In the mid twenties, aging,
impecunious, and tired, he returned reluctantly to California,
and there in 1929 he died.

The Nation, following his death, spoke of Veblen's "mordant wit, his extraordinary gift of discovering wholly new meanings in old facts," saying in a sentence what I have said here in many. Wesley C. Mitchell wrote an obituary note in the *Economic Journal*, an organ of the Royal Economic Society, then pre-eminently the most prestigious economic publication in the world. Saying sadly that "we shall have no more of these investigations with their curious erudition, their irony, their dazzling phrases, their bewildering reversals of problems and values," he also observed that the *E.J.*, as economists have long called it, had reviewed but one of Veblen's books. In 1925 it took notice of the ninth reprinting of *The Theory of the Leisure Class*, twenty-six years after its original publication.

American Heritage, Volume 24(3), (1973): 33:40

REVIEW: Raymond Vernon (1974)*

The Theory of the Leisure Class was published in 1899. Nevertheless, it qualifies as a product of the twentieth century, for that curtain-raising work carried most of the major themes that Veblen would develop in a series of ten remarkable books over the next thirty years.

Remarkable books they were, but not, it appears, very durable. Today, few graduate students of economics study Veblen seriously. Those with an eye on the computer and the econometric model find little in Veblen to carry them over the intellectual hurdles they confront. Those who are reformist or radical in mood, if they know Veblen at all, find him too aloof and old fashioned for their needs. Here and there, Veblen's detached commentary on the predatory capitalist process provides them with a catchword or a phrase for argument, but not much more than that.

Perhaps it is just as well that radicals have not taken much to Veblen. He himself had no use for radicals. *The Leisure Class*, as far as he was concerned, was not a radical tract. It was a scholarly analysis, an effort at understanding, an explanation that was an end in itself. To the extent that Veblen had social values and social preferences, he would probably have denied that they were revealed in *The Leisure Class* or in his other works. The conspicuous waste and the pecuniary emulation that Veblen attributes to the leisure class is, in his view, simply the result of a social process, entitling the actors neither to good marks nor to bad. The legitimate business-like sabotage of captains of finance is an inescapable aspect of their calling. The instinct for workmanship, the propensity for cooperation, and the avoidance of waste which he attributes to workers and engineers are no more to be admired than the characteristics of the leisure class and the captains of finance are to be condemned. Today's social activist, therefore, even if he is attracted by Veblen's ideas, would be repelled by Veblen's way of using them.

Though Veblen is little read and little quoted in the mainstream of modern economics, it would be too simple to say that he has not affected the direction of that stream. The size of his impact might well have disappointed him, but the effect is surely there.

In Veblen's time, the leading propositions of economics were still taught as a series of laws, derived by deduction from a set of absolute assumptions. To be sure, great economists like Alfred Marshall were perfectly capable of ruminating over the complexities and uncertainties of economic motivation and process, and of revealing their uncertainties in footnotes to the main text. But, on the whole, if Veblen is to be believed, economics was taught as dogma: right was right and wrong was unmentionable.

Veblen's reaction was the predictable response of the perpetually alienated scholar viewing the economics profession morosely from a precarious perch on its fringes. From that perch, he saw the leading economists as a priestly cult, ordained by the University and practicing their rites in accordance with their calling. They were, in his view, more nearly an appendage of the leisure class than of the engineers.

Veblen, on the other hand, professed to build his leading propositions not from dogma but from observations, purportedly drawn from history and anthropology. According to his perceptions, the fundamental tenet of classical economics --that man is driven by a constant weighing of pain-cost against pleasure-gain--was simply not an operational concept. Men's motivations, as Veblen saw them, were various; they were capable of being systematically described, but they were far from being explained by simple-minded hedonistic calculus. I rather suspect that Veblen's own generalizations at times would draw pained reactions from historians and anthropologists. But the question of methodology was at least as important to Veblen as that of substance.

The fact that the empirical side of economics has flourished in the last half century might on first glance be regarded as a trimuph for Veblen's views. But some of the empiricism in contemporary economics would surely have left Veblen cold and unapproving. The mechanistic slicing up of available data according to prescribed statistical procedures, so commonly presented in economic journals, was not what Veblen had in mind. That kind of empiricism, I fear, he would have regarded as akin to the ritualistic exercises in deduction which he found so dysfunctional in his contemporaries. In any case, those who abandon themselves to mechanistic data manipulation probably owe that proclivity to the advent of the Hollerith card, the computer, and the canned regression program, not to the empiricism of Veblen.

Still, Veblen's influence can be seen in his impact on key personalities. One branch of his influence is epitomized in the empirical tradition associated with men like Wesley Mitchell and Simon Kuznets; the other in the reformist tradition of such men as R. G. Tugwell and J. K. Galbraith. These men, representing profoundly different brands of empiricism, have influenced economic thinking measurably in their own times; and in the case of Kuznets and Galbraith, the impact is still palpable. It is not clear, however, how much influence empirically minded men of either variety will have on the shape of economics in the long run. Their complex and qualified propositions are in constant competition with the elegance and simplicity of propositions drawn from the deductive process. Commencing with the authoritative assertions of conventional wisdom and manipulated through the unambiguous modalities of algebraic or geometric logic, the deductions are bound to command a premium in the intellectual marketplace, even when in substance they may seem shallow.

My admiration for Veblen's splendid spirit of unremitting alienation has, I fear, shone all too obviously through these last few paragraphs. Yet, for all that, I have considerable misgiving over the intrinsic validity of Veblen's own offerings. The impact of his brilliant mind may have been good for the main drift of economics, deflecting it a little bit in more fruitful directions. But the propositions he supported in order to perform that diversionary task may not be altogether defensible.

Take Veblen's distinction between the captain of finance
and the engineer, the predatory bargainer and the productive
worker, the conspicuous waster and the rational measurer.
These delicious dichotomies, seductively appealing though they
may be, do not have much to do with the visible facts of the
modern corporation. True, contemporary society continues to
turn up an unambiguous example of the captain of finance from
time to time, a Cornfeld or a Vesco. But how are we to typify
the managers of today's great corporations? Some of their
problems, to be sure, are of Veblen's pecuniary, predatory
variety: decisions on the movement of money, on borrowing and
lending, on the advertising budget, on the tactics of bargaining with the oil sheikhs, on influencing competitors' reactions. But decisions on whether to invest in the building of
supertankers, whether to build large refineries or small,
whether to gamble in the development of commercial shale oil,
all involve engineering estimates that are too important to
be left to engineers. The teleological, rational, and non-
predatory aspects of those difficult decisions require best
guesses over the future cost of various inputs, the future
trend of government regulation, the future development of competing sources of energy, the future course of technologies
as yet unrevealed. In short, once the costs of uncertainty
and information are introduced as elements in the decision
process, Veblen's neat dichotomy is in mortal danger.

One could reply perhaps that the distinction between captains of finance and engineers still remains useful, even
though captains of finance sometimes find themselves obliged
to take a hand in the task of the engineers. But such a reply will never do. The personal values that Veblen attributes
to people in these different pursuits are so dramatically at
odds that one would be at a loss to say how they could be
encased in a single psyche. According to Veblen's definitions, an executive who was made up of one part financier and
one part engineer would run a severe risk of schizophrenia.
Yet the leaders of many large enterprises today--particularly
enterprises engaged in the large-scale development of new
processes and products--do have to perform in both of Veblen's
main modes. Veblen's taxonomy, therefore, seems to fail the
very test on which he himself would insist, namely, that of
its empirical utility.

The limitations in usefulness of Veblen's distinction
between the pecuniary and the productive can be illustrated
from a very different direction, namely, from the experiences
of the Soviet Union. Here we have an economy in which pecuniary motives, as far as most industrial managers are concerned,

are effectively subdued or altogether suppressed. Success, as
a rule, is measured according to the norms of the national
plan; and these norms are usually dominated in physical units.

In order to perform under these unexceptionable standards,
however, Soviet managers often find themselves obliged to engage in surreptitious, predatory, and pecuniary tactics. The
problem is that the central-planning mechanism does not have--
indeed, cannot have--the information needed for a wholly consistent plan; and even if the data were available, the central-
planning mechanism could not predict the random events, such
as sickness, breakdown, and flood, that throw the plan off
kilter from time to time. Accordingly, the manager hedges;
he under-reports on inventory and machinery, he swaps materials in a grey market, and he resists the center's instructions to modify products or change processes. In short, in
his efforts to operate within the plan under conditions of uncertainty and risk, the manager-engineer takes on some of the
attributes of the captain of finance.

If Veblen was wrong to place so much weight on his captain of finance as a useful archetype, he was in even greater
error to rely so much on his mythical engineer as a counter-
point. The engineer, of course, does represent a certain kind
of rationality in modern life, but like all forms of rationality, that of the engineer is restrained at its limits by a
set of unquestioned assumptions. The engineer's form of rationality, therefore, has to be weighed in terms of whether
it plays over a wide field or a narrow, and whether the assumptions that apply at the borders of his field make much
sense.

In terms of some of the social preferences of the society
of the 1970's, the engineer's values may be no more attractive
than those of the captains of finance. The skills of engineers
are generally supplied within an organization that has an assigned task; and it is notorious that engineers as a class are
not given to raising questions about the nature of the task
itself. Highway engineers build roads even if mass transit
makes more sense. Chemical plant engineers build efficient
chemical plants even if efficiency requires polluting the atmosphere. In short, the rationality of the engineer is bounded
by the task of the institution with which he is associated.

Moreover, Veblen's assumption that rationality is an in-
grained habit of mind among workers and engineers, carried
over from their daily occupations into other aspects of their
behavior, does not seem self-evident. I have never seen a

reliable breakdown of the membership of organizations whose
values are primarily predatory, honorific, nonteleogical and
wasteful, such as local poker societies, investment clubs,
drag-racing associations, and the Ku Klux Klan. But I am prepared to guess that engineers are not under-represented in any
of these organizations, as compared with commission brokers or
race horse jockeys or corporate directors. Indeed, as far as
politics is concerned, I would not be surprised to discover
that the engineer's preference for the avoidance of ambiguity
had generated a slight bias in favor of dogmatic and authori-
tarian political solutions.

It may be that in the last days of the nineteenth century
waste, leisure, gaming and the predatory instinct were more
easily associated with the captains of finance than with the
working classes. But casual observation suggests that the
association is badly eroded by now, if indeed it ever existed.
I myself prefer Linder's *The Harried Leisure Class* as an efficient framework for analyzing the leisure pursuits and preferences of captains of finance and of the modern industrial
worker.

Yet, for all the perishability of Veblen's ideas, I suspect he would have reveled in the nature of some of those very
findings of modern researchers that have tended to make his
own observations obsolete. The increased emphasis on risk
and uncertainty in the theory of economic choice, for instance,
would have given him pleasure, though some of the mechanistic
efforts to capture these ideas in simple econometric relationships might have set his teeth on edge. The attempts of the
behavioralists to throw light on the motivations of modern
business organizations would have been grist for his mill,
though I suspect he might have enjoyed Galbraith rather more
than Cyert. The idea that managers might prefer growth to
profits, status to yield, and security to practically anything
else would be in a neo-Veblenian mold, even though it might
reduce even further the utility of the conclusions of classical
Veblen.

The clue to Veblen's genius lay in his alienation, in his
resistance to the conventional wisdom of this time, and in his
indifference to the logical propositions that derived from
such wisdom. He provided that critical counterweight in the
search for human understanding which is constantly needed to
remind us that we have not yet arrived.

*Daedalus, Volume 102, (Winter, 1974): 53-57

The Theory of Monopolistic Competition
by
Edward Chamberlin

REVIEW: Morris A. Copeland (1934)*

Chamberlin's *Theory of Monopolistic Competition*[1] deserves
to rank as one of the major contributions to the theory of value
and distribution in recent years. Holding constant most of the
other assumptions of neo-classical economics that have been especially subjected to criticism of late, he proceeds to vary the
assumption that each market approximates either perfect competition or absolute monopoly. He postulates an imperfectly competitive market consisting of a number of smaller markets, each
being characterized by a seller's monopoly imperfectly isolated
from the others. He studies this imperfect market (which we
will designate the genus market) through one of the constituent
(species) markets and through two demand curves for it, which we
will call the species curve and the average genus curve. The
species demand curve represents changes in the purchases of a
species when the price of that species alone is varied. The
average genus demand curve represents changes in the purchases
of a species when the prices of all other species in the genus
also vary so as to remain "identical"[2] with that of the species
under consideration. The extent of divergence of these two demand curves is a reflection of the effectiveness of competition,
perfect competition appearing as a limiting case in which the
species demand curve is horizontal. In the other limiting case,
absolute monopoly so far as the genus under consideration is
concerned, the two curves coincide.[3] When selling costs are introduced, two types of cost curves are found necessary, too,
analogous to the two demand curves. Thus for a given price, the
species selling-cost-per-unit curve assumes the selling costs of
the competing monopolies constant; the average genus selling-
cost-per-unit curve assumes the same sales cost by each seller
in the genus market.

The (reviewer's) words, "genus" and "species," suggest
quality differences in the good dealt in. Chamberlin's theory
is intended to embrace geographical differences and differences
in terms of sale as well. Most of his theory, except the appen-

65

dix on pure spatial competition, proceeds on the assumption
that each species competes equally closely with every other,
but he deals briefly with the case of near and remote competitors under the caption of "oligopoly." In the reviewer's opinion this case is the rule, and merits more extended treatment.

While Chamberlin has by no means exhausted the possibilities
of varying the assumption regarding monopoly and competition, his
conclusions are instructive. ". . . . Under conditions of pure
competition there would be no selling costs. . . . Wherever
selling costs are incurred--and they are incurred in some measure
for almost all commodities--to cast the price problem in terms of
'competitive' demand and cost curves is not merely inaccurate; it
it impossible" (p. 174). ". . . . The curve of selling costs
which is superimposed on the curve of production costs must be a
rectangular hyperbola distributing over different volumes of product the fixed total of selling costs which defines the demand
curve. It is not a curve showing the costs of producing and
selling different volumes of product. No single demand curve
would be valid for this latter type of cost curve, for the position of the demand curve shifts with each alteration in total
selling expenditure" (p. 175). ". . . . The theory of pure competition understates both price and cost, first by understating
production costs, and secondly, by omitting selling costs altogether" (p. 175). "The conclusion that pure competition represents the scale of production as too large . . . . is highly
probable" (p. 176). This last statement calls for comment below.

Under the usual neo-classical assumptions including perfect
competition, each enterpriser pursuing his own maximum profit
(and each consumer-laborer-saver pursuing his own maximum utility) so acts as to maximize the physical volume of national income. Clearly Chamberlin's modification of neo-classical assumptions introduces one important--though not the only important--
qualification on the validity of this view that private profit
is a good index of public policy. He offers us a theory the implications of which definitely depart from laissez faire and
move toward what is variously called "social control," "public
regulation," "economic planning."

Admittedly, "The theory of monopolistic competition has not
been carried in this study beyond its beginnings" (p. 176).
Chamberlin mentions the implications for the theory of distribution. It may be in order to list some other implications which
he has not followed out and which would require amendments in
some of his statements.

(1) Economic theory has recognized but seldom explored the

concept of a buyer's monopoly. Had Chamberlin not followed this precedent in elaborating his theory of competing monopolies,[4] he might have been led to explore a market in which there is competition both among buyers and sellers, and yet in which each buyer as well as each seller enjoys some monopoly advantages. If his picture of a market is more realistic than the absolute monopoly or perfect competition of the texts, this further step should take us still further in the direction of realism. And it offers us an explanation of what is commonly recognized but cannot be adequately explained by the theory of perfect competition--differences of bargaining power as between buyer and seller. Moreover, had Chamberlin applied his theory to both sides of the market, his analysis would not have been so narrowly limited to the consumer (and investor); it would have considered the laborer, the farmer, and the borrower as well.

(2) Neo-classical competitive theory affords no satisfactory basis for distinguishing "plant" from "enterprise," hence neo-classicists have often failed to distinguish them. Chamberlin has a real place for sales effort in his theory, and hence a basis for explaining the existence of an enterprise that embraces more than one plant. Yet, curiously enough, he fails to make the distinction between plant and enterprise. This confusion is embodied in the words "scale of production" in the quotation from page 176 cited above. If an enterprise includes a number of plants, it is possible but not "highly probable" that the equilibrium scale of production for a plant will be less than the scale for which unit production cost is a minimum. And it is very unlikely that the equilibrium scale of production for the enterprise will be less than under the hypothetical conditions of perfect competition where plant and enterprise coincide. Under appropriate conditions (including unit sales cost at a minimum with a small volume of output as in the diagram on page 138) plant and enterprise will coincide and his conclusion (p. 176) appears to hold.

Failure to reckon with a unit of business organization other than the plant appears also in his discussion of oligopoly, where he says, "If no one is advertising, no one may begin, each realizing that his own aggressive policy would affect so adversely each of his competitors that they would be forced to advertise in order to protect themselves, and that in the end all would lose" (p. 170). He does not here suggest as possible alternatives either consolidation or trade association advertising.

(3) Chamberlin elaborates his theory in stages: (a) price and sales effort constant, quality varied, (b) quality and sales effort constant, price varied, etc. He warns us himself against

assuming that this method will yield a complete picture (p. 3) yet he follows it, and hence he offers no theoretical basis for distinguishing product manipulation[5] as a form of sales effort from quality competition as an anticipation of consumer demand.

(4) It is the virtue of Chamberlin's treatment[6] that he offers us a theory not of a single enterprise but of a *market* consisting on one side of competing monopolies. He does not, however, carry the analysis to its final stage--the economic system as a whole.[7] The reviewer suspects that, if it were carried to this final stage, there would be interesting and fundamentally important implications (1) for Say's Law;[8] (2) for the theory of the business cycle; (3) for the theory of the level of prices; (4) for the determinacy of the equilibrium point on the assumptions made.

The theory of monopolistic competition clearly opens new vistas for what has been called pure, abstract, or deductive economics. But its novelty is necessarily precarious. For most economists have long recognized, in mental compartments separate from what they call "theory," markets with the characteristics on which Chamberlin insists. Thus few students of railroad rate theory have sought to force the market for railroad service either into the perfect monopoly or into the perfect competition category. Hence it should be easy to read Chamberlin's *Theory* (as many appear to have read Clark's *Overhead Costs*) without recognizing its real novelty.

Nonetheless, it may be suggested that Chamberlin offers us in addition to his specific theoretical novelty important light upon the vexed question of the relative merits of induction and deduction. Neo-classical economic theory has often been criticized as being "purely deductive." In the sense in which it is "purely deductive" Chamberlin is "purely deductive" too. But he has changed one of the premises. The real criticism of neo-classical theory implied in characterizing it as "purely deductive" is that it has clung so steadfastly to a single set of premises, never really probing the logical implications of alternative assumptions.

In lesser degree this criticism applies to Chamberlin. Particularly is it to be regretted that he has accepted the usual neo-classical oversimplifications of time relationships.[9] Thus his theory gives no recognition to the competitive relationship between a present monopolistic buyer or seller and his own future self--a relationship particularly important for differences in bargaining power. Again his cost curves are all premised upon the assumption that every cost is *directly* assignable to some accounting period, that there are no overhead costs in Clark's sense. Further, although the convergence between the species and the average genus demand curve may be an adequate measure of resistance to shifting from one species market to another for the neo-classical assumptions as to time (even here to make the species curve approximately a straight line is arbitrary), it fails to take account of the time-shape of such resistance. Thus his two-dimensional diagrams do not show the relation between the cost of establishing and the cost of maintaining a business. And they do not portray the problem of fixing a single price for successive periods in which the demand schedule is expected to vary from one to another. Nor do the curves portray the relative profitableness of such a policy of price maintenance as compared to alternative policies.

All of which is to say that Chamberlin is a pioneer. If he has missed some of the paths that others have found, and if many interesting bypaths have escaped him, he has nevertheless gone far into new and promising territory--much farther than anyone else who has come to the reviewer's attention. And with few exceptions, he has traveled this new territory with an accuracy of thought that has too seldom been equaled even in the well-worn paths of value theory.

[1] Edward Chamberlin, *The Theory of Monopolistic Competition* (Cambridge: Harvard University Press, 1933). Pp. x+213.

[2] Chamberlin does not investigate what he means by "identical." If his theory is to be broad enough to include the case where the different species represent, e.g., different but competing freight hauls, "identical" appears to be the wrong word.

[3] In addition to offering us a generalized theory under which both perfect (price) competition and absolute monopoly are subsumed as limiting cases, Chamberlin's analysis implies that logically neo-classical theory should include a theory of pure quality competition, which by analogy to the conventional treatment of pure price competition in the "law of supply and demand" might lead to a "law of single quality."

[4] ". . . . The problem of value where buyers are few and sellers are many (as in an unorganized labor market) is not within the scope of this book" (p. 30).

[5]The word "product" should be here taken to include the container and the terms of sale.

[6]Contrast Robinson's *Economics of Imperfect Competition*, London, 1933.

[7]In discussing sales effort he says: "In the analysis to follow, we shall not go beyond the adjustments within the single group. It will be evident that a method similar to that applied as between the individuals in one group could be extended to systems of interdependent groups and even to the all-inclusive problem of the whole economic system."

[8]Chamberlin claims to offer an explanation of permanent excess capacity of plants (Chap. v, Sec. 5). The reviewer is still unconvinced that his market theory (as distinguished from a theory for the entire economic system) explains more than a negligible amount of permanent excess capacity. His position seems to imply (1) that the size of the enterprise at equilibrium is less than the most efficient size of plant, and (2) that it will pay the enterprise in the long run to employ a plant of such size that it would be capable of an appreciably larger continuing output without increasing the average production cost per unit.

It should be added, however, that he has explained chronic excess capacity for one factor--entrepreneurship.

[9]"The curve of selling costs has been defined without reference to the period of time and to the distinction between short-time and long-time results" (p. 139). Chamberlin even follows the classical tradition here to the extent of omitting capitalization doctrine.

Journal of Political Economy 42, (August 1934): 531-36

"On Maximizing Profits: A Distinction Between Chamberlin and Robertson": Stephen Enke (1951)*

I.--*Introduction*

The recent debate on "marginalism," which it is not intended to resurrect, appears to have overlooked an important distinction between the theories of Professor Chamberlin and

Mrs. Joan Robinson. In many respects the ideas—and as Triffin has pointed out, the language also[1]—of these two authors are often very similar. However, it is a mistake to assume that they are analyzing the same subject.[2] In many respects Chamberlin is extending the Marshallian tradition, but with a revolutionary addition; he is studying competition with product differentiation.[3] Logically, as Triffin has pointed out,[4] the advent of product differentiation destroys the concept of industries and groups, and so Chamberlin has really taken a first step towards explaining the competitive adjustments of different product-making firms within the economy. Mrs. Robinson, despite the misleading title of her celebrated book,[5] is concerned only incidentally with competitive adjustments; excepting Chapter 7, she is almost exclusively bent upon analyzing an isolated monopoly or contrasting it with competition. This distinction is important because it affects the ability of each theory to make predictions regarding the typical adjustments of sets of firms.

One of the main potential uses of value theory to the economist is as a predictive aid. This is particularly so, when as is so often the case, the economist is concerned with public policy. He wants to employ value theory to predict the average effect of this or that autonomous event—and especially of actual or proposed government actions—upon the prices, outputs, employment, etc., of some industrial or regional class of firms. Professor Chamberlin's theory of monopolistic competition—or competition with product differentiation—is in many respects a long-run theory and can make aggregate predictions without resorting explicitly to the assumption that each firm knows how to maximize profits. Mrs. Robinson's analysis of isolated monoply can be used to make predictions regarding aggregate behavior only in so far as it can be relied upon to predict individual behavior; and this in turn requires the assumption that each firm knows in advance how to maximize profits, and succeeds in doing so.

It is the contention of this paper that it is quite unreasonable to suppose that each firm acts to maximize profits. The explanation of this unreasonableness is not simple ignorance of the logic of profit-maximizing theories or the practical impossibility of knowing all the relevant functions of the moment and relating them to one another. It is also that, in the face of future uncertainty, the profit-maximizing motive does not provide the entrepreneur with a single and unequivocal criterion for selecting one policy from among the alternatives open to him. The desire to maximize profits does not constitute a clear and unique behavior prescription; consequently, the economist cannot make individual-firm predictions in the short run. In

the long run, however, if firms are in active competition with
one another rather than constituting a number of isolated monopolies, natural selection will tend to permit the survival of
only those firms that either through good luck or great skill
have managed, almost or completely, to optimize their position
and earn the normal profits necessary for survival. In these
instances the economist can make aggregate predictions *as if*
each and every firm knew how to secure maximum long-run profits.
This "as if" assumption is far more reasonable in the case of
Professor Chamberlin's theory than in that of Mrs. Robinson.

III.--*Long-Run Viability Analysis*

It does not follow, because an economist cannot predict
individual firm behavior in the short run, that he can never
predict aggregate firm behavior in the long run. The greater
the intensity of inter-firm rivalry, the more competent is the
economist to make long-run predictions of aggregate firm behavior. Perhaps, under certain circumstances, we can predict
as if firms do in fact maximize profits by consciously equating
marginal costs and marginal revenues.[13]

A firm's survival depends usually upon its ability to escape negative profits. If there is no competition, a great
many policies--all "good" but only one "best"--will permit an
isolated monopoly to survive; the fact that such a firm exists
is no reason for supposing that it is securing maximum profits.[14] However, if there is intense competition, all policies
save the "best" may result in negative profits, and in time
elimination; then firms that survive must, through some combination of good luck or good management, have happened upon
optimum policies. If environmental conditions are such that
surviving and competing firms earn zero profits, we can often
assume that they are securing maximum profits: it may then be
justifiable to pretend that these firms cleverly and deliberately equated marginal revenue and marginal costs in all the
various dimensions.[15] However, this "as if" approach can only
be validly used for the special case of intense competition in
the long run.

Unfortunately, as is well known, long-run equilibrium is
in practice never attained. The processes of long-run adjustment are always being interrupted, before their work has been
completed, by some new autonomous event. This has important
repercussions. It means that maximum possible profits of the
moment may be far in excess of zero profits. It means that
the essential condition of continued survival becomes the earning not of maximum profits (including the case of zero profits),

but of zero or positive profits (including submaximum profits). Moreover, it means that the firms that exist at any moment will include both those that are destined to survive and those that are not. Hence the economist cannot proceed to predict actual aggregate behavior, even for those firms that will survive, as if each one arranged its affairs according to the precepts of marginal analysis. If the environment is changing rapidly and unexpectedly, some poorly managed firms will survive and some well managed firms will expire.[16]

Nevertheless, long-run forces are always at work, even if long-run equilibrium is never quite attained. These long-run forces of adjustment operate in the main through the effect of altered conditions of survival and the births and deaths of firms. In most trades and industries, a considerable number of firms are born and die each year, and the existing population of firms in any locality adjusts in time to the current possibilities of survival.[17]

Consequently, so long as competition is sufficiently intense that zero profits *would* result in the long run, the economist can probably detect the direction in which average adjustments will proceed. He can predict directions of change, if he is willing to overlook the variance of individual behavior, *as if* firms always maximize profits in the end. However, he must supplement this marginal analysis with viability analysis or he may reach false conclusions.[18]

For example, some would hold that a 50 per cent profits tax on corporations, even when it is not permitted to "carry-over" losses, will not alter the output and employment of a corporation. According to marginal analysis, is not a given percentage of maximum profits always better than a given percentage of submaximum profits, and does not each corporate entrepreneur consequently ignore the tax in its decisions? The trouble with this view is that it ignores uncertainty and long-run adjustments. The mean retained profit of all corporations, and the variance of their experienced profit distributions, will presumably be reduced by the profits tax. Consequently, fewer corporations which now exist are likely to survive, and fewer new corporations are likely to come into existence. An economist naturally cannot predict which corporation will now die rather than live, or will now never be born at all, but he should be able to form a reasonable opinion concerning the incidence of a profits tax upon the number of corporations.[19]

In predicting the consequences of some environmental change, such as a new tax, subsidy, or technology, the economist can only adopt the *as if* approach, and employ marginal analysis, if there is intense competition. However, he can then employ viability analysis also; he can consider the altered conditions of survival that will now, through natural selection, affect the character of firms existing in the future.[20] Will large firms now have a better or poorer chance of survival relative to small firms? Will firms that employ skilled labor now have a poorer chance against firms that employ unskilled labor? A consideration of these questions will indicate whether firms of the future are likely to be larger and employ more skilled labor. The character of the prediction may be the same whether the marginal analysis or the viability analysis is employed, and so the issue may seem rather immaterial; however, the language of the former method seems pedagogically and scientifically inferior because it attributes a quite unreasonable degree of omniscience and prescience to entrepreneurs.[21]

IV.--*"Monopolistic Competition" and "Imperfect Competition"*

Some of the more important differences between the theories of competition with product differentiation (Professor Chamberlin) and isolated monopoly (Mrs. Joan Robinson), as they affect the ability of economists to predict entrepreneurial behavior, can now be indicated briefly.

Professor Chamberlin's theory is primarily a long-run theory; exit and entry and rivalry are an integral part of the theory, and the cost curves of his diagrams are explicitly long-run cost curves. On the other hand, Mrs. Robinson's theory, while it could be long run at times, gives the impression of being primarily concerned with the short run. It has already been pointed out that it is invalid to assume short-run profit maximization; hence her theory of "imperfect competition" is an invalid tool for predicting individual firm behavior in the short run.[22]

Mrs. Robinson has to assume that each firm succeeds always in making the most profitable adjustment possible to the situation in which it finds itself; Professor Chamberlin does not have to make such an unrealistic and rigorous assumption. Mrs. Robinson has to assume maximum profits, as she does explicitly in the quoted passage above, because "imperfect competition" does not provide any other theoretical *modus operandi*. In the case of "monopolistic competition," no explicit assumption that firms in fact always secure maximum profits is necessary for, besides firm entry and exit, it stresses inter-firm rivalry in terms of price and output, quality, and selling effort. Hence, profits are always being either eliminated or severely confined through competitive pressures, and surviving firms must in the long run adopt either optimum or almost-optimum policies. This contrast possesses significant implications.

"Imperfect competition" is a study of a firm in isolation for the most part; "monopolistic competition" is a study of the competitive adjustments, in many dimensions, of firms that sell differentiated products. Consequently Mrs. Robinson can only employ marginal analysis, whether in the short or long run, but this employment is unrealistic and unjustifiable; nor can she properly employ viability analysis. Professor Chamberlin, stressing the long run, can adopt the "as if" philosophy and make decent approximations with marginal analysis; or he can use viability analysis to secure approximations.[23]

V.--A Possible Modification of Monopolistic Competition

It would seem that Professor Chamberlin's theory of competition with product differentiation, with one important modification already intimated by Triffin,[24] provides a useful theory of value that can aid the economist in predicting the behavior of firms.

This vital modification would be to recognize that the group is co-extensive with the economy. Chamberlin's revolutionary contribution was his vision of a world of competing and differentiated products. Also, it is well known that high cross elasticities are as often among different kinds of physical products as among products of the same technological class; there may be more competition between Cadillac cars and mink coats than between Cadillacs and Chevrolets.[25] Moreover, most firms of any consequence sell many different kinds of products, and use many different kinds of inputs, so that every firm has numerous competitive fronts with many firms, some in quite different product markets. The concept of a relatively small group cannot be incorporated into a rigid theory, and employed to yield theoretical conclusions, without making many heroic assumptions.[26]

The realistic detail of "monopolitic competition" remains, but several artificial assumptions, such as similar cost curves among members of the "group," can then be sloughed off.[27] It will still be true that the product demand schedules that appear to confront a firm will be dependent upon the price reactions of other related firms: this will also be true of factor supply schedules confronting a firm. It will still be true that if one firm makes successful innovations, every other firm will in numerous ways seek to draw closer to it in imitation. It will still be true that the interdependence of firm profits exists through many links on both the output and input side, and through decisions regarding price, quantity, quality, and promotion. Monopolistic competition will then be able to look at only one firm at a time--the kind of firm depending upon the problem--but it will continue to analyze it in terms of its environment.

If one pauses to contemplate all the facets at which a single firm is confronted by the competitive pressures of the outside world, the possibility that the seller of a differentiated product can hope for continuing long-run profits, as distinct from temporary innovation profits, appears very unimportant. Either the possibility will be slight or the profits will be small. If certain firms appear to make substantial profits year after year, it is probably because they have succeeded in making a series of useful innovations, because some original windfall continues to be carried on the books at an obsolete valuation, or because of the ownership of some legal monopoly.[28]

The fundamental competition is between rival organizations of capitalists, investing money against one another, and the fact that they use physically different products and firms as instruments of their warfare is rather unimportant to the fundamental analysis. Unless rival capitalists obtain unfair advantages from the State, or are extremely lucky in some way, the attempts of each to increase his profits is likely to leave the average profits of a year rather nominal. And if there were a moratorium on external change, so that long-run equilibrium were one day attained, it is possible that all survivors would be left with almost zero profits.

If one is willing to adopt the view that long-run profits will closely approach zero, and this seems a more realistic view if one considers each firm competing with the economy rather than with some artificially restricted "group," monopolistic competition can validly proceed as if firms maximize profits in making long-run predictions. Also, to a considerable extent, what probably awaits one firm in the long run probably awaits other firms which in important respects are similarly situated. And so aggregate predictions can be made with some assurance for groups of firms, even though formal analysis involves a single unreal but representative firm, and even though it will still be impossible to predict the action of any specific existing firm.[29]

VI.--*Summary and Conclusions*

A number of distinctions must be kept in mind when confronted by the term "maximizing profits." This term may mean
that the entrepreneur desires maximum profits (probable) or
that he has always secured maximum profits (improbable).
Clearly the motive does not guarantee the result. In fact,
the motive does not even provide an entrepreneur with a criterion for preferring certain policies to others, unless he is
willing to ascribe a unique outcome to each policy; if he admits uncertainty, and even if he assumes overlapping frequency
distributions for each outcome, there is no rational and unambiguous way to determine which is the "best" policy to adopt.

Because all firms are faced by uncertainty, and most entrepreneurs are very conscious of this, an external observer such
as an economist cannot hope to predict the actions of any real
and specific firm. This inability will be true in the short
run and in the long run. It is for this reason that Mrs. Robinson's theory of "imperfect competition" may well be useless for
prediction, because it seems to depend upon the unrealistic assumption that each firm in every situation knows the most profitable policy and adopts it.

However, an economist may, if one requirement is satisfied,
predict the likely character of those firms in certain situations that survive in the long run. The requirement is that
intense competition prevails, not necessarily among firms selling the same product in the same place, but among rival collec-
tions of capital that compete in many overlapping markets.
Survivors will then tend to earn small or zero profits. The
economist can then employ viability analysis, that is his knowledge of the forces of natural selection in the economic environment, to predict those characteristics that survivors must eventually possess. These survivors, consciously or not, will have
made the right decisions; if long-run equilibrium were attained,
they would be found, whether from luck, habit, or ability, equating marginal costs and receipts. Under these circumstances an
economist can pretend that firms do succeed in maximizing profits; but this is only valid in terms of long-run analysis when
there is intense competition. It is for this reason that Professor Chamberlin's use of marginal analysis in his theory of
"monopolistic competition" is acceptable as an approximation;
surviving firms compete sufficiently that long-run profits must
be meager, and when profits are meager there is little latitude
for suboptimum policies.

The logical justification for employing marginal analysis

in monopolistic competition might be even stronger if the group concept were dropped and each firm were conceived to be in competition with various firms selling and buying different things in a variety of markets. The obvious fact of product differentiation would then not seem to suggest, so falsely but insidiously, the inevitability of monopoly profits throughout the economy. It would still be possible to make generalized predictions, applicable to a group of similarly situated firms, based on a study of a representative firm that does not exist. The characteristics of survivors can then be predicted but not the fate of any actual firm of the moment. This is one of the paradoxes of value theory.

A Note on the Uses of Marginal Analysis

The following note is appended lest "antimarginalists" should seize upon some of the preceding assertions as grist for their mill.[30]

If an entrepreneur knew all relevant facts and functions with certainty, and also possessed sufficient computational ability, a careful equating of the proper marginal values would always secure him maximum profits. Moreover, marginal analysis would be essential for indicating what facts and relationships had first to be ascertained, estimated, or assumed. The orthodox theory of the firm, granted perfect knowledge of present and future, comprises a set of logical propositions which are in themselves irrefutable. The real question, in view of the actual uncertainty of the future, relates to their applicability

As a matter of fact, a corporation economist, but not a government economist, should use marginal analysis even when dealing with problems involving the uncertain future. Once he has decided what future values to assume, for important variables and functions, he should introduce them into the formulae dictated by marginal analysis. Having made his assumptions, he needs marginal analysis to show what policies can yield what it is hoped will be maximum profits. If retrospect reveals that the realized profits are submaximum, and that other policies would have been more profitable, that will not be the fault of marginal analysis but of the disproved assumptions that were employed.

The whole situation is somewhat perplexing. As we have seen, the assumption that firms seek maximum profits does not enable the economist to predict the behavior of an individual firm. However, the fact that few if any firms ever do secure maximum profits does not mean that managers should never employ marginal analysis. Quite the contrary appears to be the case. Marginal analysis, given a set of expectations, will tend to give the greatest possible profits if the future confirms the expectations. In so far as the future can be dimly sensed, the use of marginal analysis should increase firm profits more often than not. Mrs. Robinson notwithstanding, it is not necessary to assume that firms do seek and secure maximum profits in order for marginal curves to be validly employed by *entrepreneurs*, however invalid their employment by economists at times.

Marginal analysis of unique future assumptions, that is the logic of profits maximizing, should be stressed even more in Business Administration than in Economics.

†Many of the ideas in this paper have been inspired by the thoughts and work of Professor A.A. Alchian. (*Cf.* "Uncertainty, Evolution, and Economic Behavior," *Jour. Pol. Econ.*, Vol. LVIII, No. 3 [June, 1950], p. 211 *et seq.*)

[1]Dr. Robert Triffin, *Monopolistic Competition and General Equilibrium Theory* (Harvard University Press, 1940), pp. 38-46.

[2]This has, of course, been frequently pointed out by Professor Chamberlin. It is interesting to note this is also the opinion of Professor George J. Stigler. (See his "Monopolistic Competition in Retrospect" in *Five Lectures on Economic Problems*, London School of Economics and Political Science (Macmillan Co., New York, 1950), Lecture 2.

[3]*The Theory of Monopolistic Competition* (Harvard University Press, 1935).

[4]*Op. cit.*, pp. 81-85.

[5]*The Economics of Imperfect Competition* (Macmillan, London, 1933).

[13]*Cf.* Friedman and Savage, *op. cit.*

[14]Which is the supposition of Mrs. Robinson.

[15] This is Professor Chamberlin's "tangency solution" case.

[16] In the field of biology we do not make the mistake of attributing outstanding analytical ability to those houseflies that find themselves inside a warm house on a cold night. We realize that flies that are just as clever are dying outside. Those entrepreneurs who survive are those who took a satisfactory course of action (not necessarily the best) for some reason (not necessarily the correct one).

[17] One often fails to appreciate the extent of business fatalities due to preoccupation with the success of existing firms; such myopia might be lessened if more periodicals bore such doleful names as DEATH or MISFORTUNE.

[18] These statements assume that there are always some survivors. In some trades—e.g., small roadside eating places—there may be such a relatively large and steady influx of new annual capital, supplied by perennial optimists who want to be their own bosses, that optimum policies cannot even ensure survival. Hence, while matters might settle down to some "steady-state" flows, the identity of existing firms may be constantly changing.

[19] If a firm, before the imposition of a profits tax, had an annual mean profits expectancy of zero, and a Gaussian distribution of profit and loss possibilities around zero with a standard deviation σ, the expected profit with a 50% tax on profits will be $-.2\ \sigma$. Moreover the new variance will be .53 of the old. Altogether not a very happy prospect!

[20] Some of the consequences of this viewpoint are touched upon by E.A.G. Robinson in a recent book review (*Economic Journal*, December 1950, p. 774).

[21] How many students—especially the more sensible and independently minded—have not objected to the notion that firms do maximize profits? They seem to understand the survival approach far more readily. It is the author's opinion that economics teachers will do well to combine viability and marginal analyses—the survival and "as if" approaches—in the lecture hall.

[22] However, it remains a very useful tool for managers in the

short run, for it explains what should be done to maximize profits if the management can only form some unequivocal opinion regarding the future outcome of each policy.

[23]The word "approximations" is used because, according to the original and present version of monopolistic competition theory, the tangency solution of zero economic profits is an extreme possibility and not a theoretical necessity.

[24]*Op. cit.*, p. 85 *et seq.*

[25]*Cf.* Chamberlin, *op. cit.*, p. 9.

[26]*Cf.* Stigler, p. 16, *et seq.*

[27]As Chamberlin does; *op. cit.*, p. 110 *et seq.*

[28]Professor Chamberlin has stressed the possible importance of the copyright protection of brand names as a source of continuing profits (*op. cit.*, Appendix E, p. 113, and elsewhere). This would make it seem that an economy of differentiated products is honeycombed with "monopoly" profits. Despite Coca Cola, and other hoary examples, this notion can easily be exaggerated. There are other tastes than can be cultivated--even in the cola drink trade--and other wants that can be satisfied.

[29]In practice, when predicting, one must segregate certain "similar" firms, even though in theory there may be no group. These firms will all have some similar property; for example, if one were analyzing the effect of a reduction in wool tariffs, one might consider domestic firms making textiles from wool. The "representative firm" might be an average firm, having the average employment, output, etc., of the wool-using firms of this group.

[30]The following are some of the more important references to the marginal analysis controversy, and to problems arising from uncertainty, that have appeared in the *American Economic Review*: R.A. Lester, "Shortcomings of Marginal Analysis for Wage-Employment Problems" (March, 1946); Fritz Machlup, "Marginal Analysis and Empirical Research" (Sept., 1946); R.A. Lester, "Marginalism, Minimum Wages, and Labor Markets" (March, 1947); Fritz Machlup, "Rejoinder to an Antimarginalist"

(March, 1947); H.M. Oliver, "Marginal Theory and Business Behavior" (June, 1947); F.H. Blum, "Marginalism and Economic Policy: A Comment" (Sept., 1947); L.G. Reynolds, "Toward a Short-Run Theory of Wages" (June, 1948); R.A. Gordon, "Short Period Price Determination" (June, 1948); and R.A. Lester, "Equilibrium of the Firm" (March, 1949).

*American Economic Review 41, (September 1951): 566-567; 571-578

"The Impact on Industrial Organization": Joe S. Bain (1963)*

The *Theory of Monopolistic Competition* appeared in 1933, and by the later 1930's a new approach to the empirical investigation of industries and markets emerged, the pursuit of which resulted in the development of a field of study in economics early labeled and still known as "industrial organization."

The new field differed enough from earlier related fields to be recognized as substantially novel, although it did have progenitors or parents. If a simple biological analogy were applicable, we might say that Industrial Organization was foaled out of Trust Problems by Price Theory, but in the world of ideas multiple parentage is common. In this case, I am satisfied to name price theory as the principal sire, but on the side of the dam we must look to a complex of what were frequently labeled as "institutional approaches" to the industrial economy, including that of marketing as well as that of trust problems, including descriptive studies of price and profits, and including the pioneering work of Berle and Means. However this may be, the offspring was distinctive, exhibiting as it grew the capacities to erase artificial barriers between theoretical and institutional studies of markets, to blend them in organized empirical investigations which had definite theoretical orientations and were related to full-blown sets of hypotheses, and even to generate additions to or elaborations of the theory which was its parent.

Can we be a little more specific about the percentage? I believe so, if we look at the offspring. Although scholars working in and around the field have studied and written about many things, students of industrial organization proper not only have emphasized an external view of the market conduct and market performance of groups of firms (congruent with the emphasis of price theory and differing from the internal or industrial-management view), but also have placed a predominant emphasis on the study of the market structures of industries, on interindustry differences in structure, and on associations between market structure and market performance. Their disposition to study and classify market structures clearly reflects the belief that such structures do differ significantly, in the sense that structural differences are likely to be associated with significant differences in performance. Their search for the existence of such associations can be regarded generally as attempts to confirm or disconfirm theoretical hypotheses predicting such associations, to discover needed elaborations in the system of hypotheses, or to provide empirical answers to questions concerning associations of market structures to performance which the theory of the moment asks but does not answer.

This major emphasis in the empirical study of industry, the principal concepts on which such study depends, and indeed the field of industrial organization as we now know it, all find their primary theoretical origin in Chamberlin's *Theory of Monopolistic Competition*. For it was this work which simultaneously did two very important things. It advanced expressly—really for the first time—the major and crucial theoretical construct in which an economy of enterprises was viewed as being made up of industries having a variety of distinctly different market structures, with market conduct and performance tending to differ significantly with differences in structure. And it implemented this construct by developing an uncomplicated but actually quite sophisticated classification of market structures. This classification reflected a remarkable insight into what in the world of markets was empirically relevant to price theory, was the evident parent of substantially all more elaborate market classifications which have been subsequently suggested, and provided the basic skeleton for all of them which have had appreciable merit. Suddenly, therefore, economists were presented with a sophisticated theory of markets in lieu of a theory of perfect competition with dangling appendages concerning monopoly and economic warfare.

Like many theoretical contributions of revolutionary character, Chamberlin's seems at retrospective first glance to have been quite simple, or, let us say, artistically simple. In reformulating price theory, the basic novel things that Chamberlin did were to introduce the notion that groups of rivalrous firms often sell differentiated products and explore its implications, to resurrect and reformulate a long-lost theory of duopoly, and to expand it into a major novelty, a theory of oligopoly. I would regard the general contributions embodied in his analysis of oligopoly as overwhelmingly important, and not really so very

simple. For it at once suggested the need for a theory built
to fit a substantial portion of all industries or markets in
the real economy, which would fill a gaping hole in pre-existing
price theory; developed *de novo* an original pure theory of oligopoly which was both sensible and novel; and suggested the
major principles according to which the broad oligopoly category
in a general market classification might be broken into a number
of subcategories with significantly different structural characteristics. In the twelve pages which comprise his three sections of "mutual dependence recognized," "the effect of uncertainty," and "the small group: oligopoly plus product different
ation," Chamberlin revised modern price theory drastically and
permanently. My emphasis on the importance of this aspect of
his contribution is not intended to minimize in any way the cor
relative importance of his imaginative exploration of the broad
implications for price theory of recognizing formally the existence of product differentiation, product changes, and selling
costs.

Chamberlin's basic construct and his implementation of it
were extremely important because of their obviously great empirical relevance to the actual economy of business enterprises,
which, once one thought about it, was clearly composed of a mix
ture of pure and heterogeneous oligopolies of several distinct
structural subvarieties, atomistic markets with product differentiation, and some markets with pure competition. His contribu
tion, therefore, was not "timely" (in the sense that Keynes's
General Theory was timely); it was a long way overdue, and had
ex post applicability running back to 1890 and before as well as
current and future applicability. It has occurred to me, amids
subsequent and perhaps legitimate quibbles over such matters as
how much a seller's species demand curve in monopolistic competition really slopes, that the utterly unshakeable importance o
Chamberlin's major construct and his development of it is sometimes forgotten.

This, then, was the major impact of the *Theory of Monopoli*
tic Competition on the development of the field of industrial
organization—its development and general design were really su
gested by Chamberlin's major work. His initial market classifi
cation, substantially adequate, has been fruitfully elaborated.
By providing the major outlines of a theory of oligopoly, he
identified a crucial area and direction for further theorizing
and for empirical research that have ensued. And he supplied
the crucial construct and its basic pattern of implementation.
Further, his identification of dimensions of market performance
in addition to those involving price, production cost, and output—that is, selling cost and product quality and variety—

suggested an expanded range of matters deserving empirical study within the sort of theoretical framework he had established. Further yet, he suggested several fruitful hypotheses concerning market conduct in imperfectly collusive oligopolies.

The subsequent development of the field of industrial organization of course depended on one who would grasp the broad implications of the Chamberlin construct and classification of market structures, elaborate the latter, devise means of organizing available data for the testing of hypotheses concerning structure-performance links, and encourage theortically-oriented empirical research of both the individual-industry and cross-sectional types. (Not the least of the contributions at this stage was the proposition that, since the new sort of theory of markets suggested structure-performance links, it might be confirmed or disconfirmed by comparing observable structural characteristics of markets with observable performance, without ever learning much about essentially unobservable sellers' species demand curves.) The party principally responsible for all of this is of course Edward Mason. A very large amount of progress in the field of industrial organization to date has resulted from running down leads that he initially suggested during the 1930's.

There are of course some who hold that price theory can do nicely without oligopoly and product differentiation (and thus without the *Theory of Monopolistic Competition*), and implicitly that a study of industrial organization based on a sophisticated theory of markets is not necessary. A theory of competitive price will be sufficient, or the old competition-monopoly dichotomy will do. This could follow from the proposition that the economist in a bewildering world should be content if he can hit a dinosaur with a scattergun at ten paces. Some difference in aspiration levels seems to be involved here, or some disagreement about the character of our surroundings. Chamberlin's work essentially suggested that we take a close look at our surroundings, check the calendar, and use more adequate weaponry. I am inclined to agree.

I have so far emphasized that the impact of Chamberlin's work on the development of the field of industrial organization was crucial. In so doing, I do not wish to discount the considerable correlative impact of other work in price theory which antedated or was contemporary with his. First, of course, everyone owes a debt to Alfred Marshall. Second, the formal theory of the firm and of the perfectly competitive market was greatly developed during the 1920's, and Chamberlin's work depended on it, as well as being influenced by "off-the-beaten-track" works like Zeuthen's *Economic Warfare*. In addition, the work of a number of writers, including E.A.G. Robinson and P. Sargant Florence on scale economies for the plant and firm, must be recognized as having independent importance.

It would hardly be correct, however, to say that Chamberlin merely put an obvious capstone on a pre-existing edifice. It had not been obvious (stray footnotes and isolated theorems to the contrary notwithstanding), and in any event Chamberlin rebuilt the edifice to a considerable extent.

An important independent impact (the effectiveness of which depended in considerable part on the availability of the Chamberlinian construct) was made by the work of Joan Robinson on monopsony and on price discrimination (as by later work on bilateral monopoly), which suggested elaborations of the theory of markets which have considerable empirical relevance. As to Mrs. Robinson's work in general, it may be argued that some of what Chamberlin made express is implicit in her work. The term implicit is used advisedly, since it is easy to find suggestions of the major Chamberlinian construct and its implementation in her work only after reading Chamberlin; lacking this, it is easier to find the "box of tools for the analytical economist" (to use Mrs. Robinson's words), the provision of which was the asserted purpose of her excellent work.

Acknowledging the importance of the theoretical works mentioned and of others written prior to and since 1933, it must yet be recognized that the *Theory of Monopolistic Competition*, by enunciating in express form a novel theoretical construct and implementing it to provide the essentials of an empirically relevant and sophisticated theory of markets, was *the* major contribution to price theory which set in motion the systematic development of the modern field of industrial organization, and thus a blending of abstract price theory and empirical research which aims to be scientific rather than philosophical.

American Economic Review, Vol. LIV, Number 3, (May, 1964): 28-31

"Chamberlin's Monopolistic Competition: Neoclassical or Institutional?": R. D. Peterson (1979)*

"The theory of oligopoly has been aptly described as a ticket of admission to institutional economics," and perhaps the same may be said of the theory of monopolistic competition

generally.

R.A. Gordon[1]

More than half a century has passed since Edward Hastings Chamberlin deposited his provocative thesis in the library at Harvard College.[2] Thereafter, he spent an entire academic career defending and refining his progeny. The model of monopolistic competition has been a standard topic in most principles and intermediate price theory texts for at least a generation. Written at the onset of a long period of doubt about the relevance of orthodox economics, the theory of monopolistic competition continues to be an intriguing attempt to infuse realism into the neoclassical model of the firm.

Did Chamberlin set out to reformulate orthodox theory, or did he merely try to expand the neoclassical tool kit? A clue is given by the subtitle of his classic treatise: *The Theory of Monopolistic Competition, A Re-Orientation of the Theory of Value.* Another is provided when, in its opening paragraphs, Chamberlin compared the interaction of competition and monopoly in the economic system to a chemical process.[3] Indeed, the present inquiry is directed toward understanding the ramifications of this blending process. Specifically, this article seeks to demonstrate that Chamberlin synthesized institutional *and* neoclassical methodologies in his theory of monopolistic competition. The hypothesis that Chamberlin attempted to overhaul the neoclassical chassis with institutional parts is supported as follows: He credited institutionalist influence on his writings; many institutional economists favorably received the theory of monopolistic competition subsequent to its publication; and rigorous neoclassical theorists continue to reject his methodology. These facts, plus certain institutional elements in the theory of monopolistic competition itself, suggest that Chamberlin's model contains pieces which were cast on an institutional forge.

Acceptance and Rejection of Monopolistic Competition

The institutionalist would also accept much that has been done . . . in the field of monopolistic competition.

John S. Gambs[4]

Two streams of evidence support the contention that Chamberlin's concept of monopolistic competition is compatible with institutional economics. Some is found in the writings of several economists in the profession, and Chamberlin's presentation of the theory of monopolistic competition itself contains certain elements of institutionalism. Each type of evidence will be considered in turn.

Chamberlin's Debt to Veblen

Chamberlin credited the writings of Thorstein Veblen, a dominant force in the development of institutional economics, as one of several inspirational sources for the model of monopolistic competition. These references occur in Chamberlin's main treatise and in an article tracing the genesis of his ideas. Specifically, Chamberlin acknowledged Veblen's observation that most contemporary business firms of that time possessed some degree of monopoly power.[5] This point was crucial to Chamberlin's attempt to mix the concepts of competition and monopoly. Veblen also was credited with inspiring the notion of competitively oriented prices in lines containing traces of monopoly power.[6] In addition, Veblen is associated with Chamberlin's formulation of the concept of product differentiation.[7]

Acceptance by Institutionalists

Just as institutional economists favorably reviewed J.M. Keynes's *General Theory*,[8] so did many of them consider Chamberlin's theory of monopolistic competition compatible with their views. Morris A. Copeland praised Chamberlin for dealing with some of the criticisms of neoclassical economics. Although Copeland regretted that Chamberlin had accepted some orthodox assumptions, he complimented his theoretical entrepreneurship.[9]

Corwin D. Edwards also reacted favorably to Chamberlin's treatise when he reviewed it in conjunction with Joan Robinson's classic work. In fact, Edwards saw in Chamberlin's theory the crucial role of human behavior as opposed to a mechanical treatment of economic activity.[10]

Clarence E. Ayres argues that Chamberlin's theory undermined one of the main methodological elements of neoclassical economics--equilibrium.[11] And because it challenged the concept of equilibrium, Ayres concluded that the model seriously weakened the mechanistic determinateness of price economics.[12]

As a social economist, John Maurice Clark was critical of certain aspects of neoclassical economics.[13] In his major attempt to create a dynamic framework for understanding the economic system, Clark admitted that Chamberlin's ideas strove to make neoclassical economics more relevant than did the theory of pure competition.[14] Moreover, Clark interpreted Chamberlin's work as an attempt to infuse *process* into the theory of the firm.

In a recent text avowedly written from an institutional viewpoint, Copeland suggested that monopolistic competition is more realistic than pure competition as a model of present-day capitalism because it accommodates contemporary institutions.[15] To Copeland, monopolistic competition is adaptable to institutionalism because it deals with a modernized theory of the firm.

Rejection by Neoclassical Economists

Rigid neoclassical theorists tend to reject the model of monopolistic competition for the same reason that they reject institutional economics; on methodological grounds. Institutional economics is pragmatist and instrumental, while neoclassical economics is logical positivist: It is the predictive quality of a theory which counts most, not the realism of assumptions. To the institutional economist, realistic assumptions are essential because important policy prescriptions are often based on them. Since monopolistic competition theory replaced the assumption of product homogeneity with that of product differentiation, to orthodox economists Chamberlin is guilty of the same transgression as institutionalists, namely, questioning the assumptions of a theory.

The most ardent critics of monopolistic competition have been members of the Chicago School. George J. Stigler criticized Chamberlin's theory on grounds that the group concept does not allow technically for any type of equilibrium to be attained.[16] Moreover, Stigler attacked Chamberlin for developing a reformulated theory of value based merely upon the alleged unrealism of neoclassical assumptions.[17]

Another major architect of the Chicago School, Milton Friedman, has also expressed a similar criticism. In his classic article on economic methodology, which discredited institutional economics *and* the theory of monopolistic competition simultaneously, Friedman pointed out that institutional economics is not a positive science because it challenges the realism of assumptions but neglects the empirical testing of hypotheses. And because the model of monopolistic competition altered the neoclassical assumptions of pure competition, Chamberlin's theory does not qualify as positive science for the same reasons that institutional economics does not.[18]

Finally, some neoclassical textbook authors do not regard monopolistic competition as a relevant market structure. Gary

Becker shows Chamberlin's tangency solution as only a minor
part of a section on imperfect competition, and he remarks[19]
that there are technical flaws in its application. Likewise,
Kelvin Lancaster mentions monopolistic competition only coinci-
dentally with monopoly and terms it merely a subdivision of oli-[20]
gopoly. Robert Haney Scott devotes little space to the subject, but he does warn that, although the theory is appealing,[21]
it is not very adequate as an explanatory model. The scant
treatment of monopolistic competition in these textbooks should
be compared to the extensive chapters on the subject in other
popular texts written by economists less rigid than those of[22]
the classical liberal, logical positivist ideology.

Institutionalism in Monopolistic Competition

*The great formal contribution of Chamberlin, however, was in
recognizing adequately the possible economic implications,
with respect to price, output, product, and cost, of the governing institutional framework and of market structures, and
in suggesting the necessity of an analysis employing several
variables . . . for the interpretation of actual price behavior.
So interpreted, the doctrines of monopolistic . . . competition
called for a new focus for empirical research in 'institutional
fields.*

Joe S. Bain[23]

There are two parts to the theory of monopolistic competition: Chamberlin's initial model and his revisions when the original was subjected to rigorous criticism. As he defended his
theory, he refined it; and as he refined it, he struggled to
find some cohesive means by which to salvage its internal mechanism. It is at this level--refinement and defense--that much of
the institutional flavor of the theory of monopolistic competition is found. To savor those ingredients one must concentrate
on the appendices in later editions of *Theory* as well as Cham-[24]
berlin's essays.

Some Criteria for Evaluation

Institutional economics is a collection of propositions
and insights, although some observers doubt that it is a unified
school of thought.[25] The basic postulates are scattered among
the writings of several economists. Some of its distinguishing
features are assembled below as a taxonomic framework for de-
tecting the presence of institutional thinking in Chamberlin's
theory. This framework is then used in this section as the
major mechanism for evaluating Chamberlin's model.

Dissent. Economists who call themselves institutionalists[26] share a suspicion of the relevance of neoclassical economics. Some may reject all (or most) of neoclassical theory; others may accept part of orthodox economics but build on it as a point of departure in need of additional elaboration.[27]

Evolution. Institutionalists dissent from orthodox economics because of its kinship to Newtonian mechanics. They see neoclassical methodology as a deliberate attempt to apply the operation of the physical universe to human behavior. Darwinian evolutionary biology, as opposed to Newtonian mechanics, provides institutionalists with a framework for analyzing human action and social change as a continuous process rather than as a static state.[28]

Process. Veblen attacked neoclassical economics because its analysis proceeds from a "precondition of normality," that is, there is some natural state toward which the economic system is ultimately heading (equilibrium).[29] He suggested that a theory based on a "precondition of process" would help show how the interaction of cultural factors creates flux in economic activity over time.[30]

Gestalt-Holism. *Gestalt* psychology holds that physical, biological, social, and psychological phenomena are integrated into a functional unit, having properties which are not neatly derivable from a mere summation of parts. Holistic thinking views the economic system as a whole (rather than as a collection of parts) in which all aspects of human behavior are interactive. Institutional economics builds on these precepts to form a "doctrine of organic unity" (according to John Gambs[31]) and a "systemic paradigm" (according to Allan Gruchy[32]).

Adjustment to Technology. The process of institutional adjustment to technological change is central to institutional economics. Institutionalists view economic activity as a process in which technology is applied to human and physical resources. As technology advances, society's coordinating mechanisms, called *institutions* ("ways of doing things"), lag behind because values and culture do not allow them to be applied in full force to newly developed technology.[33]

Culture. John Locke promulgated the view, adopted by neoclassical economists, that human beings are not creatures of wont and fashion; God, nature, and reason are everlasting, changeless, and enduring.[34] Cultural influences have little place in this scheme, a point of contention with institutionalists. Habits, customs, and the influence of culture are not

rigid phenomena, subject to eternal natural law, according to
John R. Commons.[35] This sort of reaction to neoclassical thinking leads institutionalists to consider economic life as an
evolving process in which people make cultural adjustments over
time.

   Valuation. The question of whether *exchange* value (price)
can be equated with *use* value (merit) has been a subject of much
discussion within the classical-neoclassical tradition. Whereas
classical economists argued that the value of a good can be explained by its cost of production, the neoclassical theory of
value is based on a hedonistic calculation of human dislike for
pain and a desire for pleasure.[36] Institutional economists, who
reject equating value with price, claim that value is "more oriented to effort actually to appraise value and less oriented to
the belief that values can be quantified, and added up, and
maximized."[37]

   Maximization. For some time, institutionalists (and others)
have questioned the relevance of the neoclassical maximization
assumptions. Piero Sraffa confronted the issue in his classic
article on the laws of returns,[38] as did Adolf Berle and Gardiner
Means with evidence on the separation of ownership from control
in large corporations.[39] Neoinstitutionalists, such as John
Kenneth Galbraith, dispute whether profit maximization is the
primary goal for decision making in the large industrial corporation.[40]

   These eight criteria may be used to evaluate Chamberlin's
theory of monopolistic competition as institutional literature.
The evidence comes from both his main treatise and the many
clarifications and defenses that he issued over the years.

Dissent

   Chamberlin's model of monopolistic competition may not
represent pure institutional dissent, but it comes quite close.
Chamberlin did not accept the black-and-white dichotomy of pure
competition and pure monopoly as market structures characterizing American capitalism.[41] Indeed, he considered monopolistic
competition to be an attack on pure competition.[42] Not only do
recent writers refer to the "monopolistic competition revolution,"[43] but also Chamberlin himself considered the model to be
a general theory of value rather than one confined to a special
case.[44] Similar to many institutionalists, Chamberlin sought
to build on orthodox theory rather than to replace it entirely.

Evolutionary Process

Chamberlin's notion of a chemical blending emerges as an institutionalist idea. Monopolistic competition is an evolving phenomenon because the blending requires continuous change and movement as elements of monopoly power alter the structure of market organization in selected parts of the economy. Chamberlin considered his theory to be evolutionary--to be a processual explanation of how a market develops. It is noteworthy that he distinguished monopolistic competition from static equilibrium concepts.[45] To Chamberlin, for example, product differentiation involves a continuous adjustment in the sense that he envisioned an unlimited number of product variations and combinations.[46] As he strove to connect theory with reality, Chamberlin became involved with the institutional concept of *process*. Indeed, his use of the word suggests a connection between evolving changes in the economic system and developmental phenomena giving rise to monopolistic competition.[47]

Chamberlin attempted to reformulate neoclassical economics within its own methodological framework. The model of monopolistic competition was originally intended to be consistent with profit maximization and to yield a determinate solution. Chamberlin's separate models, and there are more than a dozen of them (some diagrammed, some not), were generally cast in equilibrium terms. Not only did Chamberlin describe the process of adjustment toward equilibrium, but also he treated both individual and group equilibria.

Gestalt *and Holism*

Gestalt and holism are interrelated phenomena, the former referring to functional unification of a system, and the latter to the connection among the elements of a larger system. Chamberlin comes close to infusing these concepts into his analysis at two junctures. The first occurs in the original model of monopolistic competition, the second in a paper written twenty years after the publication of his famous treatise.

In the treatment of product differentiation, Chamberlin introduced three variables controlled by the monopolistically competitive firm: price, product, and selling costs.[48] At the time, these factors were a step toward a *Gestalt*-holistic approach, albeit an incomplete step. Nevertheless, Chamberlin's description of the many factors giving rise to differentiation suggests a *Gestalt*-holistic idea.

In his attempt to show how equilibrium might be attained

with product differentiation and with selling costs. Chamberlin
toyed with *Gestalt*-holistic criteria. He argued that both quantitative and qualitative factors must be considered in the
achievement of equilibrium,[49] but he admitted being unable to
enumerate them because they are so diverse.[50]

Chamberlin was quite explicit about matters of *Gestalt*-
holism in a paper elaborating the dimenstions of product variation which were introduced in his original model.[51] Not only
did Chamberlin digress on "three main determinants of products,"[52] including behavioral and physical influences, but he
also discussed the "wide range of product possibilities" which
can be derived from them.[53]

Cultural Influence

For institutionalists, construction of an evolutionary
theory must focus on the social habits and customs of a people.
The institutional belief that human beings are more cooperative
than competitive, in contrast to the neoclassical view, is embodied in product differentiation and attendant selling costs
as both relate to habits and customs. To Chamberlin, even price
was often a function of cultural influences.[54] In this regard,
he obviously did not subscribe to the neoclassical view that
people behaved as predictable consumers in the marketplace.[55]
Indeed, in Chamberlin's group equilibrium, if the product is
varied--adjusted to suit the peculiarities of buyers--then cultural influences on that variation become important.[56]

Technology

In the static equilibrium context of neoclassical economics,
it is a commonplace that technology is an exogenous variable,
given or held constant throughout both the short and the long
run. Institutionalists, however, believe that technology has
an inner logic all its own which *is* the economic problem.[57]
The Theory of economic dynamics allows for the introduction of
time, and hence technology, into a model. In *Theory of Monopolistic Competition*, Chamberlin did not indicate whether technology was to be held constant, or whether time was considered.[58]
Yet, he cast his analysis in a dynamic setting in which technology was apparently a variable. Chamberlin opened the door
to varying technology in an attempt to reformulate part of his
monopolistic competition theory.[59] Two decades after the appearance of his main treatise, Chamberlin published an important
article in which he expanded the concept of product differentiation. In it, he suggested that the constant-technology assumption could actually be relaxed when dealing with the product as

an economic variable.[60] Moreover, in that same article, he
suggested that product differentiation is a continuous, evolutionary process in which technology varies as firms make product adjustments under monopolistic competition.[61] Finally,
in a revealing passage in another paper, Chamberlin admitted
that his refinement of the neoclassical model allows for technology to vary even when long-run average cost curves are
involved.[62]

Institutional Adjustment

Institutions are coordinating mechanisms which allow technology to interact with resources to assist economic activity.
As technology advances, institutions adapt slowly. This process is one of continuous adjustment, according to institutionalists. Chamberlin's concept of product differentiation accommodates institutional adjustment directly. Being variable, the
product is not fixed; rather, it is able to change as habits
and customs evolve. Chamberlin pointed out that in group equilibrium, long-run adjustments actually change the number of
products in the economy (or at least in that segment of the
economy in which monopolistic competition happens to be opera-
tive).[63] This fact is important in an institutionalist setting
because Chamberlin's concept of a *product* is tied to human preferences, which are themselves ephemeral and fickle. Whereas
many economists include within the term "product differentiation" *both* product variation and selling costs, Chamberlin meant
two different activities: product differentiation (varying the
product itself) and selling costs (informing and influencing
prospective buyers about those variations). The former affects
the cost-of-production curve, while the latter are subject to a
law of diminishing returns in their own special way. Both activities allow for continuous adjustments because each is inherently affected by changing technology (for example, new product
development) and changes in habits and customs (such as learning
to accept, use, and desire new products once they are developed
and promoted). The key to institutional adjustment in monopolistic competition is therefore Chamberlin's abandonment of the
product homogeneity assumption in the neoclassical model of pure
competition.

Valuation

Several references in Chamberlin's works suggest that he
did not equate price with value in the traditional neoclassical
way. In this regard, he experienced some difficulty *reformulating* the neoclassical theory of value because he found it necessary to retain certain parts of the orthodox framework. Yet,

there is evidence that Chamberlin modified the identification
of price with value. This modification occurs within the concept of product differentiation because price is only one of
several variables in Chamberlin's model. The product is a
variable, too, and so is promotion (selling costs). As such,
not only price motivates buyers, but also the nature of the
product itself.[64] In *Theory of Monopolistic Competition*,
Chamberlin treated the product as a variable in terms of the
neoclassical equilibrium process, but twenty years later he
considered the product to be variable on a continuum of adjustment possibilities.[65] Product and promotion do not necessarily
yield intrinsic value, but they are value oriented insofar as
they are *important* factors in the consumer preference process.

Profit Maximization

In his attempt to reformulate the neoclassical theory of
value, Chamberlin ostensibly felt that he had to retain the
profit maximization assumption. After all, it is the touch-
stone embodying the Newtonian flavor of neoclassical economics,
especially in the sense that hedonistic calculus is its social
expression. Early in the description of monopolistic competition theory, Chamberlin committed himself to a determinate
solution which yielded the profit-maximizing output quantity.[66]
However, when *Theory of Monopolistic Competition* is considered
in its entirety, profit maximization appears to be both relaxed
and abandoned at several points in the analysis. Chamberlin
actually acknowledged that his model is not confined to maximization of profit as the sole motivator of economic behavior
in the firm.[67] For Chamberlin, monopolistic competition included the entire range of market organizations, from pure
monopoly to pure competition. Even oligopoly was merely the
"small group" case of monopolistic competition. And in this
situation, Chamberlin allowed the profit maximization assumption
to be modified.[68]

Concluding Remarks

*Chamberlin . . . could not incorporate within formal theory
all of his ideas and all of his insights. Nevertheless,
Chamberlin's work altered every aspect of price analysis which
it touched. The theory of pure competition was never quite
the same after Chamberlin's assault.*

Romney Robinson[69]

Has Edward H. Chamberlin contributed to institutional
literature? Is *Theory of Monopolistic Competition* an institutional document? Do Chamberlin's writings reflect an integration

of institutional thinking into the neoclassical model of the firm? Based on evidence presented here, it might be tempting to answer these questions in the affirmative: Chamberlin gave credit to Veblen for two key ideas in monopolistic competition theory; book reviews immediately after the publication of *Theory of Monopolistic Competition* demonstrates a favorable acceptance by institutionalists; many institutionalists since the publication of Chamberlin's treatise have considered his model compatible with their mode of thinking; and serious neoclassical theorists reject Chamberlin's monopolistic competition theory for the same reasons that they disavow institutional economics.

But this is not all. An examination of the specific elements of the theory of monopolistic competition, appraising it through the medium of an institutional paradigm, provides additional support to the hypothesis: It is a form of dissent; an evolutionary posture is evident; the analysis is compatible with *Gestalt*-holism; Chamberlin sometimes allowed technology to vary; cultural factors are important in product differentiation; institutional adjustment is accommodated; value becomes embodied in product differentiation *and* price; the profit maximization hypothesis is not rigidly followed.

Edward Chamberlin conceived the idea for monopolistic competition more than fifty years ago at a time when orthodox economics was being challenged. Institutional economics was a generation old, and the Darwinian evolutionary theory was a popular topic among social scientists. Moreover, the power wielded by the corporate form was increasing; technology was rapidly changing; real incomes were rising; consumer choices were expanding; and seeds of doubt about the efficacy of the profit-maximization assumption had been planted. In his attempt to inject realism into a reformulated theory of the firm, Chamberlin found himself inserting institutional ideas into his model. As is often the case with ideas which ultimately change man's intellectual view of the world, Chamberlin's monopolistic competition has not caught on in any widespread fashion. Nevertheless, his ideas have infiltrated economic theory, and in their insurgency, those ideas have carried the institutional banner.

It should not be concluded that Chamberlin was an institutional or evolutionary economist. Far from it. He was thoroughly orthodox, even to the point of detesting labor unions as a major element of monopoly power in the economy.[70] Suffice it to say that he exhibited some institutional leanings in his quest for realism. His genius (or his failing) was to try to weave institutional methodology into the neoclassical fabric of the representative firm. It is one thing to argue that Chamberlin was an institutional economist; it is another to suggest that the theory of monopolistic competition contains institutional elements. It is the latter contention, rather than the former, which seems most appropriate to accept.

John R. Commons once confessed in his *Distribution of Wealth* that he had "tried to mix things that will not mix," namely, Austrian marginal utility theory and his concept of social relations.[71] Likewise, Chamberlin may have attempted a methodologically impossible task, that of seeking to mix Darwinian and Newtonian ideas. That attempt undoubtedly caused the adverse reaction by the Chicago School, for Chamberlin's dilemma was manifest in mixing pragmatism with logical positivism.

Economists should look critically at recent reformulations of the theory of the firm to determine the extent, if any, of their institutional orientation. Many extensions of the market model are thought to be consistent with neoclassical economics. Yet, there may be evidence of attempts to mix institutional and neoclassical methodologies. And if there is a mixing, then institutionalists may have been successful in their endeavor to influence orthodox economic theory. Chamberlin's legacy to neoclassical economics would then have been an irreversible infusion of institutional methodology into the Marshallian system.

[1] R.S. Gordon, "Institutional Elements in Contemporary Economics," in *Institutional Economics* (Berkeley: University of California Press, 1963), p. 132. The first reference is to Edward S. Mason, "Price and Production Policies of Large-Scale Enterprise," *American Economic Review* 29 (March 1939).

[2] According to Chamberlin himself, it was in 1927.

[3] Edward H. Chamberlin, *The Theory of Monopolistic Competition*, 9th ed. (Cambridge, Mass: Harvard University Press, 1962), p. 3.

[4] John S. Gambs, *Beyond Supply and Demand* (New York: Columbia University Press, 1946), p. 5.

[5] Chamberlin quotes from Thorstein Veblen's *Theory of Business Enterprise*: "It is very doubtful if there are any successful

business ventures within the range of modern industries from
which the monopoly element is wholly absent" (Chamberlin,
Monopolistic Competition, p. 5).

[6]Edward H. Chamberlin, "The Origin and Early Development of
Monopolistic Competition Theory," *Quarterly Journal of
Economics* 65 (November 1961): 515-43. In the case "of 'competitive' markets. . . . from some price divergent from the
equating one, there would be a movement toward it. Among
the markets analyzed and compared were those by . . .
Veblen" (p. 523). The reference is again to Veblen's *Theory
of Business Enterprise*.

[7]Chamberlin, *Monopolistic Competition*, p. 60. "Veblen speaks
of monopolies 'resting on custom and prestige as frequently
sold under the name of goodwill, trade-marks, brands, etc.'"
The reference is to Veblen's *Theory of Business Enterprise*.

[8]Clarence E. Ayres, "The Impact of the Great Depression on
Economic Thinking," *American Economic Review* 36 (May 1946):
112-25; and Morris A. Copeland, "Institutional Economics and
Model Analysis," *American Economic Review* 41 (May 1951); 59-
60.

[9]Morris A. Copeland, "The Theory of Monopolistic Competition,"
Journal of Political Economy 42 (August 1934): 531-36. "Chamberlin's work is one of the major contributions to the theory
of value and distribution in recent years" (p. 531).

[10]C.D. Edwards, "Review of *Theory of Monopolistic Competition*,"
American Economic Review 23 (December 1933): 683-85." He
misses the geometrical determinateness of Mrs. Robinson's
graphs; but thus he recognizes . . . that policy in semi-
monopolistic markets depends upon belief about the way which
rival enterprises will retaliate" (p. 684).

[11]Clarence E. Ayres, *The Theory of Economic Progress* (Chapel
Hill: University of North Caroline Press, 1944): "As a matter
of fact, one of the most recent and startling developments of
price theory, that of 'monopolistic competition,' seems to be
well on the way to establishing the insignificance of equilibrium with effects which are not yet fully appreciated" (p. 67).

[12]Ibid., p. 68. "The theory of monopolistic competition is the

deductive determination of the various points at which equilibrium occurs under various conditions of restraint of trade.
This is indeed the demoralization of the concept of equilibrium. But it is the reduction of the whole classical theory
of price to an absurdity. The essence of that theory is that
the price system forms patterns which are significant, whereas
the essence of this new theory is that price patterns are
without significance" (ibid., p. 68).

[13]The term is Clark's (as cited in Allan G. Gruchy, *Modern
Economic Thought* [New York: Prentice-Hall, 1947], pp. 337-
402).

[14]John Maurice Clark, *Competition as a Dynamic Process* (Washington, DC: Brookings Institution, 1961): "This is perhaps the
culminating challenge which this latest industrial revolution
has presented to economic theory, to bring itself into closer
touch with economic processes and problems in ways that involve enlarging its scheme of variables. It is this challenge
that Chamberlin undertook to meet in his study of the theory
of monopolistic competition" (p. 39).

[15]Morris A. Copeland, *Our Free Enterprise Economy* (New York:
Macmillan, 1965): "During the past twenty-five or so years
most treatments of the theory of the firm have waived some
of the assumptions of a pure competition, long-run model.
For one thing, they have frequently replaced the assumption
of pure competition in the market in which the firm's one
product is sold with the assumption of monopolistic competition" (p. 141). "Under monopolistic competition the seller
names the price at which he is willing to sell" (p. 171).
"The theory of monopolistic competition gives a formula for
the markup on a product in terms of the price elasticity of
the demand for it" (pp. 158-59).

[16]George J. Stigler, "Monopolistic Competition in Retrospect,"
in *Five Lectures on Economic Problems* (New York: Macmillan,
1949): "It will be observed that the theory of monopolistic
competition now contains no conditions of equilibrium, only
a definition of equilibrium" (p. 18).

[17]"The sole test of the usefulness of an economic theory is
the concordance between its predictions and the observable
course of events . . . . One can but show that a theory is
unrealistic in essentials by demonstrating that its predic-

tions are wrong" (ibid., p. 24).

[18] Milton Friedman, "The Methodology of Positive Economics," in *Essays in Positive Economics* (Chicago: Phoenix Books, University of Chicago Press, 1966): "The theory of monopolistic competition offers no tools for the analysis of an industry and so no stopping place between the firm at one extreme and general equilibrium on the other. It is therefore incompetent to contribute to the analysis of a host of important problems: the one extreme is too narrow to be of great interest; the other, too broad to permit meaningful generalization" (p. 39).

[19] Gary Becker, *Economic Theory* (New York: Alfred A. Knopf, 1971): "Although the concept of monopolistic competition captures relevant dimensions of the competition prevailing in many industries, the tangency solution has serious defects" (p. 96).

[20] Kelvin Lancaster, *Introduction to Modern Microeconomics* (Chicago: Rand McNally, 1974): "Most of the market structures formerly regarded as typical of monopolistic competition. . . are now seen to involve important elements of oligopoly" (p. 191).

[21] Robert Haney Scott, *The Pricing System* (San Francisco: Holden-Day, 1973): "The theory of monopolistic competition is intuitively pleasing as an explanation of many everyday marketplace events, but as a theory that is useful in making predictions it lacks the same degree of strength that the models of monopoly and perfect competition have" (p. 246).

[22] Two good examples are Richard H. Leftwich, *The Price System & Resource Allocation* (Hinsdale: Dryden, 1973); and Donald S. Watson, *Price Theory and Its Uses* (Boston: Houghton Mifflin, 1968).

[23] Joe S. Bain, "Price and Production Policies," in *A Survey of Contemporary Economics*, edited by Howard Ellis (Homewood: Richard D. Irwin, 1948), vol. 1, p. 131.

[24] Edward H. Chamberlin, *Towards a More General Theory of Value* (New York: Oxford University Press, 1957). This volume contains sixteen papers, eleven of them reprinted from articles

in various professional journals.

[25]David Seckler, *Thorstein Veblen and the Institutionalists* (Boulder: Colorado Associated University Press, 1975), pp. 4-5.

[26]Allan G. Gruchy, "Neoinstitutionalism and the Economics of Dissent," *Journal of Economic Issues* 3 (March 1969): 3.

[27]John S. Gambs, *Beyond Supply and Demand* (New York: Columbia University Press, 1946), p. 4.

[28]David Hamilton, *Evolutionary Economics* (Albuquerque: University of New Mexico Press, 1970), pp. 27-28.

[29]Thorstein Veblen, "Why is Economics Not an Evolutionary Science?" *Quarterly Journal of Economics* 12 (July 1897): 379.

[30]Gruchy, *Modern Economic Thought*, p. 53.

[31]Gambs, *Beyond Supply and Demand*, pp. 24-25.

[32]Gruchy, *Modern Economic Thought*, pp. 550-69.

[33]Ayres, *Economic Progress*, p. 174.

[34]For example, see John Locke, *Essay Concerning Human Understanding* (Oxford: Clarendon Press, 1975), p. 204.

[35]John R. Commons, *Institutional Economics* (New York: Macmillan, 1934), p. 47.

[36]Clarence E. Ayres, *The Industrial Economy* (Boston: Houghton Mifflin, 1952), p. 335.

[37]Wendell Gordon, *Economics from an Institutional Viewpoint* (Austin: University Stores, 1973), p. 28.

[38]Piero Sraffa, "The Laws of Returns under Competitive Conditions," *Economic Journal* 36 (June 1926): 548.

[39]Adolf A. Berle, Jr., and Gardiner C. Means, *The Modern Corporation and Private Property* (New York: Macmillan, 1932), p. 122.

[40]John Kenneth Galbraith, *Economics and the Public Purpose* (Boston: Houghton Mifflin, 1973), pp. 96 and 114.

[41]Chamberlin, *Monopolistic Competition*, commenting on competition and monopoly: "On the one hand, analysis has revealed the difference between them and has led to the perfection and refinement of a separate body for each" (p. 3).

[42]"Monopolistic Competition was an attack, not on Marshall, but on the theory of perfect competition" (ibid., p. 316).

[43]See, for example, Paul A. Samuelson, "The Monopolistic Competition Revolution," in *Monopolistic Competition Theory: Studies in Impact*, edited by Robert E. Kuenne (New York: Wiley, 1967), pp. 105-38.

[44]Chamberlin stated this in both *Monopolistic Competition* and *General Theory of Value*.

[45]Chamberlin, *General Theory of Value*: "The point can be made that the fundamental question is the nature of the economy. If its structure is one of monopolistic competition, this must be true whether it is being studied as a system of static equilibrium or as one of dynamic movement, or perhaps of 'development.' Whether segments of it are being studied in isolation or whether the whole of it is being studied as a single system; whether the focus is upon the parts or upon their aggregates" (p. 9).

[46]"The importance of nonprice competition in the real economic world has become a commonplace in recent years, and one wonders how anyone could seriously maintain that the economist should have none of it. The almost endless ways in which economics opens out when this factor is admitted are discussed at length . . . they are so much and so vital a part of actual competition that it would seem that any arbitrary attempt to exclude them by ruling that the economist's province is price only would be on a par with limiting a surveyor to north and south distances, to the exclusion of east and west and up and down. No doubt the scope of economics is

greatly widened by releasing products from their status as
data and recognizing them as variables crying out for analysis. But so many narrowing influences have been at work in
economics in recent years that if the 'science' is not to
lose complete touch with reality, and even vanish in logic,
the discovery of some new worlds to conquer should be welcomed" (ibid., pp. 22-23).

[47]Edward H. Chamberlin, "The Chicago School," in *General Theory
of Value*, pp. 305-306.

[48]Chamberlin, *Monopolistic Competition*, p. 71.

[49]"One difficulty encountered in describing the group equilibrium is that the widest variations may exist in all respects
between the different component firms. Each 'product' has
distinctive features and is adapted to the tastes and needs
of those who buy it. Qualitative differences lead to wide
divergences in the curves of cost of production, and buyers'
preferences account for a corresponding variety of demand
curves, both as to shape (elasticity) and to position (distance from the x and y axes). The result is heterogeneity
of prices, and variation over a wide range in outputs (scales
of production) and in profits. Many such variations are, of
course, temporary, and are constantly in process of being
eliminated" (ibid., p. 81).

[50]"To a very considerable extent the scheme of prices is the
result of conditions unique to each product and to its market
--it defies comprehensive description as a 'group' problem,
even when monopolistic forces are given their full value in
the explanation" (ibid., p. 82).

[51]Chamberlin, "The Product as an Economic Variable," *General
Theory of Value*, pp. 105-37.

[52]Ibid., p. 118.

[53]Ibid., p. 116.

[54]Chamberlin, *Monopolistic Competition:* "Some products are in
their very essence incapable of becoming set. . . . The entrepreneur may be regarded as accepting a price generally
prevalent, one established by tradition or trade practice,

or one determined upon by an earlier decision, and to which his customers have been habituated" (p. 78).

[55] Edward H. Chamberlin, "Monopolistic Competition Revisited," in *General Theory of Value:* "There is no reason to assume that human beings always act perfectly rationally; indeed, there is good reason not to assume it" (p. 60).

[56] Chamberlin, *Monopolistic Competition:* "Each 'product' has distinctive features and is adapted to the tastes and needs of those who buy it" (p. 81).

[57] An example of this reasoning is contained in Gordon, *Economics:* "The basic force controlling the nature of the economy is technical knowledge; and the accumulation of technical knowledge is a process which has an internal dynamic of its own" (p. 5).

[58] Chamberlin, *General Theory of Value:* "Very little is said specifically about time in *Monopolistic Competition*, since it was taken for granted that the proposition that monopoly and competition are blended is logically independent of time" (p. 12).

[59] Chamberlin, "Monopolistic Competition Revisited": "It remains to indicate how the theory of monopolistic competition permits us to pass over to the study of dynamics, and in particular to the problems of development and growth . . . in the theory of the subject . . . it is significant that the entrepreneur who breaks away from the established order of things by introducing an 'innovation' . . ." (p. 62).

[60] Chamberlin, "The Product as an Economic Variable": We may discuss at this point two other explanations of short-run product rigidity logically independent of custom, yet involving it finally in the form of generally accepted, industry-wide procedures. The first is the influence of technical change on the frequency with which types or models of certain products are altered" (p. 119).

[61] "The appearance on the market of every new product creates pressure in some degree on the markets for others, and when products are variable and determined by profit maximization some of this pressure is bound to be exerted on quality in

order to maintain prices which people can afford to pay.
Thus, in a world whose technology is constantly creating new
products, it should not be surprising to find that a part of
the whole process is the deterioration of other products in
order to make room for the new ones at the mass market level
where the population is concentrated" (ibid., p. 131).

[62]Edward H. Chamberlin, "Proportionality, Divisibility, and
Economies of Scale," in *Towards a More General Theory of
Value:* The plant curves which compose the average cost curve
have, for a time, successively lower minima, and hence define
a downward course for the latter until its minimum is reached,
primarily for two reasons: (1) increased specialization, made
possible in general by the fact that the aggregate of resources is larger, and (2) qualitatively different and tech-
nologically more efficient units of factors, particularly
machines, made possible by wise selection from among the
greater range of technical possibilities opened up by the
greater resources" (pp. 175-76).

[63]Chamberlin, "Origin and Early Development," Appendix H in
Theory of Monopolistic Competition: "Thus the entry or exit
of sellers in the problem of group equilibrium for instance,
carries with it an expansion or contraction in the number of
products in the whole system instead of merely a change in
the number of producers for some given product" (p. 302).

[64]"When both 'product' and price are variable, an equilibrium
adjustment will be reached for both which is a combination
of that for each in isolation. For each variety of 'product'
possible to him there will be a price which will render his
profit a maximum relative to that 'product'" (ibid., p. 98).

[65]Chamberlin, "The Product as an Economic Variable": "One must
take it into account because products are not in fact given;
they are continuously changed--improved, deteriorated, or
just made different--as an essential part of the market
process" (p. 107).

[66]Chamberlin, *Monopolistic Competition:* "That figure will be
sought which will render the total profit a maximum" (p. 71).

[67]Chamberlin, *General Theory of Value:* "Monopolistic competition
is more general than pure competition in that it embraces policy objectives other than profit maximization" (p. 24).

[68]Edward H. Chamberlin, "Monopolistic Competition Revisited":
"Other forces, and I believe real ones may be conceptions of
'good' or 'reasonable' profits rather than maximum profits,
perhaps because of a genuine desire not to 'profiteer,' or
perhaps through a fear of adverse publicity, or of inviting
public regulation" (p. 58).

[69]Romney Robinson, *Edward H. Chamberlin*, Columbia Essays on
Great Economists (New York: Columbia University Press, 1971),
p. 67.

[70]Edward H. Chamberlin, *The Economic Analysis of Labor Union
Power* (Washington, DC: American Enterprise Institute, 1958).

[71]John R. Commons, *Legal Foundations of Capitalism* (Madison:
University of Wisconsin Press, 1968), p. vii.

*Journal of Economic Issues, Vol. XIII, No. 3, (September
1979):669-686*

The General Theory of Employment, Interest and Money
by
John Maynard Keynes

REVIEW: G. D. H. Cole (1936)*

Unemployment is, in the view of most people, the disease
that is threatening our present capitalist societies with
destruction. There are, indeed, some who protest that unemployment is not an evil, but will be a positive good as soon
as we consent to convert it into leisure and to distribute it
aright among the whole people. And there are others who maintain that unemployment is not a disease, but only a symptom
of something far more deeply wrong with the economic systems
under which we live. But against the apostles of leisure
common sense urges that, until most people are a good deal
richer than today, most of them will prefer more goods to
more leisure if they are given the choice. And against those
who regard unemployment as no more than a symptom, it can
fairly be argued that the distinction between symptom and disease is not so absolute as rhetoric can make it appear.

At all events, most statesmen and most economists profess to be in search of a cure for unemployment, and to regard this quest as at any rate one of the most important economic ends. The trouble is that they differ profoundly about
the methods that are calculated to secure their object. Of
late years quite a chorus of voices—from the City, from the
business world, and from the academic groves of Cambridge and
London—has been assuring us that the abnormally high unemployment of post-war years is the consequence chiefly of the
"rigidity" influences, in valuing their labour at higher rates
than the market will bear. Let wages fall, till they coincide
with the "marginal productivity" of the last labourer, and all
will be well. So we have been told, with so much punditory
self-assurance that it has been quite difficult for the plain
man confronted with a series of unintelligible equations, not
to begin thinking that it may perhaps be true.

There have been, of course, other voices--Mr. J. A. Hobson's for example--preaching a very different doctrine, and telling us that "under-consumption" is at the root of all our difficulties. What is wanted, on this showing, is more consulting power; for ultimately the entire volume of economic activity is necessarily limited by consumption. Investment is useless, unless there is a market for the consumers' goods which it can be applied to making; for *all* demand is, in the last resort, a demand for goods and services to be consumed. But these voices, in respectable circles, have been drowned by the outraged clamour of the orthodox. "Under-consumption" has remained a disreputable heresy; and of late, though Man himself can be quoted on its side, Communist Marxists, such as Mr. John Strachey, have denounced it with hardly less gusto than they have directed against the more orthodox view--presumably because, when they are dealing with capitalist or other non-Marxist economists, they work on the principle of "the horrider, the better."

But now there comes, from one who is no Socialist and is indisputably one of the world's leading economists trained in the classical tradition, a book which with all the armoury of the classical method pushes at one blow off their pedestals all the classical deities from Ricardo to Wicksell, and all their attendant self-canonised sprites from Vienna and the London School, and puts in their vacant places not indeed Marx, but Mr. J. A. Hobson and the late Silvio Gesell. For Mr. J. M. Keynes, after many uneasy years of wandering amid the classical abstractions--years whose *stigmata* are still upon him--has discovered that after all, in the matters which practically matter most, Richardo and Vienna and London and Cambridge have all this time been talking nonsense, whereas Gesell and Hobson (and Malthus in his most maligned moments) have had hold of the right end of the stock.

Mr. Keynes is evidently conscious of the supreme challenge which has new book offers to the entire economic practice of Capitalism, and to the relevance and conclusiveness of the fundamental economic theories put forward by most of his academic colleagues. Otherwise, he would hardly have published at five shillings a book of nearly four hundred pages which most trained economists will find stiff reading and most other people at some points wholly beyond their comprehension. By putting the book forward at such a price, Mr. Keynes is saying in effect: "This is no ordinary book. It is a book that has to be understood because it really matters. It marks an epoch in economic thought." And, in claiming this, Mr. Keynes is, without the smallest shadow of doubt, absolutely right. His new book is the most important theoretical economic writing since Marx's *Capital*, or, if only classical economics is to be considered as comparable, since Ricardo's *Principles*.

In the challenge which Mr. Keynes has thrown down to his orthodox colleagues, there are, of course, many elements that are now new. Indeed, Mr. Keynes's most signal service is that he has brought together, co-ordinated and rationalised many criticisms of orthodoxy which have hitherto been ineffective because they have been disjointed and unrelated to any clear body of fundamental theory. There are many points, at which Mr. Keynes's alternative construction is open to challenge. But it does give the critics of economic orthodoxy solid ground on which they can set their feet.

There is no space here for more than the briefest indication of Mr. Keynes's arguments. His book is in form chiefly an attempt to determine the underlying conditions which, in a capitalistically organised society, determine the actual volume of unemployment. The classical economists, either explicitly or more often by implication, have been accustomed to set out from the assumption of "full employment" as normal, and to prove their general theories without regard to the possibility of variations in total employment, treating the actual occurrence of unemployment as a deviation from the normal, due to some exceptional factor such as monetary mismanagement or the rigidity of wages. Mr. Keynes himself, in his earlier writings, had not got far from this method, though his explanation was different, for he formerly traced unemployment largely to divergences between the "natural" and the market rates of interest. But he has now seen that, for the economic system as it is, "full employment" cannot be treated as normal, and that the problem is to devise an economic order which will secure "equilibrium" on a basis of "full employment" and not by preventing booms at the cost of making semi-depression permanent.

Mr. Keynes now sees the factor which determines the total volume of employment under capitalism as the maintenance of investment at an adequate level. This seems, at first sight, to put him sharply in opposition to the "under-consumptionists"; but actually it makes him their ally. For the will to invest depends, in Mr. Keynes's phrase, on the "marginal efficiency of capital," which may be roughly translated as the marginal expectation of profit from investment over its entire life, as far as this is actually taken into account by the investor. This expectation, however, depends absolutely on the demand for consumers' goods; and accordingly the maintenance of investment at a satisfactory level depends on the maintenance of consumption.

In orthodox theories, consumption and investment stand in an antithetical relation. But Mr. Keynes is able to show the falsity of this view, except on the assumption that the available productive resources are being fully employed. More consumption, he shows, stimulates more investment, as well as more investment more consumption, up to the point at which full employment has been secured. In his earlier work, Mr. Keynes stressed the difference between "saving," which is mere abstinence from consumption, and investment, which is the positive use of the "saving" in the creation of capital. He now re-states his doctrine, so as to emphasize that, while from the collective standpoint "saving" and "investment" must be equal (for the only way of *really* saving is to invest), the processes of individual saving and individual investment are wholly distinct. Accordingly, the attempts of individuals to save can, from the social point of view, be rendered wholly abortive by the failure of entrepreneurs to borrow these savings and apply them to real investment; and this failure, wherever it occurs, is bound to cause unemployment.

Mr. Keynes believes that failure of this sort is an inherent defect of the present economic system, and that it can be cured only by public action, taking at least three related forms. He wants the State to control the supply of money so as to secure its adequacy for maintaining full employment; and this involves a repudiation of the gold standard, or of any fixed international monetary standard, and also a decisive repudiation of all those economists who wish to stabilise the supply of money. Secondly, he wants the State to control the rates of interest (mainly by adjusting the supply of money) in order to keep these rates down to a point which will make investment worth while up to the level of "full employment." This involves a complete repudiation of the orthodox view that interest rates are self-adjusting to a "natural" level. Thirdly, he wants the State largely to take over, or at any rate control, the amount and direction of investment, with the object of maintaining full employment on the basis of a balanced economic development.

These are Mr. Keynes's most fundamental points of advocacy. But perhaps most attention of all will be popularly focused on his views about wages. For he reduces to sheer absurdity the prevalent view that lower wages are a cure for unemployment. He begins by pointing out that this view rests on a fundamental confusion of thought between money wages and real wages. It assumes that, broadly, these can be spoken of

together, and that if workmen could be persuaded to accept
lower money wages, their real wages would fall. Actually, he
points out, real wages have often risen when money wages have
been reduced, and he offers reasons why this should be so.
The reduction in money wages, unless it is expected to be soon
reversed, sets up an expectation of falling costs and prices
which positively discourages investment by reducing the "marginal efficiency of capital." Thus, instead of increasing
employment, it reduces it, even if it raises the real wages of
those who remain in work. Mr. Keynes considers that the tendency of Trade Unions to keep up money wages in times of depression is positively good for the capitalist system, and
makes the depression less severe than it would be if the workmen yielded to the blandishments of Professor Robbins and his
like.

There is in Mr. Keynes's challenge an enormous amount more
than it has been possible even to mention in this necessarily
brief summary of his central argument. But enough has been
said to show that the book is one which must, sooner or later,
cause every orthodox text-book to be fundamentally re-written.
It is true that Mr. Keynes's conclusion is not that we should
destroy the system of "private enterprise," but only that we
should drastically re-fashion it. Mr. Keynes rejects complete
Socialism, and looks forward to a society in which private and
collective enterprise will live together, but the *rentier* class
will have practically disappeared--for the maintenance of full
employment with the aid of investment kept up to the requisite
point by State action will, he thinks, reduce the rate of
interest almost to vanishing point. But this part of his argument is but briefly sketched in his closing chapter and is not
a necessary deduction from his analysis. What he has done,
triumphantly and conclusively, is to demonstrate the falsity,
even from a capitalist standpoint, of the most cherished
practical "morals" of the orthodox economists and to construct
an alternative theory of the working of capitalist enterprise
so clearly nearer to the facts that it will be impossible for
it to be ignored or set aside.

The New Statesman and Nation, (February 15, 1936): 220-222

REVIEW: Horace Taylor (1936)*

Unemployment, the most conspicuous and most painful symp-

tom of unsoundness in the existing economic system, is the
central problem to which Mr. Keynes addresses himself in this
new book. His study is framed as an investigation of how it
comes that there is not full employment, and of the means by
which, in a system of free enterprise, full employment may be
achieved and maintained. While his elaborate and highly technical analysis is presented in general terms, it is apparent
that he is concerned primarily with British conditions and
British policies.

Only an outline of the broader relationships treated by
Mr. Keynes can be attempted here. Mr. Keynes assumes that a
virtually full employment of labor can be attained. Assuming
that there is less than full employment at a given time (which
it is not difficult to do), the trend of actual employment will
depend on whether the rate of investment of new capital is increasing or diminishing. This is because an increase (or decrease) in the rate of investment must carry with it an increase (or decrease) in the rate of consumption and of the
effective demand for goods. The rate of investment of new
capital, in its turn, depends on the prospective gain to be
derived from the investment ("the marginal efficiency of capital") and also on the "liquidity value" which money possesses
over other valuable things. Whether there is a sufficient
prospective gain to induce investment (and here we skip a number of steps in analysis) depends, taking industry as a whole,
on the height of interest rates and of wages.

It follows, therefore, that the amount of prospective gain
from investment (and thereby the employment of labor) can be
enhanced, at any particular time, either by a reduction of
money-wages or by a reduction of interest rates, *i.e.*, an increase in the supply of loanable funds. As between these
(essentially British) alternatives, Mr. Keynes recommends the
latter on grounds of justice, experience and expediency. He
proceeds, therefore, to the conclusion that credit should be
made easier as a means of obtaining a full employment of labor.
The maintenance of such full employment would require, during
a period of cyclical boom, the abandonment of the customary
practice of raising interest rates to check credit expansion,
and the substitution therefor of a policy of reducing interest
rates and increasing credit expansion. Following this proposal, Mr. Keynes offers a number of qualifications and says:
"If we are precluded from making large changes in our present
methods, I should agree that to raise the rate of interest
during a boom may be, in conceivable circumstances, the lesser
evil."

I hope that this summary is not so inadequate as to be unfair to Mr. Keynes. His entire analysis is hedged about with technical exceptions and special considerations. Yet his central theme, while it runs in terms of pure theory, would scarcely serve as a central theme if it were so qualified as to have a significant meaning only in highly exceptional circumstances. One or two of the special considerations must be mentioned. Mr. Keynes recognizes and stresses the conventional and habitual addiction people have to high rates of interest-- "John Bull can stand many things, but he cannot stand two percent." This consideration, added to certain administrative necessities, leads Mr. Keynes to "conclude that the duty of ordering the current volume of investment cannot safely be left in private hands." Such ordering of investment at low rates of interest clearly would require that the state do the investing. Again, when faced with the theoretical imperative of the under-consumption theorists that expenditures for consumption must be increased and savings for investment diminished, Mr. Keynes gives it as his practical judgment that both should be increased. Such a judgment would set the task of the monetary and credit authority.

Mr. Keynes's analysis adds substantially to our understanding of the process by which public investment and public ownership may--perhaps must--grow up within the system of private enterprise. Carried to its logical conclusion, such a program must mean that finally the prospectiveness of profit would cease to determine the rate of capital investment. I believe that Mr. Keynes has overstressed the power of control vested in the interest rate, and that a great variety of disparities would arise within his scheme of economic adjustment, frustrating the efforts to maintain full employment. Mr. Keynes, while apparently conscious of these probabilities, appears also to forget them at times in his discussion of policy.

Mr. Keynes's critical views are invariably interesting. When he wrote "The Economic Consequences of the Peace" he was interesting because he saw more clearly than most other people the errors made at Versailles. More recently he has been interesting for his forthright attacks on the errors which, in his own view, he himself has made. Three years ago, in a lecture on national self-sufficiency at University College, Dublin, he recognized that the grounds for his earlier support of liberal internationalism had shifted widely. Now in his latest book, while serving more positive ends than self-criticism, he courageously seeks to tidy up and to rectify certain theoretical positions he has tacitly or explicitly

assumed in earlier works. He has made several changes—notably
on the relation of saving and investment and in his cordiality
to John A. Hobson's under-consumption theory. He no longer
regards the influences of money as calling for study separate
from the general theory of demand and supply. While he approached this theoretical position in his "Treatise on Money,"
those who have followed his work will recognize, in the very
title of the present book, an association of ideas somewhat
incongruous to the Keynes they earlier have known.

Mr. Keynes undoubtedly will write other books as correc-
tives to this one. In his present study he apparently has
taken a step toward the positive position he will finally come
to occupy in the history of economic theory. But since it is
presented in a highly abstruse and mathematical fashion, "The
General Theory of Employment" probably will not add directly
to his popular prestige.

The New Republic, Volume 86, (April 29, 1936): 349

"Keynes and the General Theory," Alvin H. Hansen (1946)*

It would be a mistake, I think, to make too sharp a dividing line between pre-Keynesian and Keynesian economics.
That some line has to be drawn I do not believe will be denied
by anyone who will examine the economic literature before and
after 1936. But every contributor to any field of knowledge
stands on the shoulders of his predecessors. Specialists in
any field of knowledge know that no one man ever single handed
invented anything. In a sense there are no "revolutionary"
discoveries. Nevertheless, in the progress of man's thinking
new plateaus are from time to time case up not unlike a geo-
logical upheaval. And these *are* revolutionary developments
even though the constituent elements composing the structure
can be found elsewhere and have long been well known.

If a stranger from Mars should undertake to read the literature of economics from, say, 1700 to the present day, he
would be struck, I believe, particularly by the new direction
and outlook injected by the publication of (a) *Wealth of Nations*, (b) the works of Jevons, the Austrians, and Walras, and
(c) Keynes' *General Theory*. Scarcely has any issue of an economic journal or any serious volume since 1936 appeared which
has not been influenced by, or primarily concerned with, the
concepts and thinking of Keynes.

The record will also verify, I think, that friend and foe alike have experienced a considerable enrichment of their "mental furniture" by reason of the Keynesian contribution. This indeed is nothing new. Alfred Marshall's *Principles of Economics* was profoundly influenced by Jevons and the Austrians, though he was far from sympathetic when this "attack" on the classicals first appeared. There are plenty of parallels today.

While it is not possible now to assess the ultimate place of Keynes in the history of economic thought, it is safe to say that no book in economics has ever made such a stir within the first ten years of its publication as has *The General Theory*. And this interest continues unabated. It is further true, I believe, that economic research has tackled new problems and is better equipped with tools of analysis by reason of the work of Keynes. Moreover, a correct appraisal of Keynes' work cannot be made by confining attention to the contents of *The General Theory*. The Keynesian "revolution" is far from having been completed, and it is, accordingly, not possible this early accurately to appraise the importance of his work in relation to the great peaks of intellectual achievement which have gone before.

Keynes proved to be quite right when he predicted in his Preface to *The General Theory* that many economists would fluctuate between a belief that he was quite wrong and a belief that he was saying nothing new. This conundrum, it appears, still torments some economists; but many more, during the process of criticizing Keynes, have acquired as a by-product the new analytical apparatus. Keynes himself felt he was "treading along unfamiliar paths," and the the composition of *The General Theory* has been a long "struggle of escape from habitual modes of thought and expression." In the literature of the last 10 years one cannot fail to be impressed with the change that has occurred in the "habitual modes of thought and expression" of Keynes' critics, also.

David McCord Wright, in a recent article on the "Future of Keynesian Economics,"[1] put his finger quite accurately on the basic change in *outlook* effected by the "Keynesian Revolution." We cannot follow, he says, the main lines of Keynes's argument and say that the capitalist system, left to itself, will automatically bring forth sufficient effective demand. Keynes' ideas "derive much of their unpopularity because they form the most widely known arguments for intervention even though such intervention may be quite capitalistic in nature." It is the analysis of the problem of *aggregate demand* together

with the implications of this analysis for practical policy
which challenges the old orthodoxy.

In this connection an illuminating passage appears in the
Preface to Pigou's recent pamphlet, *Lapses from Full Employment* as follows:

"Professor Dennis Robertson . . . has warned me that the
form of the book may suggest that I am in favour of attacking
the problem of unemployment by manipulating wages rather than
by manipulating demand. I wish, therefore, to say clearly that
this is not so."

This sentence would not likely have been written prior to
The General Theory.

It has been my conviction for many years[2] that the great
contribution of Keynes's *General Theory* was the clear and specific formulation of the consumption function. This is an
epoch-making contribution to the tools of economic analysis,
analogous to, but even more important than, Marshall's discovery of the demand function.[3] Just as Marshall's predecessors were fumbling around in the dark because they never
grasped the concept of a demand *schedule*, so business cycle
and other theorists from Malthus to Wicksell, Spiethoff and
Aftalion, never could quite "reach port" because they did not
have at hand this powerful tool. It is illuminating to re-
read business cycle and depression theories in general prior
to 1936 and to see how many things settle neatly into place
when one applies the consumption function analysis--things
that were dark and obscure and confused without it. The consumption function is by far the most powerful instrument which
has been added to the economist's kit of tools in our generation. It is perfectly true that embryonic suggestions (as also
with the demand function) appear in earlier literature, but
the consumption function was never fashioned into a workman-
like instrument until *The General Theory*. This, I repeat, is
Keynes's greatest contribution. And in more general terms, the
effect of variations in income upon all manner of economic
variables has, since Keynes, become an important field for research and analysis. Income analysis at long last occupies a
place equally as important as price analysis. This part of
the Keynesian contribution will remain regardless of what happens to that which relates to policy.

Time and time again when I thought I had discovered this
or that error in the Keynesian analysis either on my own or
at the suggestion of a critic, I have been surprised to find

how often, upon examination, the point had already been anticipated and covered in *The General Theory*. I regret that I have not kept a list of these points, but only recently I came upon another interesting example which relates to the consumption function. In my *Fiscal Policy and Business Cycles* I had pointed out (p. 233 *et seq.*) that, on grounds of general reasoning and such facts as are available (Kuznets's long-run data) we may assume an upward *secular* drift in the consumption function. Later, this was elaborated more fully by Paul Samuelson.[4] This upward secular drift is often (but erroneously) cited as proof that the consumption function analysis is not valid. Until recently, I had supposed that Keynes had overlooked the secular aspect of the problem, and it was therefore of great interest for me to discover that his particular formulation does in fact (possibly inadvertently) cover the matter in a fairly satisfactory manner. The consumption function of two periods, widely separated in time, can be made comparable by correcting for changes in prices, per capita productivity and population increase.[5] This would correct for the secular drift, and if the corrected functions were found to be similar, we could say that the consumption function was stable over time. Now Keynes achieves a fairly satisfactory result by casting his consumption function in terms of wage-units. When the consumption income schedules of two different periods are cast in terms of wage units, the effect is to correct for price and productivity changes.[6] Thus the schedules become quite comparable over time, and we are accordingly in a position to determine whether or not a shift has in fact occurred in the consumption function.

The role and significance of the consumption function can be illustrated by a comparison of the *Treatise* with *The General Theory*. In the *Treatise* $\pi o = E + (I - S)$, where πo is the current income, E the normal (full employment) income, and S is the current saving which *would* be made from a normal, full-employment income. Thus the current realized income is, according to the *Treatise*, less than the normal or full-employment income by the amount that current investment falls below the potential saving at full employment. But this, of course, is wrong, since it leaves out the multiplier. The missing link is supplied by the consumption function. This in a nut shell reveals one of the great advances of *The General Theory* over the *Treatise*.

In this connection it is interesting to compare Robertson's $Y_1 = Y_0 + (I_1 - S_1)$ with Keynes' $\pi o = E + (I - S)$ in the *Treatise*. They bear a superficial resemblance. An important difference is that Robertson's is a period analysis which does not pretent to explain the *level* of Y_1, but only its relation to Y_0, while Keynes's (Treatise) equation pretends to explain the *level* of πo. By combining Robertson's formulation with the consumption function analysis (as I have done in Chapter XII in *Fiscal Policy and Business Cycles*) one arrives at a correct solution of the problem attempted by Keynes in the *Treatise*. Keynes, however, chose in *The General Theory* to implement the consumption function[7] analysis in terms of a logical or mathematical formulation involving no time-lags. Thus if the consumption function is given, the level of income is uniquely determined (time-lags assumed away) by the volume of investment.

With respect to the determinants of investment--the marginal efficiency of capital and the rate of interest--Keynes's contribution relates chiefly to the latter. The real factors, in a dynamic society, which determine the marginal efficiency of capital are largely taken for granted. The psychological and institutional aspects are indeed at points well treated, but the "real" or "objective" aspects--the dynamics of technical progress--are passed by almost unnoticed. The result is that too great emphasis is placed on the rate of interest. The rate of interest is indeed enormously important in the effective implementation of fiscal policy (debt management, lending and guaranteeing operations in such areas as housing, etc.), but as a means of increasing purely private investment it could *only* be of great importance as a determinant of income and employment if the marginal efficiency schedule were very highly elastic. And even so, once a minimum low rate of interest had been reached (Keynes's liquidity preference) nothing more could be accomplished by means of interest rate reduction. In so far as anything can be achieved (and something can within limits be done) by reducing the rate of interest, this method obviously, from the long-run standpoint, is nonrecurring and quickly runs out. The movement *along* the marginal efficiency curve would be a "once for all" movement were it not for the *upward shift* of the curve, due to growth and technical progress. It is the upward shift that provides the outlet for a *continuing* flow of investment.

The volume of investment during the last century can be accounted for mainly by growth and technical progress. "Growth" has provided vast outlets for investment of the "widening" type; technical progress has provided outlets of the "deepening" type (greater capital intensity per worker). In addition, some "deepening of capital" has been achieved[8] through some secular decline in the rate of interest. This is important in the sense that we have in consequence more nearly approached the condition of "full investment"--a fuller realization of the potentialities of technical progress. But the contribution which the secular fall in the rate of interest has made to *annual* investment over the last century is surely negligible compared with the annual investment due to growth and technical progress.

It is not necessary to argue that the marginal efficiency schedule is highly inelastic. The movement *down* the curve cannot be of great importance for *continuing* income and employment creation. What is needed in order to develop a considerable *flow* of investment is a continuing upward shift of the marginal efficiency schedule such as may be caused by technological improvements, the discovery of new resources, the growth of population, or public policy of a character which opens up new investment outlets. The effect of *lowering* the rate of interest would quickly wear off in the absence of an upward shift in the marginal efficiency schedule. Thus little can be expected for *continuing* investment from progressively lowering the rate of interest even though this were feasible. A low rate of interest is desirable nevertheless because this permits an approach to "full investment" which would mean higher productivity per worker. But in the absence of dynamic growth and innovation, a constant level of the rate of interest, no matter how low, would ultimately result in zero net investment.

The liquidity preference analysis is important as an explanation of the enormous volume of liquid assets which it is possible for an advanced and rich industrial society to hold without inflationary consequences. And while the growth of liquid assets beyond a certain point may have little effect on the rate of interest, it may nevertheless affect income and employment by raising the consumption function. How important this may or may not be depends upon certain circumstances to which I refer below. Mere *volume* alone is not the controlling factor.

Thus under-employment equilibrium may be reached, given a fairly low consumption function, not merely because of an elastic liquidity preference schedule, but mainly because of limited investment opportunities (technical progress, etc.) combined with a marginal efficiency schedule which is not highly elastic. Keynes, however, rests his case heavily on the liquidity preference analysis, from which it follows that the economy does not tend toward full employment merely through the automatic adjustment of the rate of interest.

Wage reduction, as a means of increasing employment via the fall in the interest rate (Pigou) is thus, along with other policies designed to lower the interest rate, relatively ineffective. And with respect to the effect of increased liquid assets (whether in terms of an *absolute* increase or a *relative* increase caused by wage reductions) on the consumption function, that all depends upon who it is that holds the liquid assets. If the liquid assets are largely in the possession of the rich, the consumption function can rise very little unless, indeed, the accumulation of such assets in the hands of a concentrated few is pushed far beyond the limits of tolerance in a democratic society.

It is therefore important *how* the liquid assets came into being and who it is that holds them. The method of *relative* increase in liquid assets (via wage reductions) is clearly not a realistic method of increasing the consumption function for the general population. And with respect to the method of *absolute* increase, it makes considerable difference whether the monetary expansion merely came about through monetizing assets held by investors and wealthy individuals, or whether the new money was created as part of an expansionist's program of subsidization of mass consumption--school lunches, housing and household equipment for low-income groups, family allowances, etc.--or for public construction projects which directly increase the income of workers and start a round of expenditures (multiplier effect) throughout the economy. There is no assurance that a mere increase in liquid assets (whether absolute or relative) will raise the consumption function appreciably. That depends. Thus it is that monetary policy may be relatively ineffective unless combined with appropriate fiscal policy.[10] And it is considerations such as these here under discussion that reveal the essential differences between pure monetary policy and pure fiscal policy.

After ten years of criticism the Keynesian analytical apparatus remains as essential equipment if one pretends to work on the determinants of income and employment. The consumption function has become and will remain the pivotal point of departure for any attack on the problem of aggregate demand. Moreover, with respect to policy, little reliance in the future will be placed on the notion that it matters little what the consumption function may be, since, whatever its level, a volume of investment adequate to fill the "gap" will always automatically tend to develop if only price, wage, and monetary adjustments are made. Special models set up to show how wage and price flexibility under certain conditions might so operate are notoriously unrealistic and unworkable in the

practical world and so fail to come to grips with economic
reality. Finally, a mere increase in the quantity of money,
apart from the manner in which it is created and put into circulation, and apart from its distribution among the members
of society, is not capable *per se* of raising the consumption
function to a level adequate to insure full employment. On
the other hand, Keynesian economics has itself been the means
of showing the important role of monetary expansion in conjunction with fiscal policy in the creation of adequate aggregate demand. Monetary policy is an essential instrument for
an effective full-employment program. The volume of liquid
assets and the rate of interest are indeed important, though
if applied alone relatively ineffective.

These then are the essentials of the Keynesian system and
these are the considerations with which we must grapple in
appraising its continuing effectiveness for analysis and policy. Under-employment equilibrium is not dependent upon wage
rididity (properly defined). The fundamental explanation is
to be found in (a) the consumption function, (b) investment
outlets, and (c) the liquidity preference analysis.[11] There
are no automatic processes that will produce under all circumstances adequate aggregate demand. Private consumption and
private investment outlays will not automatically produce this
result. And no other explanation for this has so far been
offered that is as satisfactory as that presented by Keynes.

It is evident that a new outlook was injected into economics, both with respect to theory and policy, by the publication of *The General Theory*. That is was not "old stuff" is
evidenced by the terrific effort it required for economists to
readjust their thinking and indeed the difficulty they had in
understanding what it was all about. Witness, for example,
the first reviews (including my own) and the endless controversial articles on concepts which, in retrospect, are rarely
a credit to the profession.[12] More and more, even those who
professed to see little in Keynes that was new or valid began
to reveal that they had experienced a rebirth despite their
protestations to the contrary. Add to this the fact that the
influence of Keynes permeates all official international gath-
erings grappling with economic problems and is present wherever
internal economic problems are under consideration (witness
postwar governmental pronouncements). It is difficult to avoid
the conclusion that nothing like it has happened in the whole
history of economics. It is too early to say, but it does not
now appear an extravagant statement, that Keynes may in the
end rival Adam Smith in his influence on the economic thinking
and governmental policy of his time and age. Both lived at

profound turning points in the evolution of the economic order.
Both were products of their times. Yet both were also powerful agents in giving direction to the unfolding process of
institutional change.

[1]*American Economic Review,* June, 1945.

[2]See my *Fiscal Policy and Business Cycles,* Chapter XI.

[3]Not until Marshall did the demand function play a significant
role in economic analysis. Yet Cournot (and perhaps others)
had formulated the principle before.

[4]See Chapter II, in *Postwar Economic Problems* (edited by
Seymour E. Harris, New York, 1943).

[5]This would amount to much the same thing as calculating each
schedule as ratios of a full-employment income in each period.
Thus the consumption function could be said to be stable over
time if the schedules so constructed had the same relation to
a full-employment income in each period.

[6]This, at any rate, is true if the schedules are reduced to a
per capita basis.

[7]It is not correct, as is often done, to identify the Keynesian
formulation with the "ex post" or "statistical" formulation.

[8]I am aware that secular upswings and downswings in the rate
of interest have occurred; these have been associated particularly with the so-called "long waves." Moreover, the rate of
interest reached a low level, roughly comparable to that of the
present period, in the eighteen-nineties.

[9] Professor Haberler's quotation from Keynes (p. 196, below)
that an "increase in employment can only occur to the accompani-
ment of a decline in the real rate of wages" fails to include
the very important conditions which must be assumed to make
this statement true, namely, no change in "organization, equipment and technique"; in other words, no change in productivity.
Moreover, Keynes (March, 1939, *Economic Journal*) explicitly
repudiated the notion that employment must increase *by or
through* a lowering of real wages and a movement *along* a declining so-called general demand curve for labor. In his view

employment is increased by raising effective demand, thereby
causing an upward *shift* in the demand curve for labor.

[10]Professor Haberler, in his contribution to this symposium,
argues that under-employment equilibrium with flexible wages
and prices is impossible since wages and prices will under
these conditions fall continually. But this is surely no
criticism of Keynesian economics. Completely flexible wages
and prices would indeed give us a system so unstable as to be
unworkable.
But this is not the question. The question is rather whether
an orderly reduction of wages and prices which are *relatively*
rigid could promote an increase in employment. And it was
presumably such a policy which Professor Haberler had in mind
when he discussed the *relative* increase of liquid assets (via
wage reductions) and the effect of this on the interest rate
or on the consumption function. Whether or not this is effective depends, as I have noted above, on circumstances. You
cannot cure unemployment *merely* by expanding the money supply
(absolutely or relatively) without regard to how this increase
is brought about or who holds the money. The position of
Modigliani, Polanyi, and others is, I think, a modern recrus-
cence of an excessive preoccupation with the mere *quantity* of
money—a preoccupation no less indefensible than the old. I
say this despite the fact that I myself place great stress
upon the importance of adequate (but not excessive) monetary
expansion as a part of fiscal policy.

[11]Professor Haberler's criticism of the elasticity of the
liquidity preference schedule seems to me to require cautious
interpretation. It relates to factors affecting a *shift* in
the schedule rather than to *elasticities* along a given schedule.
To be sure, a long-run schedule can sometimes be traced out by
determinate shifts of short-run schedules; but Haberler's
theory seems to be a special one, which denies, among other
things, that as the rate of interest gets nearer and nearer to
zero, the difficulties of lowering it further begin to increase.

[12]A recent example disclosing a number of elementary miscon-
ceptions is the pamphlet by Arthur F. Burns, on *Economic Research
and the Keynesian Thinking of Our Times* (National Bureau of
Economic Research, 1946). However, the pamphlet does strikingly
reveal (perhaps inadvertently) how economic theory—whether
Ricardian or Keynesian—serves the highly useful purpose of
pointing up what factual data are relevant to a useful investigation.

The Review of Economic Statistics, Volume 28, (1946): 182-187

"After Twenty Years: The General Theory," James R.
Schlesinger (1956)*

I. Background of the General Theory, 581. -- II. The General
Theory and its implications, 583. -- III. Contrast with the
classical position, 586. -- IV. The restoration of full employment and the Pigou effect, 588. -- V. The failure of the
General Theory, 590. -- VI. Background of the Pigou effect,
592. -- VII. Neo-Keynesian resistance to the Pigou effect,
594. -- VIII. Methodology, terminology, and policy, 598. --
IX. Conclusion, 602.

Some twenty years ago Keynes's General Theory[1] burst with
fanfare upon an expectant world. Since it was soon hailed as
the manifesto of a Revolution, it is perhaps not unfair to
examine how attitudes have changed toward the General Theory
in the intervening score of years since its publication. Three
propositions will be presented in this paper: (a) Keynes's
original thesis, based in no inconsiderable measure upon a
misinterpretation of his predecessors, has now become qualified
almost to the point of nonexistence. (b) In the area of
methodology and terminology, the Keynesian approach was notably
triumphant; this should not, however, be confused with a theoretical victory. (c) With respect to public policy, Keynes and
his followers scored a signal victory over the "price flexibility school," but contrary to popular impression (carefully
nurtured by Keynes's disciples), the latter was a rather small
and relatively powerless group.

I. BACKGROUND OF THE General Theory

In neoclassical analysis, the very existence of unemployment indicated a wage level that was excessive relative to the
full employment marginal productivity of labor. Employment
might, therefore, be stimulated by a reduction of money wages
(which presumably would reduce real wages). Considering the
clarity of the policy implications, economists were, as we
shall see, remarkably loath to advocate general wage cutting
as a remedy for depression. Predecessors, particularly among
the underconsumptionists, had antedated Keynes in his conclusions concerning the undesirability of general wage reductions,
and it is likely that the Great Depression would have destroyed,
in any event, whatever latent belief continued to exist in the
wage cutting cure. Keynes's contemporaries--the marginal pro-
ducitvity theorist, Paul Douglas,[2] and the conservative libertarian economist, Wilhelm Röpke,[3] advocated much the same
policy, but it was Keynes who brought to his analysis the time-

liness and verve which captured public sentiment as well as
the economists.

According to the classical (Ricardian) view, a reduction
in real wages implied an increase in the "residual share" of
national income--i.e., a rise in the rate of profit--which
would induce additional accumulation (investment) and thereby
increase employment. But the classical analysis remained in
terms of the *real* components of the national income, and was
not placed in a monetary framework. The implications of the
classical *equilibrium* analysis with respect to employment remained largely uncultivated until 1933 when Pigou's *Theory of
Unemployment*[4] was published, for under the division of labor
then prevailing, such problems were left to business cycle
analysis.

Keynes accepted the classical view with respect to the
effect of a reduced real wage, but argued that it was "not
open to labour to reduce its real wage by accepting a reduction in its money wage."[5] Since classical theory was so
evanescent, in order to expose the errors of "a hundred years
past,"[6] Keynes attacked the Pigovian theory--the "classical"[7]
thought which had then reigned supreme for but three years.
In dealing with the pre-Pigovian theoretical treatment of wage
reduction which was so meager,[8] Keynes could only pummel that
convenient but difficult to define strawman, Say's Law.[9] It
is questionable whether Keynes's caricature could be considered
a fair presentation of the views of his postclassical predecessors.

To illustrate the vagueness of the classical outlines,
Seymour Harris, later to become an ardent Keynesian, had
earlier suggested an entirely different interpretation in his
enthusiastic review of Pigou's book, which he then thought to
be a highly original work. It is noteworthy in light of subsequent presentations of Pigou's thought, that throughout
that review the contrast between Pigou's analysis and classical thought was emphasized.

"Professor Pigou has written one of the truly great books since
Marshall's day. Making hardly any use of the findings of
others, and striking out on lines of his own, he has contributed more to our science in this book than in any of his earlier
ones. . . That he has isolated for us the variables requiring
consideration for a concrete meaning to the concept of the real
elasticity of the demand for labor, and has suggested the
tools and manner of analysis, alone constitutes a great contribution."[10]

II. The *General Theory* and Its Implications

The fundamental proposition advanced by Keynes in the *General Theory* was not "income analysis" (as has been suggested by Keynesian revisionists in recent years), nor was it the existence of an under-employment equilibrium when wages were rigid downward. In the presence of rigid wages, the possibility of permanent unemployment would be conceded by classicists using either the quantity theory or the cash balance approach.[11] The essential feature of the Keynesian vision was that even on the level of comparative statics on which the discussion was carried, no mechanism was envisaged which would tend to restore full employment. The stagnation thesis follows directly from the Keynesian assertions concerning the shape[12] of the relevant functions; it is inherent in the analysis. Hicks in his justly celebrated paper, immediately espied this facet as the fundamental difference between Keynes and the classicists. Basically the investment schedule was too interest-elastic for a fall in the interest rate to generate full employment. Hicks refers to this as "Mr. Keynes' *special theory*"[13] and rightly concludes that "the General Theory of Employment is the Economics of Depression."[14]

Keynes's contribution was not the delineation of the savings-investment relationship. That relation had been more fully and lucidly analyzed by earlier business cycle theorists. In the final analysis what Keynes did was to incorporate the depression savings-investment relationship into an equilibrium model.

In regard to the issue of wage flexibility, the *General Theory* developed the following propositions: (1) Real wages are determined by the level of employment, rather than by money wages. (2) Cuts in money wages will be followed by equivalent price cuts, since prices will be competitively determined by marginal prime cost. (3) Wage earners are therefore not in a position to increase employment by accepting a reduction in money wages. (4) If the investment schedule is inelastic (as is likely in depression conditions), or if the "liquidity trap" has been reached, cuts in wages will lead to equal cuts in effective demand, and employment will be unaffected, for liquidity can only influence effective demand via the interest rate.

The Keynesian model was widely hailed as demonstrating the possibility of a competitive underemployment equilibrium. Keynes, himself, was not deceived as to the nature of the theory; he recognized that only a pseudo-equilibrium exists based on money wage rigidity.

"Moreover there might be no position of stable equilibrium except in conditions consistent with full employment; since the
wage-unit might have to fall without limit until it reached a
point where the effect of the abundance of money in terms of
the wage-unit on the rate of interest was sufficient to restore a level of full employment. At no other point could
there be a resting-place."

In short there could be no *competitive* underemployment
equilibrium, but full employment in Keynes's judgment could
only be restored by the stimulation of additional investment
via a falling interest rate. Even this position is, however,
qualified by the statement:

". . .moreover, there is not one of the above factors which
is not liable to change without much warning, and sometimes
substantially. Hence the extreme complexity of the actual
course of events."[16]

Among the factors subject to capricious change might be the
consumption function. If the latter is not stable, the course
of events will be "complex" and the elegant simplicity of the
Keynesian formulation disappears. Full employment might be
restored, therefore, by an upward "shift" of the consumption
function.

Irrespective of the marginal qualifications introduced,
the intent of the *General Theory* was to establish the likelihood of the proposition that (barring unlikely increases in
investment) wage cuts cannot stimulate effective demand, since
"real consumption is a unique function of real income."[17] Certain it is that if one accepts the Keynesian view concerning
the determinate nature of the consumption function, one must
conclude with Arthur Smithies that (assuming a constant interest
rate), "Real income is determined independently of changes in
money wages and prices."[18] No nonsense about "money illusion"
here; the money supply and the price level have no effect
whatsoever upon the level of real income. This is implicit
in the Keynesian model; it is rather curious then that this
influence was reached in a theory which purported to redress
the classical overemphasis on real factors by incorporating
monetary analysis into the model. As phrased by Harris, the
position developed was:

"A reduction in wages, moreover, could not improve the status
of industry, for demand would decline *pari passu* with the de-

cline of wages; favorable effects on investment, either as a result of the increased availability of money associated with falling wages or through active monetary expansion, would be excluded by the high elasticity of demand for cash in relation to falling rates of interest (as interest rates tend to fall, the public absorbs the additional cash created), and the small response of investment to any practical decline in the rate of interest."

Thus the entire burden of adjustment in case of a tendency toward unemployment was thrust upon the rate of interest, and yet, the rate of interest could not bear the burden forced upon it. By itself, the rate of interest was too weak an influence to accomplish the adjustments required of it. The anomalous condition of economic thought induced by the *General Theory* has been most succinctly and most colorfully phrased by Sir Dennis Robertson.

"Under the first impulse of Keynes's work, the rate of interest was elevated to a position of commanding theoretical importance. Roughly speaking, nothing was ever allowed to happen--money was not allowed to affect prices, wage-rates were not allowed to affect employment, I had almost added, the moon was not allowed to affect the tides--except through the rate of interest: it became as never before, the keystone of the whole theoretical arch. But it became also the villain of the piece, and a very powerful villain. It was the dragon guarding the cave of "liquidity preference"--of the ineradicable urge of capitalist society to run for cover and to play for safety; it became the rock against which the waves of social improvement beat in vain."

VIII. METHODOLOGY, TERMINOLOGY AND POLICY

In the areas of methodology, terminology, and public policy, the approach implicit in the *General Theory* was as notably triumphant as the underlying theoretical model was dubious. One recent writer, commenting on the classics from essentially a Keynesian position, has remarked on the difficulty of dissociating "Smith, the anti-mercantile-polemicist, from Smith, the economist."[21] It is similarly difficult to distinguish Keynes, the economist, from Keynes, the neo-mercantile-stagnationist. Nevertheless, Keynes's conceptual apparatus, though originally designed to convey the stagnationist proposition that effective demand was normally "inadequate," has proved itself to be sufficiently flexible to become the principal weapon of income analysis. The division of demand into components--consumption, investment, government,

and even more refined breakdowns--has proved its advantages.
It is more useful than the undifferentiated demand analysis
implicit in the quantity theory type of approach. This development has been made possible by the improvement in available
statistics, and has been aided by a new generation for statistics exuded generally by the so-called social sciences.
Income analysis, in turn, has helped to clarify the theory and
practice of social accounting. All this may be credited to
Keynes, since his was the seminal mind stirring renewed interest in income. Unhappily, this sort of apparatus has also
proved its convenience in the prophetic line, although it has
not yet been shown to be any more adequate than previous methods of astrological prediction.[22]

    The degree to which the Keynesian terminology has ousted
its predecessors is noteworthy. To my mind, the staying power
of Keynesian terminology is not unimportant, for only within
limits can it be considered "neutral." Schumpeter, for example,
felt that Keynes's model was a vehicle contrived to further
his ideology.[23] To the extent that this is true, the terms
used to describe the relevant functions are a conscious or unconscious reflection of that ideology. What has latterly been
termed the "consumption function" is a question-begging term
which assumes a stability in the relationship which it is pur-
porting to examine, and carries with it implications of a
social philosophy hinting of the sort of government interven-
tionism and antisavings attitudes that Schumpeter feared. Certainly the overpreciseness of terms like the "marginal efficiency of capital" or the "liquidity preference function,"
gives encouragement to the statistical model builders who
attempt to discover these functions in real life. It is a
grave question, whether the ideas lying behind these terms
are not so vague that the very attempt to give precision to
them destroys their intuitive reality. To the extent, however, that it is possible to dissociate the terminology from
the ideas from which it flows, the new language is, of course,
neutral and a part of the improved convenience of the Keynesian
methodological approach to income analysis.

    In the arena of public policy, Keynes and his followers
destroyed what was left of the "price flexibility school."
Probably the most interesting parts of the *General Theory* today are the *obiter dicta* on dynamics which could not be incorporated into the static model. The dynamic repercussions
of falling wages and falling prices on anticipations[24] make
virtually unassailable the Keynesian position on wage-price
policy--i.e., that "the money-wage level as a whole should be
maintained as stable as possible, at any rate in the short

period."[25] This would imply, of course, that the Pigou effect, which Pigou himself states to be of little practical importance, should not be relied upon as an antideflationary force,[26] for exactly the same stimulating influence of a mild increase in liquidity may be accomplished through an expansive monetary policy without submitting the society to the social strains of deflation. That unemployment might conceivably be reduced through hyperdeflation hardly makes the latter a desirable policy. When price and wage flexibility are removed from the simplified world of theory and introduced amidst the dynamic realities of the everyday world, they are hardly to be taken seriously from a realistic policy standpoint.

In dealing with pre-Keynesian thought, however, it must be recognized that economists did not indiscriminately advocate wage cutting as a cure for depression. It is a fallacy to identify the non-Keynesian or "classical school" with the "price flexibility school." Space does not permit any extensive treatment of attitudes prior to 1936. Many writers did advocate wage cuts during the interwar period, but many of these were thinking in terms of an "open" economy operating under the gold standard.[27] This is true of the Cannan article cited earlier. Others thought, not in terms of general wage flexibility, but in terms of structural wage flexibility--emphasizing the need for reducing the excessive wage rates in the "sheltered" trades, and bringing about a balance in the wage structure. Such writers tended to stress the massive maldistribution of labor that had come about as a result of the war.[28] It is to be remembered that Keynes himself agreed with the general tenor of this analysis, although he leaned to the view that flexible exchange rates were the best way to allow wages to fall in the "sheltered" trades.[29] In the twenties, Pigou mentioned in *Industrial Fluctuations* that in certain conditions of deep depression, wage rates (and prices) would have to be negative in order to eliminate unemployment.[30] Wage flexibility could play only a minor role--estimated by Pigou as reducing unemployment by one-eighth--and Pigou's position was, obviously, a highly qualified one. The Brookings Institution advocated expansion of output as the appropriate method of enhancing profits, and warned that wage cutting would be self-defeating.[31] E. R. Walker stressed the importance of employers' reactions, and believed that under depression conditions the prevailing pessimism would cause employers to reduce bank loans rather than employ added labor in the face of a wage cut.[32] Sumner Slichter, to be sure, advocated wage cuts but in order to correct the imbalance in the wage-price structure. He stated, moreover, that "in the face

of such conditions as existed in 1931 and 1932. . .even drastic
wage cuts accompanied by huge government spending would scarcely turn the tide."[33] Among practical statesmen, wage cutting
was always resisted, and the purchasing power theory dominated
the thought of such diverse politicians as Presidents Hoover
and Roosevelt. In general, wage cutting might be advocated
to end particular maladjustments, but there was a surprising
degree of agreement in resistance to general wage reduction.
As Röpke put it--"without a simultaneous policy of expansion
wage cutting is almost certain to aggravate the depression."[34]

Advocates of selective wage cuts were not per se advocates of wage flexibility in depression. The genuine price
flexibility school was a relatively small group, and since the
onset of the depression it has shrunk still further. At the
end of the depressed thirties, Wilford King expressed quite
concisely the view of this group:

"Employment is a function of the price of labor. There is no
indication that with wage-rates conforming to the market demand, private industry cannot readily absorb the entire available labor supply. . ."[35]

It is just such an attitude and policy as this, which, at
least in the opinion of this writer, has become untenable in
the light of the compelling argument on expectations in the
General Theory. Virtually all economists, irrespective of
their attitude toward his theoretical contribution, may gather
under Keynes's banner to endorse wage stability in the face of
depresstion conditions.

IX. CONCLUSION

At best, economic theorizing can be no more than "the
quintessence of experience," and so as the circumstances and
events which gave rise to the ideas expressed in the *General
Theory* have passed over the horizon, the book itself has become increasingly dated. While Keynes himself has surely not
been relegated to the "underworld" of economics with Major
Douglas and Silvio Gesell, Keynes's model is increasingly being
discarded by disciples who carry forward their work in his
name. Clearly the era during which, what one of my colleagues
insistently refers to as the "Revelation of St. John the Divine" was uncritically accepted as the sourcebook of all economic knowledge, is now behind us. The apparatus Keynes designed to demonstrate the common condition of chronic under-
employment or stagnation has, to be sure, been sufficiently
flexible to become the basis of income analysis. But the

General Theory was a controversial book, not because it suggested a new method of analyzing income and demand, but because of the stagnation thesis and the fact that Keynes asserted that certain functions had certain shapes. As his
followers play the stagnationist note ever more softly, the
controversy over the book has tended to fade.

Yet, in certain circles, Keynes, the symbol, marches on[36]
while Keynes, the theoretician, is being undermined by his
very disciples. Why is this so? I think it is Keynes's emotional attractiveness and not his theoretical structure that
makes him so satisfying. For many individuals, Keynes represents the Proper Attitude Toward Social Problems. As long as
those economists, whose essentially utilitarian views[37] were
shaped by the events of the thirties, remain dominant in academic circles, the symbolic Keynes will retain his present
position of veneration, for he is the continuing embodiment
of the Dreams of Their Youth—the reforming fervor of ancient
days. Actually, the model of the *General Theory* is a matter
of indifference; but the very admission of this would, for
the generation of the thirties, represent a cutting off of a
very dear part of their own lives.

*The author is indebted to Professors John Dunlop, Gottfried
Haberler, Robert Kuenne and Warren Smith for reading and criticizing earlier drafts of this paper. The present writer must,
however, bear sole responsibility for the conclusions herein
expressed.

[1] J. M. Keynes, *The General Theory of Employment, Interest and
Money* (Harcourt Brace, 1936).

[2] P. H. Douglas, *Controlling Depressions*, pp. 214-26.

[3] Wilhelm Röpke, *Crises and Cycles*, pp. 184, 190-92.

[4] A. C. Pigou, *The Theory of Unemployment*.

[5] Keynes, *op. cit.*, p. 11.

[6] *Ibid.*, p. 3.

[7] Dunlop has intimated to me that this statement is unfair to
Keynes. He points to a strong "body of oral tradition" in

favor of wage reduction and suggests that the noted article of Edwin Cannan, "The Demand for Labour" (*Economic Journal*, XLII (Sept. 1932), 357-70) is illustrative of this general attitude. Cannan's position was that the demand for labor as a whole was not easily sated, since the public desires more production. On the question of general unemployment, he incautiously concluded that "in all employments taken together demand is definitely elastic and consequently indefinite numbers can be employed if they do not ask too high a remuneration. General unemployment appears when asking too much is a general phenomenon" (p. 367). But Cannan clearly had in mind the interwar conditions in Britain in which the price level was being forced down due to the attempt to maintain the gold parity. Under these circumstances, his judgment was probably correct. In the opinion of the present writer, Keynes was guilty of attributing to his predecessors a general position which was at least partially a reflection of the exigencies of the gold standard.

[8]Keynes refers to the *Theory of Unemployment* as "the only detailed account of the classical theory which exists." (*Op. cit.*, p. 7.)

[9]*Ibid.*, pp. 18-21. Compare Hansen's sympathetic treatment of this entire question (*A Guide to Keynes*, pp. 3-20). As will appear below, I would disagree with his statement that Pigou "advanced without reservation the view that a completely plastic wage policy would abolish fluctuations of employment" (p. 16). By the time that he wrote *Industrial Fluctuations*, Pigou's position concerning the effectiveness of a wage cutting policy was a highly qualified one.

[10]S. E. Harris, "Professor Pigou's Theory of Unemployment," this *Journal*, XLIX (Feb. 1935), 322. Hick's comment is interesting in this regard (Mr. Keynes and the 'Classics,'" *Econometrica*, V (April 1937), p. 147), for he agrees with the early estimate of Pigou's work by Harris rather than the later (Keynesian) estimate. "Now *The Theory of Unemployment* is a fairly new book. . . .To most people its doctrines seem quite as strange and novel as the doctrines of Mr. Keynes himself; so that to be told that he has believed these things himself leaves the ordinary economist quite bewildered."

[11]Cf. Franco Modigliani, "Liquidity Preference and the Theory of Interest and Money," *Econometrica*, XII (Jan. 1944), 65-67.

[12] See in this regard the penetrating analysis of J. H. Williams in "An Appraisal of Keynesian Economics," *American Economic Review*, XXXVIII (May 1948), 275-76. If anyone should doubt that the stagnation thesis constitutes the core of the *General Theory*, let him examine pp. 30-32, 105-6, 164, 219-24, 253-54, 308-9, 323-24, 347-48 and 375-76.

[13] Hicks, *op. cit.*, p. 152. On pp. 308-9, the final two pages of the main body of the text, Keynes sums up the *General Theory* in virtually the same way that Hicks does—i.e., that the interest rate cannot fall low enough to stimulate sufficient investment to maintain full employment.

[14] Hicks, *op. cit.*, p. 155.

[15] Keynes, *op. cit.*, p. 252; see also pp. 229-35 and Haberler's discussion of the implications of this quotation, *Prosperity and Depression*, 3d ed., pp. 242-43. See also S. E. Harris, *The New Economics*, pp. 28-29 and 46-47 for a defense of the underemployment equilibrium concept.

[16] Keynes, *op. cit.*, p. 249. This sort of statement might well have given pause to certain enthusiastic model-builders and income-projectors, concerning the reliability of the statistical consumption function.

[17] James Tobin, "Money Wage Rates and Employment" in *The New Economics*, p. 573.

[18] Arthur Smithies, "Effective Demand and Employment," in *The New Economics*, p. 560.

[19] Harris, *op. cit.*, p. 29.

[20] D. H. Robertson, "What Has Happened to the Rate of Interest?" *The Three Banks Review*, Mar. 1949, p. 16.

[21] Jesse Burkhead, "The Balanced Budget," this *Journal*, LXVIII (May 1954), 193.

[22] For the latest in a long history of pitiful failures in prediction see the *January 1955 Economic Report of the President*,

Hearings before the Joint Committee on the Economic Report,
pp. 107-15, for a discussion by a panel of "experts" on prospects in 1955. The consensus seemed to be that a GNP at an
annual rate of $370 billion was to be expected in the last
quarter. This turned out to be a mere $32 billion off. In
the light of these results Chairman Burns's brief statement
(pp. 44-45) on why the Council would not issue numerical predictions and his warnings concerning the "limitations of economic forecasting" and the need for a flexible policy seem all
the more pertinent.

[23] J. A. Schumpeter, "Science and Ideology," *American Economic
Review*, XXXIX (mar. 1949), 355-56.

[24] A good brief statement of these dynamic considerations is
given in Martin Bronfenbrenner, "The Dilemma of Liberal Economics," *Journal of Political Economy*, LIV (Aug. 1946).

[25] Keynes, *op. cit.*, p. 270.

[26] Milton Friedman ("A Monetary and Fiscal Framework for Economic Stability," *American Economic Review*, XXXVIII (June 1948),
259) is the only writer that I know of, who has suggested
utilizing Pigou's secular device under depression conditions.

[27] See note 7.

[28] Cf. Henry Clay, "Unemployment and Wage-Rates," *Economic
Journal*, XXXVIII (Mar. 1928), reprinted in *The Problem of
Industrial Relations* (Macmillan, 1929).

[29] Cf. J. M. Keynes, "The Economic Consequences of Mr. Church-
hill," reprinted in *Essays in Persuasion*, 2d ed., pp. 252-53.

[30] Pigou, *Industrial Fluctuations*, p. 225. It should be noted
that Pigou's statement in the introduction to *Lapses from Full
Employment*, that he is not opposed to treating the problem of
unemployment from the demand side, is not a recantation as has
been frequently suggested, but is fully in line with his earlier
thought.

[31] Cf. The Brookings Institution, *The Recovery Problem in the
United States* (Washington, 1936), pp. 522-28.

[32] E. Ronald Walker, *Unemployment Policy* (Sydney, 1936), pp. 49–58; it should be noted that Walker stressed his debt to Keynes and to the Macmillan Report.

[33] S. H. Slichter, *Towards Stability*, p. 137.

[34] Röpke, *op. cit.*, pp. 190–91.

[35] Willford I. King, "Are We Suffering from Economic Maturity," *Journal of Political Economy*, XLVII (Oct. 1939), 622; see also "Wage Rates, Wage Costs, Employment, Wage Income, and the General Welfare," *American Economic Review Supplement*, XXIX (Mar. 1939); for a similar point of view see Benjamin M. Anderson, "The Road Back to Full Employment," in *Financing American Prosperity*, ed. Homan (Twentieth Century Fund, 1945), p. 70; see also Haberler, *op. cit.*, pp. 493–95.

[36] Cf. Schumpeter, *op. cit.*, p. 356, for a partially contrasting opinion, "the (Keynesian) 'creed' has petered out with the situation that made it convincing." To my mind, the Keynesian vision is still very much with us, though in *diminuendo*.

[37] Cf. Arthur Smithies, "Schumpeter and Keynes," *Review of Economics and Statistics*, XXXII (May 1951); 164–69.

Quarterly Journal of Economics, Volume 70, (1956): 581–586; 598–602

"Keynes Today," Joan Robinson and Francis Cripps (1979)*

No one should attempt to defend Keynes line by line or to apply his writings literally to the problems of today. The coverage of *The General Theory* was too narrow, and there are mistakes in it. The important point is that, in response to the experience of 1920s and 1930s, Keynes was able to move economists on from the elaboration of idealized theories that assumed full employment to the study of more practical views that allow for unemployment.

Pre-Keynesian classical economics, developed mainly in England, had reduced economic policy to a single rule—that of the gold standard. This implied fixed exchange rates between

different currencies and a fixed relationship between the
quantity of money and gold reserves. According to the classical theory, if bankers enforced these monetary rules free
market mechanisms would take care of everything else. Governments had no role in economic policy apart from providing what
are now called public goods, financed by taxation. Governments
were to accept financial disciplines imposed on them by bankers
and were to refrain from intervention in free market mechanisms.

In the 1930s very high unemployment made it obvious that
the classical theory did not work in practice. Keynes showed
unemployment was due to a deficiency of effective demand or
aggregate spending. By analyzing the relationship between
money, investment, savings, and income, he explained how a
state of demand deficiency could come about. The change in
policy advocated by Keynes was a break with the gold standard.
His *General Theory* implied that governments should plan their
own financial policies and require bankers to adjust the money
supply to the needs of a flow of spending sufficient for full
employment. The new theory also implied that foreign trade
and exchange rates should be adjusted so as to ensure that a
full employment financial policy was compatible with balance-
of-payments equilibrium.

Although these policies were interventionist so far as
the banking system was concerned, Keynes was far from being a
"radical." His declared aim was to save the free market
economy by showing how to correct its main defects. As he
put it, "whilst, therefore, the enlargement of the functions
of government, involved in the task of adjusting to one another the propensity to consume and the inducememement to invest,
would seem to a nineteenth-century publicist or to a contemporary American financier to be a terrific encroachment on
individualism, I defend it, on the contrary, both as the only
practicable means of avoiding the destruction of existing
economic forms in their entirety and as the condition of the
successful functioning of individual initiative" *(General
Theory,* p. 380).

Keynes' solution to prewar unemployment was made effective by vast public expenditures and deficit financing during
World War II and its cold war aftermath. Then in the postwar
period the center of gravity of the economics profession
moved decisively to the United States. Here, despite suspicion of government and adulation of the free market system,
Keynes' theory was taken up by some American economists and
propounded as the "neoclassical synthesis." The point of

this synthesis was to stress that, provided the government
took responsibility for maintaining full employment through
Keynesian monetary policy, free markets could function properly and secure an optimum use of resources. Unfortunately,
this provided a justification for American economists to take
up the pursuit of theorems about an ideal free market economy
at the point where the English had left off. Thus Keynes'
work, far from being the starting point for realistic study
of the imperfect market economies in which we live, became an
excuse for economists to carry on as before.

In Britain Keynesian full employment policy was practised
continuously throughout the 1950s. The unemployment rate
averaged 1.5 percent and inflation declined to 1 percent a
year. The success of the policy created a Keynesian consensus. In the United States, on the other hand, peacetime
Keynesianism was accepted by the federal government only in
the early 1960s. Meanwhile, monetarist economists, centered
in Chicago, resisted the Keynesian aspect of the neoclassical
synthesis, using the traditional bankers' argument that
monetary expansion causes inflation. There was only one important difference between the new monetarism and the old
classical economics: the monetarists made a virtue of the
massive international currency speculation that developed
during the 1960s by advocating a free market in currencies or,
in other words, floating exchange rates, in place of the
fixing of currencies to a gold standard.

Until recently American monetarism had few followers in
Britain. Though inflation worsened during the 1960s more
quickly in Britain than in the United States, it was obvious
that the main cause was a process of "cost push." In the
face of disappointing economic growth, trade union pushed
wage claims, companies raised prices, and governments increased taxes in a cumulative spiral that grew worse when the pound
sterling had to be devalued because of weak exports and fast-
rising imports. It was clear that a tight money policy would
make unemployment worse without doing much to correct the
inflation and the weak growth performance of British industry.
The remedy for inflation was therefore conceived to be "incomes policy," whose main element was institutional restraint
on trade union wage demands. Incomes policies, repeatedly
introduced by the government, were initially accepted by an
electorate worried by inflation and by the international weakness of the British economy. But in each case initial acqui-
escence was eventually followed by popular rejection. The
policies broke down because they had arbitrary and repressive
effects on particular groups of workers and because they

failed to protect full employment or secure faster growth of productivity.

The repeated breakdown of incomes policies has finally made American monetarism fashionable in Britain as an alternative theory of how to deal with the problem of inflation. But although many British academics, commentators, and politicians now talk the language of monetarism, it has little practical credibility because it ignores the reality of present-day bargaining.

Monetarism in the United States has been no more successful as a practical policy. Inflation has worsened considerably in the 1970s, the U.S. balance of payments has deteriorated drastically, and the level of employment remains insecure.

The truth is that no economists, whether in Britain or in the United States, have found a complete, workable answer to the problem of inflation in a modern democracy. It is clear that inflation is a symptom of the failure of an economy to deliver the income that workers, businesses, and governments require, and of conflicts within and between all these groups over distribution of the income that is available. In principle, part of the answer must be full employment and better use of the resources available (another part of the answer must be to seek broad agreement on the income levels toward which each social group should aim). The restrictive policies advocated by monetarist economists are no help. On the contrary, to ease inflation economic expansion is needed. Here Keynesian economics can still make a contribution if economists are willing to start again by going back to Keynes and devoloping his ideas in a different direction.

Postwar British Keynesians have made some progress at least in developing the analysis of policies to cope with many difficulties not treated fully in Keynes' theory. The main problems that needed to be tackled in Britain were the low level and slow growth of productivity, the depression and dereliction of old industrial areas, and balance-of-payments difficulties due particularly to Britain's loss of trade in manufactures. To many Americans and some British academics, it may appear that these problems have been caused by government intervention. Yet anyone who has followed economic policy in Britain at all closely will have observed that, as in other countries, government intervention has been devised belatedly in response to long-standing problems and can hardly be blamed for causing them. The unemployment and de-industrialization now occurring in Britain will grow rapidly

worse if intervention is abandoned. The question to ask is
not whether intervention is necessary buy what kind of intervention will be effective and consistent with a democratic
society. Neither classical economics, nor the neoclassical
synthesis, nor monetarism provide any guide to this since
they all assume from the outset that the problems in question
should not really exist.

The main theoretical ingredient which needs to be incorporated into Keynes' theory is a recognition of the prevalence
of imperfect or oligopolistic markets and the importance of
innovation and reorganization of production as a strategic
weapon in this form of competition. Empirical research has
shown that our economies behave in practice in an entirely
different manner from that postulated by free market theory.
Companies, regions, and even whole countries are prone to
long periods of relative success or decline, and many regular-
ities can be discovered in such processes. It is necessary
to discover which are the most useful simplifying assumptions
for the purpose of assessing policy. The choice will depend
in part on social priorities, so that analysis of this kind
is bound to have a political ingredient.

Empirical economics should not be antitheoretical. But
it should make theory an end product, a set of working generalizations which further research may show to be misconceived
in important respects and which may in any case become irrelevant as problems and social institutions change. Such an
approach is a natural development of the work of Keynes, who
was ready to be proved wrong by events or new facts because
he wanted to use economics to find solutions to real-life
problems.

Seen from a British perspective, the United States is
now beginning to suffer many of the problems that have proved
difficult to solve in Britain. Inflation, unstable foreign
holdings of dollars, and a weak trade balance, especially in
manufactures, are the symptoms of developments in the market
economy that in the British case have resulted in chronic
high unemployment, severe regional depression, stagnation of
productivity, and acute scarcity of funds for public services.
Although the realistic study of these problems is beginning
to make progress in Britain, it has come too late to prevent
deterioration of the economy from which, even with effective
policies, it would now take a decade or more to recover. If
a moral is to be drawn in the United States from the history
of postwar Keynesianism in Britain, it should be that a
major effort is needed to study problems in the real-life

imperfect-market economy without preconceptions based on perfect market theory.

A second moral from British experience concerns the international economic system. The United States, as a result of a long period of economic isolation followed by a period in which other countries were effectively on a dollar standard, formerly tended to regard international economic developments as peripheral to the internal economic situation. But the dollar has lost its special status in international money markets, the United States has become strategically dependent on imported oil, and U.S. markets have been opened to imported manufactures to the extent that the U.S. trade balance, and the fate of American industries, is closely dependent on devopments in other countries. The United States is now as powerfully affected by the international economy as Britain, Japan, and many European countries have been since long past.

It is plain that the international economy is not a self-balancing system and that both Britain and the United States are exceptionally vulnerable because of losses in manufactured trade. Neoclassical and monetarist economists will argue that such problems can easily be dealt with by flexible exchange rates--in other words, by allowing the dollar or the pound sterling to fall against other currencies. But Britain's experience has been that devaluation or depreciation of sterling is not an effective adjustment mechanism. Again, economists are arguing on the basis of idealized assumptions. In practice, in the British case the trend loss of markets has been too rapid, the beneficial effects of devaluation on trade have been too slow and weak, and the inflationary effects of devaluation on prices of imports and raw materials have been too immediate for devaluation to be a practicable remedy. After several unsuccessful experiments with devaluation, Britain is left with no recourse but to control imports by the very unpleasant method of cutting internal purchasing power at the cost of stagnation of home industries and high unemployment.

Examination of trends in trade suggests to Cambridge economists that imbalances in manufactures are now becoming even more disruptive to the world economy as a whole, and to Britain and the United States in particular, than was the rise in world oil prices in the mid-1970s. This implies that new forms of regulation of trade will be required in the 1980s and that carefully devised protection might be a necessary part of any solution to recession. The existence of a problem of prolonged imbalances in trade certainly cannot be ruled out by any abstract theory. Keynes' lesson needs to be

learned again. We must devise new and practical frameworks of
analysis within which policies to solve new problems can be
systematically investigated.

*Journal of Post Keynesian Economics, Volume II, No. 1, (1979):
139-144*

"Keynes' Politics in Theory and Practice," James Tobin (1983)*

   The hundredth anniversary of the birth of John Maynard
Keynes occurs, like the publication of *The General Theory,*
during a world depression. History has contrived to call attention to Keynes just when his diagnoses and prescriptions
are more obviously credible than at any other time since the
Great Depression of the 1930s. The current depression is
tragic, but the coincidence of timing may be fortunate. It
should help revive the credibility of Keynesian analysis and
policy within the economics profession and in the broader public arena. It may even enhance the prospects for recovery in
this decade, and for stability and growth in the longer run.

   Of course we have a long way to go, both to restore prosperity to the world and to restore realistic common sense to
discussion and decision about economic policy. But the beginnings of recovery that have brightened the economic news this
year, mainly in the United States, can be credited to Keynesian policies, however reluctant, belated, or inadvertent.
Our Federal Reserve finally took mercy on the economy about
a year ago and suspended its monetarist targets. Its easing
of monetary policy saved the world financial system from
dangerous crisis and averted further collapse of economic activity. At the same time, American fiscal measures began to
exert a powerful expansionary influence on aggregate demand.
This Keynesian policy was, of course, fortuitous in its timing and unintentional in its motivation. It was a combination
of tax cuts, rationalized by anti-Keynesian supply-side arguments, and increased defense spending. Whatever one may think
of the distributional equity and allocational efficiency of
these measures, they are increasing private and public spending on goods and services and creating jobs. Every business
economist and forecaster knows that, even if his boss's
speeches deplore federal deficits as the principal threat to
recovery.

In the battle for the hearts and minds of economists and
of the thoughtful lay public, the tide may also have turned.
The devastating effects of Thatcher policies on the United
Kingdom, and of Volcker policies in this country after October
1979, have opened many eyes and minds. The idea that monetary
disinflation would be painless, if only the resolve of the
authorities to pursue it relentlessly were clearly announced
and understood, proved to be as illusory as Keynesians predicted. Monetarism—both of the older Friedman version stressing adherence to money stock targets and of the newer rational
expectations variety—has been badly discredited. The stage
has been set for recovery in the popularity of Keynesian
diagnoses and remedies. I do not mean to imply, of course,
that there is some Keynesian truth, vintage 1936 or 1961, to
which economists and policymakers will or should now return,
ignoring the lessons of economic events and of developments
in economics itself over these last turbulent fifteen years.
I do mean that in the new intellectual synthesis which I hope
and expect will emerge to replace the divisive controversies
and chaotic debates on macroeconomic policies, Keynesian ideas
will have a prominent place.

The postwar record

A strong case can be made for the success of Keynesian
policies. Virtually all advanced democratic capitalist
societies adopted, in varying degrees, Keynesian strategies
of demand management after World War II. The period, certainly until 1973, was one of unparalleled prosperity, growth,
expansion of world trade, and stability. Unemployment was
low, and the business cycle was tamed. The disappointments
of the 1970s—inflation, stagflation, recessions and unemployment resulting from anti-inflationary policies— discredited
Keynesian policies. But after all, the Vietnam inflation
occurred when President Johnson rejected the advice of his
Keynesian economists and refused to raise taxes to pay for his
war. The recoveries of 1971-73 and 1975-79 ended in double-
digit inflation in the United States. But the Yom Kippur war
of 1973, OPEC, and the Ayatollah Khomeini were scarcely the
endogenous consequences of those recoveries or of the monetary
and fiscal policies that stimulated or accommodated them.
Indeed, the main reason for pessimism about recovery today is
the likelihood that excessive caution, based on misreading
of or overreaction to the 1970s, will inhibit policy for recovery in the 1980s. If so, we will pay dearly in unemployment, lost production, and stagnant investment to insure
against another burst of inflation.

But if we Keynesians need feel no compulsion to be apol-
ogetic, neither are we entitled to be complacent. Keynes did
not provide, nor did his various followers over the years, a
recipe for avoiding unstable inflation at full employment.
The dilemma, though it became spectacularly severe in the
last fifteen years, is an old one. It was recognized and
prophesied by Keynesians like Joan Robinson and Abba Lerner
in the early 1940s, when commitments to full-employment policies after the war seemed likely, and it was a practical
concern of policymakers throughout the postwar period. It
still remains the major problem of macroeconomic policy.
Keynesians cannot accept--nor will, I think, the politics of
modern democracies--the monetarist resolution of the dilemma,
which amounts simply to redefining as full employment whatever
unemployment rate, however high, seems necessary to ensure
price stability. But we cannot ignore the possible inflationary results of gearing macroeconomic policies simply to
the achievement of employment rates that seem "full" by some
other criterion. The politics of modern democracies will not
allow that, either. I shall return to this central issue
later.

Keynes on macroeconomic policy

It is time now to say more about what Keynesian policies
are. Actually, *The General Theory* itself contains little in
the way of concrete policy recommendations; for the most part,
those are left for the reader to infer. But Keynes was, of
course, an active participant in policy debates in the United
Kingdom in the 1920s and '30s. One evident purpose of *The
General Theory* was to provide a professional analytical foundation for the policy positions he had been advocating in
those debates.

Keynes opposed Britain's return in 1925 to the 1914 parity
of sterling with gold and the U.S. dollar. His arguments
were summarized in *The Economic Consequences of Mr. Chruchill,*
who was Chancellor of the Exchequer at the time. More from
shrewd realism than from theory, Keynes based his opposition
on a view he held consistently thereafter and formally expounded in *The General Theory*: the downward inflexibility of
money wages. He predicted, correctly in the event, that making wages costs fall to correct the overvaluation of the
pound would be difficult, socially disruptive, and economically costly. He thought that workers and their unions would
accept lower real wages accomplished by a lower exchange
value of sterling and higher prices for imports, while they
would resist the equivalent adjustment via cuts in money wages.

Once the fateful decision he opposed was taken, moreover, Keynes advocated government leadership in bringing about a smooth reduction of nominal wages. This advice, too, was ignored. Britain entered a long period of industrial strife, mass unemployment, and depression.

In 1929 the Liberal Party, led by Lloyd George, proposed during its unsuccessful electoral campaign a program of public works to relieve unemployment. Keynes supported the proposal in his pamphlet with H. K. Henderson, *Can Lloyd Géorge Do It?* There and in his later testimony before the MacMillan Committee, Keynes refuted what became to be known as the "Treasury View." In modern parlance, this View was that public works outlays, financed by borrowing, would "crowd out" private borrowing, investment, and employment one hundred percent. The U.K. Treasury, like other exponents of "crowding-out" scenarios in other countries and at other times, made no distinction between situations of idle and fully employed resources. Keynes pointed out how public and private saving generated by public works activity, and overseas borrowing as well, would moderate the crowding-out the Treasury feared, and how the Bank of England could be accommodative. Of course, only after the famous multiplier paper by Keynes' student R. F. Kahn, stimulated by this very controversy, could Keynes develop a full rationale for his position.

The reigning governments would neither adjust the exchange rate nor adopt expansionary fiscal measures. Keynes was therefore led for macroeconomic reasons to favor a general tariff, in effect a devaluation of sterling for merchandise transactions only. When Britain was finally forced to devalue sterling in 1931, Keynes lost interest in the tariff, though one was enacted anyway. Keynes was, of course, quite aware of the "beggar-my-neighbor" aspects of devaluations and tariffs, but in the British policy discussions he was a Briton. *The General Theory*, fortunately, is cast in a closed economy, interpretable as the whole world, and thus excludes nationalistic solutions.

The general characteristics of Keynes' policy interventions are clear from these examples. Keynes consistently focused on real economic outcomes, to which he subordinated nominal and financial variables, prices, interest rates, and exchange rates. He naturally and unproblematically attributed to governments the power and the responsibility to improve macroeconomic performance. Keynes was a pragmatic problem-solver, always ready to figure out what to do in the circumstances of the time. These characteristics carried through

to his policy career after *The General Theory*, his effective
contributions to British war finance and international monetary architecture.

What does *The General Theory* itself say about policy?
Fiscal policy, long regarded as the main Keynesian instrument,
is introduced obliquely as a means of beefing up a weak national propensity to spend. Keynes warns against budget surpluses
built by overly prudent sinking funds. He advocates redistribution through the fisc in favor of poorer citzens with
higher propensities to consume. He welcomes public investment, but deplores the political fact that business opposition
to productive public investments limits their scope; nonetheless, intrinsically useless projects will enrich society if
the resources directly and indirectly employed would otherwise be idle. Keynesian theory of fiscal policy was developed by others, notably Alvin Hansen and the members of his
Harvard Fiscal Policy Seminar.

The role of money

Keynes was ambivalent on monetary policy. For fifteen
or twenty years following publication of *The General Theory*,
many economists, more in England than America, used the
authority of the book to dismiss or downgrade the macroeconomic importance of money. Their reasons were first, the
apparent insensitivity of investment and saving to interest
rates during the 1930s, and second, the observed insensitivity
of interest rates to money supplies in the same period.
Keynes' own views were more subtle. Though he originated the
"liquidity trap" and exploited it in his theoretical attack
on the "classical" theory of unemployment, in his discussions
of monetary policy he did not regard it as a typical circumstance or as an excuse for inaction by central banks. Neither
did he regard investment decisions as beyond the reach of
interest rates. His skepticism arose from his belief that
the long-run expectations governing the marginal efficiency
of capital are so volatile and unsystematic that central
banks might well be unable to offset them by varying interest
rates. Yet he thought they should try, arguing for example
that mature investment booms should be prolonged by reductions
in interest rates, not killed by monetary tightening.

The same view led Keynes in *The General Theory* to advocate some "socialization" of investment. This idea is not
spelled out. Apparently Keynes had in mind not only public
capital formation and tax policies affecting private investment, but more comprehensive, though cooperative, interven-

tions in private investment decisions. Moreover, he had in mind not only cyclical stabilization but a long-run push to saturate the economy with capital and accomplish "the euthanasia of the rentier." Perhaps Jean Monnet's postwar "indicative planning" in France, where government sponsored a coordinated raising of sights to overcome pessimism and lift investment, is an example of what Keynes had in mine. Perhaps some of the Swedish measures designed to make investment less pro-cyclical are another example.

Finally, I want to call attention to Keynes' habit of regarding wage determination as subject to "policy." This is evident in *The General Theory* well as in the pamphleteering cited above. In the book, Keynes discusses stable versus flexibility. In a famous passage, he notes that monetary expansion and wage reduction are equivalent ways of attaining higher employment and observes that only "foolish" and "inexperienced" persons would prefer the latter to the former. His frequent references to "wage policy" do not fit very well with his attempt at the outset of *The General Theory* to build his story of involuntary unemployment on the competitive foundations of Marshallian economics. But in policy matters Keynes was a shrewd and practical observer, and it would not be far-fetched to infer from his hints that he expected and advocated direct government interventions in the wage-setting process.

Keynesian principles of macroeconomic policy

The theory of macroeconomic policy, the subject of bitter controversy today, really developed after World War II and after Keynes' death. The principles of what came to be known as Keynesian policies were expounded in the postwar "neoclassical synthesis" by Paul Samuelson and others. They occupied the mainstream of economics until the powerful monetarist and new classical counter-revolutions of the last fifteen years. They were the intellectual foundations of official U.S. policies in the Kennedy-Johnson years, when the media discovered them and somewhat misleadingly called them the "New Economics." They are expounded in the 1962 Economic Report of the Kennedy Council of Economic Advisers.

Let me review those principles, with particular reference to the items that are now particularly controversial, some of which are explicitly rejected by U.S. policymakers, as well as by those of other countries, notably the Thatcher government.

The first principle, obviously and unambiguously Keynesian, is the explicit dedication of macroeconomic policy instruments to real economic goals, in particular full employment and real growth of national output. This has never meant, in theory or in practice, that nominal outcomes, especially price inflation, were to be ignored. In the early 1960s, for example, the targets for unemployment and real GNP were chosen with cautious respect for the inflation risks. Today, however, a popular anti-Keynesian view is that macroeconomic policies can and should be aimed solely at nominal targets, for prices and/or nominal GNP, letting private "markets" determine the consequences for real economic variables.

Second, Keynesian demand management is activist, responsive to the actually observed state of the economy and to projections of its paths under various policy alternatives. The anti-Keynesian counterrevolutionaries scorn activist macroeconomic management as "fine-tuning" and "stop-go" and allege that it is destabilizing. The disagreement refers partly to the sources of destabilizing shocks. Keynesians believe, as did Keynes himself, that such shocks are endemic and epidemic in market capitalism; that government policymakers, observing the shocks and their effects, can partially but significantly offset them; and that the expectations induced by successful demand management will themselves be stabilizing. (Of course, Keynesians have by no means relied entirely on discretionary responsive policies; they have also tried to design and build automatic stabilizers into the fiscal and financial systems.) The opponents believe that government itself is the chief source of destabilizing shocks to otherwise stable system; that neither the wisdom nor the intentions of policymakers can be trusted; and that stability of policies mandated by nondiscretionary rules, blind to actual events and forecasts, are the best we can do. When this stance is combined with concentration on nominal outcomes, the results of recent experience in Thatcher's Britain and Volcker's America are not hard to understand.

Third, Keynesians have wished to put both fiscal and monetary policies in consistent and coordinated harness in the pursuit of macroeconomic objectives. Any residual skepticism about the relevance and effectiveness of monetary policy vanished early in the postwar era, certainly in the United States though less so in Britain. Keynesians have, of course, opposed the use of macroeconomically irrelevant norms like budget balance as guides to policy. They have, however, pointed out that monetary and fiscal instruments in combination provide sufficient degrees of freedom to pursue demand-management objectives in combination with whatever priorities a democratic society chooses for other objectives. For example, Keynesian stabilization policies can be carried out with large or small government sectors, progressive or regresive tax and transfer structures, and high or low investment and saving as fractions of full-employment GNP. In these respects, latter-day Keynesians have been more optimistic than the author of *The General Theory*: They believe that measures to create jobs do not have to be wasteful and need not focus exclusively on bolstering the national propensity to consume. The idea that the fiscal-monetary mix can be chosen to accelerate national capital formation, if that is a national priority, is a contribution of the so-called "neoclassical synthesis." Disregard of the idea since 1980 is the source of many of the current problems of U.S. macroeconomic policy, which may not only be inadequate to promote recovery but also perversely designed to inhibit national investment at a time when greater provision for the future is a widely shared social priority.

Fourth, as I observed earlier, Keynesians have not been optimistic that fiscal and monetary policies of demand management are sufficient to achieve both real and nominal goals, to obtain simultaneously both full employment and stability of prices or inflation rates. Neither are Keynesians prepared, as monetarist and new classical economists and policymakers often appear to be, to resolve the dilemma tautologically by calling "full employment" whatever unemployment rate results from policies that stabilize prices.

Every American Administration from Kennedy to Carter, possibly excepting Ford, has felt the need to have some kind of wage-price policy. This old dilemma remains the greatest challenge; Keynesian economists differ among themselves, as well as with those of different macroeconomic persuasions, on how to resolve it. It may be ironically true that, thanks to good luck and to the severity of the depression--the two Eisenhower-Martin recessions of the late 1950s helped pave the way for an inflation-free Keynesian recovery in the early 1960s, and the Volcker depression may do the same--revival of inflation is unlikely during recovery in the 1980s, just when policymakers are acutely afraid of it. But it would be foolish to count on that, even more to assume the problem has permanently disappeared.

The need for incomes policy

The need for a third category of policy instruments--in
addition to fiscal and monetary, the "wage policy" hinted in
The General Theory--is clear to me. We can and should push
other measures to reduce the expected value of the NAIRU (the
non-accelerating-inflation rate of unemployment). These include standard labor market, manpower, and human capital policies. They include attacks on the legislative sacred cows
that impart floors to some wages and prices and bias upward
the price response to aggregate demand stimulus. They include
encouragement to new arrangements for labor compensation,
substituting shares in performances and fortunes of employers
for exclusive reliance on administered or negotiated scales
of pay for labor time. They include measures to make collective bargaining more responsive to those workers with greater
risks of unemployment. But even if everything is done that
realistically can be done, politically and economically, on
these fronts, I believe we will need incomes policies in our
arsenal. The challenge is to design policies which labor and
management will accept in the interests of better macroeconomic
performance--policies which will not be so rigid and heavy-
handed in microeconomic impact as to entail heavy costs in
allocational efficiency. I myself believe that guideposts, to
which compliance is induced by tax-based rewards, offer the
greatest promise. But the subject is still wide open.

Until Keynesians design the instrument missing from their
kit of tools, we cannot press with the full conviction and
confidence merited by theory and history the superiority of
Keynesian policies to the anti-Keynesian policies of recent
experience.

Politics and ideology

In the near half-century since the debut of *The General
Theory*, Keynesian macroeconomics has been identified politically and ideologically with liberalism, in the modern
rather than the 19th century meaning of that word. Although
prior to 1979 conservative governments, Republican in the
United States and Conservative in Britain, practiced Keynesian
demand management, its main proponents have been liberal
parties: Democratic in this country, Labor in the United
Kingdom, social-democratic parties elsewhere. Certainly
Keynes has never been accepted in the ideological pantheon of
business and finance, despite the efforts of groups like the
Committee for Economic Development in the United States to
define a pragmatic synthesis. The lines are drawn more sharply

than ever now that conservative movements with ideologies explicitly condemning Keynes and Keynesian policies have gained
influence and power.

The reasons for business interests to reject Keynes are
not entirely clear. Keynes himself thought the implications
of his theory were moderately conservative. He found no
fault with the way capitalist systems allocated employed resources. (These days, with externalities more apparent and
hazardous, he might be less confident.) He wanted to employ
more resources—to the benefit of claimants to profits as
well as to job-seekers, as experience repeatedly testifies.
The fiscal and financial shibboleths he challenged, and often
ridiculed, were obstacles to general prosperity, not just to
the well-being of workers. Compared to the revolutionary institutional changes threatened by other critics of capitalism's
failures in the Great Depression, the reforms prescribed by
Keynes were mild and conservative indeed. Perhaps the instinc-
tive revulsion of conservatives was due to the suspicion that
the liberation of government from traditional norms and the
assignment to government of powers and responsibilities for
overall economic performance would expose capitalists to un-
predictable social, political, and economic hazards. Perhaps
businessmen feared that full employment would cost them more
by tilting bargaining power toward labor than it would gain
them in the fruits of prosperity. Perhaps they felt intuitively that they really were being displaced from the temples
of their civilization.

Organized labor has found Keynesian economics selectively
congenial. Its interest in jobs coincides with the full-employment emphasis on Keynesian macroeconomic policies. But
labor's support of price-increasing measures and unions' representation of senior employed workers at the expense of the
unemployed worsen the agony of the trade-off and cripple full-
employment policies. Moreover, it has been difficult, to say
the least, to obtain and maintain labor's acceptance of income
policies. Political parties that espouse Keynesian policies
are also those which depend on nonbusiness interest groups
for campaign support. The public does not make distinctions
obvious to economists, and many opponents of those interests
mistakenly associate Keynesian economics with all sorts of
dubious microecononic interventions.

There is, however, a sense in which Keynesian economics
is a natural ally of liberalism. In the same passage where
Keynes exonerated capitalism of allocational inefficiency, he
faulted it for inequality of wealth as well as for chronic

underemployment. There is nothing particularly Keynesian
about the welfare state, which in greater or lesser degree
has grown in every democratic capitalist country since World
War II. Keynesian macroeconomists could take any side of controversies about Social Security, socialized medicine, food
stamps, and the like. Nevertheless, Keynesian economics at
a minimum provides a license for welfare-state measures and
other government efforts toward redistribution of wealth.
The license is the faith that macroeconomic stabilization
and prosperity are compatible with a wide range of social
policies, that modern capitalism and democracy are robust
enough to prosper and progress while being humane and equitable. That faith conflicts with the visions of extreme
Right and Left, which agree that extremes of wealth and poverty, of security and insecurity, are indispensable to the
functioning of capitalism. Keynesian policies helped to
confound those dismal prophecies in the past; I think they
will do so again.

Challenge, Volume 26, (November-December 1983): 5-11

Social Choice and Individual Values
by
Kenneth J. Arrow

REVIEW: Harold M. Somers (1952)*

This book constitutes a carefully worked out consideration of the feasibility of constructing an acceptable social
welfare function. Its appearance will reinforce the stimulus
that has been given to welfare economics during recent years
by such books as Little's *Critique of Welfare Economics*,
Reder's *Studies in the Theory of Welfare Economics*, Myint's
Theories of Welfare Economics, Samuelson's *Foundations of
Economic Analysis*, Lerner's *Economics of Control*, and numerous
articles in the technical journals.

"Nonmathematical" economists may be prepared to welcome
a Cowles Commission monograph that does not use geometry,
trigonometry, calculus, difference equations, or determinants.
But anyone who expects an hour or two of easy reading is doom-
ed to disappointment. Like most of Von Neumann and Morgen-
stern's *Theory of Games and Economic Behavior* this book employs
a particular form of symbolic logic, and the level of concentration required is about the same in both cases.

Arrow sets up in rigorous form five conditions that an
adequate social welfare function should fulfil. They may be
stated informally as follows: (1) for some sufficiently wide
range of sets of individual orderings of alternative social
states; (2) the social ordering responds positively to alterations in individual values, or at least not negatively; (3)
irrelevant alternatives (i.e., those not concerned in the comparison under consideration) should not influence the choice
among relevant alternatives; (4) there should be citizens'
sovereignty in the sense that no decision shall be imposed by
custom, thus preventing the free choice by the individual;
and (5) there should not be dictatorship, that is, social
choice conforming only to the will of one man. Arrow also
suggests an interesting distinction between individual *tastes*
and individual *values*. Individual tastes are concerned with
the goods and services enjoyed directly by the individual and

available to him in the market. Individual values are concerned with general standards of equity about which he may
voice an opinion in the political arena but which is not directly open to him for decision through the market mechanism.

Arrow finds it impossible to construct a social welfare
function that satisfies all five conditions unless some highly
restrictive, special assumptions are made. He finds that the
Bergson welfare function and the Hicks-Kaldor compensation
principle contradict one or more of these conditions. In the
special case where there is "single-peakedness"—that is, all
individual orderings of preferences are similar—all five conditions can be satisfied. However, if there is not unanimity
or at least a general consensus as to desirable policy, it is
impossible to have social choice that conforms to the five
conditions. Another complication he points to is that the
decision process itself may be a value. This leads to the
possibility that, even if the democratic decision-making procedure does not give the same material goods and services as
other systems, it may nevertheless be desirable because the
process has a value to the individual in and of itself. The
limiting case may be considered that of "give me liberty or
give me death."

This is a challenging and disturbing book that demands
the attention of everyone concerned with economic policy. Do
we have a sufficient consensus to determine specific lines of
policy? Or do our policy-makers fall into the error of im-
puting social preferences that do not actually exist? It would
be well for all economists to follow Arrow and pause to reflect on the problems involved in jumping from individual
tastes and values to the question of social choice.

*Journal of Political Economy, Vol. 60, (April 1952): 170-171

REVIEW: Irving M. Copi (1952)*

Arrow's is No. 12 of the monographs prepared by the Cowles
Commission for Research in Economics. It should be of great
interest to social scientists in general, and to ethical and
social philosophers as well, for the problem with which this
book deals is an important and pervasive one. That problem
can be formulated somewhat as follows. Societies as well as
individuals continually must choose between alternative courses
of action. The individual members of a society will have their
own preferences as to which of the alternatives should be

chosen. Arrow is interested in the relationships which can obtain between the set of individual preferences, on the one hand, and the social choice, on the other. A process or rule which for every set of individual preferences or orderings determines a social ordering is called a "social welfare function."

It is obvious that any number of social welfare functions, in this sense, could be arbitrarily defined. Arrow's interest, however, is in the conditions which such a function could reasonably be expected to satisfy. The problem can be posed now in this way: If each individual makes a *rational* ordering of the alternatives, what social welfare functions are there, if any, which will yield a *rational* ordering by society? For this question to be handled in any precise fashion, what is meant by a "rational" ordering must be precisely specified. Arrow explains that "the concept of rationality used throughout this study is at the heart of modern economic analysis" (p. 19). An ordering of alternatives is said to be rational provided that, (1) of any two alternatives x and y, either one is preferred to the other or else they are regarded as indifferent, and (2) the ordering is transitive, i.e., for any alternatives x, y, and z, if x is either preferred or indifferent to y and y is either preferred or indifferent to z, then x must be either preferred or indifferent to z.

It is again clear that an arbitrary ordering, imposed perhaps by custom, would satisfy the formal conditions of rationality and that this imposition would constitute a social welfare function in the specified sense despite a complete absence of any connection between society's choice and the preferences of the individuals composing that society. Such a social welfare function is said to be "imposed." Another social welfare function which would yield a rational social ordering for any set of rational individual orderings could be obtained simply by specifying some one individual whose ordering would automatically become the ordering for the group. The individual specified would in effect be an absolute dictator, and Arrow calls such a social welfare function "dictatorial." Although they satisfy the formal requirements of rationality, these imposed and dictatorial social welfare functions are repugnant. The question naturally arises: Can a rational social welfare function be constructed by way of democratic processes?

Some doubt is raised by the "paradox of voting." To say that a group should prefer one alternative to another if a majority of its members prefer the first alternative to the

second plunges us into the following situation. Suppose there
are three individuals in a group, 1, 2, and 3, and suppose that
that there are just three alternatives A, B, and C. Suppose
further that individual 1 prefers A to B and B to C (and hence
A to C), that individual 2 prefers B to C and C to A (and
hence B to A), and that individual 3 prefers C to A and A to
B (and hence C to B). Now a majority prefer A to B, and a
majority prefer B to C. But a majority prefer C to A, so that
if the social preference between pairs of alternatives is to
conform to the preferences of a majority, then the social ordering is nonrational, since preference is not transitive in
this case.

Arrow's main conclusion can be regarded as a generalization of the paradox of voting--although the generalization is
neither simple to state nor easy to prove. A number of perfectly natural and reasonable conditions are laid down for the
social welfare function to satisfy, and then a general possibility theorem is demonstrated. That theorem asserts that if
there are at least three alternatives which the individual
members of society are free to order in any way, then any social welfare function which satisfies two prima facie reasonable conditions and yields a rational ordering of the alternatives for society must be either imposed or dictatorial
(p. 59).

That the implications of the general possibility theorem
are unwelcome to Arrow is shown by the fact that the latter
part of his book is devoted to the problem of searching out
conditions under which a democratic social welfare function
is possible. Some very special cases are satisfactorily resolved, but the general question remains unsolved. Perhaps
one method of escaping the unhappy conclusion is by way of
challenging the prima facie unobjectionable conditions which
Arrow lays down for the social welfare function. That avenue
seems not very promising to this reviewer. Another way might
be to challenge the definition of "rationality" stated by
Arrow. Of interest to ethical theorists is the fact that certain assumptions about individuals' evaluations suffice to
permit a satisfactory (i.e., democratic) social welfare function to be constructed. A careful study of such assumptions
should lead to more precise and persuasive discussions of the
role of the individual in a democratic society and to the
limitations on the freedom of individual citizens which membership in a democratic state requires.

Of interest to many philosophers will be the use which
Arrow makes of symbolic logic. Adopting the notation of the

logic of relations enables the author to state his conditions
in highly perspicuous form and to demonstrate his conclusions
with complete rigor. The present book shows that the methods
of symbolic logic are profitably applied to areas whose non-
quantiative nature prevents the use of more ordinary mathematical techniques. No previous knowledge of symbolic logic
is required for reading this book, however, for all the symbols used are carefully and lucidly explained as they are introduced.

On the negative side, the reader of this book will encounter more technical economic jargon than he might like.
But the message of the book is well worth the trouble of
going through the moderately difficult passages.

Arrow is to be congratulated on having written a book
which is instructive and stimulating to both philosophers and
social scientists.

Ethics 62, (1952): 220-222

"Arrow and the 'New Welfare' Economics--A Restatement,"
E. J. Mishan (1958)*

Since Mr. Davis's remarks suggest that my paper may have
given rise to misapprehensions, it may be worthwhile summaris-
ing, in a paragraph, my view of the recent history of welfare
criteria in order to have Arrow's contribution, and my criticisms of it, in proper perspective.

The principle of compensation: (a) that a change which actually made some better off and no one worse off was an improvement in social welfare, was supplemented in 1939 by a criterion
introduced by Kaldor and Hicks which marks the inception of the
new welfare economies, a criterion based on hypothetical compensation; (b) a change which *could* make some better off without
making any worse off was to be regarded as an advance in the
community's welfare. It was put forward in the spirit of an efficiency indicator by whose measure, on the scale of "better" or
"worse," we might agree to abide. Once Scitovsky had uncovered
a mechanical defect in this indicator, it was extended, on the
suggestion of Samuelson and others, to take the form (c), that a
situation II was to be regarded as better than I if everyone
could be made better off in II than in I *for every distribution
conceivable* in the I situation. A sufficient condition for the
fulfilment of this criterion, which eradicated the possibility

of any ambiguity, was that the situation II contained more of
some goods (resources) and no less of any good (resource) than
existed in the I situation.

But having got this far, the new welfare economics led to a
further development. Samuelson summarised the individual welfare possibilities latent in a collection of goods, or resources,
in a utility possibility frontier--a boundary encompassing all
the possible combinations of individual welfares. Consistent
with the spirit of the original Kaldor-Hicks essay, we might now
regard as an improvement for the community any outward movement
of the complete utility possibility frontier. Alternatively--
and this is very much to the point--we might argue that the acceptance of an outward movement of the utility frontier as an
improvement in social welfare, on the grounds that everyone
could be made better off, is a tacit acceptance of a Paretian-
type social-welfare function of unspecified form. And though
such a welfare function be widely acceptable, it is, in a sense,
arbitrary; of only limited use, not being specified; and only
one of an indefinite number of such functions. Thinking along
these lines, we might prefer to adopt a method (d), which is to
regard the utility frontier as having no welfare implications of
itself but, instead, embodying the requisite "technical" data
prior to imposing any chosen social-welfare function--if a satisfactory one could be constructed--which reflected the ethics
of the individuals in the economy.

Arrow, I take it, was concerned to discover whether or not
such a thing as a social-welfare function could, in general, be
constructed in a "satisfactory" manner given all the conceivable
ways in which the individuals might rank any given alternative
social states. His conclusion, with which I agree, was that--
granted the "reasonable" conditions such a function had to meet
--in principle this was not possible, though, I might add, this
does not rule out the possibility that in some circumstances the
alternatives facing society are such that, with the particular
individual orderings, a solution which meets Arrow's requirements may be found.

Where do we stand today? As a consequence of ambiguities
in the original Kaldor-Hicks-Scitovsky tests, (b) has given way
to (c). As a result of Arrow's research, any hope for reaching
(d), on his "reasonable" conditions, has to be abandoned. Some
would like to amend one or more of his conditions in the endeav-
our to construct a social-welfare function which works. Others
may feel content to hold on to the new welfare economics in the
form of (c).

What I wished to make plain in my paper was that, although welfare economics was indeed vulnerable to various sorts of criticism, nothing that Arrow had written need weaken our decision to adopt welfare criterion (c), the contrary impression notwithstanding. For, while I agree that Arrow was experimenting with the idea of using the principle of (hypothetical) compensation for the passage from individual ordering to the social ordering of alternatives, to dismiss it on the ground that "Scitovsky indifference is not transitive" is, first, to suggest that the principle itself is in error and, therefore, does constitute an attack on the new welfare economics, and, secondly, to dismiss it for manifestly wrong reasons, since the compensation principle in its (c) form goes beyond the Scitovsky criterion. In any case, few would endorse Scitovsky's footnote suggesting that self-contradicting community indifference curves might be taken to indicate a state of indifference for the community.

On the other hand, my strictures on Arrow's Possibility Theorem, as I see them now, were perhaps a little severe. What I wished to establish was that its conclusion had no real bearing on the traditional welfare economics. This proposition may have been apparent on a close examination. But a cursory impression could easily mislead on a matter which I hold to be important. Of related significance is the superficial view that the theorem demonstrates that if individuals have opposing interests any assumed derivation of a social-welfare function which meets Arrow's conditions necessarily leads to a contradiction. Though, admittedly, it suffices for Arrow's thesis, we should be aware that contradiction is no more than a possible outcome. It seems useful to me to point this up, since, despite Arrow's resolution, interpersonal comparisons may be seen lurking about his consequence 3 (If $x^{\prime}P_1y^{\prime}$ and $y^{\prime}P_2x^{\prime}$, then $x^{\prime}Iy^{\prime}$) and a conclusion may be drawn, wrongly, that any welfare economics which chose to proceed on the assumption that interpersonal comparisons were possible was fated to perish through contradictions.

[1]The Editors apologize for the omission of this note from the September issue. A rejoinder to it by Mr. Mishan was printed in that issue.

[2]E.J. Mishan, "An Investigation into some Alleged Contradictions in Welfare Economics," ECONOMIC JOURNAL, September 1957.

[3]London; Chapman & Hall, 1951.

[4]Mishan, *op. cit.*, p. 452.

[5]Arrow, *op. cit.*, p. 37.

[6]Mishan, *op. cit.*, p. 454.

*Economic Journal, Vol. 68, (September 1958): 595-597

"Kenneth Arrow's Contribution to Economics," Carl Christian von Weizsäcker (1971)*

6. Social Choice and Individual Values

The work which made Arrow's name better known than any of his other contributions is his book on *Social Choice and Individual Values* (first edition 1951, second edition 1963) (A1). It was by this book that certain deep difficulties in developing satisfactory mechanisms for arriving at social choices became known to economists interested in welfare economics and related questions. The voting paradox, known earlier, was thereby generalized to a general impossibility theorem about the existence of a function relating individual preferences to social "preferences" or choices, if this function were to fulfill certain conditions. The conditions stipulated by Arrow were

1. The function should have a domain containing all logically possible combination of individual preferences with respect to at least three alternative choices for the society, A, B, C.

2. If a certain alternative becomes preferred to some other alternative with certain people which this had not been the case before and if this alternative was socially preferred to the other one before, then it should ceteris paribus a fortiori be preferred socially after this change of preferences (positive association of social and individual values).

3. A change in individual preferences only with respect to third alternatives should have no influence on the social preference ordering with respect to two given alternatives (independence of irrelevant alternatives).

4. A given social preference of one alternative over the other cannot prevail for every conceivable combination of individual preference orderings (the social preference is not

allowed to be imposed independently of individual preferences).

5. There is no dictator dictating his preferences to society as a whole.

Arrow proves that there exists no social choice function fulfilling all these conditions although each of them appears to be a reasonable requirement for such a social choice function. Since the existence of social choice functions seemed to be a necessary requirement for any kind of rational social decision making. His theorem was a great challenge to those who were interested in the foundations of welfare economics and, indeed, political theory.

It was particularly the third axiom (independence of irrelevant alternatives) which was criticized and scrutinized, since it seemed to exclude the introduction of the criterion of intensity of preference: If 51 people just barely prefer A to B and 49 are willing to pay a high price to have B instead of A, then this appears to be different from a situation in which the same 51 people intensely prefer A to B and the 49 prefer B to A, but very mildly so. Indeed, it is reasonable to except that a sufficiently coherent democratic society will in the first case choose B and will in the second case choose A, and many would not object to this difference of outcomes. Yet Arrow's condition 3 implies that the decision has to be the same in both cases. Murakama [B9], Sem [B10] and others have pointed out that condition 3 really contains two conditions: one which says that the ranking of third alternatives as such should not have an influence on the social ranking of any given two alternatives; and another one which says that the social ranking of two alternatives should only depend on the *ordinal* individual ranking of the alternatives. It is this second condition which causes doubt: in so far as the "intensity" of preferences between two alternatives is measured by their relative position with respect to other alternatives, the third condition of Arrow may be too strong. The appropriate formulation of axioms for social welfare functions replacing Arrow's condition 3 is still a debated subject. Since Arrow's axiom is inconsistent with traditional utilitarianism and the "new welfare economics", the central place of this debate in the field of normative economics is obvious.

Another attempt to bypass the impossibility theorem is to try to reduce the scope of the socail welfare function, which means not to accept Arrow's condition 1. Tullock argues in his book [B11] that it is empirically irrelevant to try to find a social welfare function covering all logically possible pref-

erence relations of individuals, since the variety of preferences of reasonable voters is much smaller; and he tries to
convince the reader that, whenever the number of (reasonable)
voters is large, single majority voting will work satisfactorily. However such a basic problem as income distribution
cannot be solved by majority voting, as Arrow notes in his
review of Tullock's book [A24].

The discussion of these problems seems even to be increasing in recent years. So it should be expected that other introduction and survey of the state of the art on social welfare
function by Sen [B10] shows clearly how much this field and
hence the foundations of welfare economics as well as of
political entory own to Arrow's pioneering work.

Swedish Journal of Economics, No. 4, (1972): 498-500

REVIEW: John Broome (1984)*

Kenneth Arrow's collected papers are being published in
several handy volumes, selected by subject. This is the first.
Arrow, with his famous impossibility theorem (in his *Social
Choice and Individual Values*, Wiley, 1951), more or less invented social choice theorem and most of the fifteen papers
in this volume are to do with the theorem and developments
from it. There are some useful presentations and explanations
of the theorem itself, as well as discussions of its interpretation and significance. There are some more recent papers
presenting new formal results in social choice theory, chiefly
intended to take account of the value of equality. And there
are less formal discussions of various topics that come broadly
under the heading of 'justice.' Justice between generations
emerges as one of Arrow's particular recent interests.

Besides being a landmark in welfare economics, Arrow's
impossibility theorem was, of course, one of our century's
major contributions to political philosophy. In it Arrow
brought the theory of preferences, basically a tool of economics, to bear on a question with a much wider scope than
economics. And this is one of his great skills. He uses, not
just the technical tools, but also the substantive conclusions
and insights of economics, to shed light on wider issues. This
book is full of examples; two of the best are reviews of Rawls'
Theory of Justice and Nozick's *Anarchy, State and Utopia*.
Economics has lessons to teach about human relations that
philosophers sometimes forget; Arrow reminds us of them, and

draws important conclusions. Several of the papers in this book are addressed to philosophers and other social scientists rather than economists, and in them Arrow speaks up deliberately and well for the point of view of economists.

One point of view he speaks up for is 'ordinalism', the idea that what should count in social decision-making is people's preference orderings only rather than some measure of the degree of their well-being or something else. This collection makes it plain that a commitment to ordinalism has been one of Arrow's guiding principles throughout his career. From the start he thought of a social welfare function as a function of people's orderings, and ordinalism-liberalised now and accommodating a sort of inter-personal comparison-motivates the latest papers too. One might almost say that this whole book documents a collision between this doctrine and Arrow's equally strong and at first sight conflicting belief in equality. The source of Arrow's ordinalism is his conviction that ordinal preferences are epistemologically more secure than degrees of well-being; he sometimes even doubts the *meaningfulness* of cardinal measures of 'utility'. Preferences, he says, can be made 'operational'; by defining them in terms of choice. 'State x is preferred to state y' he defines as 'State x would be chosen if the only two feasible states were x and y' (p.164). The *definiens* here is a subjunctive conditional statement that does not seem particularly secure epistemologically. Its truth is certainly not directly observable except on the rare occasions when the condition is satisfied, and often the condition is so remote from reality that even the meaning of the statement is unclear. Arrow, for instance, is willing to count as operational such statements as 'If I were to have a choice between being me in state x and you in state y I would choose the former' (Pg. 169-60). Who, I wonder, would I be when I do the choosing? It is odd that Arrow should feel more comfortable with this statement than with such an innocent remark as, say, 'A square meal would do Lazarus more good than Dives'.

Ordinalism, though almost exclusively the property of economists, is a philosophical theory. It needs a philosophical justification. But Arrow, so adept at turning economics to problems in political philosophy, is less adept at turning philosophical arguments to support his economics. I found his arguments disappointingly imprecise. To take a different example: a central issue in interpreting Arrow's work is whether social choice should be based on people's self-interested preferences or on preferences that depend on their moral opinions. Arrow's discussion of this question often equivocates on the meaning of 'satisfaction' (e.g. pp. 54-5, 66, 148-9). Satisfying either type of preference Arrow takes to give a person 'satisfaction', which he treats as a benefit to the person. So he seems to think that either type has a similar sort of claim to being satisfied. But actually if one of my moral preferences is satisfied I need not *feel* satisfaction, or be in any way benefited. The reason why it may be right to satisfy one of my moral preferences is not that doing so brings me satisfaction, but that the moral belief underlying the preference may be correct. Arrow takes no account of this point.

This book shows Arrow illuminating important questions of justice and social choice from the standpoint of economics. If doubts can be raised about his philosophical assumptions, that does not lessen this achievement.

Quarterly Journal of Royal Economic Society, Vol. 95, No. 377, (March 1985): 210-211

Imperialism: A Study by J. A. Hobson
and
Imperialism: The Highest Stage of Capitalism by V. I. Lenin

REVIEW: Paul S. Reinsch (1908)*

Mr. Hobson's study of the forces and motives of imperialism is not a piece of original investgation but an examination of the tendencies and principles, political and economic, underlying the present movement in world politics. While, therefore, no new material is adduced and while the principles considered are fairly familiar, the grouping of considerations is nevertheless very original and constitutes a most striking representation of the anti-imperialist position, supported by a telling array of arguments. Many new points of view are suggested and the significance and mutual relations of world-wide movements are explained.

Mr. Hobson begins by distinguishing imperialism from nationalism, internationalism and colonialism. He especially dwells upon the difference between colonial movements, through which the population of the nation expands over new territory, and the modern imperialism, in which there is very little displacement of population, and in which the attempt is made to establish political control for economic purposes. The economic basis of contemporary imperialism is the development of natural resources through investment rather than through commerce. The author holds that imperialism represents an extensive economic policy, and he believes that national energies would be better spent in the *intensive* culture of national resources. In this he holds the same view of the essence of civilizing activities as does Ratzenhofer - the constant improvement of the basis of economic life, as opposed to the mere seizing upon resources for the purpose of rapid exploiation *(Raubwirtschaft)*. It must, however, be said that the great Austrian sociologist holds also that a civilizing policy is further characterized by the creation of a constantly increasing surplus over consumption. From this point of view the question would be whether a rational exploitation of the tropics by European capital would· not produce a far greater surplus than a more intensive culture of European economic resources. Mr. Hobson holds, in Chapter VI, that it would be far better to effect a change in the distribution of wealth

so as to enable the poorer classes to absorb the surplus
wealth which is now seeking an outlet in foreign investment.
It may be an open question as to whether better social
service could be obtained by distinctly improving the income
of the working classes than by using the capital for the
acquisition of tropical products; or in other words, whether
society would benefit more by paying its working classes
better than by purchasing products which the national
territory cannot produce. The author admits that we need
tropical products in ever-increasing quantities, and even
that we are justified in politically directing the development
of the tropics. In Chapter II, or Part II, he seems to
abandon the argument of the sufficiency of mere intensive
development of national resources. This apparent incon-
sistency does not, however, detract from the value of
emphasizing the prime importance of intensive development
and the danger of relying instead upon streams of wealth.
pouring in from dependent regions.

Politically, the author considers the most characteristic
feature of modern imperialism to be that competitive, and that,
while the various empires are avowedly executing a trust
for civilization, they are, in fact, engaged in an intense
competition for national wealth and power. This results
in a serious set-back to the efforts to strengthen the
feeling of common interests coextensive with humanity. The
author seems to think that the economic basis of imperialism-
the development of backward regions- would be justifiable
were it not for the fact that a class of International
capitalists who are impatient to make quick profits are
pushing the European states into selfish and reckless action.
The natual growth of economic interests is thus anticipated
and the arts of diplomacy and politics are used to preempt
fields for investment and to create an artificial control
over wide territories which can be developed only very
gradually. The two most serious consequences of this
reckless haste to secure fields for investment are the
threatened enslavement of the black race and the break-up
of Oriental civilization. The imperialists are unwilling
to wait for the operation of the natural causes which are
transforming the negro tribes of Africa into a working
population . They advocate such means as taxation, destruction
of tribal bonds, and the formation of artificial "location"
for the purpose of forcing the growth of a labor supply in
Africa, to the ineffable injury of the black race. It
admits of no doubt that the world is in danger of having
to fight the slavery issue again. It would seem that the
expansion of national societies to a world-basis is bringing

with it a recrudescence of slavery in substance, though
not in form, and that an attempt is being made to reduce
the black race in Africa to absolute servile dependence
upon white employers. As the imperialist movement in Africa
shows a great disregard of the rights of the natives, so in
the Orient it has interfered most recklessly with long-
established civilizations. Outside of the political order
introduced by Britain into India, the author believes that
the only consequence of Western interference in the Orient
is the ruining of Oriental art by the introduction of cheap
processes of manufacture.

The author has carefully scrutinized the facts upon
which his argument is based. It is a matter for regret that
he did not develop more fully his evidence as to the existence of an international group of capitalists who mould
public opinion and direct public action in order to be
able to profit by the fluctuations of the stock market.
These forces and manipulations deserve most careful and
detailed study. A few minor points are subject to criticism.
On page 307 the author seems to imply that Alexander the
Great had actually established his *peace* throughout India;
and the reference to the zemindary system on page 314
is misleading.

Mr. Hobson has effectively pointed out the most serious
dangers inherent in imperialism,-- a reckless exploitation
threatening the natives and civilizations of dependent
territories, and the creation of a parasite class-- in fact,
even general parasitism in the European countries. His
condemnation, though often caustic, is not extreme, and
though his views are plainly colored by the especially
reckless manifestation of imperialism which he himself
witnessed in South Africa, his views must be taken account
of in any constructive policy of the period. While he admits
the theoretical justification of a sane imperialiam, he seems
to despair utterly of its realization as long as nations
have no other judge but themselves in the execution of the
"trust for civilization." By those who admit that imperialism
is a natural and inevitable movement, everything that the
author has said should be considered in an attempt to
establish a true civilizing policy of colonial administration.

*Political Science Quarterly, Vol. XVIII, No. 3, (1908):
531-533*

REVIEW: *The Economist* (1939)*

The latest contribution to Marxian exegesis* takes the
form of an expansion of a tract by one of the Early Fathers,
supplemented by a commentary. Lenin's original pamphlet
on Imperialism is reprinted in full on the left-hand pages
and on the facing pages are new statistical and other data
collected by Messrs Varga and Mendelsohn. This arrangement somewhat reduces the effect of Lenin's clear and vigorous style, but faculutates the comparison of his statistics
with more recent information. It also brings out plainly the
main point which the present editors desire to establish,
namely, the fulfilment of Lenin's prophecies.

The final effect of the extension of the statistical
tables of the original pamphlet down to recent times is
indeed striking. Writing in 1916, Lenin set out to illustrate
with somewhat exiguous material the increasing concentration
of production in modern industry, the growth of monopolies,
the strengthening of the connection between the banks and
industry, and the division of the world's markets between
industrial and financial combines on the one hand and the
principal imperialist Powers on the other. Messrs Varga and
Mendelsohn faithfully demonstrate, with statistics which are,
with a few exceptions, taken from the most reliable "bourgeois"
sources, that
> the facts and figures of capitalist economy during the
> subsequent twenty years not only corroborate the tendencies
> that were indicated in the data indicated by Lenin;
> they also reveal that these tendencies have become more
> marked and developed.

The arrangement of the new data follows strictly the plan
of Lenin's original work. There is no direct statement that
his figures have been verified by the editors, but there is

some indirect evidence to the effect and, in any case,
Lenin himself indicated his sources in almost every instance.

In fact, the principal criticism of this work lies, not
in the facts which it presents, but in the interpretation
which is placed upon them by Lenin himself and accepted
without question by the editors. Few investigators would
disagree with the purely statistical aspect of the thesis
set out in Lenin's first six chapters. The occupation of an
increasing proportion of the industrial and financial field
by large scale enterprise is an incontrovertible fact, and
the extension of imperialist domination in the past seventy
years is also inquestionable. But arguments to the effect
that the whole process follows the set lines of Hegeliam
dialectic, and involving the decay of capitalism and the
growth of "parasitism" within it, are less acceptable.
They outrun the solidly cased inference that the tendencies
examined involve a whole series of new problems of control,
and go straight on to condemn the process outright. The
intermediate steps in the reasoning are not to be found in
Lenin's work. And, if it be argued that logical detail of
this kind is inappropriate in a pamphlet, the natural reply
can only be that the re-publication of the pamphlet, with
all the trappings of statistical research, would also be
inappropriate by the same token.

The fact is that Lenin's book is something more than a
pamphlet despite its perverse terminology (for example,
the use of "combined production" instead of the clearer and
generally accepted "vertical combination"), and its occasional false parallels, such as that which is drawn between
the relation of the banks to industry in Germany and in
Great Britain, it is stimulating work of energetic scholarship. Moreover, the figures compiled by the present edition
have an interest of their own, and will inevitably provide
a re-examination of the tendencies which they illustrate.
The editors are at their best when they are simply collecting
figures on the lines laid down by Lenin. They are less
happy when they attempt to supplement his invective--
directed equally at capitalism and the "bourgeois" economists
who apologise for it--with the familiar phrases of present
day Communist propaganda.

Apart from the expansion of Lenin's figures, there are
two new sections--a collection of supplementary data (pages
225-264) and an essay by Mr. Mendelsohn at the end of the
volume in which he emphasises the lesson of Lenin's teaching.
The former is the weakest part of the book. Forsaking the

salutary guidance of Lenin's thesis, the editors embark on an
excursus of their own in which they include some curious items
such as "Victims of White Terror, 1925-35-12,978,000" as an
example of "Direct and Indirect Destruction of Labour Power."
The final essay is well written, but adds little to the argument. The data it contains could have been more conveniently
included in the body of the work.

The Economist, Vol. 136, (August 5, 1939): 268

"The Meaning of Economic Imperialism," James O'Connor (1970)*

Against the view that dissociates capitalism and imperialism, Marxist economists have put forward many variations on
the same fundamental argument. The second doctrine if imperialism, also inspired by European expansionism in the late
nineteenth and early twentieth centuries, holds that monopoly
capitalism, imperialism, and colonialism are basically the
same phenomena. Perhaps it is more accurate to call this view
"new-Marxist," because those who hold it have inherited few
clear theoretical guidelines from Marx himself. In the three
volumes of *Capital*, apart from the brief concluding chapter
in Volume 1, there are only two or three references to the
economics of colonialism, the gist of which is that commodities
produced under conditions of high labor productivity and sold
in countries where labor productivity is low will command an
abnormally high rate of profit. Marx's relative silence on
the economics of imperialism may have handicapped the development of Marxist theory, or it may have been a blessing in
disguise. The absence of any theoretical precedent has forced
(and continues to force) Marxists back on their own experiences
and intellectual resources. Thus older interpretations of
imperialism as far apart as those of Lenin and Rosa Luxemburg,
and modern theories as disparate as those of Paul Baran and
Joseph Gillman, have arisen from basically the same critical
tradition.

Nothing succeeds like success, however, and Lenin's ideas
have dominated the field. Yet Lenin owed much to John A.
Hobson's *Imperialism*, published in 1902, a book which is frequently (and legitimately) read as the precursor of Lenin's
study. Thus we will begin by sketching out the main ideas of
Hobson and Lenin, later subjecting them to analysis on the
basis of theoretical and historical studies published in recent
years.

Hobson and Lenin wrote about imperialism during the heyday of colonialism (1885-1914), which naturally enough appeared to be the most significant economic-political phenomenon of the time. By making colonialism their focal point, however, both men equated imperialism and colonialism and thus failed to understand the significance of the "imperialism of free trade"--an expression coined to describe British economic expansion from the 1840's to the 1880's. Moreover, they barely acknowledged United States expansion and could not anticipate future modes of imperialist controls which have proved to be even more effective than formal colonial rule.

The distinctive feature of Hobson's theory is his conception of colonialsim as the reflection of the unfulfilled promise of liberal democracy. As Hobson saw it, inequalities in the distribution of wealth and income in Britain dampened the consumption power of the British working classes, which in turn made it unprofitable for capitalists to utilize fully their industrial capacity. Unable to find profitable investment outlets at home, British capitalists subsequently sought them abroad in the economically underexploited continents. Britain therefore acquired colonies as a dumping ground for surplus capital. The end of imperialist conquest and de-colonization would come about only when the British working classes acquired more economic and political power through trade unionism and parliamentary representation, which would set the stage for a thorough-going redistribution of income and hence the development of a home economy in which the volume of consumption corresponded more closely to the volume of production.

Hobson supported his thesis not only by his faith in the promise of liberal democracy, but also by reference to changes in Britain's trade and investments. He tried to show that the expansion of the empire during the last two decades of the nineteenth century, when most of the world not already independent or under European rule was carved up among the European powers, resulted in a *decline* in British trade with her[10] colonies in relation to trade with noncolonies. He also underlined the obvious fact that the new colonies in Africa and Asia failed to attract British settlers in significant numbers. Through a process of elimination Hobson thus hit on what he considered to be the crucial element in British overseas investments rose from 785 million pounds in 1871 to 3,500 million pounds in 1911 and annual not foreign investments were frequently greater than gross domestic fixed investments--with the frantic struggle by the European powers for colonies, and inferred that the former causes the latter. The political struggles for profitable investment outlets, and the explorers, missionaries, traders, and soldiers of the period were seen as the puppets of London's financial magnates.

Lenin agreed with Hobson that the prime cause of capital exports was the vast increase in the supply of capital in the metropolitan countries, especially Britain, and played down the role of the demand for capital in the underdeveloped regions. He also, like Hobson, casually linked foreign investments with the acquisition of colonies. The distinctive element in Lenin's theory related to the *cause* of the surplus of capital.

Lenin understood that imperialism is a *stage* of capitalist development, and not merely one possible set of foreign policy options among many. In particular, imperialism is the monopoly capitalist stage, and exhibits five basic features:
(1) The concentration of production and capital, developed so highly that it creates monopolies which play a decisive role in economic lift.
(2) The fusion of banking capital with industrial capital and the creation, on the basis of this financial capital, of a financial oligarchy.
(3) The export of capital, which has become extremely important, as distinguished from the export of commodities.
(4) The formation of the international capitalist monopolies which share out the world among themselves.
(5) The territorial division of the whole earth complete by the great capitalist powers.[11]

The key element is the formation of local and international monopolies behind high tariff barriers in the metropolitan countries. Monopolistic organization develops "precisely out of free competition" in essentially four ways. First, the concentration (growth in absolute size) of capital leads to the centralization (growth in relative size) of capital. Second, monopoly capital extends and strengthens itself by the seizure of key raw materials. Third, financial capital, or the investment banks, "impose an infinite number of financial ties of dependence upon all the economic and political institutions of contemporary capitalist society," including nonfinancial capital. Fourth, "Monopoly has grown out of colonial policy. To the numerous 'old' motives of colonial policy, the capitalist financier has added the struggle for the sources of raw materials, for the exportation of capital, for 'spheres of influence,' i.e., for spheres of good business, concessions, monopolist profits, and so on; in fine, for economic territory in general." In short, the new colonialism opposes itself to the older colonial policy of the "free grabbing" of territories.

The cause of the surplus of capital and capital exportation, and of monopolistic industry, is the tendency of the rate of profit to fall.[12]   Two underlying forces drive down the rate of profit in the metropolitan country. First, the rise of trade unions and social democracy, together with the exhaustion of opportunities to recruit labor from the countryside at the going real wage. Second, labor saving innovations increase the organic composition of capital. Monopoly is this in part formed in order to protect profit margins. At the same time, economies of large-scale production (internal expansion) and mergers during periods of economic crises (external expansion) strengthen pre-existing tendencies toward monopolistic organization.

Meanwhile, in the economically underexploited regions of the world, capital yields a substantially rate of return. For one thing, the composition of capital is lower; for another, labor is plentiful in supply and cheap; and, finally, colonial rule establishes the preconditions for monopolistic privileges. Rich in minerals and raw materials required by the development of metals, automotive, and other heavy industries in the metropolitan powers, the underexploited regions naturally attract large amounts of capital. Consequently, foreign investment counteracts the tendency for the rate of profit to fall in the metropolitan economy. On the one hand, high profit margins in the colonies pull up the average return on capital; on the other hand, the retardation of capital accumulation in the home economy recreates the reserve army of the unemployed, raises the rate of exploitation, and, finally, increases the rate of profit.

Pushing this thesis one step forward, the precondition for a truly "favorable" investment climate is indirect or direct control of internal politics in the backward regions. Economic penetration therefore leads to the establishment of spheres of influence, protectorates, and annexation. Strachey suggests that the backward regions assumed a dependency status (last step before outright control) in relation to the metropolitan powers chiefly because the former were in debt to capital goods in world trade was the colony-to-be needed long-term credits or loans to pay for the capital goods, and that, finally, the relationship between the backward country and the metropolitan country became one of debtor and creditor, and from this it was but a small step to dependence and domination.

Whatever the exact sequence of events which led to colonialism, Lenin's economic definition of colonialism (and imperialism) is monopolistically regulated trade and/or investment abroad at higher rates of profits than those obtained in the metropolitan country. "As soon as political control arrives as handmaid to investment," Dobb writes, "the opportunity for monopolistic and preferential practices exists." The essential ingredient of colonialism therefore is "privileged investment: namely, investment in projects which carry with them some differential advantage, preference, or actual monopoly, in the form of concession-rights or some grant of privileged status."[13]

The criticisms of Hobson's and Lenin's theories, and the alternative views which have been put forward, do not constitute a new theory so much as a catalogue of historical facts which are not fully consistent with the older theories. These criticisms bear on three key aspects of Lenin's theory, two of which also figured importantly in Hobson's thought.

One line of criticism is that Lenin ignored the theme of continuity in European expansionism and was too eager to interpret the partition of Africa and the Pacific as a qualitatively different phenomenon. Alexander Kemp has shown that throughout the *entire* nineteenth century British net capital exports in relation to national income amounted to just over 1 percent during recession periods and about 6 to 7 percent during boom years.[14] Pointing to a similar conclusion is Richard Koebner's judgement that British "imperial responsibilities were enlarged step by step by a hesitant government."[15] Gallagher and Robinson also reject the idea that there were important qualitative differences between British expansionism in the first and second parts of the nineteenth century. In both periods the formula was "trade with informal control if possible; trade with the rule if necessary."[16] In Egypt and South Africa, for example, they maintain that Britain was only responding to internal upheaval and that traditional controls no longer be relied upon.

Lenin was aware of the continuity in European expansionism but maintained that the development of monopoly capitalism led to a break in this continuity. In principle Lenin had solid earth under his feet because the generation of business savings and their absorption by new investments are governed by different laws in a competitive capitalist society than under monopoly capitalism. But in practice it is by no means certain that Lenin was right when he asserted that at the beginning of the twentieth century, monopolies have acquired complete supremacy in the advanced countries.[17]

In the most powerful imperialist country, Great Britain[18] there were few trusts or cartels of any consequence in 1900. One highly qualified economic historian maintains that the British economy failed to enter the monopoly stage until the early 1930's.[19] Lenin was aware the British capitalism was far from a model of monopoly domination, but slurred over the problem by referring to a "monopoly" of a few dozen companies and by interpreting Chamberlain's Imperial Preference System as Britain's reply to the European cartels. The German economy was not thoroughly trustified until after 1900, even though bank control of industry was established at a much earlier date. As for the United States economy, recent research has thrown doubt on the received idea that the great merger movement around the turn of the century resulted in the cartelization and trustification of heavy industry, and has substituted the thesis that the economy was more competitive in the first decade of the twentieth century than in the last decade of the nineteenth.[20]

The same line of criticism developed from a different perspective also casts doubt on Lenin's major thesis. The truth is that British capital exports to Africa were mobilized by small-scale speculators, not mainly by the big London banking houses. For the former, although not for the latter, foreign lending was a precarious undertaking. One of the first of the African companies, The Royal Niger Company, "had to ... enlist subscribers in order to make certain that the Company would be equal to its administrative undertaking."[21] Similarly, subscribers to the Imperial British East Africa Company and Cecil Rhodes' South African Company were mainly small-scale savers, such as pensioners and retired military officers. If monopoly capitalism is essentially a post-Lenin phenomenon, it is readily understandable why the African companies were financed by small capital. The interesting point in this connection is that capital exports to the under-developed regions today conform closely to the Leninist vision. It is not the small investor attracted to an empire builder like Rhodes who provides the savings for foreign investment, but the giant multinational corporations such as Standard Oil, General Motors, and General Electric.

The second line of criticism challenges directly the thesis of Hobson and Lenin that vast amounts of capital from Britain flowed into new colonies. As Cairncross has shown in his definitive study, the great mass of British foreign investments penetrated India and what Ragnar Nurkse has termed the regions of recent settlement--the United States, Canada, Australia, Argentina, and South Africa.[22] These areas contained primary commodities, chiefly agricultural goods, which Britain required and which in turn needed a steady flow of foreign capital, mainly to finance railroad construction, to exploit. This analysis lays great stress on the increase in the demand for capital (and is sometimes called the capital-pull thesis) and plays down the significance of the capital surplus which Hobson and Lenin saw piling up in the metro-politan countries.

Maurice Dobb has countered this reasoning with the obser-vation that Britain's need for foodstuffs and raw materials was specific to Britain and in no sense characteristic of the other imperial powers. Thus while the demand for British capital may have increased more rapidly than the supply, the same conclusions cannot be applied to France or Germany. What is more, repatriated interest and dividend payments on invest-ments "pulled" from Britain in the early years of the colonial epoch may have been during later decades "pushed" out into both the old and new colonies. Fieldhouse has pointed out that there were no important differentials between home and foreign interest rates during the pre-World War I colonial era, con-cluding that capital could hardly have been attracted by colo-nial superprofits.[23] Taken at face value, this conclusion supports the Nurkse-Cairncross "capital-pull" thesis. But the conclusion is fallacious because it was precisely the vast outflow of capital which depressed interest rates abroad and kept them form at home.

The new colonies did fail to attract many investments during the period directly before and after their conquest. Egypt's indebtedness to Britain was a factor, to be sure, but it was the collapse of the Egyptian government which led Britain to occupy that country in 1882 in order to protect Suez and the routes to the east.[24] As for the rest of Africa, British enterprise in the nineteenth century was restricted mainly to the palm oil trade on the west coast, and moderate investment activity in the Transvaal and Rhodesia. As Robin-son and Gallagher have shown, Africa provided little trade, less revenue, and few local collaborators, and Britain supplied little capital and few settlers. Certainly, until the twen-tieth century British ruling-class opinion held widely that there was no real economic reason for the partition of Africa.[25] In the Pacific, large-scale investments in Malayan tin and rubber were made considerably after the annexation of that country, and other late nineteenth-century conquests in Asia and the Pacific failed to attract new investments in any sig-nificant quantity. This of course does not prove that these acquisitions were not economically motivated, but only that investors may have had over-optimistic expectations.

Lenin's description of the chief characteristics of the new colonial era--foreign investments, seizure, monopolistic preferences--was therefore largely accurate. A single, or simple, theoretical pattern, however, cannot be imposed on the complex sequence of events which revolutionized the world capitalist system between the 1880's and World War I. More often than not, in Orbinson and Gallagher's words, the "extension of territorial claims ... required commercial expansion." Certainly the attitudes expressed by the German Colonial Congress in 1902 suggest that in point of time investment and trade followed the flag, rather than vice versa: "The Congress thinks that, in the interests of the fatherland, it is necessary to render it independent of the foreigner for the importation of raw materials and to create markets as safe as possible for manufactured German goods. The German colonies of the future must play double role, even if the natives are forced to labor on public works and agricultural pursuits." Similar sentiments were expressed in one form or another by Joseph Chamberlain, Theodore Roosevelt, and a host of lesser leaders and ideologists of imperialism.

We have finally to discuss a criticism of Lenin's thesis which arises from the experiences of Britain in the period directly after World War II. Although domestic investment had been considerably in excess of foreign investment (thus reversing the pre-1914 ratio of home to foreign investment),[26] capital exports did not come to a complete halt with the political independence of Britain's colonies. It has been inferred from this that formal colonial rule was not necessary to provide profitable investment outlets. In defense of Lenin, the argument has been raised that British economic stagnation in the immediate postwar era can be attributed to the decline in repatriated earnings from foreign investments, and therefore a decrease in the rate of profit, in turn due to the removal of British economic interest from their monopoly over trade, banking, agriculture, and other branches of politically independent ex-colonies.[27] The empirical work published by Michael Barratt-Brown tends to confirm this line of reasoning: Brown estimates that after deducting payments to foreign owners of property, net earnings from overseas investments in the postwar period amounted to only 1 percent of Britain's national income.[28]

These estimates, and the conclusion implicit in them, have been questioned by Hanza Alavi, who argues that informal economic control exercised by the advanced capitalist countries can be as effective, and as profitable, as formal political rule.[29] In our subsequent interpretation of contemporary imperialism we lay great stress, and develop in detail, this idea. Alavi challenges the estimates on three grounds. First, he maintains that the gross return, not net return, on capital invested abroad is the relevant figure on the grounds that Britain incurred her liabilities independently. Second, he rightly stresses that profit remittances represent but a portion of the return flow on foreign investments. Although it proved impossible to arrive at any accurate estimates, income remitted in the form of monopolistic prices, "services" such as commission royalties, and head office charges, should be included in the return flow. Lastly, Alavi states that income remissions in relation to the domestic economic surplus (and not relative to national income) is the relevant comparison for measuring the impact of foreign investments on the metropolitan economy. Alavi calculates that gross income from overseas investments in the postwar period (excluding the disguised income remissions listed above) amounted to 3.3-4 percent of the national income and 40-50 percent of domestic net investment. Clearly, if Britain financed perhaps one-half of her home investment from overseas profits, foreign asset holdings must have been a decisive element in the maintenance of the rate of profit at home.

[1] Margery Perham, *The Colonial Reckoning* (London, 1963), p. 1.

[2] Joseph Schumpeter, *Imperialism and Social Classes* (1919; reprint ed., New York: Augustus Kelly, 1951), pp. 98, 128. It should be stressed that the above paragraph fails to capture the subtleties and complexities of Schumpeter's thesis, and aims chiefly to provide a point of comparison with the other two doctrines.

[3] Hans Kohn, "Reflections on Colonialism," in Robert Strausz-Hupe and Harry W. Hazard, eds., *The Idea of Colonialism* (London, 1958). The different kinds of political control are as follows: (1) The metropolitan power can grant the subject people full autonomy, with the exception of foreign relations. (2) Subject peoples can be granted full citizenship, and assimilated into the foreign culture. (3) Indigenous peoples can be annihilated or expelled. (4) Subject peoples can be maintained in an inferior status. (5) The metropolitan power can tacitly claim the right to oust an unfriendly government.

[4] An excellent review of mercantile thought and practice is provided by Eric Roll, *A History of Economic Thought*, 3rd ed. (Englewood Cliffs, N.J.: Prentice-Hall, 1957), Chapter II.

[5] Charles Wilson, *Power and Profit: A Study of England and the Dutch Wars* (London, 1957).

[6] This changeover set the stage for the ruin of Indian manufacturing industries, and can be roughly dated from the abolition of the East India Company's trade monopoly in 1813. The East India Company had provided an umbrella for India's weaving industry, which could not survive the massive importation of British cotton manufactures.

[7] This is not meant to imply that there are no important conflicts between international-minded capitalists and national-minded power elites.

[8] This, of course, does not exhaust the motives for colonial conquest. In the conquest of Mexico and Peru, the search for precious metals was of foremost importance. The east coast of Africa was at first seized for strategic reasons. But the characteristic sequence was followed in India and West Africa. In the latter region, Portugal had acquired a monopoly over trade based on coastal fortifications. Cloth, metal, and glass were exchanged on favorable terms for gold, ivory, and, above all, slaves. In the middle of the seventeenth century Portugal's monopoly was broken by the Dutch, and then by the British and French.

[9] *Capital*, Kerr ed., Volume III, pp. 278-279.

[10] Cairncross has shown on the basis of more and better data than those available to Hobson that there was a relative increase in empire trade, most of it, however, with the older colonies such as India. See J. Cairncross, *Home and Foreign Investments, 1870-1913* (Cambridge: Cambridge University Press, 1953), p. 189. Cairncross's findings refine but do not contradict Hobson's argument.

[11] V. I. Lenin, *Imperialism: The Highest Stage of Capitalism* (New York, 1926), pp. 71-76. By comparison, Rosa Luxemburg's *The Accumulation of Capital* bases its analysis of capitalist expansion abroad on Marx's models of expanded reproduction

which assume a *competitive* economy. Luxemburg saw imperialism as a necessary result of competition between capitalist enterprises which drove capitalism outward in search
of new markets in areas which were not incorporated into the
world capitalist system. Lenin, as we have noted, stressed
the export of capital, not commodity exports. Moreover, Lenin
viewed imperialist rivalries over areas already integrated
into world capitalism as extensions of the struggles between
the European powers over the underdeveloped continents.

[12] In the following paragraph we will rely not only on Lenin's
theory of the causes of imperialist expansion, but also on
Maurice Dobbs' and John Strachey's readings of Lenin. See
"Imperialism," in *Political Economy and Capitalism* (London,
1937); *The End of Empire* (New York: Praeger, 1960).

[13] Dobb, *Political Economy and Capitalism*, pp. 239-234.

[14] Alexander Kemp, "Long-Term Capital Movements," *Scottish
Journal of Political Economy*, vol. 13, no. 1 (February 1966),
p. 137.

[15] R. Koebner, "The Concept of Economic Imperialism," *Economic
History Review*, 2nd series, II (1949), p. 8.

[16] Nevertheless, these historians believe that reasons must be
found to explain the *pace* of colonial conquest from the 1880's
on. Fieldhouse's explanation--that there was an overriding
need for military security after 1870 because Europe had become an armed camp--they consider inadequate by itself. To
the spillover from rivalries in Europe, they add the following
reasons: the collapse of Western-oriented governments under
the strain of previous European influences; the changing importance of Africa for British geopolitical strategy; and the
need to relieve economic depression, especially relief from
tariff increases by Germany in 1879 and France in 1892. As
we have seen, the final "reason" itself was explained by Lenin.
See R. Robinson *et al., Africa and the Victorians* (New York:
Doubleday, 1968), p. 181.

[17] See Lenin, *Imperialism: The Highest Stage of Capitalism*,
pg. 24.

[18] D. K. Fieldhouse, "Imperialism: A Historiographical Revision,"

Economic History Review, 14 (1961), *passim*.

[19] Richard Pares, unpublished manuscript.

[20] Gabriel Kolko, *The Triumph of American Conservatism: A Re-interpretation of American History, 1900-1916* (Chicago: Quadrangle, 1967).

[21] Koebner, "The Concept of Economic Imperialism," p. 12. The evidence brought to light by D. C. M. Platt suggests that with regard to Latin American loans, only the small lender, not the large financial interests, bore great financial risks. "British Bondholders in Nineteenth-Century Latin America--Injury and Remedy," *Inter-American Economic Affairs*, vol. 14, no. 3 (Winter 1969).

[22] Cairncross, *Home and Foreign Investment*, p. 185.

[23] Fieldhouse, "Imperialism: A Historiographical Revision," p. 198.

[24] Robinson, *Africa and the Victorians*.

[25] *Ibid.*, p. 15.

[26] Kemp, "Long-Term Capital Movements." In 1964, a year of high capital outflow, long-term capital amounted to only 9 percent of gross domestic investment.

[27] Palme Dutt, *The Crisis of Britain in the British Empire* (London, 1953).

[28] Michael Barratt-Brown, *After Imperialism* (London: Heinneman, 1963).

[29] Hanza Alavi, "Imperialism Old and New," *Socialist Register 1964* (New York: Monthly Review Press, 1964), pp. 108-109.

*Imperialism and Underdevelopment, (1970)L 107-115

"Lindsey's Lenin and the Problem of Imperialism," Mark
Obrinsky (1984)*

Imperialism: The Highest Stage of Capitalism is undoubtedly the best known of Lenin's works on political economy, and
perhaps the most widely read of all his writings. A short
pamphlet (just over 100 pages), considered by Lenin a "popular
outline" and largely descriptive in character, it is the
starting place and focal point for Marxist discussions of imperialism and has been influential in many non-Marxist circles
as well. Perhaps because of its brevity and the need to clear
the Czarist censors, controversy has arisen concerning this
analysis of imperialism. Debate has centered on only whether
Lenin's theory is valid, but also whether there really is a
coherent theory here at all.[1] Charles Lindsey is the latest
to make the claim that Lenin fails, in *Imperialism*, to present
a theoretical explanation of the causes of imperialism (Lindsey
1982; see also Brewer 1980: 109-110).

As Lindsey sees it, Lenin "attempted to interweave two
theories--a theory of monopoly and a theory of imperialism,"
and while the former theory is "sound," the latter is "found
lacking" (Lindsey 1982:1). Specifically, Lindsey finds no
adequate rationale in *Imperialism* for casually tying monopoly
to imperialism (that is, for attributing the latter to the
former). The use of the term "imperialism" is at odds with
Lenin's, however, and underscores the difference in approaches.
Lindsey considers imperialism as "the relationship of a ruling
or controlling power to those under its domination" (Lindsey
1982:3). This notion raises several problems. Included here
could be the relation of slaveowner and slave in the antebellum
United States, of serf and lord in medieval Europe, even of
bully and bullied--though Lindsey apparently does not use the
word this broadly. Similarly, the ancient Athenian, Persian,
and Roman empires would here be placed alongside the modern
British, French, and Czarist Russian ones as examples of the
same phenomenon, thus elevating apparent similarities of form
above the very different underlying realities.[2] Clearly, this
abstract and vague conception is devoid of any class character.

Remarkably, Lindsey suggests Lenin would not find this
definition objectionable. Actually, Lenin flatly rejected a
definition of imperialism rather similar to Lindsey's.[3] Instead, Lenin views imperialism as an historically concrete
phenomenon: economically, it is a stage of capitalism characterized by monopolies, finance capital, export of capital,
division (and attempts at redivision) of the world, and parasitism. The analysis which let to this characterization of

imperialism as a new phase of capitalism also led Lenin to
argue that imperialism is the last, the "highest" stage of
capitalism, and therefore also "the transition from the capitalist system to a higher socio-economic reader" (Lenin 1964a:
298).[4]

These differences aside, the question can still be asked:
Does Lenin, in *Imperialism*, present a clear analysis of the
causal connection between the domestic emergence and domination of monopolies in the advanced capitalist countries, and
the colonial (and perhaps neo-colonial) partition of the
world? While Lenin demonstrates causality, Lindsey will apparently accept only a mechanical, one-way causation from monopoly
to imperialism (in his sense), thereby ruling out both interaction and the possibility that both are consequences of the
same cause.[5]

These methodological problems are at the root of Lindsey's
failure to grasp Lenin's analysis. In fact, Lenin does present theoretical grounds for connecting monopoly and imperialism, even in *Imperialism*. Before examining those grounds,
however, it is necessary to review Lindsey's specific contentions.

Lindsey's Critique
Lindsey looks at the various elements singled out by Lenin
as characteristic of this stage of capitalism—viz., monopolies,
finance capital, capital export, international cartels and
syndicates, and the division of the world among imperialist
states—with an eye toward locating a causal link between
domestic and foreign economic developments. Capital export
alone is considered a possibility, and must be examined.

Lindsey accepts Lenin's assessment of the monopolistic
development of capitalism—viz., that monopoly has grown out
of competition, out of the very nature of capitalism and the
pursuit of profit.[6] He makes light, however, of the significance Lenin attaches to monopolistic banks and finance capital. Regarding Lenin's listing of the impact of monopolization in banking—including control of credit, formation of
holding companies, and takeovers of businesses—Lindsey
comments:

> an impressive list, but is it one that should be
> limited to banks? As financial intermediaries,
> bank capitalists no doubt can perform these func-
> tions, but so can other capitalists. Centraliza-
> tion of capital—the rise of monopoly—and *not*

banks or, for that matter, finance capital is
the key (Lindsey 1982:4).

Finance capital is thus eliminated from further consideration
here. International cartels are not discussed by Lindsey,
leaving only monopoly to explain capital export, and therewith imperialism.

The export of capital arises, in Lenin's view, because
of "an enormous 'superabundance of capital,'" interpreted by
Lenin as "a considerable stock of money capital available to
be used for direct investment or to be lent by those who control it, but is idled for lack of profitable opportunities"
(Lindsey 1982:4). It is necessary, therefore, to explain why
there are no profitable investments. Lindsey identifies three
candidates for an explanation. First is the "long term or
secular falling rate of profit hypothesis" (Lindsey 1982:4).
This is rejected on four counts: there is allegedly no theoretical reason the "causally link the secular falling rate of
profit with ... monopoly"; a falling profit rate would produce
not a surplus but a shortage of capital; Marx's falling rate
of profit thesis is false; and anyway, Lenin nowhere mentions
the falling rate of profit in *Imperialism* (Lindsey 1982:4).

Alternatively, the lack of profitable investments can be
explained "in terms of an underconsumption of (perhaps) a dis-
proportionality theory of crisis." Lindsey finds this explanation wanting because "crises also occur in capitalism under
more competitive conditions," as does, therefore, "superabundant" capital (Lindsey 1982:5). Capital surplus, that is,
may be greater under monopoly conditions, because crises are
more severe, but it is not new, and therefore not "explained"
by monopoly.

Finally, this lack "can also be interpreted in a relative sense: there is a lack of profitable opportunities domestically when compared with opportunities elsewhere." This
requires examining the capital-importing countries as well as
the capital-exporting ones. However, "Lenin treated the backward countries as essentially passive, waiting for the monopoly stage of capitalism in order to become the receptacle of
capital exported from the industrialized nations." And the
"demand for capital" in the former countries has nothing at
all to do with the existence of monopolies (Lindsey 1982:5).

Lindsey also regards as misguided Lenin's analysis of
income redistribution and its impact. While indicating that
"if capitalism could develop agriculture ... and could raise

the living standards of the masses ... there could be no question of the surplus of capital, "Lenin also suggests that rentiers in various guises increase their income share and that a part of the working class is "bribed" under imperialism (Lenin 1964a:241). The latter are treated by Lindsey as income transfers which, however unintentionally, lessen crises and make capital surplus even harder to explain. In addition, the corrupting of a section of workers is made possible not by imperialism, but rather by monopoly (See Lenin 1964a:193-194, 301).

Finally, Lindsey cannot understand Lenin's periodization of colonization. He quotes Lenin referring to imperialism as the stage *after* the colonialist division of the world, but also as viewing monopoly and finance capital as motivating forces in the *drive* for colonies, an apparent contradiction. Lenin also suggests the turn of the century as the year monopoly capital supercedes the old capitalism and finance capital's domination is established. This Lindsey sees as excluding monopoly and finance capital from the explanation of Great Britain's colonial expansion, which began forty years earlier, or of that of France and Germany, occurring twenty years earlier (Lindsey 1982:6).

If all this is true, one cannot but conclude as Lindsey does: *Imperialism* offers little theoretical analysis, and nothing to suggest anything more than correlation, or historical coincidence, between monopoly and imperialism. "Modern" imperialism is no doubt rooted in the nature of capitalism, but it is not qualitatively altered" (Lindsey 1982:8).

In fact, however, *none* of this is correct. Not only are the specific points of Lindsey's critique not accurate, the overall conclusion does not hold up. Even within the limits Lenin sets for himself in writing a short work of this kind (and set for himself by censorship), a coherent theory of imperialism *does* emerge, one that *does* causally connect monopoly and the division of the world, as well as finance capital and capital export.

Finance Capital and the Problem of Capital Export

Is it true that the "extent to which financial capitalists or industrial or commercial capitalists (if they are truly separable) play the dominant role in the functions Lenin discussed" is only "a historical question," of no theoretical importance (Lindsey 1982:4)? Putting the question thus already misunderstands Lenin's point. Finance capital repre-

sents "the merging or coalescence of banks with industry,"
and is the "merger, or ... coalescence, of bank and industrial
capital" (Lenin 1964a:226, 223). The development of what
Veblen called the "absentee owner," as stockholder-rentier,
landowning capitalist, or monopolistic banker, represents a
new quality in the capitalist economy that Lenin refers to as
finance capital (Lenin 1964a: 238). It is not separable from
monopoly; it is the concentration and centralization of money
capital that enables banks to play their "new role" as not
mere financial intermediaries but rather as a controlling
force in economic affairs and it is the development of monopoly
in reference to productive capital that puts large sums of
money capital in the hands of formerly entrepreneurial industrialists and effects their transition to "coupon-clippers"
(Lenin 1964a: 210, 213-215, 206-207, 238-239). It is not only
an historical question, but also a theoretical one. In particular, it is wrong to look in Lenin for an explanation of
imperialism solely in terms of monopoly, if monopoly is to be
understood as something different from, and independent of,
finance capital.

Even so, the connection between monopoly as such and
capital export is stronger than Lindsey admits. It is pre-[9]
cisely because of monopoly that a capital "surplus" exists."[9]
The ability of monopoly to increase prices (or to resist lowering them) stems from its ability to restrict production.
The relative sheltering from competition obviates the need to
reinvest profits in the production of relative overproduction.
This is, in fact, one important ground for the establishment
of monopolistic practices.[10] Lenin therefore writes:

> although commodity production still "reigns"
> and continues to be regarded as the basis of
> economic life, it has in reality been undermined
> and the bulk of the profits go to the "geniuses"
> of financial manipulation (Lenin 1964a: 206-7).

The concentration and centralization of capital puts large
enough amounts of money capital in few enough hands to make
possible such manipulation, while the relative protection
from competitive pressures "allows" capital to be used otherwise than to lower costs (i.e., otherwise than as investment
in productive facilities). Hence, a capital "surplus" (see
Etherington 1983: 40, 51).

This is related to the *tendency* for the profit rate to
fall, but not along the lines suggested by Lindsey. It is to
escape the working of this tendency that the surplus value

previously realized is not reinvested in expanding production: if this surplus value to follow Marx's circuit of productive capital in the industry from which it came, the rate
of profit *would* fall. Hence the pressure to find another outlet for this capital, including its export.[11] This further,
along with Marx's other "counteracting influences," helps
account for the lack of statistical evidence of an actual
long-run decline in the rate of profit, a situation Lindsey
seems to interpret as disproving Marx (Lindsey 1982: 9n).
Though Lenin makes no explicit mention of the falling rate of
profit tendency, his repeated references to the actual activities of monopoly and finance capital designed to increase the
rate and mass of profit assume familiarity with this part of
Marx and is clearly incorporated.

   It is unclear what Lindsey has in mind in suggesting that
a falling rate of profit could produce only a *shortage* of
capital. This would seem to hold only if a falling rate also
meant a falling mass of profit, at least compared to something like available investments. But, firstly, this is not
true: the rate and mass bear no direct relation. And secondly,
a falling rate of profit leads capitalists to withhold capital
from investment and produce a crisis; this would mean not too
little but "too much" capital.

   Lindsey's suggestion that some of Lenin's discussion of
capital export better fits an underconsumptionist or dis-
proportionality crisis theory is misleading. Lenin is quite
clear in rejecting both underconsumption and disproportion-
ality as crisis explanations, when these are understood
separately. Asking whether Marxism denies "the fact of a
contradiction between production and consumption," Lenin
answers:

> *Of course not.* It fully recognizes this fact,
> but puts it in its proper, subordinate, place ...
> It teaches us that this fact cannot explain
> crises, which are called forth by another and
> more profound contradiction ... namely the con-
> tradiction between the social character of
> production and private character of appropriation
> (Lenin 1960: 168; see also Lenin 1964b: 57-58).

This fundamental contradiction manifests itself in various
ways, including the inability of the market for consumer goods
to absorb all the consumer goods produced--"underconsumption."

   This does not exclude crises from the explanation of

capital export. These several elements are linked: crises
lessen, through bankruptcies, the number of competitors; the
fact of fewer competitors both is, and facilitates, monopolistic development; monopolistic practices restrict supply (to
prevent relative overproduction and maintain prices and
profits); the restriction of supply "frees" capital which was
otherwise destined for immediate productive investment: this
"freed" capital now seeks alternative investment, including
in other nations--capital export. This many-sided process
involves as well the development of finance capital; it is no
longer solely (or even primarily) productive efficiency that
determines profit, but rather market power; marker power is
largely a function of financial prowess (i.e., of the "business"
side of affairs, as opposed to the "engineering" side, to use
Veblen's terms once again); the existence of substantial sums
of money capital (consisting in part of this now "free" capital) concentrated in few hands, furthers the control of the
monopolists/finance capitalists. And despite all this, crises
continue, and become more severe.

Lindsey's claim that because crises existed prior to the
era of monopoly capital they must be excluded from explanation
of capital export is not well-founded. Monopolies, of course,
also existed before the era of monopoly capital, but should
hardly be excluded from the explanation of the latter. More
to the point, while it is certainly true that crises existed
in the earlier period, they necessarily take on a different
character under the domination of monopolies; bot only do the
latter *wish* to prevent crisis-caused bankruptcy and destruction
of (their) capital--competitive firms have the same wish--but
they also *can* do so, at least to a certain extent. Lindsey's
tacit assumption that crises are the same in both periods,
except possibly in severity, is methodologically unsound, and
at odds with Lenin's entire perspective.

Finally, in suggesting that Lenin may mean a *relative*
lack of investment opportunities domestically with abroad,
Lindsey wrongly asserts that Lenin treats these other countries
as passive. Lenin is trying to understand a phenomenon that
originates in the developed capitalist countries; the other
countries have been forced into capitalist system by the
dynamics of capitalism, not through their own internal development. To be an unwilling participant, however, is not to be
a passive one.[12] An explanation that focuses on the demand
for capital abroad may have been, it is changes in the conditions of capital "supply" that are fundamental for understanding imperialism.[13]

Redistribution and Surplus Capital

Lindsey's view of income redistribution and its effect on capital surplus and crises shows similar failure to comprehend what is at issue. It is true that finance capital (the rentier class) grows in importance in the imperialist era, that its income expands through various means (e.g., monopoly profits and interest on increasing loan capital), and that this can be considered an income transfer. Insofar, however, as this income is transferred from one capitalist sector to another and therefore is a change in the distribution of the same surplus value, there is no obvious impact on aggregate demand and crises. Indeed, since this transfer serves to increase the concentration of income in the hands of finance capital, the sector least likely to use it productively, and consisting of the wealthiest individuals, the greater income of rentier comes at the expense of the working class—representing a greater extraction of surplus value—this would directly worsen the conditions necessary for the realization of surplus value.

Regarding the corruption of the "upper stratum of the labor aristocracy" or of "certain sector of workers, and for a time a fairly considerable minority of them," there are two possibilities (Lenin 1964a: 194, 301). If Lindsey is correct in claiming that this process is a result of monopoly rather than imperialism, then the income received by workers is just a portion of the extra surplus value appropriated by capital because of its monopoly position. This would ease the potential for overproduction only if this received income were greater than that extra taken from workers by monopoly, plus that part of the income lost by other sectors of capital which would have been spent.[14] There is no obvious reason to think this is the case (indeed it is unlikely that monopoly would give up so much of its differential advantage), nor does Lindsey present any rationale for this to occur.

But while monopoly profits may provide some possibility for buying off a section of the working class, imperialism greatly increases that possibility for buying off a section of the working class, imperialism greatly increases that possibility by expanding the base for the production of surplus value. By reaching abroad, capital is able to go beyond the "narrow" limits of profit-earning power represented by its "own" workers. This increased mass of profit can certainly be used, in part, to gain influence. This may improve domestic sales potential and to that degree ease crisis pressure (though there are no grounds for thinking this would overcome

the previously stated tendency to exacerbate crises). In any
case, nothing here would cause the problem of surplus capital
to diminish: it is only a part of the repatriated profits that
are going to some workers, while the rest *add* to the existing
difficulty of finding "profitable" investments.

Colonization

The final part of Lindsey's critique is just as wide off
the mark. In reference to colonialism, Lindsey's mechanical
approach fails to appreciate the significance of social development, of processes. It is no contradiction to assert, as
Lenin does, that monopoly and finance capital became *dominant*
only in the twentieth century, and also that monopoly and
finance capital were *influential* well before 1900; in fact,
the former presupposes the latter. It is, therefore, not contradictory to argue that although imperialism is definitely
established in ther period *after* the preceding period, both
monopoly and finance capital—aspects of one development process—are important in the push of colonies. Furthermore,
Lenin does not argue for a simplistic, unidirectional causation between monopoly and colonialism. Rather, a symbiotic,
or dialectical, relationship is envisioned; while monopolies
strive for colonial possession, colonial expansion also pro-
motes the development of monopolies, for example by ensuring
control of raw material supplies.[15] It is therefore the
transitional period—between the high point of competitive
capitalism and the definite takeover of monopolies and finance
capital—that is particularly marked by the striving colonies.
In Lenin's words, "capitalism's transition to the stage of
monopoly capitalism, to finance capital, *is connected* with the
intensification of the struggle for the partitioning of the
world" (Lenin 1964a: 255).

One may argue with this explanation, but surely there is
no flaw in the logic.

Conclusion

The rejection of Lindsey's critique carries with it the
connotation that Lenin does offer a coherent theory of imperialism. It is true that the greater part of *Imperialism*
is devoted to descriptive material (though there is more in
this than Lindsey makes of it), and that it has a particular
political purpose for Lenin, viz., explaining the underlying
cause of World War I and of the opportunism and conservatism
of a good deal of the labor movement. It is also true that
little space is given over to detailed exposition of the inter-

action of the various characteristics of imperialism identified by Lenin. But the elements of such interaction are
there, sufficient to understand that these phenomena are parts
of a whole.[16]

   This is not to suggest that *Imperialism* presents the last
word on imperialism. Its brevity alone marks it as a *basis*
for study and analysis, and the actual economic development
since its publication equally invites further work. That is
another issue, however. What Lenin does provide is a logically
consistent framework for the theoretical understanding of imperialism, not just "slogans, rhetorical phrases, and quick
summaries" (Lindsey 1982: 8). Lindsey thinks that a "theory
of imperialism that took monopolies into account would be a
contribution to understanding the present world economy,"
such can be found in Lenin (Lindsey (1982: 8).

NOTES

[1]It is not entirely clear why serious scholars have so confined their attention to *Imperialism*. In particular, there
would seem to be no reason not to look at the *Notebooks on
Imperialism* (Lenin 1968) as well as Lenin's other writings on
imperialism which were not subjected to censorship—not only
to help clarify, if necessary, the summary analysis in *Imperialism*, but also to get a better, more well-rounded picture
of Lenin's overall view of imperialism.

[2]Of course, this is itself a conclusion which one could con-
test: why not begin with similarities of appearance until
analysis process them different? Such an approach, along the
lines of empiricism rather than Marxism, is ill-designed to
comprehend Lenin, however.

[3]See his critique of Kautsky (Lenin 1964a: 268).

[4]Lindsey quotes Lenin on such a characterization; his assertion that Lenin would accept his own version, indicated above,
is thus even more incomprehensible (Lenin 1964a: 265, 298, and
passim; see also Szymanski 1981: 6).

[5]Lindsey acknowledges the problem of mechanistic interpretation quoting Magdoff on "the compression of Lenin's theory ...
into a rigid model," Magdoff continues by calling these models
formally similar to "the kind bourgeois economists delight in,"
while stressing that "Lenin himself never engaged in such
formilae construction games" (Magdoff 1978: 95-96. Lindsey is

unconvinced, arguing that "if there is a theory to be associated with Lenin, it is not unreasonable to desire to know what it is and to what extent it is coherent" (Lindsey 1982: 1).

[6]Though he regards Marx as providing the basis for theory on this point, and Hilferding as the first to "incorporate" monopoly into Marxist economy, Lindsey does acknowledge Lenin's recognition of a monopolistic *stage* of capitalism (Lindsey 1982: 2).

[7]This is not a summary of Lindsey's critique here, but rather is the entire critique; no evidence is provided for either of the first two points, while the third is covered by a footnote and two references.

[8]This timing for colonial expansion is given by Lenin (Lenin 1962a: 225).

[9]This is only a relative, not an "absolute" surplus of capital if the latter means there are no *needed* projects to invest. But as meetings needs is not the purpose of capitalism, "if capitalism did these things it would not be capitalism" (Lenin 1964a: 241). Of course, capitalism could be *forced* to make such investments, but that is another question.

[10]See Lenin's citation and his summary of cartels' activity (Lenin 1964a: 199-200). A classic example from United States history is the short-lived Wire-Nail Association (Dillard 1967: 407).

[11]Marx first mentions this (Marx 1966: 237-239). This does not imply that because capital export preceded monopoly capital, it is not a special characteristic of monopoly capitalism. It is the qualitatively new significance of capital export, and its overtaking of commodity export, that Lenin is pointing to.

[12]While the nature of the other social systems is relevant in determining whether capitalism would *succeed* in bringing these countries into its orbit, the point is still the capitalist countries initiating the process.

[13]Rosa Luxemburg "incurred Lenin's disapproval for what he considered, in her biographer's words, her "whole attempt to transport the problems of imperialism into foreign and colonial territories—instead of leaving them at home where they belonged'" (Stokes 1969: 297).

[14]This is in regard to aggregate spending and production and does not address the problem of correct proportions required for realization.

[15]Lindsey implies that Lenin asserts, or must assert, that monopoly is *the* motivating factor in colonialism (Lindsey 1982: 6). In fact, Lenin never goes this far. Eric Stokes, in trying to rescue Lenin from criticisms more accurately directed at Hobson, also suggests that Lenin does not provide an explanation for nineteenth century colonial expansion. But he argues that this is not Lenin's intent anyway, and that his theory is sound for the twentieth century (Stokes (1969: 288-292).

[16]It is worth recalling that just prior to his taking up the question of imperialism, Lenin was studying Hegel, leading him to suggest that it "is impossible completely to understand Marx's *Capital*, and especially its first chapter, without having thoroughly studied and understood the *whole* of Hegel's *Logic*" (Lenin 1961: 180). This certainly suggests that Lenin was very much aware of understanding the world dialectically, especially in seeing the interrelationship and contradictions present in, *inter alia*, economic reality.

REFERENCES

Brewer, Anthony, 1980. *Marxist Theories of Imperialism*, London: Routledge & Kegan Paul.
Dillard, Dudley, 1967. *Economic Development of the North Atlantic Community*, Englewood Cliffs, N.J., Prentice-Hall.
Etherington, Norman, 1983. The Capitalist Theory of Capitalist Imperialism, *History of Political Economy* 15 (1): 38-62.
Lenin, V.I. 1960 *A Characterization of Economic Romanticism*. Vol. 2: *Collected Works*. Moscow: Progress Publishers.
_____. 1961 *Philosophical Notebooks*, Vol. 38: *Collected Works*, Moscow: Progress Publishers.
_____. 1964a. *Imperialism: The Highest Stage of Capitalism*. Vol. 22 *Collected Works*, Moscow: Progress Publishers.
_____. 1964b *The Development of Capitalism in Russia*. Vol. 3 *Collected Works*, Moscow: Progress Publishers.
_____. 1968 *Notebooks on Imperialism*. Vol. 39: *Collected Works*. Moscow: Progress Publishers.
Lindsey, Charles W. 1982. Lenin's Theory of Imperialism, *Review of Radical Political Economics* 14:1-9.
Magdoff, Harry, 1978. *Imperialism: From the Colonial Age to the Present*. New York: Monthly Review Press.
Marx, Karl, 1966. *Capital*, Vol. 3. Moscow: Progress Publishers.

Stokes, Eric 1969. Late Nineteenth-Century Colonial Expansion and the Attack on the Theory of Economic Imperialism: A Case of Mistaken Identity? *The Historical Journal* XII, No. 2: 285-301.

Szymanski, Albert, 1981. *The Logic of Imperialism*, New York: Praeger.

Review of Radical Political Economics, Vol. 16 2/3, (1984): 211-219

"Hobson, Wilshire, and the Capitalist Theory of Capitalist Imperialism": Peter J. Cain (1985)*

Professor Norman Etherington's recent demonstration of some of the capitalist sources of the "classical" theories of economic imperialism is undoubtedly one of the liveliest contributions to its subject for many years.[1] His rediscovery of Wilshire, and of the capitalist press in the United States which inspired and informed him, certainly shows that theories of capitalist imperialism have independent American roots. Where Professor Etherington goes wrong is in assuming that J. A. Hobson was dependent upon Wilshire for the essentials of his own theory.

Etherington is far too good an historian to fall into the trap of assuming that Hobson's critique of imperialism was wholly inspired by American sources. He recognized that Hobson's own work "was in a fairly advanced stage when he discovered Wilshire's tract. It confirmed rather than inspired his misgivings about imperialism and contributed to only one chapter of a multi-faceted study of what Hobson fully realized to be a complex phenomena" (Etherington, 48). Nonetheless, Etherington does appear to believe that the economic reasoning which is central to the argument of *Imperialism: a study* came directly from a reading of Wilshire. He claims that Hobson's article, 'The economic taproot of imperialism,' published in the *Contemporary Review* in August 1902 and the incorporated, without essential changes, into *Imperialism, a study*, is a "paraphrase"[2] of an article written by Wilshrie in 1901 and that it was his reading of the "source" (Etherington, 61) which helped Hobson to pull together the strands of his own anti-imperialist thinking and give it a coherent economic base. In this way, Hobson became indebted for the crucial elements in his theory not only to Wilshire but to the American capitalist sources which lay behind Wilshire and which, according to Etherington, were written during 1899.[3] The difficulty here

is that this account ignores "the fact that Hobson had actually laid out his own theory in skeletal form in a *Contemporary
Review* article of 1898, well before Wilshire wrote, 'The significance of the trust' and at the same time as the *U.S. Investor*, Wilshire's own main source, was propounding its views.
In the article of 1898 Hobson explicitly confronted the argument that the continued expansion of foreign trade and new
over seas markets was essential to national prosperity and
that the search for outlets necessarily involved an aggressive
militarism in a highly competitive world. He argued that even
if an expansion of foreign trade was needed, imperialism was
not. The development of the world market by other imperialist
powers would generate growth which would have spin-off effects
on British trade; and anyway, the extra military costs involved
in imperialism were far in excess of any likely gains from
trade.[4] More important than this, however, was Hobson's claim
that there was not obvious correlation between foreign trade
and growth. The crucial need of the times was to expand the
domestic market to tap the enormous potential demand of the
mass of the population in industralised countries, something
which had hitherto been blocked by maldistribution of property
and income in advanced countries. It was at this point that
Hobson went on to make the essential link between underconsumption and the urge for financial imperialism:

> Though a potential market exists within the United
> Kingdom for all the 'goods' that are produced by
> the nation, there is not an 'effective' demand, because
> those who have the power to demand commodities for
> consumption have not the desire, since their material
> needs are amply satisfied, whilst those who have the
> desire have not the power ... The upper and a large
> section of the middle classes, who own an excessive
> proportion of goods that are produced, do not desire
> themselves to purchase or consume, and, since they
> cannot find a sufficient home market amongst the
> workers, are compelled to struggle with classes of
> other nations in the same predicament for foreign
> markets ... If direct testimony to this fact and its
> consequences is desired, it is found in that large
> surplus of our national income which, being needed
> neither for home consumption nor for capital in home
> industries, seeks foreign investment ... Thus, in the
> first resort, it is the excessive purchasing power
> of the well-to-do classes which, by requiring foreign
> investment, forces the opening up of foreign markets,
> and uses the public purse for the purpose of private
> profit-making.[5]

Hobson thought that the "growing pressure for foreign investment must be regarded as the most potent and direct influence in our foreign policy" and that the choice of the future was between social reform and a growing domestic market or "a militant imperialism animated by the lust for quantitative growth as a means by which the governing and possessing classes may retain their monopoly of political power and industrial supremacy" (Hobson, 'Free trade,' 178-79).

Given that he had reached this advanced point in his argument in 1898, the inference must be that Hobson and Wilshire came to similar conclusions independently and on the basis of separate streams of evidence. The reasons for Hobson's exuberant reaction in 1902 to Wilshire's article may simply reflect his own intellectual generosity and express the gratification which an embattled author feels when he finds that his most cherished--but hardly popular--ideas have found a response elsewhere. Wilshire's work also had a particular usefulness to Hobson at that time, who in 1898 had written only of Britain, a country where the small firm was still the dominant form and where industry and the major financial institutions were still separated. The British economy could not provide Hobson with the materials for a theory of economic imperialism based, as was Wilshire's, on the existence of what Lenin later termed 'monopoly capitalism.' By 1902 Hobson was trying to widen his critique and to investigate imperialism on a global basis. The demonstration of a relationship between American big business and overseas expansion was just the kind of material he was looking for.[6]

If Hobson does not derive from Wilshire and the *U. S. Investor*, must we put him down simply as an original and leave it at that? In welding together a theory of underconsumption and attack on financial imperialism in 1989, Hobson was certainly doing something new; but at the same time, he was building on a rich tradition of radical protest in Britain.

Radicalism, in its eighteenth-century origins, was founded on a distinction between a 'natural society'--capitalist industry, commerce, and farming--and an 'unnatural' one formed our of the artistocracy's monopoly of land and their control of government.[7] Natural society was open to plunder--firstly, because government was used to extract more from the productive sectors of the economy through various forms to taxation for, amongst other things, the prosecution of wars and the extension of colonialism. Hostility towards aristocratic government was firmly tied in with antagonism to the growth of the

public debt in the eighteenth century and during the Napoleonic
Wars and with the rise of what Cobbett called the paper
aristocracy.'[8] Landed and financial wealth were intermingled
to such an extent within the system of 'Old Corruption'--the
manipulation of taxation and patronage by an aristocratic
Parliament[9]--that radicals simply regarded monopoly corporations like the East India Company, the Bank of England, large
parts of the City fed on government stock, and the rentier
populations (mainly on the South) living upon it, as 'out-
works' of the system, elaborate extensions of a governmental
machine intent on amassing unproductive wealth. Such was the
growth of the debt by the early nineteenth century that John
Wade, the radical publicist, could argue in a widely read book
that Britain was faced with an attempt to replace 'the feudal
aristocracy, from which Europe has suffered so much, with a
monied aristocracy more base in its origins, more revolting
in its associations and more inimical to general freedoms and
enjoyment.'[10]

Opposition to 'Old Corruption' in both its landed and
financial forms was capable of uniting middle-class and working-class radicals to some degree. Cobden, one of Hobson's
great heroes, tirelessly emphasised the evils of land monopoly
and government extravagance, and clearly saw "the banker and
money mongers" of the City as extensions of the hated aristocracy, the more so because British overseas loans in midcentury often went to prop up feudal regimes in Europe and
were used, according to Cobden, "in obstruction industry."[11]
Working-class emphases differed: as well as complaining about
Old Corruption and land monopoly, they pointed to a link
between these phenomena and underconsumption. They were also
more likely to view concentrations of industrial capital as
an additional form of exploitation and to object to please
for freer trade and the manufacturers' stress on the need for
export markets for industrial goods, seeing them as ways of
diverting attention from the problem of inadequate domestic
demand.[12]

After midcentury the underconsumptionist argument, both
as an element in economic theorising and as a weapon in the
radical political armoury, disappeared for reasons which are,
at present, something of a mystery. Emphasis upon the evils
of concentrated financial wealth also died out. Old Corruption was eliminated as the British state adjusted to a much
more limited view of its role in the economy. The City and
the money market shifted their international economy away
from government stock to the running of the growing international economy of which Britain was the centre, adopting

in the process the same enthusiasm for free trade and the
minimalist state as animated the industrial capitalists. By
the 1880s radical protest was confined largely to the issue
of land distribution, as the success of Henry George's campaign indicates.[13] The first, faint stirrings of a renewed
interest in the relationship between financial wealth and
British overseas expansion came as a result of the occupation
of Egypt in the early 1880s: but the radical response to the
crisis was purely Cobdenite, lacking in any serious attempt
to analyse the nature of the 'stockjobbing' which supposedly
lay at the root of the problem.[14]

Like the Fabian,[15] Hobson in the early 1880s developed
his theory to demonstrate that the unearned increment could
arise from land but from any factor of production in short
supply or protected by privilege and monopoly; and that, in
this sense, much financial and undustrial wealth was unearned
and a part of the 'unproductive surplus' which could be fruitfully redistributed through progressive taxation.[16] Hobson's
other crucial contribution was to reintroduce the long-lost
idea of underconsumption--a phenomenon which, in his view,
arose as a result of the existence of the surplus--and to link
this with an insight into the structure of wealth holding in
modern Britain and its implications for overseas expansion.[17]
Hobson emphasised the importance of surplus arising from
finance rather than industry and his concentration on the former reflected the fact that whereas in the earlier part of the
century, radicals could assume that financial capital was
merely an adjunct, albeit an important one, of landed wealth,
by 1900 financial wealth--based on overseas trade and overseas
investment rather than any direct connexion with British in-
dustry--was at the centre of the economic stage in Britain.
In Hobson's view, best expressed in a little-known article
of 1910 but implicit in many of his earlier works, the chief
owners of surplus capital in Britain were the rentiers of the
South of England, once succoured by the National Debt but now
dependent upon overseas investments which were both a direct
result of underconsumption and lack of domestic demand and a
means of propetuating these problems. The rentier class were,
therefore, the chief source of economic difficulties at home,
of misguided attempts to solve them by foreign adventure, of
"Imperialism, Militarism, Protection, Oligarcy."[18] Hobson
recognised that many industrial export interests were indirectly in alliance with the owners of financial wealth in
search for markets abroad; but he assumed that the small
industrial firm was still the norm in Britain, that it was
mainly interested in the domestic market, and that it was
naturally in alliance with the propertyless masses in the

fight for underconsumption and imperialism.

In identifying a rentier class as the main source of Britain's economic troubles, both domestic and foreign, Hobson was, whether he was ware of it or not,[19] elaborating upon a long and complicated British radical tradition. In the context of this tradition, the addition of Wilshire's material and insights although helpful in getting Hobson to understand the nature of American imperialism, probably had its costs. Chapter 6 of *Imperialism: a study*, the "Taproot" chapter, does leave the unfortunate impression that the structure of capitalism in Britain was similar to that in the United States; and it was only occasionally thereafter—as in the article of 1910—that Hobson took sufficient care to express his theory in such a way as to bring out the unique elements in the British case.[20]

[1] Etherington, Norman, 'The capitalist theory of capitalist imperialism,' *History of Political Economy* 15.1 (1983): 38-62.

[2] Etherington. 46; "Hobson's paraphrase of Wilshire in the 'Taproot' chapter opens a narrow window on the first capitalist discussion of investment-powered imperialism."

[3] Etherington, 39-45, Etherington's claim is also asserted in the paragraph beginning "Hobson thus had ready to hand in 1902 ..." on p. 59.

[4] J. A. Hobson, 'Free trade and foreign policy' *Contemporary Review* 74 (1898): 169-76.

[5] Ibid. 177-78. The first scholar to draw attention to the importance of this article in Hobson's thought was B. Porter in *Critics of empire* (London, 1968).

[6] In a book published in 1984 Professor Etherington has noticed Hobson's 1898 article but claims that it only 'vaguely' suggests the developed views of *Imperialism: a study* since it "ignores trusts and cartels and mentions foreign investment only as an incidental byproduct of the struggle for foreign markets" (N. Etherington, *Theories of imperialism, war conquest and capital*, 1984, 45). As for Hobson's failure to mention big business in his 1898 article, it is clear, as argued above, that this was irrelevant in the British context; and the extracts from the article quoted here also contradict the "by-product" notion.

[7]The classic early expression of this is in Tom Paine's *The rights of man*, first published in 1793.

[8]G. D. H. and M. Cole, *The opinions of William Cobbett* (London, 1944) 68-69.

[9]W. D. Rubenstein, 'The end of "Old Corruption" in Britain 1780-1860, *Past and Present*' 101 (1983).

[10]J. Wade, *The Extraordinary black book* (London, 1831) 377.

[11]J. Bright and J. E. Thorold Rogers, eds., *Speeches on question of public policy by Richard Cobden, M.P.*, vol. 2 (London, 1870), 193-94, 195; P. J. Cain 'Capitalism, war and internationalism in the thought of Richard Cobden,' *British Journal of International Studies* 5 (1979); 244-34.

[12]J. E. King, "Perish commerce": free trade and under-consumption in early British radical economics *Australian Economic Paper* 20 (1981). See also R. V. Clements, 'British trade unions and popular economy 1850-75, *Economic History Review*, 2d ser. 14 (1961).

[13]A good example of the limited scope of radical political economy in the 1880s is provided by J. Chamberlain et. al., *The radical programme* (1885; ed. D. Hamer, 1971). See especially the summary of major objectives on pp. xv-xvi.

[14]See, for example, H. Richard, *Mr. Chamberlain's defence of the war* (1882?).

[15]D. M. Ricci, 'Fabian socialism: a theory of rent as exploitation, *Journal of British Studies II* (1969).

[16]The development of Hobson's concept of surplus is discussed in J. Allen, *The New Liberalism: the political economy of J. A. Hobson* (1981), ch. 3. See also W. H. Richmond 'John A. Hobson: economic heretic, *American Journal of Economics and Sociology* 37 (1978).

[17]Whether there was any significant theoretical development in radical economic thinking between the Egyptian crisis and Hobson's 1898 article, and to what extent this thinking was fertilized by contact with the developing socialist critique of society offered by organizations like the Social Democratic Federation and the Fabian Society, are matters

for future research. The only work to offer anything of interest on this question at the moment is Porter's *Critics of empire*.

[18]'The general election: a sociological interpretation, *Sociological Review* 3 (1910): 114.

[19]Hobson was aware of Paine's work--on which see his essay in J. A. Hobson, *The modern outlook* (1910)--and his knowledge of Cobden was extensive, as is clear from the 1898 article. He later wrote an extremely valuable book, *Richard Cobden; the international man*, first published in 1919. Whether he had any awareness on the 1890s of the underconsumptionist strain in earlier radical thinking is more doubtful. For the links between Hobson's work and the mainstream of classical economic thinking see P. J. Cain, 'International trade and economic development in the work of J. A. Hobson before 1914, *History of Political Economy* II (1979) at 420-23.

[20]I have attempted to put some flesh on the bare bones of the argument of the final two paragraphs in P. H. Cain, J. A. Hobson, financial capitalism and imperialism in late Victorian and Edwardian Britain, *Journal of Imperial and Commonwealth History* 13 (1985).

*History of Political Economy, 17:3, (1985): 455-460.

The *Modern Corporation and Private Property*
by
A. A. Berle, Jr. and Gardiner C. Means

REVIEW: I. Maurice Wormser (1932)*

This book, obviously, stems from the work of Professor
William Z. Ripley. It is devoted to establishing, factually,
that "ownership of wealth without appreciable control and
control of wealth without appreciable ownership appear to be
the logical outcome of corporate development."   (p. 69.)

These propositions are satisfactorily established by a
wealth of evidence, doubtless collected by the able and
industrious Dr. Means. (pp. 47-119) No quarrel can be
found with the factual conclusions that the desires of corporate organizers, as well as the vast sums of money necessary
to establish and carry on large corporations, result in the
concentration of managerial control in the hands of those
who own but a minority of the stock.

The legal views set forth, in respect of this situation,
may be challenged, however, as failing entirely to recognize
the adaptability of the common law itself, in comfronting the
problems resulting from the separation of ownership from
managerial control. At page 335, for example, it is stated:
"Since powers of control and management were created by law,
in some measure this appeared to legalize the *diversion* of
profit into the hands of the controlling group."

This assertion, to say the least, is most astounding.
The profits of a corporate enterprise may properly be disbursed,
only in accordance with the contractual relations created be-
teen the corporation and its stockholders, as set forth in
the certificate of incorporation. In this respect the certificate of incorporation is a contract between the corporate
body and its stockholders. If the corporate profits are disbursed in accordance with the provisions of the certificate
of incorporation, such a payment of profits cannot, in any

honest sense of the word, be considered a "diversion." If, in contravention of the contractual relations of the provisions of the certificate of incorporation, the profits should be diverted into the hands of the controlling group, such a diversion would be a conversion for which the law affords ample redress to objecting stockholders. It follows that the authors' generalization is more sensational than meritorious.

In an attempt to propound a means of maintaining a proper equation between the managerial group and the stockholders at large, the authors suggest the application of what they style the theory of "Corporate Powers as Powers in Trust." (p.354.) These loudly proclaimed "Powers in Trust" are no new "discovery." They are nothing but rules of the common law and equity already in existence. If, occasionally, the courts may have failed correctly to adjudicate conflicting claims arising between the managerial group and the stockholders at large, the fault lies with the particular court, and not with the law itself, for the legal rules are sufficiently comprehensive to prevent any abuse of power by the managerial group. The unjust implication of the authors to the contrary is, therefore, not justified by the existing state of the law itself.

Equally astonishing is the statement (p. 354):

"In direct opposition to the above doctrine of strict property rights is the view, apparently held by the great corporation lawyers and by certain students of the field, that corporate development has created a new set of relationships, giving to the groups in control powers which are absolute and not limited by any implied obligations with respect to their use."

Certainly, no competent lawyer or student in the field properly can subscribe to any such notion. The courts, with striking unanimity in the past, have controlled improper actions of those who have managerial control as the result of stock ownership. Just as they have not hesitated to protect minority stockholders against any abuse of power on the part of majority stockholders, so they do not, and will not, hesitate to interfere with improper actions of those who have managerial control without majority of the stock ownership. Any authors who suggest that the power of the managerial group, or of a majority of the stock, is unlimited, ignore the fundamental rule that while no trust relation, in a technical sense, may exist as between the stockholders of the corporation, the majority cannot, nevertheless, exercise their power so as to deprive the minority of their essential rights.

The authors say (pp. 355-6): "The control groups have, rather, cleared the way for the claims of a group far wider than either the owners or the control. They have placed the community in a position to demand that the modern corporation serve not alone the owners or the control but all society."

The right of society exists, but not as the result of the separation of control, as these professors suggest. If society has any claims, they may be found to rest in a different source--the "police power" of the state, which gives the state the power of regulation, not because of the separation of ownership and control, but if and when the public interest so demands. The exercise of that police power is for the legislature, and not for the courts, in advance of legislative action.

Much of Book II of this work has, in substance, appeared previously in Berle, "Studies in the Law of Corporation Finance."

The failure to quote, or even refer to, Judge Cardozo's recent epoch-making opinion in the case of People v. Mancuso, in Chapter V, dealing with "The Legal Position of Management," is a bad oversight. The rules there laid down establish that "directors must direct," and, if comprehended and applied, would render unnecessary a large part of the authors' rhetoric and new legal "discoveries."

The last two sentences of the work are:

"The future may see the economic organism, now typified by the corporation, not only on an equal plane with the state, *but possibly even superseding it as the dominant form of social organization.* The law of corporations, accordingly, might well be considered as a *potential constitutional law for the new economic state,* while business practice is increasingly assuming the aspect of economic statesmanship." (Italics the reviewer's.)

The only adequate comment as to these blood-curdling prognostications is--in the vernacular--"applesauce."

*The Management Review, (1932): 347-349

REVIEW: Stuart Chase (1933)*

There may have been a better book than this published in 1932, but I did not see it. By "better" I mean more significant, clearly organized, lucid, scrupulously documented. It is seldom one finds such epoch-shattering material clothed in such scholarship.

It fixes the place of the great corporation in American economic life as it has never been assessed and fixed before. In fixing it, the place of the stock market swings into focus, the investor, the management, the "control" and, most important of all, the alarming revolution in the whole concept of private property. The Fourteenth Amendment to the Constitution still stands on the books, but if Messrs. Berle and Means are right, it is law from which reality has fled, or is rapidly fleeing. The day by day behavior of two hundred mammoth corporations has put it on a greased slide. It is not too much to expect, in face of such exquisite evidence as this, that even the Supreme Court may become aware of the fact in another decade or two.

Mr. Means, the economist, begins the book with a statistical gallery of our two hundred finest--the blue chips of the late new era. All the relevant facts about them are set forth with care and lucidity. In articles printed elsewhere by Mr. Means, we have had a glimpse at his gallery, but here one finds the full-length portraits. The blue chips own one-half the corporate wealth of the country. Do the stockholders of the blue chips own them? In theory, but hardly in fact. Mr. Berle, the lawyer, takes up the story and devotes the last half of the book to the legal status of the millions of stockholders, and of the 2,000 gentlemen who "control" these astronomical properties. When he ends his closely reasoned and documented analysis, there is little left of either definitive ownership or control. The stupendous assets swing in a sort of legal vacuum, not really owned by anybody, not really controlled. They have thrust their great shoulders out of nineteenth-century concepts of property. They have crashed through the law as a bear breaks through morning cobwebs; and with the same blundering blindness. They have not flouted the law--save here and there in detail--they have simply grown too large for it altogether:

> Corporations have ceased to be merely legal devices through which the private business transactions of individuals may be carried on. The corporation has, in fact, become both a method of property tenure and a means or organizing economic life. Grown to tremendous proportions, there may be said to have evolved a "corporate system"--

as there once was a feudal system—which has attracted to
itself a combination of attributes and powers, and has attained a degree of prominence entitling it to be dealt
with as a major social institution.

On January 1, 1930, our two hundred largest nonbanking corporations possessed gross assets of eighty-one billions of dollars—49 percent of all corporate wealth; 38 percent of all
business wealth; 22 percent of all national wealth. Fifteen of
them were in the billion-dollar class; the American Telephone
and Telegraph Company leading the list with gross assets of
$4,228,000,000. These companies have been growing more than
twice as fast as all other non-financial corporations, controlling an ever greater proportion of the national wealth. It is
all but impossible for an American citizen to perform the simplest act—eat, sleep, read, communicate, move—without becoming
involved with the products or services which they dispense.
They are warp and woof of the national life.

Much of their output, furthermore, is produced for use and
not for sale, in that they are suppliers to the manufacturers of
end products. Thus it is to the advantage of the Telephone Company to obtain the best possible vacuum tubes from the Western
Electric Company. This factor is operating steadily to decrease
the normal tendency toward shoddy, quick replacement goods.
This is cheery—though not immediate—news for the ultimate consumer. The development may reach him in time.

These vast companies have changed the nature of capital.
It is no longer composed, in many cases, of tangible goods, but
of functioning organizations. "Even the value of tangible goods
tends to become dependent upon their organized relationships to
other tangible goods composing the property of one of these
great units." Particularly interesting to me, as an accountant,
is the fact that the balance-sheet valuation of physical assets
is fast losing meaning. They have value only *if the company
continues to function*. In liquidation, they are likely to foot
up to so much junk. Years ago when businesses were small, if
they fell into difficulties, there was a market for a factory
building, a loom, a store, simple inventories. The assets had
value in themselves. If the A.O. Smith Corporation should fall
into difficulties, its glorious automatic frame mill, which cost
many millions, would bring, I suspect, scrap-iron prices, unless
the buyer wanted to *operate* it. This distinction is one which
accountants have tended to overlook. Books are kept on the assumption that we are still living in Adam Smith's days of petty
traders.

In 1900, sixty-two billions of corporate stock was owned
by 4,400,000 holders--including *all* corporate issues in the
country. In 1928, ninety-two billions of corporate stock was
owned by 18,000,000 stockholders. Average holdings fell from
140 shares to 51 shares. Small holders have thus been prolifer-
ating. "Ownership has passed from the managing few to the investing many." Of all the 1929 dividends 26 percent went to
people with incomes of less than $5,000; 50 percent to people
with incomes of less than $25,000. The corporate system has
been drawing to itself not only a large but an increasing percentage of the national savings. Meanwhile ownership, in becoming dispersed, has become *passive*. The share owner no longer
controls the physical property or admits any responsibility for
it. He is powerless to affect it. He has a piece of paper and
a set of expectations. The spiritual values of ownership are
gone. Those satisfactions of *doing something* with one's land,
one's houses, one's horses, one's tools--satisfactions quite
apart from revenue--have evaporated. Property is no longer an
extension of one's personality. It is a ticket, and contact
with a ticket, from which the stockholder must wring what human
compensations he may. Even as the industrial revolution deprived the worker of interest in his job, the great corporation
has deprived the owner of interest in his property.

He cannot control the "control" of the company in which he
owns stock; he cannot control a sensitive and capricious stock
market. "Value" thus comes to depend upon the vagaries and manipulations characteristic of the marketplace. Value not only
fluctuates constantly but is subject--through the stock market--
to constant appraisal. Wealth has become extremely liquid. It
can be converted into other forms of wealth instantly. Sell
Steel; buy Coca Cola! Only through sale in the market can the
owner obtain direct use of his wealth. *He is thus tied to the
market as never before*. At last one can understand the tran-
scendent importance of the stock market in the modern corporate
system. It is the wheel around which the new concept of property revolves.

"Ownership of wealth without appreciable control and
control of wealth without appreciable ownership appear to be
the logical outcome of corporate development." The first
clause is proved with a wealth of citation and evidence. In
a sense it does not need to be proved. How much control do
your 25 shares of Steel Common net you? How regularly do
you send in your proxy; and what good does it do you if you
send it? A proxy, according to our authors, is not a means
whereby an owner controls his property, but a means whereby
control is taken away from him. The second clause is readily

proved in the following figures for the two hundred largest
corporations:

    Control by self perpetuating management... 44%
    Control by legal device[1].................. 21
    Control by minority interest.............. 23

    Total control without majority ownership $\overline{88\%}$

In brief, 88 percent of these companies are controlled
by persons other than their owners. In some cases the control
actually owns a substantial block of stock; in other cases a
qualifying share or none at all. What is control? The increasing number of unorganized stockholders and their dispersion "almost necessarily implies a mediary group--analogous
to a political boss. Such groups have appeared; they are
called by the financial community 'control.'" The trend of
control is toward self-perpetuating management groups--which
in 1930 accounted for 44 percent of the two hundred companies.
"It will remain outside the normal cognizance of the law."

Control is answerable to God alone. Its interests may
be--and frequently are--diametrically opposed to those of the
impotent owners of the property. "Profits at the expense of
the corporation become practically clear gain to persons in
control, and the interests of a profit-seeking control run
directly counter to the interests of owners." Sometimes this
goes so far as to wreck the enterprise, e.g., the Chicago and
Alton Railroad, the Pere Marquette, the Rock Island, the New
Haven and the 'Frisco. More frequently it takes the forms of
shifting profits from parent to subsidiary companies in which
the control has a large interest; in diverting profits from
one class of stock to another; in "inside information" enabling the control to buy low from present stockholders and sell
high to future stockholders; in the issuing of misleading
financial statements; in juggling of books, primarily in the
accounting for depreciation and capital outlays; in amending
the corporate charter. Practically the only curb on control
in this connection is that created by the future necessity of
obtaining more money from stockholders through subscriptions
to new issues. A company which flouts stockholders too out-
rageously may have difficulty in raising fresh capital. Even
when personal profit is not the dominant incentive of the controlling group, it may damage stockholders by paying high
wages, maintaining good working conditions, or improving the
quality of the product above the line of maximum return.
The owner is thus likely to lose out whether the control is
selfish or professionally altruistic.

Industrial enterprise is made up of three main functions:
(1) Ownership of the property, (2) power over it, (3) work in
respect to it. The pre-machine owner-worker possessed all
three functions, as do many farmers today. The industrial
revolution early combined ownership and power in one person,
the entrepreneur or capitalist, leaving the function of work
to the new proletarian class, which owned nothing and had no
voice in directing operations. Now comes the great corporation to drive a wedge between owner and manager. Thus
property has come to be an entirely different sort of thing,
and ownership an entirely different sort of function. (It
is interesting to note that Marx wrote his great treatise
before this final split had taken place.)

In what a splendid impasse this lands the rugged individ-
ualists! Consider it calmly. If the hope of profit is still
to be considered the holy gunpowder of progress, the only
group with power to use the incentive is the "control'."
In so far as they esteem personal profit above everything else,
these few hundred men, dominating half of industry, line
their own pockets at the expense of the consumer, the worker,
the community and *the owner.* The alternative under the classic doctrine, is to give the owner more power over his own
property, so that the porfit motive will operate more
effectively through him. Many well meaning reformers are
agitating for uniform accounting, more truthful reports, curbs
on the use of "inside information." But Mr. Berle proves
beyond all argument the folly of trying to force eighteen
million irresponsible stockholders back into the entrepreneur
psychology of a century ago. They have passed through that
stage and cannot return. Better reporting will not reverse
the clock.

Where, gentlemen, does this leave us? The owner has all
but surrendered control, the "control" cannot claim all
profits over a "conventional return" without the grave danger
of damaging, if not wrecking, the enterprise itself. Witness
Mr. Samuel Insull. Fortunately there is a third alternative.
These great properties are rotten ripe for collective ownership and management. Where owners refuse responsibility,
and where control cannot be trusted, the community must sooner
or later step in--for on the smooth functioning of two hundred
corporations, our community life depends. The community has
been placed "in a position to demand that the modern corporation serve not alone the owners or the control, but all
society."

The rise of the modern corporation has brought

a concentration of economic power which can compete on equal terms with the modern state--economic power versus political power. The state seeks in some aspects to regulate the corporations, while the corporation makes every effort to avoid such regulation. Where its own interests are concerned, it even attempts to dominate the state. The future may see the economic organism, now typified by the corporation, not only on an equal plane with the state, but possibly superseding it as the dominant form of social organization.

Such is undoubtedly the trend. Observe that it is not quite the trend prophesied by Marx. The bulbous capitalist is at the mercy of either a rapacious or an admirably professional inner group--often owning nothing but brains and a claim to high salaries. Unless the state forces its creature, the corporation, to serve community needs, we are faced with a new brand of feudalism, in which the owner suffers with the worker and the consumer. As the depression drags on however, the blue chips lose their Olympian assuredness, the state is forced deeper and deeper into economic activity. The third choice may be in nearer prospect than Messrs. Berle and Means suppose. It might just be that some of the more professional of the controlling groups would welcome the change. It would at last give them opportunity to operate their beautiful machines on the principles of sound engineering and the ballanced load.

[1] Including pyramiding, non-voting stock, stock with excessive voting power, voting trust.

The New Republic, (January 25, 1933): 299-301

REVIEW: Charles A. Beard (1933)*

In the time to come this volume may be proclaimed as the most important work bearing on American statecraft between the publication of the immortal "Federalist" by Hamilton Madison, and Jay and the opening of the year 1933. Being narrower in scope and less daring in grasping destiny by the forelock it will not have the place in world thought possessed by the "Federalist" but if there is any intelligence among Americans supposed to be intelligent, "The Modern Corporation and Private Property" will mark a sharp turning point in fundamental deep-thrusting thinking about the

American State and American civilization. Nothing less
should be said in introducing to the public this masterly
achievement of research and contemplation.

For practical purposes the volume may be considered under
three heads. The first part deals with the actual tendencies
in American industrial development. On the basis of wide-
reaching, statistical investigations of the highest order,
it reveals the concentration of industrial wealth under
great corporations, the dispersion of ownership among millions
of stock holders, and the centralization of control in the
hands of small managing directorates.

With respect to centralization of industrial wealth
under corporations, the prime conclusion is as follows:
A careful but necessarily rough estimate indicates that at
least 78 percent and probably a larger proportion of American
business wealth (apart from banking) is corporate wealth,
two hundred largest corporations control (on or about January
1, 1930) about 49 percent of all corporate wealth and 38
percent or more of all business wealth; these two hundred
largest corporations control about 22 percent of the total
wealth of the country. These figures are not absolute, but
are as accurate as the state of our statistical information
admits.

While this concentration of business under large corporations has been taking place there has been an astounding
diffusion of ownership. Between 1900 and 1928 the estimated
number of book stockholders increased from 4,400,000 to
18,000,000. This is not the number of stockholders in the
country but an estimate of the combined stockholder lists.
The same person may hold stocks in a number of companies.
Nevertheless the available figures on ownership indicate a
strong tendency toward ever wider distribution of ownership.
And this finding is supported by collateral evidence showing
the distribution of dividends among various high and low income groups. Hence there can be no doubt that ownership is
being diffused among nameless millions.

So much for concentration of industries and diffusion of
ownership. How are the concentrated industries controlled
and managed? Our authors answer: 65 percent of the two
hundred largest companies and 80 percent of their combined
wealth are controlled either by the management or by a legal
device involving a small proportion of the ownership. Only
11 percent of the companies and 6 percent of their wealth
are controlled by a group of individuals owning more than

half of the stock outstanding.

Grand conclusion: immense and increasing concentration of business wealth (apart from banking) under two hundred corporations, diffusion of ownership among millions of stockholders, and centralization of management in the hands of a relatively small group of men who own only a small fraction of the business they direct. In the long history of property, nothing like this has happened before.

The second part of the volume deals with the law and the practice under the color of law by which this transformation in economy and ownership and management has taken place. This part, freighted with multitudinous details and revealing a microscopic acquaintance with actuality as distinguished from legal theory, shows, to speak summarily, how the corporation, once defined with considerable precision as to set-up rights and obligations, has become largely emancipated from strict state control. Here are discussed its power over participations accruing to shareholders, its power over the routing of earnings as between shares of stock, its power to alter the original contract rights of security holders, and the independence of management and control from the state on the one side and the owners on the other. Nothing like this has ever happened before in the history of property management and earnings distribution.

The third part of the volume compares the stark realities of these economic facts with the conceptions long dominant in political economy. The political economy framed by Adam Smith--and still generally regnant in the schools and among most practical business men and politicians-- is based on the assumption that wealth is tangible goods in the hands of owners; that owners direct the use of their porperty; that the motive of profit keeps them going; that private and individual enterprise furnishes the dynamic of business; and that active owners and managers receive the earnings of their property, enterprise, and managerial labors. When the theory of political economy is set over against the hard facts presented in parts one and two described above, the unreality of the theory becomes apparent to any one who can think at all.

And for politics, what is the upshot? The state may legislate to protect stockholders against management. It may frankly recognize the actual position of management and authorize it to go ahead, routing earnings more or less at pleasure, especially if it will take care of its employees. Or the state may demand that the corporation serve not only the owners or control "but all society."

What will happen in fact? The future is veiled, though we are moving with the swiftness and inevitability of Niagara. The corporation may attempt to dominate the state. It may supersede the state as the dominant form of social organiza- tion. The law of corporations may be the potential constitu- tional law for the new economic state, business practice in- creasingly assuming the aspect of "economic statesmanship." Our authors are cautious; they do not attempt to forecast too closely the coming events.

If any criticism may be brought against this solid and imposing piece of work, it is that the conception has been too industrial and too legal. After the American fashion, it gives little attention to politics in the grand and realistic manner of Aristotle, Machiavelli, Adam Smith, Hamilton, Madi- son, Webster, Calhoun, Marx, Lenin and Mussolini. What will happen in the United States lies hidden not merely in indus- try and law; it lies hidden in industry, law, banking, agri- culture and that movement of ideas and culture which we call world history. When banking and agriculture have been studied with the same assiduity and in the great tradition has been brought to bear on the findings, the way will be prepared for action on an imposing scale.

New York Tribune, Vol. 9, No. 24, (February 19, 1933): 1

"The Corporation Gap," Robert Lekachman (1968)*

Two tests of a book's classic status in the social sciences are easily passed by "The Modern Corporation and Private Property": its major conclusions have been so generally ac- cepted that their source has been mislaid, and though every- body has heard the title almost no one has recently read the book. In this reissue, separate prefaces by the two authors and a new statistical appendix by Mr. Means have been attached to the unchanged original text. The 36 years since original publication have certainly not diminished the social signif- icance of the large corporation, any more than time has weak- ened the power of Berle's and Means's analysis of its opera- tions. But the book's major influence has perhaps been in a direction unforeseen by its authors and its earliest read- ers.

The two authors came to three main conclusions about
the American corporation: First, economic power was becoming increasingly concentrated as larger and larger percentages
of business wealth fell into fewer and fewer corporate hands.
Second, the ownership of these huge corporations was increasingly dispersed among a swelling army of stockholders.
Third, the separation of ownership and control had gone very
far and was likely to proceed still farther.

Berle, a Columbia Law School professor soon to be a
member of Roosevelt's Brain Trust and then of his administration, and Means, a Harvard-trained economist, based their
judgments upon an elegantly analyzed body of statistical information revealing the size and ownership characteristics
of corporations, and an equally impressive interpretation of
the case law applicable to modern business. Little by little,
Berle demonstrated the courts had nibbled at the powers of
stockholders over corporations which legal myth if not legal
fact entitled them to run in stockholder interests. The
judges had simultaneously expanded the discretion of managers
who owned little or no stock in the huge institutions over
which they exercised something approaching plenary power.

On the whole these empirical findings have stood up well
over the years, although economists still amuse themselves
by debating whether corporate concentration has or has not
increased. The authors were boldest when they came to evaluate the significance of their conclusions. The transformed
corporation, by its very success, they declared, had "cleared
the way for the claims of a group far wider than either the
owners or the control. They have placed the community in
a position to demand that the modern corporation serve not
alone the owners or the control but all society." The issue
was one of legitimacy.

Yet, even though Berle and Means were convinced that
"the rise of the modern corporation has brought a concentration of economic power which can compete on equal terms with
the modern state -- economic power versus political power,
each strong in its own field," they did not proceed to a
program of nationalization or even extensive public control
in the manner of liberal commentators like Stuart Chase, who
hailed the book in The New Republic and Ernest Gruening
(now the senior Senator from Alaska), who praised it in The
Nation.

The authors' own somewhat vague and general preferences
were for a voluntary reinterpretation of corporate goals by

the corporate managers themsleves. Their key statement contained an implicit appeal to executive statesmanship:

"When a convincing system of community obligations is
worked out and is generally accepted, in that moment the
passive property right of today must yield before the larger
interests of society. Should the corporate leaders, for
example, set forth a program comprising fair wages, security
to employees, reasonable service to their public, and stabilization of business, all of which would divert a portion of
their profits from the owners of passive porperty, and should
the community generally accept such a scheme as a logical
and human solution of industrial difficulties, the interests
of passive property owners would have to give way. Courts
would almost of necessity be forced to recognize the result
. . . ."

How faithfully has business followed this prospectus?
What impact have Berle and Means had upon academic economics?
Although John Kenneth Galbraith has said of "The Modern Cor-
poration and Private Property" that "with Keynes' 'General
Theory of Employment, Interest and Money,' (it is) one of
the two most important books of the 1930's." Berle and
Means did not, as Keynes did, revolutionize economic theory--
at least as the theorists practice its mysteries.

Although Berle and Means believed that the logic of
profit maximization had been fundamentally altered by the
tendencies they documented, most economists continue to
believe that managers maximize profits very much as owners
do. Corporate officials may aim directly at growth rather
than profit and they may even appear to perform the political
role of harmonizing the interest groups -- labor unions,
suppliers, stockholders, customers and the anti-trust division of the Department of Justice -- that affect the corporation's environment. But the managers' conduct is or at least
can be made to seem consistent with the pursuit of all the
profits that can be squeezed out of the market.

For economists, Professor Ben Lewis's 1935 review in
the Journal of Political Economy probably stated the case
best. It was his judgment that the study "will be productive
of more pronounced and sustained results in the field of law
and public policy than in the realm of economic theory."
One such substantial result was the Securities Exchange legislation whose detailed provisions and regulations rested
very heavily indeed upon the analysis of the stockholder's
situation in Book Three of "The Modern Corporation and Pri-

vate Property." Public regulation of the stock exchanges is
a large monument to any book.

The comparative freedom from major scandal that the
securities industry has enjoyed since the 1930's owes much
to the vigilance of the Securities and Exchange Commission.
In turn the continuing dispersion of stock ownership, the
emergence of "People's Capitalism," and the refurbished
reputations of investment bankers and brokers all flow from
a new public confidence created by the cleansing of the
Augean stables of finance. Berle and Means identified a
trend toward stock dispersion. The reforms they stimulated
undoubtedly accelerated that trend.

It is time to return to the harder questions Berle and
Means posed and in part, answered. Should corporations as
gargantuan as General Motors be allowed to operate without
explicit federal supervision? Is Berle's and Means's
favorite proposal of corporate self redefinition feasible?
Has it indeed occurred? Should corporations "as the dominant
institution of the modern world," be responsible for eliminating poverty, rescuing the cities, restoring the countryside, and placing social welfare on a paying basis? Where
is the public consensus that might guide corporate executives
in the preformance of their new duties?

The mere statement of such questions should remind us
what a very short distance has been traveled toward explicit
and acceptable redefinition of the corporation's legitimate
role. Here is one illustrative puzzle this summer the
steel industry did its very best to raise prices by five percent, in the wake of a moderately expensive settlement with
the steelworkers. Presidential wrath, reinforced by threats
to take defense contracts away from the offenders, led to a
compromise increase of about half the industry's original
change.

Query: by what legal right does a President intervene
in the pricing decisions made by private corporations? In
fact President Johnson did not have a legal leg to stand upon.
Nevertheless, the episode is symbolic of a change in public
and even business opinion that dates from President Kennedy's
successful showdown five years ago with the leaders of the
same industry. The men who run the steel industry have
come grudgingly to accept the power, if not the right, of
Federal government to oversee steel-pricing policy. What
steel does substantially influences other prices and the
balance of payments. Therefore steel, in common with other

large concentrated industries, is seen to be affected with a
public interest.

Or consider another of the role conflicts in which large
enterprises get entangled. The major life-insurance companies
have committed $1 billion to urban slum investment, at inter-
est rates said to average 1 per cent below the market. One
per cent of $1 billion is $10 million annually. A tax of
$10 million has been assessed upon the owners of the life-
insurance companies without their consent. What entitles
the life insurance executives to take such action?

The still inchoate doctrine of social responsibility
upon which Berle and Means rested so much hope is possibly
surfacing here. It is obvious, however, how far from general
acceptance this doctrine is. Business finds it so uncomfort-
able that they are often constrained to conceal their good
deeds under the cloak of normal greed. A Henry Ford explains
his company's serious and costly attempt to recruit hard-core
blacks from the Detroit slums with the argument that such
action is a protection against a recurrence of last summer's
Detroit riots. Now while it is undeniable that the fortunes
of Ford and Detroit are connected, it is hard to believe that
Ford's action alone will really protect Detroit (and Ford)
against the possiblity of future riots.

A different sort of redefinition of corporate goals
appears more significant, and in it profit retains its traditional primacy. Many alert business leaders seem to have
identified social welfare with a new and promising market.
Litton and Philco among others have managed job camps.
U.S. Gypsum seeks to boom sales of its products by dramatic
demonstrations of instant rehabilitation of dilapidated slum
structures. Innkeepers enter the nursing home industry,
bolstered by medicare benefits to the elderly. Alert plumb-
ing-equipment concerns restyle themselves for the growing
anti-pollution market. Businessmen have discovered a new
set of public markets.

An important factor in encouraging business committment
to these new ways of making money is the drastic change in
old, New Deal ideological animosity between government and
business. A sophisticated grasp by each party of the potential benefits of partnerships between business and government
made possible the love affair between the Johnson Administration and many of the most prestigious members of the business
establishment. Of the varieties of such corporation there is
no end. Major defense contractors like McDonnell Douglas and

General Dynamics are almost subdivisions of the Pentagon.
Supersonic transport is being developed partly by public and
partly by private research and development. One current and
fashionable tendency is legislation encouraging business housing and plant investment in the slums by intricate combinations of tax incentives, credit guarantees, and direct subsi-
dies.

The traditional logic of profit maximation is not seriously
jarred by slum-investment programs that guarantee returns to
private corporations of 12 to 14 per cent. Profit maximization may be a tougher beast, and social responsibility a more
distant prospect, than Berle and Means believed.

Berle and Means made a final major contribution in their
classic study. Their analysis struck a blow, possibly decisive, at the school which has sought early and late to break
up large corporations and restore a regime of atomistic competition. For even in describing desirable corporate reforms,
Berle and Means were affirming the legitimacy of the large
corporation as very nearly a sovereign economic power.

Modern critics of the large corporation usually take for
granted its inevitability. Galbraith's imaginative analysis
of the technostructure that manages the corporations really
centers upon increasing its enlightenment and enlarging the
government's capacity to supervise it in the interest of objectives the corporations neglect. The anti-trust movement
has come on sad days because most Americans and even many
economists judge large corporations to be useful, important,
efficient, and occasionally even benevolent. For better or
for worse, Berle and Means played a large role in the evolution of the corporation's good contemporary reputation.

Somewhat paradoxically, then, the largest influence
these two critics of corporate practice have had is their
contribution of the legitimacy of the giant corporation.
Even political liberals are inclined to accept the giant corporation as an inevitable fact. The more cheerful among them
do their best to see the corporation as potentially a powerful
engine of social as well as economic progress. The liberals
of the 1930's interpreted "The Modern Corporation and Private
Property" as a radical tract. As matters have turned out, this
book has done as much to promote a healthy capitalism as
Keynes's "The General Theory of Employment, Interest and
Money."

*New York Times Book Review, (September 15, 1968): 9-14

"The Literature of Economics: The Case of Berle and Means,"
George J. Stigler and Claire Friedland (1983)*

> ...the question that was not asked during the great
> socialism *versus* capitalism has now been answered:
> ownership has been split off *de facto* from internal
> control. [Robert A. Dahl, *After the Revolution*,
> Yale Univ. Press, 1970, p. 125]

There are not many books fifty years old whose central
argument is identified for modern economists simply by nam-
ing the work, but Berle and Means's *The Modern Croporation
and Private Property* is surely one. Every schoolboy, as
Macaulay would say, knows that they discovered or asserted or
proved or were otherwise joined to the proposition that ownership and control have been separated in the large corporation.
Moreover this separation had large, but not easily recalled,
effects on the conduct of corporate enterprise.

This essay will examine the reception of this book, particularly by the economics profession, in its first decade.
Our interest will be not so much in the novelty or validity of
the book's message as in how it was understood and received.
The process of which a proposition of great potential scientific and political significance gets established in a discipline is fascinatingly mysterious. Our investigation will
support the view that doctrines and theories congenial to
an intellectual milieu are accepted quickly and widely, although not necessarily as uncritically as the work of Berle
and Means was accepted.

I.   The Theses of Berle and Means

The authors present the main theme of their work early
in the book:

> It has been assumed that, if the individual is protected
> in the right both to use his property as he sees fit and to
> receive the full fruits of its use, his desire for personal
> gain, for profits, can be relied upon as an effective incen-
> tive to his efficient use of any industrial property he may
> possess.

> In the quasi-public corporation, such an assumption no
> longer holds. As we have seen, it is no longer the individual
> himself who uses his wealth. Those in control of that wealth,
> and therefore in a position to secure industrial efficiency
> and produce profits, are no longer, as owners, entitled to the

bulk of such profits. Those who control the destinies of the typical modern croporation own so insignificant a fraction of the company's stock that the returns from running the corporation profitably accure to them in only a very minor degree. The stockholders, on the other hand, to whom the profits of the corporation go, cannot be motivated by those profits to a more efficient use of the property, since they have surrendered all disposition of it to those in control of the enterprise.[1]

The theme of the book--that we are entering a new era of economic organization because of the separation of ownership and control of the modern corporation--rests on three propositions:

1. The large corporation is owned by so many stockholders that no one or even no score of them typically own a significant fraction of the outstanding stock.[2] In three corporate giants of the time--Pennsylvania Railroad, U.S. Steel (how are the mighty fallen!), and American Telephone and Telegraph-- no stockholder owned so much as 1 percent of any of these companies. There was no effective stockholder control in at least 44 percent of the two hundred largest nonfinancial corporations, and if one makes allowances for devices such as the holding company, a majority of companies and of stockholders, even measured by dollars, had no effective voice in the management of their corporations.

The evidence, no doubt the work of Means, was scattered and fragmentary, but this proposition seemed a valid generalization and one that was becoming even more descriptive with time.

2. Corporate officers in general own a very small fraction of the stock of their corporations. This proposition is a corollary of the first, and--no doubt because of data limitations--it was given no separate documentation until a later time.

3. The third and crucial proposition is that the interests of management and stockholders diverge widely. The actual incentives and behavior of corporate officials received no systematic attention in the entire volume, and the burden of supporting this proposition was assumed in a peculiar fashion by Berle.

He made a study of the changing statute and case law with respect to the rights and duties of stockholders and corporate directors and officers (bk. II). The relaxation of in-

corporation statutes, the reduction in the rights not only
of voting but of participation by the stockholders, and the
growing prerogatives of the management to control investments,
corporate structure, and disbursement of profits, and the
like, were held to have eliminated most legal restraints on
managerial prerogatives. The ambiguous legal boundaries of
permissible behavior are of course no necessary description
of actual behavior, and the authors so concede from time to
time. "With control over earnings, as in the case of control
over asset values, it is impossible to determine the use made
of the power by directors, and by or at the instance of the
'control.'"[3]

The inconclusiveness of the support for the third proposition is emphasized by a late chapter on "Corporate Powers
as Powers in Trust." There we are told that "no form of
words inserted in a corporate charter can deny or defeat"
the insistence of the courts upon equitable treatment of
stockholders. Only difficulties of bringing and financing
effective suits by stockholders pervent the courts from employing their powers, which are wholly adequate to deal with the
problems raised by separation of ownership and control. Again,
the need of the corporation to sell securities to raise additional capital "sets a very definite limit on the extent to
which those in control can abuse the suppliers of capital."

Thus the actual effects of the separation of ownership
and control are left undetermined, and even unstudied. Yet
the book closes on the fear of "corporate plundering" by the
non-owning controllers.[4]

The Modern Corporation is not a tightly written volume,
and in particular it contains several subthemes that are
analytically independent of the main themes.

There is, first, the emphasis on the growing concentration of economic power in large corporations. Means, presents
a list of the two hundred largest nonfinancial corporations
in 1930, holding 49 percent of nonbaking corporate wealth--
the forerunner of Fortune's 500. There are hints that these
firms have market power simply because of their absolute size
and that duopoly is becoming the proper model of market
organization.[5] The concentration thesis is of course no
necessary part of the separation of ownership and control,
but it served to emphasize the social urgency of the problem
of controlling the large corporation.

There is, second, a strangely casual account of the

securities markets. The rules imposed by the NYSE on disclosure of information are praised, but the competence of the
market in appraising earnings or the effects of corporate
financial practices is frequently challenged.[6]

The probable behavior of the corporate manager is not
identified with what is now called the agency problem. The
single owner of an enterprise, with no attention to its size,
simply manages it efficiently: "Even though [the owner]
employs a manager to carry on the immediate activities of the
business, his desire for profits presumably induces him to
select the most efficient manager available and to require
him a high standard of performance." [7] The problems posed
by the employment of agents are thus ignored except in the
context of ownership's relationship to management, and even
in that narrower context no attention is paid to incentive
systems of remuneration of management.

II. The Previous State of Public Knowledge

Suspicion and fear were no doubt expressed before the
first large corporation was created, and surely a scholar with
nothing better to do could find such suspicions expressed in
every year of recent centuries. It is quite sufficient to
listen to Adam Smith:

The trade of a joint stock company is always managed
by a court of directors. The court, indeed, is frequently
subject, in many respects, to the control of a general court
of proprietors. But the greater part of those proprietors
seldom pretend to understand any thing of the business of
the company; and when the spirit of faction happens not to
prevail among them, give themselves no trouble about it, but
receive contentedly such half yearly or yearly dividend, as
the directors think proper to make them. This total exemption from trouble and from risk, beyond a limited sum, encourages many people to become adventurers in joint stock
companies, who would, upon no account, hazard their fortunes
in any private copartnery. Such companies, therefore, commonly draw to themselves much greater stocks than any private
copartnery can boast of. The trading stock of the South Sea
Company, at one time, amounted to upwards of thirty-three
millions eight hundred thousand pounds. The divided capital
of the Bank of England amounts, at present, to ten millions
seven hundred and eighty thousand pounds. The directors of
such companies, however, being the managers rather of other

people's money than of their own, it cannot well be expected, that they should watch over it with the same anxious vigilance with which the partners in a private copartnery frequently watch over their own. Like the stewards of a rich man, they are apt to consider attention to small matters as not for their master's honour, and very easily give themselves a dispensation from having it. Negligence and profusion, therefore, must always prevail, more or less, in the management of the affairs of such a company. It is upon this account that joint stock companies for foreign trade have seldom been able to maintain the competition against private adventures. They have, accordingly, very seldom succeeded without an exclusive privilege; and frequently have not succeeded with one. Without an exclusive privilege they have commonly mismanaged the trade. With an exclusive privilege they have both mismanaged and confined it.[8]

This is the place to quarrel with Berle and Means, not with Smith, so we shall merely note in passing our doubts of the failure of monopolists to conduct their affairs efficiently.

Of course the theses of Berle and Means, that often stock ownership was diffused and management had small stockholdings in large corporations, were "facts" of wide currency by the 1920s. In the preceding years, as several reviewers of the book pointed out, Thorstein Veblen had developed a congenial theory of the development of corporate structure in *Absentee Ownership and Business Enterprise in Recent Times* (1923). Berle and Means themselves acknowledge a debt to William Z. Ripley's *Main Street and Wall Street* (1927). But even if we could--as we no doubt can--find a hundred such discussions, none was presented with remotely the effectiveness of Berle and Means's. It is difficult to know how much to credit the success of their reception to their statistics and the arsenal of legal cases. We would give much weight to the fact that there was no better date in modern history to launch an attack on large corporations than 1932, and no better place than New York City.

We shall briefly survey the noneconomists' reception before we turn to the economists.

III.   The Lawyers (and Other Amateurs)

Almost without exception the lawyers received the book warmly, and often extravagantly. Jerome Frank began his review: "This book will perhaps rank with Adam Smith's

Wealth of Nations as the first detailed description in admirably clear terms of the existence of a new economic epoch."[9] Thus only a "perhaps" separated Berle and Means from equality with the book that Buckle had said was the most important book in the history of the world.[10]

The acceptance of the economic theses of the book was well-nigh complete: we give some illustrative quotations from reviews in Table 1. *(Please note that all references to tables and diagrams have been excluded. Please refer to the original article if such information is desired.)* It is not surprising that findings accepted without serious reservation by the economists (as we shall see) were convincing also to the practitioners of a nonquantitative discipline. There were only a few misgivings. That at least eighteen of the two hundred corporations on Means's list were already in receivership by early 1933 cast some doubt on their omnipotence.[11] The neglect of the control possibly exerted by banks was remarked.[12] The intimation by Berle and Means that the corporate giants acted as an integrated group was rejected.[13]

The legal doctrines of Berle were naturally received more critically. Berle's suggestion that the time was ripe to view corporate directors as trustees, not only for stockholders but also for other interested groups such as consumers and laborers, seemed unrealistic. Joseph V. Kline observed that "one cannot doubt that hopeless confusion and lack of uniformity would result from the inexperienced efforts of innumerable courts to adjust such matters [as wages and other matters of public interest] for the larger corporations."[14] Wormser denied that the law permitted many of the abuses alleged by Berle.[15] Dodd complained at the neglect by Berle and Means of the administrative controls over corporate officials by the ICC and other bodies.[16]

A casual inspection of the historians and social scientists other than economists indicates that the Berle-Means theses were accepted by many, ignored by some, and denied by none.[17]

IV. The Passage of the 1933 and 1934 Securities Acts

The Securities Act of 1933 and the Securities Exchange Act of 1934 initiated a regime of close federal supervision of the security markets and corporate behavior. To what extent did *The Modern Corporation* contribute to the passage of these acts?

One could find evidence suggesting powerful influence. Samuel Rayburn, chairman of the House Commerce Committee, presented the 1933 bill in language that could have been, and in a sense was, provided by Berle and Means:

Where the stock is widely distributed, as in the case of so many American corporations, the officials of the company, through the use of proxies and the advantages they have in obtaining proxies, are able to continue in office without much regard to their efficiency. . . . Two hundred companies own 75 percent of the total wealth of the United States.

The management of these big corporations, as a rule, own an insignificant percentage of the outstanding voting stocks.[18]

Again, the two hundred corporations reappeared in President Roosevelt's letter to Rayburn asking for the Securities Exchange Act in 1934.[19]

The presumption, however, is that the book was at most minor influence on the formulation and passage of the securities acts. The great crash of 1929 and the disastrous decline of the markets in the next four years would surely overshadow any book or books. In addition, the book itself appeared only in the latter part of 1932, and it requires a longer period of time and a good deal of wide discussion before any study reaches the level of public and legislative influence. We are not prepared to estimate the long-run influence of the book upon attitudes of legislators and members of regulatory bodies toward corporations and security markets.

V. The Economists

If economists were the professional audience for the economic theses of *The Modern Corporation*, they seldom displayed a deeper understanding of the work than the audience we have labeled "amateur." Ben Lewis, in his review article, was warm enough in his compliments:

The implications of this development challenge many of the basic assumptions of current thought: it is necessary now to think in terms of immense non-competing business units; the principles [?] of duopoly have become more important than those of free competition;... and economic forces are being supplanted by the conscious activity of a handful of individuals in the governing and control of production...

By and large the conclusions offered by the book are well grounded in the evidence.[20]

Lewis nevertheless believed that the traditional logic of entrepreneurship, in which the stockholder's role did not extend to management, was simply being carried to its conclusion.

There was little distinction between the attitudes of the textbooks on economics and those of the historians which we have just noted: support and neglect were common, opposition was nonexistent.[21]

The two economists who devoted much attention to the book deserve fuller attention.

W. L. Crum

W. L. Crum made the first attack on the assertion of the dominant role of the giant corporation in the American economy.[22] He made one objection that presumably should be characterized as psychological: inclusion of railroads and public utilities by Means led to an exaggerated view of the role of large corporations in the remainder of the economy. A second, and rather more cogent, criticism of the treatment of corporations that had no net income in Means's measurement of the growth of the role of large corporations, completed his main complaints.[23]

In a subsequent study, Crum confirmed the dominant role of large corporations on the basis of income tax returns.[24]

Robert A. Gordon

Gordon became the leading academic student of the ownership and control of large corporations, writing a series of articles in the 1930s that were later brought together and supplemented in *Business Leadership in the Large Corporation*. The SEC's requirement of the disclosure of stock ownership allowed him to make a direct study of the stockholdings of 107 listed (NYSE) industrial companies.[25] He found that the median share of voting stock held by all officers and directors was less than 10 percent and was less than 4 percent in the largest corporations. (Of course, the most tightly held corporations were not eligible for listing.) Moreover, the market value of the major officers' holdings had a median value of only $137,000, presumably a modest stake in profit maximizing even in absolute terms.

Then comes the customary leap:

...income to passive owners is not entrepreneurial income and may be to some extent functionless in nature. This solution would imply considering as functional profits part or all of the income of the entrepreneur derived from the concern regardless whether such income was received through ownership, salaries, financial manipulation, or in some other manner.... This sort of analysis may have considerable bearing on ortho-dox equilibrium theory....
    [The small stake of management] may indicate that progress of a fairly rapid order is possible without the incentive of profits in the usual sense.[26]

Gordon subsequently analyzed the ownership of stock by management and control groups, again using the new data provided by the SEC.[27] His conclusion assigns a dominant role to managerial control: "it seems improbable that much more than 15 percent of the total ownership of these 155 corporations can be said to be associated with control."[28] The SEC's data on officers' compensation was also exploited to demonstrate that "[n]either dividend income nor possibilities of appreciation in the value of their negligible stockholdings can compare with compensation as a source of income."[29]

At no point did Gordon address the question whether his findings were associated with any effects on the mangement of corporations or the determination of the compensation of their executives. In assuming the answers to these questions he went somewhat beyond the practice of the profession in his undocumented assertions about the behavioral effects of the separation of ownership and control:

The chief executive is in a sense his own employer. Within broad limits he frequently sets his own compensation.[30]

This much, however, is clear. Even after allowing for the heavy income taxes paid by leading executives, their compensation is considerably greater than that which would be available to them in any other vocation.[31]

However, the traditional reward of the business leader--the profits arising from business ownership--is not a primary incentive to the majority of top executives in our largest corporations.[32]

We shall postpone the impact of the Berle and Means book on general economic analysis to our concluding section.

VI. The Untested Theory

Berle and Means had challenged the applicability of the traditional theory of business behavior to the most prominent form of business organization in the modern age. A large and increasing share of the largest corporations were asserted to be effectively controlled by self-perpetuting managers. These managers controlled their own economic destinies and treated their stockholders, at best, like complaisant creditors.

It is surprising, and also depressing, to discover that at no time in the next years was there a serious attempt by anyone to discover whether the main tenets of *The Modern Corporation* were correct. Even in more recent times the most vigorous attack on Mean's statistical findings has come, not from defenders of the private enterprise system, but from Marxists: a villain is apparently even more important to a theory than a hero.[33]

Three issues will be discussed: Who controlled the large corporations? Did management-controlled corporations treat their executives differently from executives in owner-controlled corporations? and Did corporate profits behave differently in the two types of corporations? The discussion will be confined within the limits of data and theory available in the 1930s.

Who Has Control?

Berle and Means defined the control of a corporation as the power to select a majority of the board of directors.[34] In fact their criterion of control is literally applicable only in three of their control categories: private ownership; majority control; and control through a legal device (chiefly pyramiding). Some sixty-three of their industrial corporations fall in these classes.

Minority control is the control by holders of a substantial fraction, but less than half, of the voting stock. A corporation no doubt usually belongs here if 40 percent of its stock is closely held and the remainder is widely dispersed, but where to draw the line? (In practice, Berle and Means set 20 percent as the minimum holding by one or a few groups.)[35] Direct information on actual control over the selection of directors is usually not public knowledge, although often a matter of street gossip.

Because the management-controlled corporations are the
residual category, it would seem essential to devise a more
objective criterion of management control. How does one know
whether a minority of the management is in de facto control?
It is remarkable that even much later students of this problem
have followed the same subjective procedure as Berle and
Means.[36]

Of course "control" is a word that invites loose usage,
and Means accepted the invitation. In a comment at a session
of the American Economic Association devoted to financial control of large corporations, he said: "I shall use the term
economic control ... to refer to relationships between individuals or groups and a producing unit such that the former
can influence the economic policies of the latter."[37] On this
view, control includes, for a wage rate decision, "union
pressure of fellow members of the chamber of commerce, the
supply of labor, demand for the corporation's product, a
telephone call from an important creditor, and a dozen other
influences".[38]

The majority of the voting stock is the ultimate control
over a corporation even if that stock is diffused among many
owners. The stock may be acquired by a small group by stock
purchases if the shares become an attractive speculation, so
in an ultimate sense ownership and control cannot be separated.
It is a mystery of the literature of the 1920s and 1930s that
the takeover and the unfriendly merger are simply not discussed. It is not for lack of precedent,[39] although the frequency of changes in management so achieved is unknown.

In the absense of a struggle for control, one cannot know
whether a given management or set of stockholders controls the
selection of the board, or indeed whether they are a single
coalition. We suggest a test of de facto control: if the
membership of the board of directors changes substantially,
normal retirement aside, but the senior officers remain in
office, again normal retirement aside, then management is in
control. With the reverse pattern, the stock ownership is in
control. This test, which we have not made, is probably applicable only in times of serious crisis, but it is usually
only in such periods that a major change in policy or personnel
is called for.

The Compensation of Executives

The primary thrust of R. A. Gordon's studies of executives'
compensation, as we noted, was to demonstrate that their stock-

holdings yielded income that was only a small part of their
direct compensation. No attempt was made by Gordon, or that
prolific writer of the 1930s on executive compensation, John C.
Baker, to relate compensation to type of corporate control.

This scientific myopia was all the more surprising in that
a decade earlier F. W. Taussig and W. S. Barker had broached
this particular question.[40] They had collected data on executives and their compensation from some four hundred corporations for the "normal" period 1904-14. They found that the
executives usually owned little stock, especially in large
corporations, and were not representatives of friends or rela-
tives. They found that salaries were a much larger fraction
of invested capital in companies, the larger the share of stock
held by the executives (but not holding company size constant).[41]

Three bodies of data were available in the 1930s to test
portions of the Berle-Means argument pertaining to executive
compensation.

The FTC Study of 1928-32. In 1933 a Senate resolution
requested the Federal Trade Commission to collect salary schedules of officers and directors of large corporations listed
on the New York Stock Exchange. Data on compensation (including
bonuses) were collected retroactively through 1928, and they
are the basis of the present section.[42] The data, including
material from the financial manuals, are presented in Table Al.

The scatter diagram of the 1928-29 relationship between
average pay of the top three executives and the logarithm of
assets of each company is given in Figure 1, with the type of
control of the corporation given by Berle and Means indicated.
A regression of salaries on the logarithm of assets and a
dummy variable for type of control (D = 1 if the corporation
has management control) reveals no relationship of compensation to type of control (t = .35).[43] A comparable analysis
of the data for 1931-32 again shows no relationship of compensation to type of control (t = .54).

We may also compare the percentage changes in profits and
in executive compensation from 1928-29 to 1931-32. The literature commonly asserted that the officers could set their own
compensations rather independently of the corporation's profitability. The early years of the Great Depression offer no
support for this hypothesis. As the scatter diagram reveals
(Figure 2), there was a weak positive association between the
two variables, but the type of corporate control had no significant effect upon it.[44]

The SEC Data for 1934 and 1935. In 1936 the data on executive compensation collected by the SEC began to appear, and from this source we are able to obtain the average compensation of the two best-paid officers in seventy-seven of the 106 industrial corporations on the Berle-Means list. We present the basic data in Table A2, and a scatter diagram of the combined compensation of the two highest paid executives against the logarithm of total assets of the firm in 1934-35 is presented in Figure 3. In the figure, each corporation is again distinguished by whether it is owner or management controlled according to Berle and Means. The relationship between executive pay and type of control is nonsignificant and negative (the regression coefficient has a t-value of -1.03).[45]

We have 1934-35 data on fourteen petroleum companies in the Berle-Means list, and these companies have been analyzed separately because they are relatively homogeneous in their industrial characteristics. Again no relationship of executive pay to type of control is observed.

The TNEC and SEC Data for 1937-38. For this later period we have a new (1937) list of large corporations newly classified as to type of control constructed for the Temporary National Economic Committee (TNEC).[46] This new listing was based primarily upon a compilation of the stock ownership of each of the twenty largest stockholders in each company. We have condensed their data into two classes: (1) management controlled, which includes "no dominant stock interest" with or without "considerable minority blocs"; (2) nonmanagement control, which consists of all others, including majority and predominant minority control. Minority control usually involved 10 percent or more of the voting stock. No attention is paid to control devices (such as the holding company), unlike the Berle-Means procedure. For 1937-38 we again have SEC data for ninety-two companies on executive salaries and on corporate assets and profits. In addition we can use the 1937 share of the corporation's voting stock owned by the twenty largest stockholders as an *inverse* measure of officer control. The basic data are presented in Table A3, and the scatter diagram of the compensation of the three top executives[47] versus the logarithm of corporate assets is shown in Figure 4, excluding two outliers.[48] Again we find no relation between executive pay and type of control, after allowing for the logarithm of corporate assets (the t-value of the regression coefficient is .20). If we use the share of voting stock hold by the twenty largest stockholders as an inverse measure of the probability of management control, the same lack of a relation between executive salaries and type of control is observed (t = -.96).[49]

The Profitability of Corporations

The type of corporate control was asserted to have an important influence upon the goal of management. The owner-controlled corporation would seek maximum profits, while the management-controlled corporation would be much more concerned with safety because major reverses could lead to a stockholder revolt, and in any event large profits little benefited the management. Accordingly we examine the effect of type of control on the relationship between profits and investment. We use profits after charges but including interest.

The regression of corporate profits on corporate assets and type of control are presented for all four periods in Table 2. In addition we present the scatter diagram for the first period, 1928-29, in Figure 5. Type of control has a significant effect in only one of the five regressions (no. 4), although it is of the predicted sign in every case.[50] The same analysis was applied to seventeen petroleum refining companies--the only industry with a considerable number of firms in the list--again without finding any effect of type of control.

VII. Conclusion

The reception of *The Modern Corporation* in the 1930s was astonishingly uncritical. The charge that the economy was being captured by giant corporations, which in turn had been captured by a self-perpetuating corporate bureaucracy, would encounter, one might have thought, vigorous challenge at every point. The effects of large corporations on competition, the degree to which corporate officials were free to pursue personal goals, the way in which they would conduct corporate policy, the defenses investors would develop against exploitation--none of these questions received close analysis. The leading academic student, R. A. Gordon, was content to dot a few *i*'s and cross a few *t*'s in the original indictment.

Moreover, the Berle-Means theses were given a most narrow application. If they were true, should there not be pronounced effects in labor markets, research investment, product innovation, advertisement? Neither Means nor his many disciples paid any considerable or systematic attention to the operation of the economic system. One is entitled to suspect that they believed that the control over economic organizations was all that mattered: the organizations then simply did whatever their controllers wished.

We must recall that the practice of testing economic

theories was still extremely uncommon in the 1930s. Certainly no one dreamed of subjecting Chamberlin's *Monopolistic Competition* or Keynes's *Treatise* to a formal empirical test. Still, there was more incentive than usual to apply statistical tests to the conjectures of Berle and Means. Means' work was nakedly empirical: he had no systematic theory of the causes or consequences of the separation of ownership and control.

We know, of course, that people are more critical of the things they do not want to hear than of those they find pleasing. The 1930s was a period of accelerating movement away from a competitive, unregulated economic system. Reasons for distrusting such a system or, better yet, bidding it a respectful adieu were in demand for the new rhetoric of public policy, and Berle and Means nicely met that need.

In fact with respect to the new rhetoric Means can properly be counted among the most influential economists of our century. Consider his legacy: the belief that the economy was no longer effectively competitive; the belief that ownership and control were fully separated in most large corporations; the strategic role of giant corporations in the economy; the beginning of measurement of concentration of production, using census data; and the belief that prices of large companies were unresponsive to the conditions of demand and supply (administered prices). Of course, none of these ideas was invented by, or solely promulgated by, Gardiner Means, but it would be difficult to name an equally influential exponent of them.

A much more modest role must be assigned to the book if we look for its effects on professional economic analysis. The most immediate implication of their work for economic theory was that the maximizing of the present value of a firm should be modified to take account of the separate interest of the management. It is not evident what the modification should be. Should the firm maximize officers' gains or minimize the risk to the officers of being replaced by action of the creditors? If the theory had no implications for the incentive structure of large corporations, why should we view the separation of ownership and control as of real importance in the operation of business?

A mixture of recollection and selective review of important theoretical work of the 1930s has not uncovered any important instances of this kind of change in economic theorizing. The Chamberlins, Robinsons, Hickses, Keyneses, Kaldors, and confrères continued to apply traditional profit-maximizing theory as if Berle and Means had never written.

We are not prepared to set the influence of the book on technical economic analysis at nought. It is plausible that *The Modern Corporation* helped to bring forth works such as Corwin Edwards's theory of the conglomerate firm, William Baumol's theory of the sales-maximizing oligopolist, and much of the life work of J. K. Galbraith.[51] That these works have received wide attention is reliable testimony to the popularity of the underlying philosophical outlook.

Our own statistical analyses, using only data and methods familiar to economists of the time, yield no clear evidence that the management-dominated corporations differed much from owner-dominated companies in practices of executive compensation or in the utilization of assets to produce profits. The main tradition of economic theory was perhaps instinctively recognizing these facts when it continued to work in complete disregard of *The Modern Corporation*.

[1] Adolf A. Berle & Gardiner C. Means, The Modern Corporation and Private Property 8-9 (1932).

[2] *Id.*, bk. I, ch. IV.

[3] *Id.* at 205; also 335.

[4] *Id.* at 280-81, 355.

[5] *Id.* at 32-33, 45

[6] *Id.* at 167, 169, 201.

[7] *Id.* at 342, n. 4.

[8] 2 Adam Smith, The Wealth of Nations 741 (Glasgow ed. 1976). See Gary M. Anderson & Robert D. Tollison, Adam Smith's Analysis of Joint Stock Companies, 90 J. Pol. Econ. 1237 (1982).

[9] Jerome Frank, Review, 42 Yale L. J. 989, 989 (1933).

[10] Charles Beard was equally generous: "this volume may be proclaimed as the most important work bearing on American statecraft between the publication of the immortal Federalist ... and the opening of the year 1933." Book Review, Herald Tribune, February 19, 1933.

[11] Norman L. Meyers, Review, 42 Yale L. J. 997, 998 (1933).

[12] *Id.* at 999.

[13] Jerome Frank, *supra* note 9 at 993.

[14] Joseph V. Kline, Review, 33 Colum. L. Rev. 557, 560 (1933). See also E. M. Dodd, Jr., Review, 81 U. Pa. L. Rev. 782, 783 (1933).

[15] I. M. Wormser, Review, 19 A.B.A.J. 113 (1933).

[16] E. M. Dodd, *supra* note 14, at 784.

[17] The acceptances include 3 Charles A. Beard & Mary R. Beard, America in Midpassage 872-75 (1939); H. U. Faulkner, American Economic History 522-23, 718 (4th ed. 1938); F. A. Shannon, America's Economic Growth 587, 594 (rev. ed. 1940); C. W. Wright, Economic History of the United States 671-74 (1941). The neglect is illustrated by E. L. Bogart Economic History of the American People (2nd ed. 1935); A. M. Schlesinger, Political and Social Growth of the United States (3rd ed. 1941).

[18] 4 The Economic Regulation of Business and Industry 2615-16 Bernard Schwartz, ed. 1973).

[19] *Id.* at 2715.

[20] Ben W. Lewis, Berle and Means on the Modern Corporation, 43 J. Pol. Econ. 548, 548-49 (1935).

[21] Examples of acceptance are R. T. Bue & W. W. Hewett Applied Economics 93-106 (4th ed. 1947); F. R. Fairchild, 2 E. S. Furniss, & N. S. Buck, Elementary Economics 301-5 (5th ed. 1939). Those ignoring Berle-Means include R. T. Ely & R. H. Hess, Outlines of Economics (6th ed. 1937); and the influential book by A. S. Dewing, The Financial Policy of Corporations (4th ed. 1941).

[22] W. L. Crum, On the Alleged Concentration of Economic Power, 24 Am. Econ. Rev. 69 (1934). It is followed by a reply by Gardiner Means and a rejoinder.

[23]To measure the growth in the role of large corporations, Means used estimated incomes of the largest 200 corporations as a share of total corporate income for 1920-29 (Berle & Means, *supra* note 1, at 37). These 200 corporations will not be the same as those ranked by assets, and indeed some of the latter will have negative incomes. The effect of this selection on the trend of the share of large corporations was not studied. Means apparently did not understand the criticism.

[24]W. L. Crum, The Concentration of Corporate Control, 8 J. Bus. (1935). He concludes that "a very large part of American industry is subject to control, as respects current operations and long-run planning, by executives of a very small number of great corporations." *Id*. at 283.

[25]Robert A Gordon, Stockholdings of Officers and Directors in American Industrial Corporations, 50 Q. J. Econ. 622 (1936).

[26]*Id*. at 654-55.

[27]Robert A. Gordon, Ownership by Management and Control Groups in the Large Corporation, 52 Q. J. Econ. 367 (1938).

[28]*Id*. at 395.

[29]Robert A. Gordon, Ownership and Compensation as Incentives to Corporate Executives, 54 Q. J. Econ. 455, 466 (1940).

[30]Robert A. Gordon, Business Leadership in the Large Corporation 277 (1945).

[31]*Id*. at 279.

[32]*Id*. at 312.

[33]See M. Zeitlin, Corporate Ownership and Control: The Large Corporation and the Capitalist Class, 79 Am. J. Soc. 1073 (1974). Also R. Fitch & M. Oppenheimer, Who Rules the Corporations?, 1 Socialist Revolution: pt. 1, July-Aug. 73; pt. 2, Sept.-Oct. 61; pt. 3 Nov.-Dec. 33 (1970) Perhaps Paul M. Sweezy initiated this tradition in The Illusion of the "Managerial Revolution," 6 Sci. and Soc'y (1942), reprinted in his The Present as History (2d ed. 1970).

[34] Berle & Means, *supra* note 1, at 69-70.

[35] *Id.* at 93.

[36] See Robert J. Larner, Management Control and the Large Corporation (1970).

[37] Gardiner C. Means, Financial Control of Large-Scale Enterprise, 29 Am. Econ. Rev. uppl. 110, 111 (1939).

[38] *Id.* at 113.

[39] Thus, Barrons for March 25, 1929 (at 25) reports "Barber Group Controls Childs Company." The story follows:
"On January 20, 1929, at the quarterly dividend meeting, with the Childs family firmly in control of the board, Mr. Childs suddenly executed a 'coup d' état' by ousting Mr. Smith and other representatives of the syndicate [formed in 1928 to revise the management], and elevating individual members of the Childs family to all official positions of the company, thus precipitating the subsequent struggle for control. At the next meeting, a group backed by the du Ponts replaced William Childs, Luther Childs, E. Ellsworth Childs, W. Sterling Childs, J. Herman Childs, Mrs. Victoria Childs, and S. Tydeman."

[40] F. W. Taussig & W. S. Barker, American Corporations and Their Executives: A Statistical Inquiry, 40 Q. J. Econ. 1 (1925).

[41] *Id.* at 27.

[42] Report of the Federal Trade Commission on Compensation of Officers and Directors of Certain Corporations, 1928-32, 15 vols., typewritten (1934) unpublished. We are indebted to the Commission for access to the data (which were used by Crum, Baker, and Gordon in the 1930s).

[43] We exclude two outliers (Paramount and Bethlehem) for which average compensation exceeded $500,000.

[44] The regression equation (excluding three cases with profits less than $1 million in 1928-29) is (t-values in parentheses):

% change in pay (1928–29 to 1931–32) = 19.05
                                        (1.70)
+ 0.122% change in profits (28–29 to 31–32) + 5.52D (con-
                                                    trol).
(1.27)   (.61)

[45] If we exclude one outlier (General Motors, whose average salary for the top two executives exceeded $275,000), the t-value becomes -.67. We have separately examined the fifty corporations classified by Berle & Means as "presumably" management or minority controlled. These presumed classes also have nonsignificantly lower salaries in the management-controlled corporations.

[46] Raymond W. Goldsmith & Rexford C. Parmalee, The Distribution of Ownership of the 200 Largest Nonfinancial Corporations, TNEC Monograph no. 29 (1940).

[47] Fuller salary data are available for this period, so we use average salary of the three top executives.

[48] The outliers are Loews and Paramount, with average salaries exceeding $275,000.

[49] If the two outliers referred to in note 48 are included, the t-value for type of control is 1.51 and the t-value for share of stock held by the twenty top shareholders is -1.20.

We have also examined the tenure of top executives, for the period 1960–76, in a sample of seven owner-controlled and twenty-nine management-controlled corporations, as classified by Larner (*supra* note 36). The results vary with the period of tenure covered (retroactive, forward, completed, uncompleted), but average tenure is consistently longer in owner-controlled corporations.

[50] As a rough check for bias resulting from the unavailability of profit data for failed companies, we examined all 106 industrials on the Berle-Means list for failures in 1930–39. Using information in the Commerce Clearning House Capital Changes Reporter and Moody's Industrial Manuals, we find that 13 percent of owner-controlled companies and 9 percent of management-controlled companies were in receivership at some time in this period.

[51]See Corwin Edwards, The Conglomerate Firm, in Business Concentration and Price Policy (1955); William Baumol, Business
Behavior, Value and Growth (1967), ch. 6; and John K. Gailbraith, Monopoly and Concentration of Economic Power, in A
Survey of Contemporary Economics (Howard S. Ellis ed. 1948),
American Capitalism, the Concept of Countervailing Power (1952)
and The New Industrial State (1967), for example.

*Journal of Law & Economics, Vol. XXVI, (June 1983): 237-249;
252; 254; 258-259*

Capitalism, Socialism and Democracy
by
Joseph A. Schumpeter

REVIEW: Charles R. Walker (1943)*

Though Professor Schumpeter's thesis is that capitalism
cannot survive in the United States and that socialism is
bound to succeed it, it appears to this reviewer that the author avoids many of the most decisive dilemmas which both a
capitalist and a collective society face in the real world.
This is surprising in view of the proven powers of observation
and logic so often demonstrated by Professor Schumpeter in his
other works. The most cogent and admirable portions of the
book are, I think it is fair to say, introductory or tangential to the main thesis.

In the early part of the book, for example, there is a
penetrating analysis of the "maturity" theory of American
capitalism, namely, that new inventions and a fresh technological change are not to be looked for. In refutation of
this thesis, Professor Schumpeter's analysis of many contemporary critics of capitalism is acute and convincing. Professor Schumpeter thereupon projects his own brand of capitalist maturity into an unknown future, on the basis of which he
predicts capitalism's decline and its replacement by socialism. If a logic inheres in this argument, it is difficult to
follow. At the very least, one may ask that Professor Schumpeter take the reader into his confidence and account for all
of the cogent arguments he has already produced to show that
capitalism is *not* mature in an economic sense. The same criticism, I feel, is also valid of his refutation and later re-
turn--in the prophetic side of his book--to theories of monopoly or "fettered" capitalism, concentration, and lack of investment opportunity. Professor Schumpeter also adds psychological arguments for the collapse of capitalism. For one who
later argues the superior advantages of socialism, it is curious how little conviction this section of the book carries.
The essential impression conveyed is that capitalism will collapse largely because the short-sighted masses don't appreciate it.

On the whole, Professor Schumpeter's critical faculties seem to have been most usefully stimulated when dealing analytically with the real advantages of capitalism and their short-sighted critics. It is surprising, therefore, that when turning to his blueprint of socialism, there is little awareness of the problems which students of every ideological tendency—I think it fair to say—have long considered basic. Professor Schumpeter's concept of democracy, for example, in a socialist society is concerned solely with formal aspects: elections, Cabinet ministers, parliamentary rule. No discussion is introduced upon the basic freedoms which these formal aspects are supposed to implement but often do not, either in such capitalist or collectivist societies as we know. Other writers *pro* and *con* collectivist tendencies in society argue either that democratic freedoms *can* be preserved when political and economic power merges in a socialist state, or argue that they will be destroyed. In short, they recognize the existence of a problem. Professor Schumpeter merely terms such a combination of powers "an advantage of prime importance." If the approach to his central thesis seems to this reviewer both unsatisfactory and illogical, it is important to repeat that there are many admirable tangential chapters in the book, notably the author's sixty-page summary of the teachings of Karl Marx and his acute analysis of recent economic theory.

Yale Review, New Series, (1943): 597-598

REVIEW: Ralph H. Blodgett (1943)

As Professor Schumpeter says in his preface, "this volume is the result of an effort to weld into a readable form the bulk of almost forty years' thought, observation and research on the subject of socialism." In the first division of the book, which deals with Marxian socialism, Marx is described as a great genius. In the field of economic theory, Marx was a "very learned man" and his theory was truly scientific, though the author gives many parts of the theory a thorough beating. Marx is also described as a great prophet, but it turns out that Professor Schumpeter has little use for the Marxian predictions concerning the declining rate of profits and the increasing misery of the proletariat. However, the predictions concerning business cycles and the concentration and centralization of capital are approved in general, and above all, the Marxian prediction of the inevitable downfall of capitalism (which coincides with Professor Schumpeter's conclusion in the matter) showed remarkable vision, even though

it rested on a faulty basis. Marx's economic interpretation
of history was "doubtless one of the greatest individual
achievements of sociology to this day" (p. 10), and his analysis of social classes was nearly as valuable, although it
exaggerated the definiteness of the classes and of the antagonism between them. On the whole, the author's verdict on
Marx is unusually favorable, and there is some tendency to
suggest that the weaker parts of the Marxian analysis should
never have been taken seriously, and to point out that Marx's
conclusions were right even though the bases on which they
rested were unsatisfactory.

In the second part of the volume Professor Schumpeter
decides that the breakdown of capitalism is inevitable, in the
sense that present trends, if continued, will produce this
result. While the actual and prospective working of the system is such as to deny that it will break down because of economic failures, its very success is leading to its downfall.
Perhaps because of this viewpoint, the author presents a glow-
ing account of the accomplishments of capitalism and is quite
willing to attribute these accomplishments to the system itself
rather than to extraneous and fortuitous factors. After sharp
criticism of the popular theory of vanishing investment opportunity, the prospective breakdown of capitalism is attributed
to such factors as the decline of the entrepreneurial function,
the political helplessness of the bourgeoisie in the face of
modern problems, the tendency of the capitalistic system to
destroy its own institutional framework (especially property
and free contracting), the general internal atmosphere of
hostility to the system, and the decline of the bourgeois
family. However, Professor Schumpeter is unwilling to venture
a prediction as to when the breakdown of capitalism may occur.

It seems rather certain that socialism can "work," assuming that the system in which it is attempted is sufficiently
mature and that the problems of transition can be solved.
After stating that there is nothing wrong with the pure logic
of socialism, the author gives the usual description of the
manner in which it would be possible for rational economic
decision-making to occur under socialism. Some economists,
while admitting that it would be theoretically possible for
rational decision-making to occur under socialism, are inclined to think that the process involved would be so difficult
that the planners would probably rely largely on their own
judgment in making basic decisions. Professor Schumpeter contends that the process would be rather simple and would almost
certainly be used. He also thinks that technical efficiency
in production might well be better under socialism than under

capitalism, though he avoids saying that the productive results attained would be an "optimum" or would result in the
greatest possible satisfaction of basic human wants. In dealing with the human element under socialism, the author real-
izes that his ground is less sure, but he is inclined to think
that adequate incentives would be provided for all and that
problems of labor discipline would not be insuperable. Finally, a peaceful, constitutional transition to socialism
would probably be possible for a mature capitalistic economy.
It seems hardly necessary to say that Professor Schumpeter is
more enthusiastic than most economists in describing the probable accomplishments of socialism.

After a severe criticism of the classical definition of
democracy, which is held to have little or no significance in
most modern situations, a new definition of democracy--as "that
institutional arrangement for arriving at political decisions
in which individuals acquire the power to decide by means of
a competitive struggle for the people's vote" (p. 269)--is
stated and defended. It then becomes clear that between socialism and democracy there is no necessary relationship and
no necessary incompatibility. Professor Schumpeter recognizes
that in practice it may be difficult to reconcile the enormous
powers of economic planners and officials in the economic
sphere with responsibility to the people as a whole in the
political sphere, and he says that "as a matter of practical
necessity, socialist democracy may eventually turn out to be
more of a sham than capitalist democracy ever was" (p. 302).
However, he does not seem greatly concerned by the fact that
this development would ruin the socialistic system from the
point of view of large numbers of people. The final section
of the book, which presents a historical sketch of socialist
parties, is interesting, but it does not seem necessary to the
rest of the book, and is in the nature of an anticlimax.

On the whole, this is an excellent book. To be sure, part
of the economic analysis depends quite heavily on some of Professor Schumpeter's favorite doctrines, such as the innovation
theory of interest, the theory of the beneficence of large-
scale and quasimonopolistic business under modern capitalism,
and the theory of the decline of the entrepreneurial function;
but this is not unexpected. The book may be somewhat difficult
for the general reader, but individuals with adequate background in the general field will find that it is charmingly
written, that its arguments and analyses are developed in
thorough and intensely interesting fashion, and that Professor
Schumpeter's outstanding scholarship is evidenced on every
page. The literature in this important field has been enriched

by the publication of this book.

*The Annals of the American Academy, 228, (July, 1943):
126-127*

"Schumpeter as a Teacher and Economic Theorist," Paul A.
Samuelson (1951)*

There were many Schumpeters: the brilliant *enfant terrible*
of the Austrian School who before the age of thirty had written
two great books; the young Cairo lawyer with a stable of
horses; the Austrian Finance-Minister; the social philosopher
and prophet of capitalist development; the historian of economic doctrine; the economic theorist espousing use of more
exact methods and tools of reasoning; the teacher of economics.

From the long-term viewpoint the first of these roles is
the most important. Schumpeter will unquestionably be labeled
by future historians of thought as a business cycle theorist
who placed primary stress on the role of the innovator. Of
this he was well aware. He always remained faithful to his
youthful vision, not only because of its intrinsic merits, but
also - I venture to think - because he was too self-conscious
an artist to let old age clutter up the aesthetic life line
laid down by the genius of youth.

But enough will be written of this long-term contribution
of Schumpeter. Here I should like to concentrate on Schumpeter
as a teacher, and on Schumpeter as a patron of economic theory.
It was in these two capacities that I knew him best. But aside
from that, you might say of Schumpeter that, although he had
an absolute advantage both as a scholar and a personality, his
comparative advantage was if anything almost greater as a personality. His books speak for themselves but only his pupils
can recapture the impact of his colorful personality.

II

I saw Schumpeter for the first time at the 1934 Christmas
meetings of economists in Chicago when, as an undergraduate,
I accidentally walked in on a meeting where he was speaking.
I saw him for the last time at the 1949 New York meetings,
where in marvelous form he was expounding good sense about
the Walrasian theory of money and bringing life back to an

audience wilted by two hours of confusing technical discourse. The intervening fifteen years constituted almost half my life-time – the important years according to Schumpeter's strong view on the biology of scholars. For Schumpeter these same fifteen years constituted less than a quarter of his life-span; and it is remarkable in view of his own theories on the aging of the creative impulse that they did not represent an anti-climax to his career.

This was the period of his two-volume *Business Cycles*, of his *Capitalism, Socialism, and Democracy*, and of his yet-to-be published *History of Economic Analysis*. A grand work on eco-nomic theory was part of his plan: a work on Money, and a sep-arate volume on Banking; a book on mathematical logic for his old age, his seventies. And as relaxation for really old age, he spoke of writing a sociological novel in his eighties. He even once did field work on the latter: after a long and rather tiring walk, Mrs. Schumpeter with some difficulty persuaded him to ride on the subway back to Harvard Square. This, he reported, had been a very interesting experience; and what was more, when he came to write his sociological novel, he was going to do it again.

Professor Smithies, who knew him much more intimately than I ever did, has indicated in his obituary essay the importance in Schumpeter's life of having been born in the closing era of the Austro-Hungarian empire. With the disappearance of that world, he became completely qualified to play the important sociological role of the alienated stranger. The America of Mickey Rooney and coca-cola he knew almost nothing about; in 1913, while at Columbia, he first saw a football game, and that was enough to last him the rest of his life; if anything, he went out of his way to exaggerate his naïveté with respect to all such matters. As a judge of short-term events, this could not help but prove a serious handicap; in compensation, his long-term view may have gained.

On the psychological side, Schumpeter's was a temperament not uncommon among gifted minds, and perhaps peculiarly characteristic of those who have been precocious in their youth. Obviously, he was ambitious to make his mark and it was no accident that the figure of the innovator should have intrin-sically appealed to him. There was in him a consciousness of great powers, and this served as an irritant urging him toward creative activity. Moreover, this was not an irritant that ceased to operate on weekends and holidays; I don't suppose that he ever crossed the Atlantic without spoiling the trip by taking along a book on tensor calculus or partial differen-

tial equations, which inevitably he succeeded neither in reading nor ignoring.

This feeling of great personal powers was of course of
tremendous importance in connection with his professional work.
It also showed itself in every aspect of his life: he was quite
prepared to talk expertly on anything from Etruscan Art to
medieval law; to read, or feel that he could read, Italian,
Dutch, and Scandinavian; to outline a theory of metaphysics.
This lack of inhibition was extremely important in giving him
the freedom to make daring and interesting sociological hypotheses concerning phenomena on the fringes of politics and
economics.

The one field in which he did show real humility was in
connection with mathematics – a statement that may seem surprising to some. It is true that he never tired of pointing
out to the non-mathematical the virtues for economics of
mathematics. It is also true that he would often refer with
a wave of his hand to quite difficult problems as if they were
elementary and easy. But nonetheless he was quite aware of
his own lack of facility with mathematics and cheerfully admitted the difficulties he had in mastering and retaining
mathematical techniques.

I think to the end he regarded it as a slightly mystical
fact that a mixed-difference-differential equation of the
Frisch-Tinbergen type involves complex exponentials which a
miraculous manner give rise to sinusoidal periodicities. He
waited eagerly (the uncharitable might almost say credulously)
for some new mathematical method to turn up that would solve
the mysteries of the ages: the tensor calculus, linear operators, symbolic logic, etc.

Moreover, it was his conviction that mathematics itself
had grown up as a servant of physics and was not adapted to
economics; so that real progress in economic theory would require new methods tailor-made to economics. In this expectation he foreshadowed in a sense what actually came to pass in
the von Neumann-Morgenstern *Theory of Games*, which dispenses
completely with the tools of modern mathematical physics and
falls back upon the more fundamental notions of point-set
theory and topology. Schumpeter held this expectation all the
more confidently because of his conviction that the processes
of logical thought had themselves been biologically developed
in the human species as the result of a Darwinian process in
which man had to learn to solve successfully the *economic*
problems of living: Schumpeter expected therefore that logic

and economics would turn out to be closely interrelated.
Such an interence may have a slightly far-fetched
flavor but it illustrates the character of his speculations.
It is not unrelated to Schumpeter's views concerning
the naturalness of econometrics; in an early issue of
*Econometrica,*he argued that the economic marketplace
is by its nature concerned with monetary magnitudes of a
measurable sort so that while other disciplines may
gradually feel their way toward exact quanitative analysis,
economics has this problem thrust upon it from the very
beginning.

Call this faith of Schumpeter's naive if you will.
Still it was a beautiful thing to see. Audit kept him
young. Every scholar, as he grows in years, experience,
and judiciousness, faces two insidious enemies which in the
end usually take over: disillusioned skepticism and
loss of enthusiasm. Schumpeter held these at bay. Only
in the last year of his life did Schumpeter express
the National Bureau of Economic Research Conference
on Business Cycles the view that mathematical models
in business-cycle research had been relatively sterile:
that as between the alternative methods of cycle research. (1) theoretical, (2) statistical, and (3)
historical, last was by far the most important. It is
not necessary here to ask whether there is any antithesis
between these alternative methods, whether there is not
one single problem of empirical induction which is
necessarily to be attacked by means of hypothesis
formation and abstraction so that (2) and (3) are methodologically indistinguishable in principle and both
inseparably intertwined with (1), with the only real
issue being the pragmatic one of degree. The only
point of the incident is that it represents one of those
rare occasions when Schumpeter gave what was from his
viewpoint "comfort to the enemy." For the real enemy
to him was first and foremost those who opposed--
and I now employ the words uttered a thousand times by him
in the classroom--"the use of exact methods in economic
analysis."[1]

Patron of mathematical economists is perhaps the
best way of describing his rôle. He was quite the
opposite of those celebrated scholars who rarely make
an error and who instill in their best students an in-
feriority complex. Schumpeter's very imperfections
gave hope and drive to his students.

Conscious of his scholarly achievements outside
of mathematical economics, he very wisely refused to make
small contributions to this field. Subconsciously he
may have realized that the last part of the 19th century
was a bad time for a theorist to be born. It was either
too late or too soon--too late to lead the pack in the
1870 "revolution," and too soon to participate fully
in the post-1925 era. In Austria, England, and America
the first quarter of the 20th century proved fairly arid
for economic theory.

However, if a bad time for theory, the first
years of this century were tremendously fertile for trade-
cycle analysis, culminating around the beginning of World
War 1 in a series of brilliant studies by Spiethoff,
Schumpeter, Aftalion, Mitchell, Hawtrey, and Robertson.
Primarily as a pioneer in this development will Schumpeter
be remembered.

III

Let me turn to Schumpeter as a teacher. Schumpeter
was a great showman. In all probability he spoke
before other scholars in history, so I do not have to try
to describe his manner. But good as was his average performance, he was really at his best in his own classroom.
I don't suppose that in his life he *read* a paper in the
literal sense. He spoke from notes only very rarely. On
really serious occasions, such as his Presidential
Address at the 1948 Meetings, he was in a sense caught
between stools and his best spontaneous speaking was
inhibited.

What his German speech was like I cannot judge. His
English was, of course, easy, grammatical, and flowery;
but with an accent that was *sui generis*. On that
occasion at the 1934 meetings referred to above, he was
quite incomprehensible to one who had never been out of
the Middle West. On every subsequent occasion my ear
seemed to have acquired the proper key so that I never
again had the slightest difficulty. This experience,
however, seems to have been quite typical.

Schumpeter liked to talk too well to be at his best
in leading a small seminar. He loved to lecture!
And to large audiences. If left to himself, he would
probably have swallowed up imperialistically all fields of
economics and lectured on all subjects. At Harvard, I

dare to think, he was not left to himself in this respect; but, nonetheless, for the semester after his death he had been scheduled to give a course on Economic Theory, one on History of Economic Thought, and one on Socialism--and all this when he was past the age of retirement!

In 1935 when he first took over Taussig's famous Ec-11, the basic Harvard graduate course in economic theory, the class met at 2 o'clock in Emerson Hall. After, and not before, the students had assembled for the class hour, in would walk Schumpeter, remove hat, gloves, and topcoat with sweeping gestures, and begin the day's business. Clothes were important to him: he wore a variety of well-tailored tweeds with carefully matched shirt, tie, hose, and handkerchief. My wife used to keep track in that period of the cyclic reappearance of the seemingly infinite number of combinations in his wardrobe: the cycle was not simple and it was far from random.

The hour after lunch is the most dangerous of all to the lecturer, but no one ever felt tempted to enjoy a siesta in his class. Humor always eludes description and defies analysis. In Schumpeter's case it is clear that he never told jokes and had no prepared-in-advance booby traps; he was never dead-pan and ingenuous, but somehow made the class itself seem witty, so that even Radcliffe students felt themselves to be engaging in brilliant sortie and repartée. He was free of the congenital vice of the veteran college prefessor: he never repeated his stories, as I know from careful count kept over a span of years. Only after some years of teaching have I learned to appreciate the real significance of this.

I do not know what the effect has been of the postwar flood of graduate students, but back in the 1930's his typical class was about 50 in number. He did not lecture in the strict European sense of a unilateral monologue. He called on people in the class, and he was constantly interrupted by his audience. If anything, he tolerated too many interruptions from grade-chasers, fools, and exhibitionists. In the beginning years when he was carrying on Taussig's famous course, he aimed particularly at carrying on the Socratic method of Taussig.

This requires some explanation, which I offer with some diffidence since I was the very first of the post-Taussig generation. The year 1935-36, my first at Harvard, was also the first year of the age of Schumpeter: Taussig

had given one half of Ec-11 the previous year; Bullock too
had just finished his last course; Gay had still one more
year to go, and Carver was long-since emeritus. The
Socratic method of teaching, which Taussig had perfected
to its highest art, had tremedous prestige and was
universlly imitated--even down to the rawest instructor
in elementary economics.

   What did it consist of? For one thing, the teacher
never presented the answers to questions to the student.
The student was supposed to work out all answers by himself, but he was never to be told whether he had or had not
arrived at the correct answer. Furthermore, different
members of the class were called upon to discuss the
question at issue, and it was part of Taussig's greatness that he would plan out his campaign in advance,
knowing exactly who could be counted on to give the
appropriate stupid reply and who must be avoided lest he
give the show away. Taussig, himself, was a rather austere
gentleman of the old school so that most of the class sat
in fear and trembling until he had announced his immediate victim, whereupon all the rest relaxed to enjoy
the fun.

   All this is course grossly over-simplified and not a
balanced view of the method, but it will suffice for the
present purpose. What shall we conclude about the Scoratic
method? That it represented a performance of consummate
skill and artistry on the part of Taussig, none can
deny; and, apparently, those who went through it had an
unforgettable experience. It is equally clear that in the
hands of most teachers--and not just beginners-- it was
a disastrous method: disastrous both to students and
teacher. Moreover, even at its best it was not-- and
here I am expressing my own opinion-- a very good method
for teaching graduate economic theory of the modern type.
If you believed as Taussig did that economics consisted
of a few great thorny problems-- such as "the" index-
number problem, "the" problem of value etc.--that no one
had ever solved and that no one ever would solve, but
concerning which there were a number of aspects to be
explored along the lines laid out by Ricardo and others--
then it was a good method. You never got anywhere very
fast, but since there was nowhere to get to anyway it
didn't really matter very much, just so long as you had a
good ride through the traditional back-country.

   All this that I am saying is, I realize, heresy.

I have never said it before, but I have thought it; and
so too did many of the people of my generation, who had
constantly thrown at them the almost-mystic accounts of the
Taussigian method which none could describe but to the
excellence of which all testified.[3]

Schumpeter was perhaps not at his best in conducting
a first course in graduate economic theory and after
two or three years he confined himself to more advanced
courses. For one thing, he was considered too difficult
for an important fraction of the class, many of whom had
scarcely heard of Marshall and J.B. Clark before coming
to Harvard, to say nothing of Pigou or Frisch. Aside from
the intrinsic difficulties of economic theory,there was
the added fact that Schumpeter darted about, "opening
door" on new theories and topics. Furthermore, he was
addicted to the cardinal vice of introducing mathematical
symbols into the economic classroom; and it must be confessed the his blackboard equations were not a model of
neatness. Sometimes we spent half an hour looking for a
lost Walresian equation or getting rid of a redundant one.

I have said that he was consistently amusing and in a
way that counted against him. Whereas he never gave a
lecture that a one-day visitor would have found dull, the
regular class attendant became a little more systematic
instruction. At the time I was a fairly conscientious
note taker, but I find not infrequently in my class notes
the following type of entry for a full hour's lecture:

A. Particular Expenses curve: Array (cumulative)
of average cost of different firms. It is not a
supply curve.

And that is all.

But now that I have stated the case against him,
let me restore the balance. His 1935 theory course
more nearly resembled the courses now being given in every
graduate school that did any course then being given in
America, excellent as were many of the contemporaneous
courses. He took you out of the flat dull text book world
and into the three dimensional world of living economics
and economists; his enthusiasm over the latest article
to appear in the *Review of Economic Studies* on the elasticity of substitution was real and carching. In the last
anaysis, the poor students were the ones who were critical.
The good ones--and in the long perspective isn't it they

who primarily matter?--found his course the most valuable
of all. I believe it was David McCord Wright who once
summed up the general reaction: a year or two after taking
Schumpeter's course, you began to appreciate what you had
got.

The subject matter of his 1935-36 Ec-11 course was
excellent. It involved readings in Marshall, Wicksell,
Pigou, Böhm-Bawerk, Knight, and Wicksteed. In addition,
much was made of Chamberlin, Robinson, and current
journal articles by Hicks, Harrod, Sraffia, and others.
Such advanced authors as Cournot, Edgeworth, and Hotelling
were at least sampled. The "Cost Controversy" was, understandable for the time, given great weight -- probably
too much weight we would now say. Monopolistic competiton
received a great deal of attention, as one could expect
from the time. The order of topics followed was:
Individual Firm,Industry, Monopolisitic Competation, General
Equilibrium, Marginal Productivity (including capital
theory), Welfare Economics (which he never got to by the
year's end). In awarding final grades. he completely
depreciated the currency by his liberality, as has become legendary.

Curiously enough, he rarely mentioned his own
theories. The nature of entrepreneurship and profits was
discussed; but only once did I hear him discuss the reasons
why the interest rate would be zero in a stationary state,
amd then in an advanced seminar and under heavy pressure
from Paul Sweeny and others.

Although he departed from the practice of his teacher
Böhm-Bawerk, in that he rarely bothered to answer criticisms
alleging the impossibility of a zero rate of interest, he
never abandoned his early views.[3] On the occasion of his
sixtieth *festschrift,* I had occasion to review the various
logical contradictions allegedly involved in his notion of
a zero rate of interest. None of the following stood up
under careful logical analysis: (1) the bizarre notion
that a zero interest rate has the logical implication
that all good must be free; (2) the incorrect belief that
at a zero rate of interest capital will necessarily not
be maintained or replaced; (3) the quaint belief that someone who has *no* intention of ever repaying his debts will
at a zero rate of interest borrow an infinite amount
and squander it on riotous living, but will at a positive
rate of interest borrow none or only a finite amount; (4)
the terror that an asset, such as land, which over perpetual

time will yield a perpetual yield, should, in the absence
of a discount factor, fail to have a finite value something horrendous or absurd, and as of this same mathematical
infinity were necessarily avoided by[4] the usual assumption
of an ever falling rate of interest; (5) the dogmatic
extrapolation of the laws of technology and of tastes so
that the question (of non-vanishing net productivity) is
begged by revealed hypothesis. One may consider attainment of a zero unlikely or even (under likely
empirical assumptions) impossible, but this is no warrant for the still-frequently indictment of deductive
error and logical contradiction.

In his general views on economic theory, he seemed
surprisingly un-Austrian. On the whole, he was much
more Walrasian. He always referred to Léon Walras as
by far the greatest economist of all time.[5] He usually
spoke of Marshall as "Papa Marshall", and although he was
always respectful toward Marshall's worth, he obviously
regarded him as overrated. Edgeworth he thought underrated,[6]
partly because he had written articles rather than books.
As a man, he found Irving Fisher a little comical; as a
scientist, he revered his achievement. This was typical
of Schumpeter; although himself a genius, he paid exuberant
tribute to talent and promise; rather fastidious in his
personal likes and dislikes, he never let these stand in
the way of giving real encouragement to able economists,
whatever the color of their haberdashery.

[1]Aside from the merits of Schumpeter's view, I do not
think we have to invoke old age as an explanation for this
uncharacteristic performance. He loved to oppose the
popular side; and in the Cowles Commission, I respect-
fully suggest, he met a faith not less fervent than his
own, thereby reversing completely his usual motivation.

[2]I am the more emboldened to say it because once when
Taussig was a dinner guest at the Society of Fellows, a
year or two before his death he told me that in his own
opinion his economic theory course had not, since the
time of the First World War, been very good. Caught up
in war-time duties, he felt himself getting out of touch
with developments in economic theory; and being about 60
years old at the war's end, he preferred to throw himself
into International Trade rather than pick up the modern
theoretical developments.

[3]See Professor Haberler's essay below.--Ed

[4]A concrete case will illustrate the point. Suppose total labor and land are fixed and inventions cease so that the interest rate is determined by the "net productivity of capital" as given by the marginal-productivity partial derivative of a Cobb-Douglas production function with exponents .75 for labor, .13 for land, and .12 for capital. If such a society always accumulates 15 per cent of its income, the interest rate will fall toward zero but never reach it. Nonethless, if we evaluate the requisite integrals, we find that under conditions of certainty any dollar or perpetual income (such as a consol or land) will in this case have *infinite* present discounted value. Shall we hurriedly shoot the mathematician lest the world come to an end? Or infer that the rate of possible accumulation must be limited relative to technology so as to avoid the infinity?

[5]By virtue of Walras' vision of general equilibrium. In In the next rank, Schumpeter placed Smith, Cournot, and (strangely) Quesnay. As a scholarly personality, Kurt Wicksell was his ideal.

[6]He used to tell of visiting Edgeworth in the *ante bellum* Edwardian days and having rock pheasant and champagne at breakfast in All Souls, which was adequate recompense for the dullness of Edgeworth's lectures. At about the same time, Schumpeter, in the full flower of his brilliant youth, visited Marshall only to be advised not to continue work in economic theory! On another pilgrimage, he asked Mrs. Foxwell whether her "father" was at home. Later when he asked to see the famous library, Foxwell, grieving over his recent necessitous sale of it, merely pointed sadly to his two young children and the shoes on their feet.

The Review of Economics and Statistics, Vol. 33, (1951): 98-103

"Address to the Entering Class at Harvard College, 1972,"
D.P. Moynihan (1973)*

It is an honor to be a member of the Freshman class of
Harvard College, and not less a distinction to be asked to
present one of the first of the many lectures that now await
you. This is a venerable form of instruction and not, perhaps,
the most efficient; but it is the way we do things here.

To be sure, other forms of instruction await you also:
seminars, laboratories, above all, libraries; but lectures remain our preeminent mode of presenting ideas. They will matter
most to you if you come with some information of your own on
the subject to be presented so that the occasion becomes in
effect an exchange: you not only listen, but respond.

Let me, then, present my first thought for the evening,
which is that this rarely happens. As you know, I asked that
in preparation for this lecture you each read Joseph A. Schumpeter's *Capitalism, Socialism, and Democracy*, and Lionel Trilling's *The Middle of the Journey*. I will estimate that one in
ten of you has done this and that another tenth, wishing it
had, imagines it has.

A show of hands indicates that the hypothesis is confirmed.

Now to the main work of the evening. Yom Kippur was over
at sundown. It is in this spirit that I address you. The sins
of the past are shrived, and we begin anew. And yet the past
remains with us as knowledge of the future. There will be
sins enough to atone for when the cycle comes round once more.
There is not much in human experience that any longer appears
to us as uniquely human. Those of you going into science will
spend a good share of your time extrapolating the behavior of
rats into that of people. Still, a sense of what will come,
especially that death will come, would seem to be singular in
our species.

A sense of what is coming is the central experience to be
had from both Schumpeter's and Trilling's books. There is a
temptation to describe this as an intellectual experience in

the case of the economics text, and an aesthetic one in the
case of the novel; but these are uncertain categories. It is
enough to see that here are two modes of anticipation, each
analytic, each rigorous, each having a claim to being considered a possible instance of social theory with true predictive qualities. Schumpeter, the economist, is absorbed with
the complex impact of technology on thought; Trilling's concerns move in rather the opposite direction, as might be expected of a literary critic. But in the end, each evolves a
singular vision that partakes of many disciplines. Your education at Harvard, as at any such institution, will divide up
intellectual life and lead you to assume that there are profoundly different ways of knowing, and perhaps there are; and
yet I would not settle too quickly into that convention.

I have asked you to read Schumpeter and Trilling because
you are living in the future about which they wrote. No two
men, to my thinking, have done this so well as they; but you
need not share this view in order to agree that they did what
they set out to do well enough for the two books to be taken
as benchmarks respecting a past which has flowed into the
present.

Each book is set in the late 1930s in America. (If we
are to discuss them together, we will find ourselves alternat-
ing between the vocabularies of science and of literature,
doing some injustice to both. But this we can claim to be a
cost others have imposed on us; alternatively, a dilemma others
have devised for us.) The 1930s is a period that matters to
you, for it was the time when most of your senior professors
were taught. (I think of the "period" as lasting into the
mid-1950s.) It was the time in which your parents were taught,
and so it has already pressed itself heavily upon you. But
now you will encounter it as the climate in which the formative intellectual experiences of your college teachers took
place, unavoidably influencing your own formation.

The fascination of that time goes beyond the intergenera-
tional tie, for it was a period that was formative to the
American political culture generally and reverberates down to
this moment in much the manner that the 1920s has attained to
the affective culture. Each era seems to go on repeating itself in however attenuated a manner. Any why ought they not?
Those are the two decades in which the present world took
shape.

The world into which Joseph Schumpeter was born ended
just as those decades began. There is a sense of the *douceur*

de vivre of the Austro-Hungarian Empire that lent its own dimension to his detachment as a social scientist from the events
and tendencies about which he later wrote. He made his way by
many stages to Harvard and made a large impression when he
finally arrived. I never knew him, but hanging about Cambridge
on the G.I. Bill during the 1940s it was impossible not to
know of him. It was said he would tell his classes that as
a young man he had resolved to become three things: the world's
greatest economist, the world's greatest lover, and the world's
greatest horseman; but that as advancing age constricted the
horizons of possibility, he was learning to accept the fact
that he would not achieve his third ambition.

And yet he had: for our purposes. His book, which he
described as "an effort to weld into a readable form the bulk
of almost forty years' thought, observation, and research on
the subject of socialism," is a work of analysis and passion
on a level few can sustain; but it is more than that. It is
the work of a man who has been around horses. I do not know
this actually to have been true, but his stepfather is described in the *Encyclopedia of the Social Sciences* as a "high-
ranking officer in the Austro-Hungarian Empire," and it ought
to have been true. Schumpeter was not of the view that horses
or riders are all alike. Dams counted and sires counted,
training and daring counted, resolution counted, and a tenth
of a second could make all the difference in life. How to explain the beginnings of capitalism? A simple matter for
Schumpeter: the "Supernormal intelligence and energy" of the
early entrepreneurs brought success in nine cases out of ten.
How to account for the appeal of socialism? Again, simple.
Socialism, in scientistic guise, formulated "with unsurpassed
force that feeling of being thwarted and ill-treated which is
the auto-therapeutic attitude of the unsuccessful many. . . ."

(I would assume that many of you take exception to such
views, and you have every right to do so. But if you think
Schumpeter wholly wrong in such matters, let me offer you at
the outset what could prove the best advice you will ever get
at Harvard College. Stay away from race tracks.)

Schumpeter wrote both to praise Marx *and* to bury him.
His purpose was to test the scientific validity of the great
Marxist thesis which has been so central to twentieth-century
politics and thought. He praised Marx the Sociologist and
Marx the Economist. Even so, he thought the Marxian scenario
altogether wrong. Capitalism as the organizing principle of
the economy and the underlying structure of the culture would
not go through the stages Marx had predicted. There would be

no immiserization of the masses, no wars of colonial expansion. And yet--and here we see the daring of the man, the exhuberant intellectual elegance--he concluded that Marx was right about what in the end would happen, was indeed right "that a socialist society will inevitably emerge from an equally inevitable decomposition of capitalist society." This was his "paradoxical conclusion"--that "capitalism is being killed by its achievements."

He saw this as resulting from the interaction of two phenomena. First, the very success of capitalism would lessen the importance of the entrepreneur and lessen the perceived value of the one thing capitalism indubitably creates, which is material wealth. Those men of "supernormal intelligence and energy" would gradually be replaced by managers of only marginally greater competence than the managed. One recalls Herman Wouk's description of the Navy in World War II: A system devised by geniuses to be run by morons. Further, as any good economist ought to have been able to foresee, there would come a period of diminishing utility of increased consumption *or* increased production. An economist would know this: a Schumpeter would know also that the phenomenon would first appear in the most affluent classes, thereby acquiring social prestige. Nowhere does he say so, but I choose to be confident that he quite foresaw the day when the children of the rich would go about in ragged dungarees and that on ceremonial occasions college students would bury automobiles, combining in a sense the aristocratical ways of the court of Marie Antoinette and the Kwakiutl Indians.

(Allow me, parenthetically, to note that Schumpeter was thinking in a very long time perspective. At the time he wrote it had been roughly two centuries from the period when capitalism had got going; it could well be, he judged, two centuries more before it had quite disappeared. My own estimate would be a half century from now, in part because the rate of increase in wealth has quite surpassed even Schumpeter's forecast; and he was most bullish for his time.)

The second of Schumpeter's master propositions is more subtle, and for me more difficult to follow. In essence he states that capitalism is rationalism. It began by challenging the right of kings and barons and popes and bishops to exist: it would end by challenging its *own* right. I follow *this*, and I can see how the defense would be difficult. But Schumpeter goes further. He suggests that the capitalist assault on itself will come not just from a habit of mind, a tradition of contentiousness and innovation, but also from far more ominous impulses.

He seems to argue that there is an innate contrariness in
human nature--an irrational destructiveness--which far from
being quelled by rationalist conditioning, merely uses it as
the most effective possible device by which to attain irrational ends. Here is the key passage.

> It is an error to believe that political attack
> arises primarily from grievance and that it can be
> turned by justification. Political criticism can-
> not be met effectively by rational argument. From
> the fact that the criticism of the capitalist order
> proceeds from a critical attitude of mind, i.e.,
> from an attitude which spurns allegiance to extra-
> rational values, it does not follow that rational
> refutation will be accepted. Such refutation may
> tear the rational garb of attack but can never
> reach the extrarational driving power that always
> lurks behind it. Capitalist rationality does not
> do away with sub- or super-rational impulses. It
> merely makes them get out of hand by removing the
> restraint of sacred or semisacred tradition. In
> a civilization that lacks the means and even the
> will to discipline and to guide them, they will
> revolt. And once they revolt it matters little
> that, in a rationalist culture, their manifesta-
> tions will in general be rationalized somehow.
> Just as the call for utilitarian credentials has
> never been addressed to kings, lords, and popes
> in a judicial frame of mind that would accept the
> possibility of a satisfactory answer, so capitalism
> stands its trial before judges who have the sen-
> tence of death in their pockets. They are going
> to pass it, whatever the defense they may hear;
> the only success victorious defense can possibly
> produce is a change in the indictment. Utili-
> tarian reason is in any case weak as a prime
> mover of group action. In no case is it a match
> for the extrarational determinants of conduct.

Now I do not fully understand this. Why is it that "Capitalist rationality does not do away with sub- or super-
rational impulses"? Rather, what is the nature of these impulses, and what is the evidence for them? Hearsay, mostly,
albeit impressive hearsay. One thinks of Robert Warshow's
comment on the nihilism of the Marx Brothers, men who "spit
on culture." They are popular among middle-class intellec-

tuals, he writes, "because they express a blind and destruc-
tive disgust with society that the responsible man is com-
pelled to suppress in himself."* This was written more than
a quarter century ago, but is surely as true of the present.
Hardly a day goes by when one or another Marx Brothers movie
is not being shown somewhere within a quarter mile of Harvard
Square. And this curious mixture was part also of the Greek
experience. So there it is: something we see happening, even
if such as I do not fully comprehend it.

I have suggested that any good man might have made these
points. Schumpeter's glory lies in having identified the peculiar agent which capitalism would create for its own destruction, which is to say the intellectuals. (Of which, one
could add, Marx himself was an exemplar; indeed, in the patronage of the manufacturer Engels, a prototype.) Any why
would it do this? Here, there is just the least touch of
melancholy in a not especially sentimental man. Capitalism
would create a vast intellectual class because it believed in
such a class, because it derived its own vitality from intellectual processes. And so capitalism would protect intellectuals, even as they shrieked of oppression and hurled anathe-
mas at their protectors: "any attack on the intellectuals must
run up against the private fortresses of bourgeois business
which . . . will shelter the quarry." Capitalism, alone of
social systems, will subsidize and reward its mortal enemies:
bound by its own rationale to do so. Its morale will begin to
be affected.

Perhaps the most striking feature of the picture
is the extent to which the bourgeoisie, besides
educating its own enemies, allows itself to be educated by them. It absorbs the slogans of current
radicalism and seems quite willing to undergo a
process of conversion to a creed hostile to its
very existence.

Schumpeter asked no quarter of life, and yet one is glad somehow that he died in 1950 and was not on hand two decades later
when one of Harvard's most distinguished officers, an avowed
and courageous opponent of the Vietnam war, collapsed in the
midst of a particularly brutal political demonstration just
as some scion of the upper middle class was describing him on
the bullhorn as a "running dog of imperialism."

*Robert Warshow, *The Immediate Experience* (New York, Doubleday
& Co.), 1962, p. 50.

I speak of melancholy because Schumpeter had a sense of
what was being lost: first language, then something akin to
liberty, for the collectivist society would ineluctably narrow
the limits of what is permitted and what is encouraged.

> Radicals may insist that the masses are crying
> for salvation from intolerable sufferings and
> rattling their chains in darkness, and despair,
> but of course there never was so much personal
> freedom of mind and body *for all*, never so much
> readiness to bear with and even to finance the
> mortal enemies of the leading class, never so
> much active sympathy with real and faked suffer-
> ings, never so much readiness to accept burdens,
> as there is in modern capitalist society; and
> whatever democracy there was, outside of peasant
> communities, developed historically in the wake
> of both modern and ancient capitalism.

To this assertion he adds an equally apt footnote:

> Even Marx, in whose time indictments of this
> kind were not anything like as absurd as they
> are today, evidently thought it desirable to
> strengthen his case by dwelling on conditions
> that even then were either past or visibly
> passing.

Schumpeter defined socialism as "conquest of private industry and trade by the state." He did not consider that this
would have to be a precipitous sequence, nor yet that there
need be a totalitarian outcome. He had no illusions about
capitalism: "the civilization of inequality and of the family
fortune." And yet this new State: how different a regime it
would be from that of *Die Fledermaus* where Eisenstein, having
insulted a government official, must go to jail for eight
days, but can put it off just long enough to attend Prince
Orlofsky's ball.

A quarter century later there are some things Schumpeter
appears to have got wrong, but, in the main, events have gone
precisely as he foresaw. The power of private enterprise remains formidable but its morale and its reputation, in places
where it matters, are quite shattered. The conquest of the
private sector by the public proceeds apace, abetted by the
extraordinary dynamic of inflation, a point Schumpeter made
in his address "The March into Socialism," delivered at the
end of 1949 just eight days before his death. Wage and price

controls, he forecast, would return and would "play an important part in the eventual conquest of the private-enterprise
system by the bureaucracy."

*Essays on the Practice of Government, Random House, (1973):
405-419*

"Schumpeter," Peter F. Drucker (1983)*

The two greatest economists of this century, Joseph A.
Schumpeter and John Maynard Keynes, were born, only a few
months apart, a hundred years ago: Schumpeter on Feb. 8, 1883
in a provincial Austrian town, Keynes on June 5, 1883 in Cambridge, England. (And they died only four years apart--Schum-
peter in Connecticut on Jan. 8, 1950, Keynes in southern England on Apr. 21, 1946.) The centenary of Keynes' birth is
being celebrated with a host of books, articles, conferences
and speeches. If the centenary of Schumpeter's birth were
noticed at all, it would be in a small doctoral seminar. And
yet it is becoming increasingly clear that it is Schumpeter
who will shape the thinking and inform the questions on economic theory and economic policy for the rest of this century, if
not for the next 30 or 50 years.

The two men were not antagonists. Both challenged long-
standing assumptions. The opponents of Keynes were the very
"Austrians" Schumpeter himself had broken away from as a student, the neoclassical economists of the Austrian School. And
while Schumpeter considered all of Keynes' answers wrong, or
at least misleading, he was a sympathetic critic. Indeed, it
was Schumpeter who established Keynes in America. When Keynes'
General Theory came out, Schumpeter, by then the senior member
of the Harvard economics faculty, told his students to read
the book and told them also that Keynes' work had totally
superseded his own earlier writings on money.

Keynes, in turn, considered Schumpeter one of the few
contemporary economists worthy of his respect. In his lectures he again and again referred to the works Schumpeter had
published during World War I, and especially to Schumpeter's
essay on the Rechenpfennige (i.e., money of account) as the
initial stimulus for his own thoughts on money. Keynes' most
successful policy initiative, the proposal that Britain and
the U.S. finance World War II by taxes rather than by borrowing, came directly out of Schumpeter's 1918 warning of the
disastrous consequences of the debt financing of World War I.

Schumpeter and Keynes are often contrasted politically, with Schumpeter being portrayed as the "conservative" and Keynes as the "radical." The opposite is more nearly right. Politically Keynes' views were quite similar to what we now call "neoconservative." His theory had its origins in his passionate attachment to the free market and in his desire to keep politicians and governments out of it. Schumpeter, by contrast, had serious doubts about the free market. He thought that an "intelligent monopoly"--had a great deal to recommend itself. It could afford to take the long view instead of being driven from transaction to transaction by short-term expediency. His closest friend for many years was the most radical and most doctrinaire of Europe's left-wing socialists, the Austrian Otto Bauer, who, though staunchly anticommunist, was even more anticapitalist. And Schumpeter, while never even close to being a socialist himself, served during 1919 as minister of finance in Austria's only socialist government between the wars. Schumpeter always maintained that Marx had been dead wrong in every one of his answers. But he still considered himself a son of Marx and held him in greater esteem than any other economist. At least, so he argued, Marx asked the right questions--and to Schumpeter questions were always more important than answers.

The differences between Schumpeter and Keynes go much deeper than economic theorems or political views. The two saw a different economic reality, were concerned with different problems and defined "economics" quite differently. These differences are highly important to an understanding of today's economic world. ...

Classical economics considered innovation to be outside the system, as Keynes did, too. Innovation belonged in the category of "outside catastrophes" like earthquakes, climate or war, which, everybody knew, have profound influence on the economy but are not part of economics. Schumpeter insisted that, on the contrary, innovation--that is, entrepreneurship that moves resources from old and obsolescent to new and more productive employments--is the very essence of economics and most certainly of a modern economy.

He derived this notion, as he was the first to admit, from Marx. But he used it to disprove Marx. Schumpeter's *Economic Development* does what neither the classical economists nor Marx nor Keynes was able to do: It makes profit fulfill an economic function. In the economy of change and innovation, profit, in contrast to Marx, is not a *Mehrwert*, a "surplus value" stolen from the workers. On the contrary, it

is the only source of jobs for workers and of labor income.
The theory of economic development shows that no one except
the innovator makes a genuine "profit," and the innovator's
profit is always quite short-lived. But innovation in Schumpeter's famous phrase is also "creative destruction." It makes
obsolete yesterday's capital equipment and capital investment.
The more an economy progresses, the more capital formation will
it therefore need. Thus what the classical economist--or the
accountant or the stock exchange--considers "profit" is a genuine cost, the cost of staying in business, the cost of a future in which nothing is predictable except that today's profitable business will become tomorrow's white elephant. Thus,
capital formation and productivity are needed to maintain the
wealth-producing capacity of the economy and, above all, to
maintain today's jobs and to create tomorrow's jobs.

Schumpeter's "innovator" with his "creative destruction"
is the only theory so far to explain why there is something we
call "profit." The classical economists very well knew that
their theory did not give any rationale for profit. Indeed,
in the equilibrium economics of a closed economic system there
is no place for profit, no justification for it, no explanation
of it. If profit is, however, a genuine cost, and especially
if profit is the only way to maintain jobs and to create new
ones, then "capitalism" becomes again a moral system.

Morality and profits. The classical economists had
pointed out that profit is needed as the incentive for the
risk taker. But is this not really a bribe and thus impossible to justify morally? This dilemma had driven the most
brilliant of 19th-century economists, John Stuart Mill, to
embrace socialism in his later years. It had made it easy for
Marx to fuse dispassionate analysis of the "system" with the
moral revulsion of an Old Testament prophet against the "ex-
ploiters." The weakness on moral grounds of the profit incentive enabled Marx at once to condemn the "capitalist" as
wicked and immoral, and assert "scientifically" that he serves
no function and that his speedy demise is "inevitable." As
soon, however, as one shifts from the axiom of an unchanging,
self-contained, closed economy to Schumpeter's dynamic, growing, moving, changing economy, what is called "profit" is no
longer immoral. It becomes a moral imperative. Indeed, the
question then is no longer the question that agitated the
classicists and still agitated Keynes: How can the economy be
structured to minimize the bribe of the functionless surplus
called "profit" that has to be handed over to the "capitalist"
to keep the economy going? The question in Schumpeter's economics is always: Is there sufficient profit? Is there ade-

quate capital formation to provide for the costs of the future, the costs of staying in business, the costs of "creative destruction"?

This alone makes Schumpeter's economic model the only one that can serve as the starting point for the economic policies we need. Clearly the Keynesian--or classicist--treatment of innovation as being "outside" and in fact peripheral to the economy and with minimum impact on it, can no longer be maintained (if it ever could be). The basic question of economic theory and economic policy, especially in highly developed countries, is clearly: How can capital formation and productivity be maintained so that rapid technological change as well as employment can be sustained? What is the minimum profit needed to defray the costs of the future? What is the minimum profit needed, above all, to maintain jobs and to create new ones?

Schumpeter gave no answer--he did not much believe in answers. But 70 years ago, as a very young man, he asked what is clearly going to be the central question of economic theory and economic policy in the years to come.

And then, during World War I, Schumpeter realized, long before anyone else--and a good ten years before Keynes did-- that economic reality was changing. He realized that World War I had brought about the monetarization of the economies of all belligerents. Country after country, including his own still fairly backward Austria-Hungary, had succeeded during the war in mobilizing the entire liquid wealth of the community, partly through taxation, but mainly through borrowing. Money and credit, rather than goods and services, had become the "real economy."

In a brilliant essay published in a German economic journal in July 1918--when the world Schumpeter had grown up in and had known was crashing down around his ears--he argued that, from now on, money and credit would be the lever of control. What he argued was that neither supply of goods, as the classicists had argued, nor demand for goods, as some of the earlier dissenters had maintained, was going to be controlling anymore. Monetary factors--deficits, money, credit, taxes-- were going to be the determinants of economic activity and of the allocation of resources.

This is, of course, the same insight on which Keynes later built his *General Theory*. But Schumpeter's conclusions were radically different from those Keynes reached. Keynes came to the conclusion that the emergence of the "symbol economy" of money and credit made possible the "economist-king," the scientific economist, who, by playing on a few simple monetary keys--government spending, the interest rate, the volume of credit or the amount of money in circulation--would maintain permanent equilibrium with full employment, prosperity and stability. But Schumpeter's conclusion was that the emergence of the "symbol economy" as the dominant economy opened the door to tyranny and, in fact, invited tyranny. That the economist now proclaimed himself infallible, he considered pure hubris. But, above all, he saw that it was not going to be economists who would exercise the power, but politicians and generals.

And then, in the same year, just before World War I ended, Schumpeter published *The Tax State* ("The Fiscal State" would be a better translation). Again, the insight is the same Keynes reached 15 years later (and, as he often acknowledged, thanks to Schumpeter): The modern state, through the mechanisms of taxation and borrowing, has acquired the power to shift income and, through "transfer payments," to control the distribution of the national product. To Keynes this power was a magic want to achieve both social justice and economic progress, and both economic stability and fiscal responsibility, because it eliminated all economic safeguards against inflation. In the past the inability of the state to tax more than a very small proportion of the gross national product, or to borrow more than a very small part of the country's wealth, had made inflation self-limiting. Now the only safeguard against inflation would be political, that is, self-discipline. And Schumpeter was not very sanguine about the politician's capacity for self-discipline.

Schumpeter's work as an economist after World War I is of great importance to economic theory. He became one of the fathers of business cycle theory.

But Schumpeter's real contribution during the 32 years between the end of World War I and his death in 1950 was as a political economist. In 1942, when everyone was scared of a worldwide deflationary depression, Schumpeter published his best-known book, *Capitalism, Socialism and Democracy*, still, and deservedly, read widely. In this book he argued that capitalism would be destroyed by its own success. This would breed what we would now call the "new class": bureaucrats, intellectuals, professors, lawyers, journalists, all of them beneficiaries of capitalism's economic fruits and, in fact, parasitical on them, and yet all of them opposed to the ethos

of wealth production, of saving and of allocating resources
to economic productivity. The 40 years since this book appeared have surely proved Schumpeter to be a major prophet.

And then he proceeded to argue that capitalism would be
destroyed by the very democracy it had helped create and made
possible. For in a democracy, to be popular, government would
increasingly become the "tax state," would increasingly shift
income from producer to nonproducer, would increasingly move
income from where it would be saved and become capital for
tomorrow to where it would be consumed. Government in a democracy would thus be under increasing inflationary pressure.
Eventually, he prophesied, inflation would destroy both democracy and capitalism.

When he wrote this in 1942, almost everybody laughed.
Nothing seemed less likely than an inflation based on economic
success. Now, 40 years later, this has emerged as the central
problem of democracy and of a free-market economy alike, just
as Schumpeter had prophesied.

The Keynesians in the Forties ushered in their "promised
land," in which the economist-king would guarantee the perfect
equilibrium of an eternally stable economy through control of
money, credit, spending and taxes. Schumpeter, however, increasingly concerned himself with the question of how the
public sector could be controlled and limited so as to maintain political freedom and an economy capable of performance,
growth and change. When death overtook him at his desk, he
was revising the presidential address he had given to the
American Economic Association only a few days earlier. The
last sentence he wrote was: "The stagnationists are wrong in
their diagnosis of the reason the capitalist process should
stagnate; they may still turn out to be right in their prog-
nosis that it will stagnate--with sufficient help from the
public sector."

Keynes' best-known saying is surely, "In the long run we
are all dead." This is one of the most fatuous remarks ever
made. Of course, in the long run we are all dead. But Keynes
in a wiser moment remarked that the deeds of today's politicians are usually based on the theorems of long-dead economists. And it is a total fallacy that, as Keynes implies,
optimizing the short term creates the right long-term future.
Keynes is in large measure responsible for the extreme short-
term focus of modern politics, of modern economics and modern
business--the short-term focus that is now, with considerable
justice, considered a major weakness of American policymakers,

both in government and in business.

Schumpeter also knew that policies have to fit the short
term. He learned this lesson the hard way--as minister of
finance in the newly formed Austrian republic in which he,
totally unsuccessful, tried to stop inflation before it got
out of hand. He knew that he had failed because his measures
were not acceptable in the short term--the very measures that,
two years later, a noneconomist, a politician and professor
of moral theology did apply to stop the inflation, but only
after it had all but destroyed Austria's economy and middle
class.

But Schumpeter also knew that today's short-term measures
have long-term impacts. They irrevocably make the future.
Not to think through the futurity of short-term decisions and
their impact long after "we are all dead" is irresponsible.
It also leads to the wrong decisions. It is this constant
emphasis in Schumpeter on thinking through the long-term consequences of the expedient, the popular, the clever and the
brilliant, that makes him a great economist and the appropriate guide for today, when short-run, clever, brilliant
economics--and short-run, clever, brilliant politics--have
become bankrupt.

In some ways, Keynes and Schumpeter replayed the best-
known confrontation of philosophers in the Western tradition--
the Platonic dialog between Parmenides, the brilliant, clever,
irresistible sophist, and the slow-moving and ugly, but wise,
Socrates. No one in the interwar years was more brilliant,
more clever than Keynes. Schumpeter, by contrast, appeared
pedestrian--but he had wisdom. Cleverness carries the day.
But wisdom endureth.

*Keynes and Schumpeter, Forbes, (May 23, 1983): 124, 125, 126,
127-128*

The Road to Serfdom
by
Friederich A. Hayek

REVIEW: Charles E. Merriam (1944)*

This volume is characterized by the distinguished author
in his Preface as a "political book" and as a variation from
the "more strictly academic work" to which he is accustomed
and inclined. Such a study is necessitated, he explains, by
the alarming extent to which public opinion in our day is
guided by "amateurs and cranks," by people with an ax to grind
or a panacea to present. The sum and substance of the essay
is defense of what the writer terms "economic liberalism."
The author vigorously denounces any and all forms of planning,
expresses his reservations about mass democracy, and holds as
suspect "conscious social control."

Planning is anathema to Dr. Hayek and is consigned to the
lower limbo, without benefit of clergy. The author blandly
brushes aside all the many forms of city planning, state planning, regional planning, national planning, with one broad
sweep of his pen. Since the socialists have employed the term
"planning," it must be placed on the black list. All planning,
as he sees it, is essentially "economic planning" of a totalitarian type, and none other is admissible, he concludes. That
there are scores of planning agencies actively at work in England and the United States does not disturb the author in the
least. In this adventure in politics he waves them all aside
and substitutes his own terminology. But this is not argument, academic or nonacademic. It is, indeed, a piece of
arrogance from the point of view of the very large body of
planners, both public and private, who have for a long time
used the word "planning" in quite a different context and
meaning. When Hayek says that this is "what our planners demand," the student of planning may merely smile and inquire
by what authority the author twists accepted terminology. On
what meat does this our Caesar feed in his "political book,"
derived from certain ultimate values"? If he wishes to discuss economic planning, the world is wide and the way is open,
but why confuse the terms widely accepted by both public and

private agencies in great sections of the modern world?

Nor is there any security in democratic planning as seen
by Hayek. In any case, we must not make a "fetish of democracy." In his chapter on "Why the Worst Get on Top," Hayek
states clearly his attitude as to mass rule. In a democracy
the common good apparently can never be the work of persons
of "education and intelligence" but only of a mass of people
from the "regions of lower moral and intellectual standards
where the more primitive and 'common' instincts prevail" (p.
138). Such persons are at the same time "docile and gullible"
and agree most readily upon a negative program, such as hatred
of the enemy or envy of those better off. When the writer in-
quires, "Is there a popular writer or speaker who dares to
suggest to the masses that they might have to make sacrifices
of their material prospects for the enhancement of an ideal
end?" (p. 214), one wonders in what world Mr. Hayek is living
that he has not heard of the incredible sacrifices now offered
for human freedom, for a free way of life.

The only home of freedom in the Hayek philosophy is the
open market place. Unmindful for the moment of monopolies,
cartels, depressions, economic concentrations, and exploita-
tions, he finds the market the source from which all blessings
flow. If evils develop in the market, it is because the market
is not working well.

Economic power, he asserts, is "never exclusive or complete power, never power over the whole life of a person" (p.
146), whereas political power is or tends to be essentially
complete--totalitarian. The fact that power over an individual's employment, wages, prices, and living and working conditions reduces living often to a narrow scope of freedom apparently does not disturb Dr. Hayek.

His root error lies, of course, in the assumption that
the essence of the political is violence, while that of the
economic is freedom of choice. He further errs in alleging
that economic power is associated with decentralization and
political power with centralization and unity. It does not
occur to him that organization and centralization may under
certain conditions be protections and guaranties of freedom
as well as the contrary under other conditions. It is not the
principle of unity or the existence of organization that is
per se dangerous to human freedom. There are petty one-man
absolutisms scattered over human history, some of them land-
lords and some war lords, and some czars of industry, alike
in public and private government.

In his discussion of "Planning and the Rule of Law," the
author is ill at ease, particularly in dealing with administration and notably in the field of administrative management
and discretion. The muddled passages in which administration
is considered indicate little knowledge of either the theory
or the practice of administration (pp. 76-77 in particular).
It is, of course, impossible for a government to foresee precisely all the detailed consequences of its rules, and consequently the administrator must be given a degree of latitude.
But this field is not the domain of the arbitrary and unreasonable, as Hayek seems to think, but an area of administrative discretion, reason, judgment. Sound administration does
not interfere with the "Rule of Law" but is supplementary to
and co-ordinate with reasonableness and justice. That administrative problems are such as we "decide by tossing a coin"
(p. 76) is a fantastic conception of administration corresponding to nothing in public or private administration, scarcely to be taken seriously.

But the fundamental object of the author's distrust is
what he terms "conscious social control"--another anathema in
his creed. As elsewhere stated, Hayek declares "the fact that
no single mind can know more than a fraction of what is known
to all individual minds limits the extent to which conscious
direction can improve upon the results of unconscious social
processes" (*Economica*, XI, 37). If nothing can be done unless
and until someone knows all that might be known, the conclusion
is anarchistic, for nothing could ever be done in government
or in economics or in human relations.

Yet now comes the conclusion that the inherent virtues of
the market place do not preclude the possibility of political
action to preserve its life and spirit. Many forms of regulation are admissible if they are not christened "conscious
social control" or "planning." For example, the use of "poi-
sonious substances" in industry may be regulated by law; working hours and sanitary arrangements may be set by law. Sign-
posts on the road may safely be provided, since they cannot
well be paid for by the individual user. Fraud and deception
may be suppressed without impending tyranny--and without administrative management. Even more, there may be established
minima of food, shelter, clothing, health, capacity to work,
through schemes of social insurance, if not called plans. The
government may properly aid in struggling with an obstinate
business business cycle, perhaps through monetary policy. What
we cannot plan (*sic*) for . . . . is protection against diminu-
tions of income. But even at this point it would be permissible for the state to provide some voluntary labor service on

military lines with guaranteed work and minimum income. Indeed, Hayek finally says that "wherever communal action can mitigate disasters against which the individual can neither attempt to guard himself nor make provision for the consequences, such communal action should undoubtedly be taken" (p. 121). But, of course, this must not be called "planning."

We know by observation and reflection that the ends of government are external security, order, justice, welfare, freedom. For the attainment of these ends men are planning and will continue to plan. For out of skillful planning will come human freedom in larger measure, the growth of the human personality, the expansion of the creative possibilities of mankind. Conscious creative evolution—mastery rather than drift—marks the way to higher levels and higher orders of human life. The road to serfdom is not planning but drift, unwillingness to change, incapacity for adaptation to new possibilities of human emancipation, worship of the status quo.

American Journal of Sociology 50, (November 1944): 233-235

REVIEW: Henry Hazlitt (1944)*

In "The Road to Serfdom" Friedrich A. Hayek has written one of the most important books of our generation. It restates for our time the issue between liberty and authority with the power and rigor of reasoning that John Stuart Mill stated the issue for his own generation in his great essay, "On Liberty." It throws a brilliant light along the direction in which the world has been heading, first slowly, but now at an accelerative rate, for the last half-century. It is an arresting call to all well-intentioned planners and socialists, to all those who are sincere democrats and liberals at heart, to stop, look and listen.

Mr. Hayek, an internationally known economist, is a native of Austria. He was director of the Austrian Institute for Economic Research and lecturer in economics at the University of Vienna during the years in which Hitler was building up his instruments to seize power. He has lived in England since 1931, however, when be became Professor of Economic Science at the University of London. In 1938 he became a British citizen.

This experience has given him a type of insight not granted to the usual American or English economist or student of
political affairs. "The following pages," as he writes, "are
the product of an experience as near as possible to twice living through the same period. *** When one hears for a second
time opinions expressed or measures advocated which one has
first met twenty or twenty-five years ago, they assume a new
meaning as symptoms of a definite trend. They suggest, if not
the necessity, at least the probability, that developments will
take a similar course. It is necessary now to state the un-
palatable truth that it is Germany whose fate we are in some
danger of repeating."

But this danger, as Mr. Hayek sees it, comes from a direction far different from the one habitually suspected by the
great bulk of "liberal" and "progressive" Americans and En-
glishment. Whenever the latter think of the danger of fascism
they always see it as coming from the conservatives. Whenever
they write novels about the rise of an American dictator they
always make him (in spite of our most outstanding native example of the type, Huey "Share-the-Wealth" Long), the darling
of the chambers of commerce. But it is no accident, Mr. Hayek
points out, that in Europe so many of the leading Fascist
leaders from Mussolini downward (and not excluding Laval and
Quisling) began as Socialists before they ended as Fascists
or Nazis. As late as February, 1941, Hitler found it expedient
to declare that "basically National Socialism and Marxism are
the same."

Mr. Hayek's central contention, in brief, is that fascism,
and what the Germans correctly call National Socialism, are
the end products not of "nineteenth-century liberalism" or of
individualism, which represent their opposites, but of the
growth of State control and State power, of national "planning"
and of socialism.

Students of the currents of ideas [he writes] can hardly
fail to see that there is more than a superficial similarity
between the trend of thought in Germany during and after the
last war and the present current of ideas in the democracies.
There exists now in these countries certainly the same determination that the organization of the nation which has been
achieved for purposes of defense shall be retained for the
purposes of creation. There is the same contempt for nineteenth-century liberalism, the same spurious "realism" and
even cynicism, the same fatalistic acceptance of "inevitable
trends." And at least nine out of every ten of the lessons
which our most vociferous reformers are so anxious we should

learn from the last war and which have done much to produce
the Nazi system. *** Although ones does not like to be reminded, it is not so many years since the Socialist policy of
that country was generally held up by progressives as an example to be imitated, just as in more recent years Sweden has
been the model country to which progressive eyes were directed.

The supreme tragedy is still not seen that in Germany it
was largely people of good-will, men who were admired and held
up as models in the democratic countries, who prepared the way
for, if they did not actually create, the forces which now
stand for everything they detest. Few are ready to recognize
that the rise of fascism and nazism was not a reaction against
the Socialist trends of the preceding period but a necessary
outcome of those tendencies. This is a truth which most people
were unwilling to see even when the similarities of many of
the repellent features of the internal regimes in communist
Russia and National Socialist Germany were widely recognized.
As a result many who think themselves infinitely superior to
the aberrations of nazism, and sincerely hate all its mani-
festations, work at the same time for ideals whose realization
would lead straight to the abhorred tyranny.

Mr. Hayek's book is so compactly written that it is impossible adequately to summarize the closely woven argument
by which he seeks to prove this thesis. He shows how the very
success of liberalism in the nineteenth century became the
cause of its decline. The miracles of production and social
advance to which it led caused the world to take this enormous
progress for granted, to forget the policy of freedom on which
it rested, and to become impatient because the unprecedented
pace of progress was not still greater. Although we had been
warned by some of the greatest political thinkers of the nineteenth century, by de Tocqueville and Lord Acton, that socialism means slavery, we have so completely forgotten the warning that, even when this new form of slavery rises before our
eyes, it scarcely occurs to us that the two things may be
connected.

Mr. Hayek points out how England, the great center from
which for more than two hundred years the world had been taking its political and economic ideas, became at about 1870
the importer of its political and economic ideas from Germany.
He tries to point out how socialism by its very nature must
be anti-liberal and anti-democratic, and how national "planning" can seem to be successful only as it progressively re-
moves all freedom of choice from the individual. He seeks to
show how the individual must necessarily become enslaved be-

cause, as Leon Trotsky once put it, "in a country where the
sole employer is the State, opposition means death by slow
starvation." He argues that under a collectivist and totalitarian system the worst men get to the top not by some horri-
ble accident, but almost inevitably, because only such men
will have the ruthlessness necessary to carry on a central
plan to its logical conclusion.

Liberal opposition to "national planning" and socialism,
Mr. Hayek insists, must not be confused with a dogmatic *laissez
faire* attitude:

The liberal argument is in favor of making the best possible use of the forces of competition as a means of coordinating human efforts, not an argument for leaving things just
as they are. It is based on the conviction that, where effective competition can be created, it is a better way of guiding
individual efforts than any other. It does not deny, but even
emphasizes, that in order that competition should work bene-
ficially a carefully thought-out legal framework is required
and that neither the existing nor the past legal rules are
free from grave defects. *** The fundamental principle that
in the ordering of our affairs we should make as much use as
possible of the spontaneous forces of society, and resort as
little as possible to coercion, is capable of an infinite
variety of applications.

The temptation to quote is irresistible, but it must be
said that no one can realize the full force and persuasiveness
of this book except by reading it through. Even if the author
were not a foreigner by birth, one would say that his English
style is remarkably fine. He has a gift for weighty aphorism.
His tone is dignified, temperate and conciliatory. (As he
writes in a preface: "My opposition to these [Socialist] views
is not due to their being different from those with which I
have grown up since they are the very views which I held as
a young man and which have led me to make the study of economics my profession.") It is a strange stroke of irony that
the great British liberal tradition, the tradition of Locke
and Milton, of Adam Smith and Hume, of Macaulay and Mill and
Morley, of Acton and Dicey should find in England its ablest
contemporary defender--not in a native Englishman but in an
Austrian exile.

The New York Times Book Review, (September 24, 1944): 1, 21

"Freedom, Planning, and Totalitarianism: The Reception of **F. A.**
Hayek's *The Road to Serfdom*," Theodore Rosenof (1974)*

One of the classic issues of politics has been that of
the relationship of the state to the economy. A long tradition in the western world has held that the relationship should
be kept as minimal as possible, that a free economy is the
very basis of economic progress and prosperity, that economic
freedom is essential to all other freedoms – including political liberty and democracy. This tradition, and these assumptions, were partially challenged and modified by the movements
for progressive reform and democratic socialism which developed
in the late nineteenth and early twentieth centuries. But the
greatest challenge came during the severe depression years of
the 1930s: the belief was widespread among radicals during the
first half of the decade that the end of an era was at hand,
that capitalism and its ethos had run their course, and that
the socialist cooperative commonwealth was now within reach.

In a depression era socio-economic concerns were foremost
in most radicals' minds; civil liberties and constitutionalism
were less emphasized. These beliefs, of course, were not widely accepted on the progressive liberal left, which rallied in
1933-34 to support the New Deal even as radicals and socialists
rejected the New Deal as a last futile effort to save the dying capitalist system. The New Dealers, while advancing programs for increased state economic intervention, and retaining
a firm faith in America's democratic political tradition,
nonetheless asserted that programs calling for greater intervention than they themselves supported would lead to total-
itarianism--even as their conservative critics insisted that
the New Deal's own programs would lead to totalitarianism.
The New Dealers, offering programs of limited, partial
planning, and dogmatically rejecting programs for central
planning and public ownership of key industries, thus accepted,
albeit in a modified way, the traditional conservative assumption that "too much" government economic intervention led to
political autocracy.[1]

This New Deal position grew increasingly popular in the
later 1930s. As it became clearer to radicals and socialists
that the New Deal was not the last gasp of a dying capitalism,
that, whatever its limitations, the Roosevelt Administration
had brought needed socio-economic reforms within the tradition
of political democracy and liberty, that the Soviet Union was
less a socialist commonwealth than a police state, and that
totalitarianism of the right as well as left was rampant in

Europe, the epochal mood of the early 1930s receded. Some
radicals and socialists became New Deal liberals (or even conservatives); others, while still professing socialism, placed
increased emphasis on the relationship between economic planning and political liberty.² Norman Thomas, for example, conceded in 1938 that "the weightiest argument of the most recent
critics of socialism is that, whatever socialists may intend,
the economic planning which their system requires ... will of
necessity bring us the totalitariam state."³

The World War II years further evidenced this intellectual trend - as did the post-war era. It was, for the left,
a period of disillusionment, of the vogue of Koestler and
Orwell, of pessimism, fear, and uncertainty. And it was in
this setting that Friedrich A. Hayek's *The Road to Serfdom*
was published in 1944. Hayek himself was a man of the right
(classical liberal version). An Austrian economist who had
emigrated to England in 1931, he was a devotee of the school
best represented by Ludwig von Mises. His book, which he
described as frankly "political,"⁴ was a surprising success
in America, commercially as well as intellectually. It was
purchased and distributed by business organizations, appeared
in a condensed version in the widely read *Reader's Digest*, and
launched the professorial Hayek on a national lecture tour.
To American conservatives it provided proof that the New Deal's
was the road to totalitarianism - a view long held and zeal-
ously preached. More subtly, and more importantly, its reception highlighted ideological shifts on the democratic left,
shifts which evidenced the transition from the mood of the depression years to the mood of the cold war era.⁵

The book raised some very basic issues. Hayek held, in
brief, that England was following the path to serfdom that
Germany had earlier followed; that the ideas in vogue in
England in the forties were the ideas that in Weimar Germany
had paved the way for national socialism; that these ideas -
calling for central economic planning - inevitably led to political despotism and the end of the libertarian tradition of
western civilization. This thesis brought fundamental questions to the fore. What was the relationship between economic
planning and political autocracy? How could the misery of depression be resolved - when depression seemingly evolved out
of the context which Hayek regarded as essential in liberty?
What were the sources of political freedom? Were political
and economic freedom separable or inseparable? Were capitalism and democracy antagonistic or inextricable?

The failures of capitalism in the 1930s helped to shape

the contours of the debate of the 1940s, helped indeed to explain why an economist was writing a "political" book. As
Norman Thomas put it, the pre-depression case for capitalism
"was always stated in economic terms"; capitalism alone "could
progressively increase the production of goods and arrange
their smooth distribution." But the case was now made on essentially political rather than economic grounds - that capitalism was essential to the preservation of liberty.[6] Con-
versely the older argument against socialism - that it could
not work economically - now gave way to the political argument: socialism inevitably led to statist tyranny.[7] It was
in this context that a "tired radical" such as Max Eastman
could proclaim The Road to Serfdom "the most important book on
political economy in our generation...."[8]

     One crucial cleavage between Hayek and his critics came
over the very nature of the liberal tradition. To the Hayekians the tradition was unitary; it was one of political and
economic freedom. These freedoms were indivisible; they had
developed together, and were historically and culturally linked; economic freedom and capitalism could not be sacrificed
without also sacrificing political liberty and democracy. To
Hayek's critics this view of the liberal tradition constituted
an arbitrary linkage of discrete traditions; capitalist freedom and political liberty were contemporary, they granted, but
not indivisible. One could restrict one kind of freedom without restricting the other; moreover, the freedoms had quite
different value: the capitalist freedom to exploit and to ag-
grandize could not be set alongside the political freedom of
speech and of the press. The debate, in brief, here centered
on the nature of the liberal tradition and on the divisibility
of economic and political freedom.

     Hayek, arguing that economic and political freedom were
inseparable,[9] conceived of socialism not merely as a mode of
economic organization but as a cultural pattern, asserting that
it marked a sharp "break not only with the recent past but with
the whole evolution of Western civilization...."[10] It was this
evolution - best exemplified by nineteenth century liberalism -
which unleashed the freedom and spontaneity which in turn ushered in the modern era of progress and prosperity.[11] In this
schema "liberalism and democracy, capitalism and individualism" were all inextricable parts of a cohesive whole.[12] It
was this tradition which Hayek saw challenged by a socialism
which was incompatible with political liberty, and which was
the road to political autocracy.

     Hayek's supporters, such as Henry Hazlitt and John Cham-

berlain, almost invariably emphasized their hero's place in
the English libertarian tradition, a tradition which they then
sharply contrasted with "German" and continental ideas of socialism, economic planning, and political autocracy. The
cleavage was seen as one between John Locke, John Stuart Mill,
Lord Acton - and Friedrich Hayek - on the one hand, and Karl
Marx, Adolf Hitler, and Benito Mussolini on the other. It was
English liberty versus German statism, individualism versus
collectivism, capitalism versus socialism, historic liberalism
versus the regimented orders of nazism, fascism, and communism.
It was a question of two sharply opposed traditions; a case of
either-or, one or the other; there could be no mixture, no
selectivity, no synthesis.[13]

A central point made by the Hayekians in this general context was this state power because of its inclusiveness was the
most dangerous form of power of all. Monopoly power, they
conceded, might have its evils; concentrated private economic
power was not necessarily benign; but such power was not capable of the general and pervasive control over the individual
and over *all* private institutions that state power could bring
to bear. As Hayek put it, "the 'substitution of political for
economic power' now so often demanded means necessarily the
substitution of power from which there is no escape for a power
which is always limited. What is called economic power, while
it can be an instrument of coercion, is, in the hands of private individuals, never exclusive or complete power, never
power over the whole life of a person. But centralized as an
instrument of political power it creates a degree of dependence scarcely distinguishable from slavery."[14]

Hayek and his supporters, consistent with their concept
of a unitary liberal tradition, denied that freedom could be
maintained - or even expanded - in society's other areas if
the economic sphere was subjected to central controls.[15] Thus
to those who argued that economic planning could promote individualism and initiative in all other realms by providing
a base of economic security upon which individuals could more
freely exercise their talents, Hayek replied that "the suggestion that, by giving up freedom in what are, or ought to be,
the less important aspects of our lives, we shall obtain
greater freedom in the pursuit of higher values" was erroneous.
"Economic control," he emphasized, "is not merely control of
a sector of human life which can be separated from the rest;
it is the control of the means of all our ends."[16]

Others pointed to the actual as well as theoretical qualifications and equivocations of socialists in the realm of

political freedom and civil liberties. What came first for
democratic socialists, socialism or democracy? If democracy
provided a barrier rather than a conduit to a socialist order
that might otherwise be in their grasp should democracy then
be "temporarily" suspended? Was political liberty somehow
"hollow" without freedom from capitalist inequity and injustice? If so, was it then to be set aside if necessary in the
quest for socialist freedom? Insofar as socialists put their
socialism before democracy, and their commitment to economic
equity before their commitment to political liberty, they were
sharply criticized by the Hayekians - as well as by others
sympathetic to Hayek on this if not on other grounds.[17]

Critics of Hayek rejected the validity of the concept of
a unitary liberal tradition. They distinguished between economic and political freedom; they argued that the idea that
economic planning would end in political autocracy was an arbitrary and abstract assertion, that the one did not necessarily follow from the other. Norman Thomas, for example, held
that for American business "The basic freedom ... has never
been 'the right to know, to utter and to argue freely according to conscience' but only freedom to acquire and to own."[18]
Social commentator Victor S. Yarros added that "The notion that
planning and socialization of certain industries will inevitably be followed by the suppression of civil liberties ... is
wholly arbitrary. What connection is there between free
speech, trial by jury, the habeas corpus safeguard, and the
socialization, as in Britain, of the Bank of England, the coal
mines, transportation ...? None is discernable."[19]

The question of the historical roots of Hayek's unitary
liberal tradition had a curious and subtle twist. This related to the question of whether the tradition of political
liberty *antedated* the tradition of economic liberty (as defined
by Hayek). One critic, for example, found it "surprising to
read Dr. Hayek's invocation of Milton, Locke, and Hume in defense of freedom of enterprise and ... competition since those
ideas were unknown to those men. Those writers were concerned
with human rights and *political* freedom and would have been
incapable of understanding what is meant by *economic* freedom,
since that idea was not developed until almost the end of the
eighteenth century."[20] Hayek himself, curiously enough, implied that in some respects the tradition of political freedom
preceded the economic. Writing of "The gradual transformation
of a rigidly organized hierarchic system into one where men
could at least attempt to shape their own life," he held that
starting from "the commerical cities of northern Italy," this
"new view of life spread with commerce to the west and north,

through France and the southwest of Germany to the Low Countries and the British Isles, taking firm root *wherever there was no despotic political power to stifle it.*"[21]   Here was a suggestion that the absence of political despotism paved the way for acceptance of economic freedom rather than *vice versa.* Hayek also stated that "The subsequent elaboration of a consistent argument in favor of economic freedom was the outcome of a free growth of economic activity which had been the undesigned and unforeseen by-product of political freedom."[22] Here again was the idea that economic freedom grew out of a pre-existing tradition of political freedom.

This seeming incongruity in Hayek's argument as to the origins of the unitary liberal tradition had far-reaching implications. If political freedom antedated economic freedom (in the Hayekian sense), if indeed political freedom paved the way for economic freedom, then clearly much of Hayek's argument could be called into question at least so far as the historical aspects of its rationale were concerned. It further opened the way to the arguments of democratic socialists, who wanted to synthesize socialist economics with political liberty, who asserted that economic socialization was an extension of political democracy, and who contended that social and economic democracy was more compatible with the essence of the liberal tradition than was capitalist industrial autocracy. Finally, this question of the validity of the concept of a unitary liberal tradition raised questions about the basic *contemporary* historical assumption upon which Hayek's book rested, indeed the assumption which was his very rationale for writing the book: that the ideas in vogue in England in the early forties were those in vogue in Germany in the twenties,[23] and that these ideas led to the Nazi horror.   For if the political factor underlay the economic, then one could argue that socialist economics did not lead to Nazi political autocracy, but rather that the Nazis' seizure of political power allowed them to institute their schemes of economic collectivism.

This question of the alleged parallel between Germany in the twenties and England in the forties provided another major area of debate, an area focusing on differing national political-cultural traditions. Hayek maintained that "it would be a mistake to believe that the specific German rather than the socialist element produced totalitarianism. It was the prevalence of socialist views and not Prussianism that Germany had in common with Italy and Russia...."[24] Hayek's critics strongly disputed this analysis. They argued that Hayek overestimated the influence of vogue ideas in historical causation,

that the existence of a certain set of ideas in Germany in the
1920s - or in England in the 1940s - did not necessarily lead
to the Nazi triumph in the former case or presage a road to
serfdom in the latter. They contended that Hayek's analysis
postulated a single factor cause, ignoring all other variables
including the historical context out of which Nazism arose and
of which the ideas under the Hayekian lens were but a part.
It was the depression of the early 1930s, they pointed out,
which lent a great impetus to the Nazis' rise to power in
Germany. Most crucially, critics focused upon the differing
political-cultural traditions of the nations of which Hayek
wrote. They stressed that Germany had a strong statist-au-
thoritarian tradition, and a relatively weak democratic-par-
liamentary tradition, quite apart from any socialist ideas
that may have been in vogue in the Weimer era; they stressed
that communism in Russia followed a long tradition of czarist
autocracy - and a very limited and weak tradition of parlia-
mentarianism; and they stressed that in Italy, too, parliamentary government had had a troubled and unsteady existence.
This, they argued, was what Germany, Russia, and Italy really
had in common: not "socialism" or "collectivism" per se, but
a political culture in which political autocracy could thrive -
be it nazi, communist, or fascist. In contrast to these countries, critics maintained, other countries - such as Britain
and America - had long and strong traditions of political democracy and liberty; "socialist" economic measures in such
countries could be democratically instituted and developed
within the culture of political liberty; the key thus lay in
differing political-cultural traditions.[25]

This alleged Hayekian tendency to stress the impact of
ideas per se and to deemphasize or even ignore the role of
concrete conditions was sharply questioned in a more general
context. Critics argued that Hayek's book was too abstract,
that it had little relation to actual societies, that the
realities were far less neatly defined and packaged that
Hayek's black-and-white, either-or, this "system" or that
"system" theorizing. They contended, for example, that the
competitive free market never really fully existed apart from
classical theory, and that Hayek's golden liberal era in England was actually one of industrial strife and suffering. In
the real world, they insisted, "pure" capitalism and socialism
was not the rule; nations faced choices between varities of
programs and not wholly different "systems"; various countries,
among them America, Britain, Sweden, and New Zealand, had combined varying degrees of economic planning with political liberty and democracy. In fact the American economy during World
War II was very thoroughly planned - but with no diminution of

the Bill of Rights, a diminution which would follow in Heyek's logic and theory but did not follow in actuality.[26]

What critics centered on most importantly was the overall schematic quality of Hayek's argument, the way in which it was presented as a "system of thought," a cohesive and interrelated whole - logical in itself but with questionable relation to reality. Hayek himself complained of a "tendency to pick and choose from what I regard as [a] unitary philosophy which must be accepted or rejected as a whole."[27] It was in this sense - in his view of inclusive "systems" - that Hayek could ask: "How many features of Hitler's system have not been recommended to us for imitation from the most unexpected quarters, unaware that they are an integral part of that system and incompatible with the free society we hope to preserve?"[28] Hayek's critics responded that Hitler did not have any such "system" - only Hayek did. They contended that Hayek's either-or ism obscured the fact that there were many varieties of planning, and that compromise and moderation could shape and modify the planning process. To those who thus invoked the Anglo-American "genius for compromise" to deny Hayekian logic, Hayek responded that "The peculiar point about these invocations of the genius for compromise is that they are produced in reply to an argument which ... was a defence of the very institutions which have created this trait...."[29] This raised the question of whether the institutions created the trait, or the trait the institutions. If the latter was the case, it would imply that planning, too, could be shaped and guided by the Anglo-American "genius for compromise."

This alleged Hayekian either-or thinking, emphasis on abstract "systems" rather than concrete realities, was clearly evidenced in the key debate over differing concepts of economic planning. Hayek used the term in the sense most common in the 1930s) of general, centralized, detailed production planning by government. This, he argued, was the traditional socialist usage. Such planning, he held, could not be instituted democratically, for in a free society the common agreement essential to its implemention would not be possible. Thus such planning would necessarily be totalitarian.[30] Hayek, given his concept of economic planning, here dichotomized planning and the democratic state. Planning became not the will of the people expressed democratically through the instrumentality of the state, but the phenomenon which required the state despotically to suppress liberty and to regiment the people. The planning state per se thus became democracy's antithesis - a concept of the state directly in conflict with the critics' concept of the state not as an entity in itself but as an entity reflecting and partaking of the people, history, traditions, and culture of the nation.[31]

Ironically, however, while they challenged Hayek's view that economic planning had led to totalitarianism, denied that there were pure and inviolable economic "systems," and asserted that compromise and choice among various economic alternatives was both possible and wise, one of the most interesting things about Hayek's critics – most of whom were New Deal liberals and democratic socialists – was the extent to which they shared Hayek's fear of the totalitarian specter and warned against "too much" government economic intervention. The logic of the New Deal–democratic socialist arguments regarding the key role of differing political–cultural traditions – that in a democratic country the government would respond to the economic will of the people – was that even central planning in or approaching the Hayekian sense could be instituted democratically. The logic of their rejection of the Hayekian concept of a unitary liberal tradition led to the conclusion that central economic planning need not imply any relation to much less curtailment of the basic political freedoms. Yet New Dealers and democratic socialists also vehemently rejected central economic planning in what seemed like Hayekian terms. While in the early and mid-1930s, when the horrors of depression and poverty were foremost in social democrats' minds, many stressed the need for central planning to meet the economic crisis, now, in the 1940s, with the impact of totalitarianism foremost, they rejected central planning as a harbinger of political autocracy – even though the logic of their own case against Hayek led elsewhere. The kind of planning they called for illustrated the narrowing of the debate in the 1940s; they called not for detailed economic planning by government but only for certain basic decisions to be publicly made; they looked not to central planning in the 1930s sense as a model but rather to autonomous public corporations such as the Tennessee Valley Authority, stressing administrative decentralization.[32]

New Dealers and democratic socialists in the 1940s felt themselves caught between the Scylla of monopoly and poverty and the Charybdis of statism and autocracy. They wanted to make government strong enough to correct the evils of capitalism, but not so strong as to become a threat in itself; and their fear of the latter made the former seem benign by comparison – a central Hayekian point. They wanted to combine political liberty and social justice, political democracy and economic equity, but given their fear of totalitarianism – though not the logic of their view of democracy as expressed

in their criticism of Hayek - they knew not quite what to do.
Their overall mood was one of perplexity and pessimism. George
Orwell, the Englishman soon to write *1984*, the ultimate reflection of the social democratic horror of totalitarianism,
well-captured this mood and "predicament. Capitalism leads
to dole queues.... Collectivism leads to concentration camps
.... There is no way out ... unless a planned economy can be
somehow combined with the freedom of the intellect...."[33]
"The rise of totalitarianism," the theologian-social philosopher Reinhold Niebuhr added, "has prompted the democratic world
to view all collectivist answers to our social problems with
increased apprehension."[34]

These apprehensions resulted in the "liberal socialism"
and "mixed economy" concepts of the 1940s, concepts which
largely displaced the emphasis on central planning of the previous decade. But Hayek, while focusing on the 1930s concept
in his book, responded to the left's retreat from the planning
positions of the 1930s effectively and astutely. He was unconvinced that the new formulae would obviate the totalitarian
threat, yet argued that these new formulae reflected the fact
that the left saw the validity of the very point he was making -
that the threat of totalitarianism was a real and viable one,
that central economic planning had indeed been associated with
political autocracy in Russia, Germany, and Italy. He thought
that the limited planning now proposed would prove ineffectual
and if continued lead to central autocratic planning, but his
basic point - that the social democrats had in the context of
the forties drawn back as (if not as far as) he had urged -
was essentially valid.[35] He noted in 1946, for example, how
the "socialist writer, Lewis Corey, ... anticipated ... a large
part of my central thesis when he went out of his way to emphasize that 'the separation of economic from political power
is the basis on which democratic freedoms arise,' ... and that
'all available evidence shows that an absolute planned economy
is of necessity totalitarian.'"[36]

Corey, a leading proponent of the "liberal socialism" of
the 1940s, did indeed argue that totalitarianism inhered in
excessive economic collectivism.[37] So did Will Herbert, another liberal socialist.[38] So did Arthur Schlesinger, Jr., a
leading Americans for Democratic Action liberal,[39] as did many
other leftists of the postwar era.[40] The reception of Orwell's
1984 only further illustrated this ideological characteristic
of the democratic left.[41] The crucial point here was that
modern liberals and democratic socialists accepted the basic
thrust of Hayek's argument - even as they rejected his historical explanation of the origins of totalitarianism. Hayek,

Orwell, Corey, and Schlesinger, for example, differed in degree but not in their basic assumption: that "too much" collectivism imperiled liberty, that totalitarianism inhered in
government economic intervention per se. Rather than viewing
political liberty as discrete and separable from a given economic structure, the democratic left here viewed them as intertwined - as did the right. And by stressing the alleged
totalitarian implications of the expansion of state economic
power per se, they provided ammunition for conservative attacks on modern liberalism and democratic socialism.

The left, therefore, in the late 1930s and into the 1940s,
moved closer to acceptance of basic conservative assumptions.
But Hayek himself modified traditional (classical) liberal
dogma, and thereby served also to narrow the debate of the
1940s. Contemporary observers often pointed out the distinction between Hayek's qualified views and the arguments of some
of his more vehement supporters in America - and how the latter accepted the main thrust of Hayek's case while ignoring
his approval of certain forms of increased government economic
intervention. Hayek favored government "planning for competition," by which he meant government action to provide a
framework in which competition could operate. In response to
depression he favored government monetary action. Some supporters of Hayek, such as John Davenport of *Fortune* saw Hayekian formulae and Keynesian fiscal formulae as consistent and
compatible. Various New Dealers, moreover, were now emphasizing indirect Keynesian fiscal controls, and themselves calling
for government action to keep the economy competitive. Ironically, some of Hayek's other critics contended that "planning
for competition" was far more utopian than any planned economy
could be, that to undertake it would require far more planning
and bureaucracy than the plans of those whom Hayek most strongly attacked.[42]

Hayek stressed, as did his New Deal critics, that liberal
doctrine had to be modified to meet the exigencies of the age,
and that to adhere dogmatically to the old liberal concepts
might lead in the end to the demise of basic liberal values.
Liberalism, he emphasized, must realize "that in order to keep
alive it has constantly to rethink its principles and to re-
state them in the light of what we are learning."[43] Of course
New Dealers - who conceived of themselves as modern liberals -
argued that they were doing precisely what Hayek suggested:
reinterpreting liberalism in the light of current realities,
retaining the essence of liberalism while sloughing off its
outdated loctrines - but that Hayek himself encouraged a dogmatic and dangerous adherence to just such outdated doctrines.

The Hayekians rejoined that the New Dealers had gone so far
by way of reinterpretation as to cease truly to be liberals,
that they had rejected liberalism in favor of planning, collectivism, socialism - the road to serfdom.

Hayek's alterations of traditional liberalism, the distinction between his avowal of certain kinds of government
economic intervention and the more rigidly negative stances
of some of his supporters, raised further questions. Hayek
argued that his "system" was unitary and had to be accepted
as a whole, but - given his qualifications and modifications
of traditional liberalism - was his system consistently "liberal" or merely Hayekian? Did it partake in a degree of the
patchwork quality that Hayek saw in the 1940s speculative
schemes of New Dealers and democratic socialists? Moreover,
since Hayek granted, indeed insisted, that liberalism would
have to be modified to meet modern conditions, and since New
Dealers said that this was precisely what they were doing,
who - once one departed from traditional liberal doctrine -
was to say which departure, Hayek's or the New Dealers', was
the more efficacious? Who, once one granted that a departure
was necessary, was to say which better met the exigencies of
the age? Some New Dealers, for example, hoping to take advantage of the Hayekian vogue, argued that the planning envisioned in the Keynesian-inspired Full Employment bill of 1945
was "good planning" in the Hayekian sense; but opponents, of
course, sharply disagreed, insisting that it was the road to
serfdom.[44]   English social democrats such as E. F. M. Durbin
could insist that they were socialists economically because
they were liberals philosophically,[45] that socialism would
give reality to basic liberal humanitarian values, but to
Hayek, of course, this constituted the very essence of the
socialist tragedy: well-meaning humanitarians turned to methods which inevitably led to autocracy.[46]

To a considerable extent, then, the debate over *The Road
to Serfdom* took place in a kind of shadow world. Hayek based
his case upon a critique of the variety of economic planning
which was in vogue in the 1930s - but not in the 1940s. He
stood for a free market system which seemed to have little
reality in a world of state and monopoly capitalism. His argument, for all its historical references, was abstract and
basically ahistorical. He himself noted that his contentions
were "mainly based not on historical" parallels but on a theoretical argument which tends to show why, in the circum-[47]
stances, the development which took place was inevitable.
Specters also haunted the social democratic world. While some
could argue, consistent with their criticism of Hayek, that in

a democracy "The state is what public sentiment and opinion make it,"[48] a George Orwell could see in "the negative part of Professor Hayek's thesis ... a great deal of truth. It cannot be said too often ... that collectivism is not inherently democratic, but, on the contrary, gives to a tyrannical minority such powers as the Spanish Inquisitors never dreamed of."[49] But did collectivism per se "give" anyone anything? Was not autocratic collectivism a result of the seizure of political power by a tyrannical minority? The fear of totalitarianism among New Dealers and democratic socialists gave their arguments theoretical incongruity: they rejected the Hayekian idea that economic planning led to political autocracy, yet they drew back from the implications of that rejection: the 1930s horror of poverty had given way to the 1940s horror of statist tyranny.

Hayek was accused by critics of subsuming all concrete phenomena under the aegis of inclusive "systems," traditions, and cultural patterns. Yet this was in a sense a variant of a Marxist and socialist mode of thought. Hayek did indeed touch a sensitive nerve when he suggested that socialists were sometimes too willing to deemphasize the value and import of political liberty in their fight against political liberty as "not worth having" in a socio-economic system of capitalist inequity. For socialists, too, sometimes tended to subsume all social, economic, and political phenomena under the aegis of an all-inclusive "system" - that of capitalism. The key question here was whether there was indeed a unitary tradition in the socialist or Marxist sense - or whether the political and economic traditions of western countries could best be understood as autonomous and separable, with varieties of economies existing alongside political liberty and parliamentary government.

To those who looked upon these political and economic traditions as separable, and who moreover saw a value in the political tradition of liberty and democracy that was lacking in the economic tradition of capitalism, the use of the political process to alter the economic process flowed both from their analysis and their values. Yet the democratic leftists' fears of statist tyranny led to dogmatism and prevented them from following through on these implications. Their planning schemes were of a limited sort, and the question was whether they were too limited to counteract the basic power of business. With much of the power of business left inviolate, how could business, as the most powerful segment of the society, be prevented from exercising undue influence upon the public controls? This was the classic problem and dilemma of public

economic regulation or planning in what remained an essentially capitalist economy. How could the economic power of the
state be made strong enough to implement the will of the people in the economic arena without - given the fears of the
forties - creating a too-powerful and therefore potentially
tyrannical bureaucratic state? This remained a unresolved
New Deal-social democratic dilemma.

In a broad historical sense, of course, the movement toward socialism flowed from essentially liberal-humanitarian
values. Economic socialization came to be seen by some as the
most efficacious means of fighting poverty and social injustice. In Europe democratic socialism was widely seen as the
heir of the liberal tradition - rather than as the Hayekian
destroyer of liberalism. Here, again, the question of a unitary liberal tradition was relevant and indeed key to an understanding of the problem. Hayek, for example, charged that
"the people of the West continued to import German ideas and
were even induced to believe ... that the political ideals of
England and America were hopelessly outmoded and a thing to be
ashamed of."[50] But Hayek here, in keeping with his concept of
a unitary liberal tradition, refused to distinguish between
economic ideas and political ideas - and one who rejected the
concept of a unitary liberal tradition could thus accept "German" socialist economic ideas while also adhering to liberal
Anglo-American political ideas. Only in terms of Hayek's logic
did acceptance of the former require rejection of the latter.

From an historical perspective perhaps the most interesting thing about *Serfdom's* reception was the degree of consensus
that it revealed. Theoretically the gulf was great; yet given
the historical context, the fear of totalitarianism, and Hayek's
alterations of liberalism, points of approach and even convergence were reached. John Davenport, for example, in a review
lavishly praising Hayek, noted that "The liberal conception
of the state is one wherein the state attempts to lay down the
rules of the game, not to play it."[51] This was precisely what
New Dealers - and critics of Hayek - were also saying at mid-
decade. And the road which America was following in the 1940s
proved to be not that of serfdom, though Hayek still had his
doubts,[52] but that of the Keynesian-welfare state. This was
conceived as the alternative both to extensive state economic
planning and to the inequities and injustices of the capitalist
economic system. But the Keynesian-welfare state could also
be seen as an evasion both practical and philosophical: economically as a palliative, an ameliorative device which confronted not the causes but rather the effects of the basic
problem, philosophically as a skirting of the question of the

compatibility of central economic planning and political liberty and democracy. It was a classic example of the compromise choice, the middle way. The question remained whether it was enough.

[1] On this particular point, see Theodore Rosenof, "Roads to Recovery: The Economic Ideas of American Political Leaders, 1933-1938" (Ph.D. Thesis, University of Wisconsin, 1970), *passim*.

[2] For these general intellectual developments see Daniel Bell, *Marxian Socialism In the United States* (Princeton, 1967), 164 Note 291, 168; Alfred Kazin, *On Native Grounds* (Garden City, N.Y., 1956 Doubleday Anchor ec.), 393-4; Morton White, *Social Thought in America* (Boston, 1957 Beacon ed.), 250-255-7; Walter B. Rideout, *The Radical Novel In the United States 1900-1954* (N.Y., 1966), 253-4; Murray B. Seidler, *Norman Thomas: Respectable Rebel* (Syracuse, 1967), 124, 178-9, 184-8, 226, 286, 302; Bernard K. Johnpoll, *Pacifist's Progress: Norman Thomas and the Decline of American Socialism* (Chicago, 1970), 185, 202-3, 245-6; Frank A. Warren, III, *Liberals and Communism* (Bloomington, 1966), 32-3, 61-2, 87, 106, 191-2; Matthew Josephson, *Infidel in the Temple* (N.Y., 1967), 106; James Burkhart Gilbert, *Writers and Partisans* (N.Y., 1968), 158, 197, 201-3; Arthur A. Ekirch, Jr., *Ideologies and Utopias: The Impact of the New Deal on American Thought* (Chicago, 1969), 122, 238-9; Ellis W. Hawley, *The New Deal and the Problem of Monopoly* (Princeton, 1966), 51, 169, 288; Arthur M. Schlesinger, Jr., *The Age of Roosevelt: The Crisis of the Old Order* (Boston, 1957), 211-12; Arthur M. Schlesinger, Jr., *The Age of Roosevelt: The Coming of the New Deal* (Boston, 1959), 472, 477; Murray Kempton, *Part of Our Time* (N.Y., 1967 Delta ed.), 170; Rexford G. Tugwell, *The Democratic Roosevelt* (Garden City, N.Y.), 545; Richard H. Pells, *Radical Visions and American Dreams* (N.Y., 1973), 53, 64, 112-13, 307, 309, 311, 351, 354-8, 396; R. Alan Lawson, *The Failure of Independent Liberalism 1930-1941* (N.Y., 1971), 129, 133-4, 149, 221, 231, 237, 241, 246-8, 260, 271; Chester E. Eisinger, *Fiction of the Forties* (Chicago, 1965 Phoenix ed.), 7, 87, 118-19.

[3] Norman Thomas, *Socialism on the Defensive* (N.Y., 1938), 210.

[4] Friedrich A. Hayek, *The Road to Serfdom* (Chicago, 1944), ix.

[5] Gilbert, *Writers and Partisans*, 254-5, 257, 266-71, 276; Ekirch, *Ideologies and Utopias*, 256-7; Arthur A. Ekirch, Jr., *The Decline of American Liberalism* (N.Y., 1967), 310-11; Louis Hartz, *The Liberal Tradition in America* (N.Y., 1955), 273; Robert Allen Skotheim, *Totalitarianism and American Social Thought* (N.Y., 1971), 1; Charles C. Alexander, *Nationalism in American Thought 1930-1945* (Chicago, 1969), 162-3,225-6; Eric F. Goldman, *Rendezvous With Destiny* (N.Y., 1959 Vintage ed.), 324-5; Eric F. Goldman, *The Crucial Decade--And After* (N.Y., 1961), 7-8; Laurence R. Frank, "The Rising Stock of Dr. Hayek," *The Saturday Review of Literature, XXVIII* (May 12, 1945), Stuart Chase, "The War of Words," *Common Sense, XII* (Nov. 1942), 383; Stuart Chase, "Back to Grandfather," *The Nation, CLX* (May 19, 1945), 565; Abba P. Lerner, "Planning and Freedom," *The New Leader, XXVIII* (Jan. 20, 1945), 7.

[6] Norman Thomas, "Hayek, Socialism and Freedom," *Common Sense, XIV* (May, 1945), 38.

[7] Lerner, "Planning and Freedom," 7.

[8] *Congressional Record*, 79 Cong., 1 Sess., Appendix 4122.

[9] Hayek, *Serfdom*, 13, 100.

[10] *Ibid.*, 13, 20.

[11] *Ibid.*, 14-17.

[12] *Ibid.*,22.

[13] Louis M. Hacker, "Threatened Submergence of the Individual," *New York Herald Tribune Weekly Book Review*, Oct. 29, 1944; Henry Hazlitt, "An Economist's View of 'Planning'," *The New York Times Book Review*, Sept. 24, 1944, 1, 21; John Davenport, "Books and Ideas," *Fortune, XXX* (Nov. 1944), 218; William Henry Chamberlain, review of *Serfdom, The Atlantic Monthly, CLXXIV* (Dec., 1944), John Chamberlain, "Foreword," in Hayek, *Serfdom, vii*; Harley L. Lutz, "A Short Cut to Serfdom," *Public Service Magazine* (Oct., 1945), 40, 43.

[14] Hayek, *Serfdom*, 145-6. See also Chamberlain, review of

Serfdom, 149; Rufus S. Tucker, "The Return to 'Enlightened Despotism'," *Vital Speeches, XI* (April 15, 1945), 395.

[15]See, for example, Max Eastman, "The Notion of Democratic Socialism," *The New Leader, XXVIII* (Feb. 10, 1945), 5.

[16]Hayek, *Serfdom,* 88, 92.

[17]Chamberlain, review of *Serfdom,* 149; "Books and Ideas," *Fortune, XXXII* (Dec., 1945), 254; Joseph A. Schumpeter, review of *Serfdom, The Journal of Political Economy, LIV* (June, 1946), 269.

[18]Thomas, "Hayek, Socialism and Freedom," 39, 41.

[19]Victor S. Yarros, "Social Workers *v.* Hayekism," *The Social Service Review, XX* (March, 1946), 107. See also Maxwell S. Stewart, "Freedom and Economics," *Tomorrow, V* (March, 1946), 68; "'The Road to Serfdom'," *The University of Chicago Round Table,* Number 370 (April 22, 1945),; Victor S. Yarros, "Revival of Pseudo-Individualism: The Hayek Case," *Unity, CXXXI* (July, 1945), 73-4; Herman Finer, *Road to Reaction* (Boston, 1945), 24.

[20]Frank, "The Rising Stock of Dr. Hayek," 26.

[21]Hayek, *Serfdom,* 14-15. My emphasis.

[22]*Ibid.,* 15.

[23]*Ibid.,* 2-4, 181.

[24]*Ibid.,* 9.

[25]Thomas, "Hayek, Socialism and Freedom," 39-40; Finer, *Road to Reaction,* 3-5, 29-30; 87-8, 105-6; Frank, "The Rising Stock of Dr. Hayek," 5-6; Lerner, "Planning and Freedom," 7; Alvin H. Hansen, "The New Crusade Against Planning," *The Republic, CXII* (Jan. 1, 1945), 11-12; Joseph Mayer, review of *Serfdom, The Annals of the American Academy of Political and Social Science, CCXXXIX* (May, 1945), 202; Eric Roll, review of *Serfdom, The American Economic Review, XXXV* (March, 1945), 179; Carl J. Friedrich, review of *Serfdom, The Ameri-*

can *Political Science Review*, *XXXIX* (June, 1945), 578; Joseph J. Spengler, review of *Serfdom*, *The Southern Economic Journal*, *XII* (July, 1945), 51-2; Sidney Hook, "Freedom and Socialism," *The New Leader*, *XXVIII* (March 3, 1945), 5; Louis Gottschalk, "Some Recent Countersocialistic Literature," *The Journal of Modern History*, *XVII* (Sept., 1945), 222, 224-5; F. A. Hermans, "Economic and Political Liberty," *The Review of Politics*, *VII* (Jan., 1945), 110; Mary Sydney Branch, review of *Serfdom*, *The Social Service Review*, *XIX* (March, 1945), 147; "Is American in Danger of Going Fascist?" *Town Meeting: Bulletin of America's Town Meeting of the Air*, *X* (Feb. 8, 1945), 7-8; Edwin G. Nourse, review of *Serfdom*, *Journal of Farm Economics*, *XXVII* (May, 1945), 485-7; Max Lerner, *Actions and Passions* (N.Y., 1949), 157; Melchior Palyi, review of *Serfdom*, *Chicago Sunday Tribune Books*, Oct. 8, 1944, 9; T. V. Smith, review of *Serfdom*, *Ethics*, *LV* (April, 1945), 224, 226.

[26] Hansen, "The New Crusade Against Planning," 9, 11-12; Roll, review of *Serfdom*, 178-80; Friedrich, review of *Serfdom*, 575; Thomas, "Hayek, Socialism and Freedom," 39-40; "'The Road to Serfdom'," *The University of Chicago Round Table*, 8; Yarros, "Social Workers *v.* Hayekism," 106-7; Finer, *Road to Reaction*, 108, 123-5, 133, 180; Chase, "Back to Grandfather," 565; Nourse, review of *Serfdom*, 484; Edwin G. Nourse, "Serfdom, Utopia, or Democratic Opportunity?" *Public Administration Review*, *VI* (Spring, 1946), 178-9, 181-2; Irving H. Flamm, "Hayek and the Reactionaries," *The Chicago Jewish Forum*, *III* (Summer, 1945), 244.

[27] *Congressional Record*, 79 Cong., 1 Sess., Appendix 2324.

[28] Hayek, *Serfdom*, 6.

[29] F. A. Hayek, "'Genius for Compromise'," *The Spectator*, *CLXXIV* (Jan. 26, 1945), 75.

[30] "'The Road to Serfdom'," *The University of Chicago Round Table*, 3, 5, 7, 10-11; Hayek, *Serfdom*, 64, 68-9.

[31] On the critics' concept see Frank, "The Rising Stock of Dr. Hayek," 6; Thomas, "Hayek, Socialism and Freedom," 40; "'The Road to Serfdom'," *The University of Chicago Round Table*, 10; Nourse, "Serfdom, Utopia, or Democratic Opportunity?" 181; Yarros, "Social Workers *v.* Hayekism," 107; Yarros,

"Revival of Pseudo-Individualism: The Hayek Case," 73; Finer, *Road to Reaction*, 64-7, 154; Lerner, *Actions and Passions*, 157; Reinhold Niebuhr, "The Collectivist Bogy," *The Nation*, *CLIX* (Oct. 21, 1944), 478, 480; J. Donald Kingsley, "Retort to Reaction," *The New Republic*, *CXIV* (Jan. 28, 1946), 130; Seymour E. Harris, "Breaking a Lance with Mr. Hayek," *The New York Times Book Review*, Dec. 9, 1945, 16.

[32]Chase, "Back to Grandfather," 566; Thomas, "Hayek, Socialism and Freedom," 40; Smith, review of *Serfdom*, 226; "'The Road to Serfdom'," *The University of Chicago Round Table*, 8-11; Yarros, "Social Workers *v.* Hayekism," 107; Stewart, "Freedom and Economics," 68; Ben B. Seligman, "Dice, Dr. Hayek and the Consumer," *Commentary*, *I* (March, 1946), 84; "The Reuther Plan," *Common Sense*, *XIV* (Nov., 1945), 19; "Are National Planning and Government Control a Threat to Democracy?" *Town Meeting: Bulletin of America's Town Meeting of the Air*, *XI* (May 17, 1945), 4, 7, 21; "Are We Moving Toward a Government Controlled Economy?" *Town Meeting: Bulletin of America's Town Meeting of the Air*, *XII* (May 30, 1946), 18; A. R. Sweezy, "Textbook for Reactionaries," *PM*, Nov. 5, 1944, M 16; Gertrude Himmelfarb, "Socialism *vs.* Bureaucracy," *The Call*, Nov. 17, 1944, 4.

[33]"Review," in Sonia Orwell and Ian Angus, eds., *The Collected Essays, Journalism and Letters of George Orwell*, *III*, *As I Please 1943-1945* (N.Y., 1968), 119.

[34]Niebuhr, "The Collectivist Bogy," 478.

[35]"'The Road to Serfdom'," *The University of Chicago Round Table*, 9-10; Hayek, "'Genius for Compromise'," 75; Hayek, *Serfdom*, 40 Note 2; Friedrich A. Hayek, "Tomorrow's World: Is It Going Left?" *The New York Times Magazine*, June 24, 1945, 12.

[36]F. A. Hayek, "Socialists Must Face Dangers of Statism," *The New Leader*, *XXIX* (August 24, 1946), 9.

[37]Lewis Corey, "Economic Planning Without Statism," *Commentary*, *IV* (August, 1947), 145-7.

[38]Will Herberg, "There Is a Third Way," *The Antioch Review*, *VI* (Dec., 1946), 616-17.

[39] Arthur M. Schlesinger, Jr., "The Mixed Economy," *The New York Times Book Review* (June 26, 1949), 6; Arthur M. Schlesinger, Jr., *The Vital Center* (Boston, 1962 Sentry ed. [orig. pub. 1949]), 153, 182; Arthur Schlesinger, Jr., "The Politics of Democracy," *Partisan Review*, XVIII (March-April, 1951), 245-6, 251.

[40] See, for example, August Gold, "C.C.F. and the Co-ops," *The Call*, Jan. 1, 1945, 4; Victor G. Reuther, "Look Forward Labor," *Common Sense*, XIV (Dec., 1945), 10; Robert Bendiner, "Revolt of the Middle," *The Nation*, CLXIV (Jan. 18, 1947), 66; McAlister Coleman, "Why I'll Vote for Thomas," *The Nation*, CLXVII (Oct. 2, 1948), 369-70; Sylvia F. Porter, "Can Socialism Be Democratic?" *Socialist Call*, Jan. 7, 1949, 2; Ben B. Seligman, "The Devil Theory," *The New Republic*, CXXIII (July 3, 1950), 19; Will Herberg, "What Happened to American Socialism?" *Commentary*, XII (Oct., 1951), 339; Irwin Ross, *Strategy For Liberals* (N.Y., 1949), 8, 44-5.

[41] See, for example, Arthur Schlesinger, Jr., "The Horrors of Utopia," *The Reporter, I* (August 2, 1949), 36-7; Diana Trilling, "Fiction in Review," *The Nation*, CLXVIII (June 25, 1949), 716-17; Irving Howe, "'1984' - Utopia Reversed," *The New International*, XVI (Nov.-Dec., 1950), 366-68.

[42] Davenport, "Books and Ideas," 221; Hacker, "Threatened Submergence of the Individual," 3; Thomas, "Hayek, Socialism and Freedom," 39; Smith, review of *Serfdom*, 225; "'The Road to Serfdom'," *The University of Chicago Round Table*, 6; *Congressional Record*, 79 Cong., 1 Sess., Appendix 2324; Hayek, *Serfdom*, 121; Frank, "The Rising Stock of Dr. Haeyk," 27; Nourse, "Serfdom, Utopia, or Democratic Opportunity?" 178-9; "Are National Planning and Government Control a Threat to Democracy?" *Town Meeting: Bulletin of America's Town Meeting of the Air*, 4, 8, 17; Finer, *Road to Reaction*, 78-9; Ben B. Seligman, "Hayek Ignores History," *Labor and Nation, I* (Oct., 1945), 59; C. Hartley Grattan, "Hayek's Hayride: Or, Have You Read a Good Book Lately?" *Harper's Magazine*, CLXXXXI (July, 1945), 46; R. F. Harrod, *The Life of John Maynard Keynes* (London, 1963), 437; Benjamin L. Masse, "Dangerous Curve Ahead," *America*, LXXII (Oct. 28, 1944), 76; *New York Times*, Jan. 6, 1945, 10; "Editorial: Liberalism on the Loose," *Common Sense*, XIII (April, 1944), 151; Theodore Rosenof, "The Economic Ideas of Henry A. Wallace, 1933-1948," *Agricultural History*, XLI (April, 1967), 149-50; Alonzo L. Hamby, *Beyond the New Deal: Harry S. Truman and American*

Liberalism (N.Y., 1973), 9-12; Dwight MacDonald, *Memoirs of a Revolutionist: Essays in Political Criticism* (N.Y., 1958 Meridian ed.), 287-90.

[43] *Congressional Record*, 79 Cong., 1 Sess., Appendix 2324. See also Hayek, *Serfdom*, 17.

[44] See, for example, *New York Times*, Jan. 6, 1945, 10; Lutz, "A Short Cut to Serfdom," 29; Henry Hazlitt, "Should Government Guarantee Full Employment?" *Independent Woman, XXIV* (Sept., 1945), 267; Stephen Kemp Bailey, *Congress Makes A Law* (N.Y.- 1950 [Vintage ed.]), 54-5.

[45] E. F. M. Durbin, "Professor Hayek on Economic Planning and Political Liberty," *The Economic Journal, LV* (Dec., 1945), 357.

[46] Hayek, *Serfdom*, 32-4.

[47] Friedrich A. Hayek, "Planning and 'The Road to Serfdom'," *The Chicago Sun Book Week*, May 6, 1945, 1.

[48] Yarros, "Social Workers *v.* Hayekism," 107.

[49] "Review," in Orwell and Angus, eds., *Collected Essays*, 118.

[50] Hayek, *Serfdom*, 23.

[51] Davenport, "Books and Ideas," 218.

[52] Friedrich A. Hayek, "Foreword," *The Road to Serfdom* (Chicago, [1956] Phoenix ed.), Hayek also provides here his own later response to the book's reception.

The Canadian Review of American Studies, Vol. V, No. 2, (Fall 1974): 149-165

The Affluent Society
by
John Kenneth Galbraith

REVIEW: David M. Potter (1958)*

"Wandering between two worlds, one dead, the other powerless to be born"--the phrase was Matthew Arnold's but the predicament is distinctively our own. The fault is partly our
own also, for we sometimes force the potentialities of the unborn world into the mold of institutions and concepts which
fitted its deceased predecessor. Rarely can we break through
the crust of familiar ideas and view our transformed universe
with a vision as fresh as its conditions are new.

One observer with this rare talent for the unfettered
view is John Kenneth Galbraith, professor of economics at
Harvard. Twice now, Galbraith has subjected the American
economy to a remarkably fresh analysis. In 1951, in "American
Capitalism," he argued that the process which makes our economy
work is no longer the free interplay of innumerable small
units--farmers, workers, and businessmen--in an open market,
but rather the accommodation to one another of major "countervailing" forces (such as unions, farm blocs, chain distribu-
tors, and large-scale producers) as their respective pressures
come into balance and reach stability. Now, in "The Affluent
Society," Professor Galbraith takes a fresh look at our economic goals and contends that the fierce and indiscriminate
emphasis upon production for its own sake, which was suitable
to an age of scarcity, is no longer appropriate to an economy
of affluence or abundance. In an age of scarcity the production of goods generally met gross physical needs, and was
therefore self-justifying. But today production often creates
goods of such marginal usefulness that an artificial need has
to be created by psychological manipulation of the consumer,
and we depend upon full production more as a means of providing
employment and preventing depression than as a necessity for
meeting direct physical needs.

How does our tenacity in clinging to the old goals deprive
us of the potentialities of the world unborn? In the most

stimulating, novel--and controversial--part of his presentation, Galbraith makes a forcible argument that a relaxation
of our productive pace might reduce the violence of economic
oscillations between boom and depression, and might avoid the
chronic inflation which results when wages and prices, both
stimulated by high productivity, push each other up in a re-
ciprocating spiral. Having reached a stage at which we value
full productivity mostly because it brings full employment,
it is time for us to break the vicious link which binds the
two by providing alternative activities and incomes for workers, so that their salvation will not depend upon the maintenance of high-pace production. Only when we do this can we
control production instead of letting it control us. Mr. Galbraith also deplores our overvaluation of private spending and
our undervaluation of public spending, leading to the imbalance
by which we feed our children superbly at private expense but
educate them poorly at public expense, or steadily improve our
homes while we let our cities deteriorate.

The author presents these ideas with notable force and
originality, and develops their implications with constructive
imagination. For example, he argues that unemployment pay
rates should rise as unemployment increases and decline as it
diminishes. He argues that continuing public functions, such
as education, should be supported by long-range appropriations
and not be subjected to biennial legislative whims. He believes that conservatives will always construe any measures
which are to be paid for by higher income taxes as disguised
attempts to expropriate wealth, and therefore that his proposals should be paid for by a sales tax to avoid their being
stalled in a liberal-versus-conservative deadlock.

As a blueprint--or dream, as the case may be--of a better
world, this book has an apt title. But in terms of content
the title is a misnomer, for the study takes more account of
economics than it does of society. Though he is always lucid
and nontechnical in doing so, Galbraith devotes extensive, and
perhaps disproportionate space to discrediting certain conven-
tions of economic thought, such as the assumption that it is
impossible to discriminate economically between the social
value of different forms of production, or that private purchase of goods (*e.g.,* 300 horsepower automobiles) is in itself good and to be encouraged but that public purchase of
goods (*e.g.,* school desks) is in itself wasteful and must be
suspiciously watched. So far so good, but with fuller attention to society Mr. Galbraith might have reckoned with the
fact that our Puritan aversion to idleness and our pioneer
urge to subdue a new continent have contributed more than

economic theory to our obsession with productivity, and that
the one-horse individualism of our agrarian past has done more
than classical economics to breed distrust of extensive community services. He might have taken more account also of the
fact that a democracy adopts given economic measures because
organized groups believe it will be to their advantage to do
so, and not because of any criterion of optimum social good.
To readers who are sympathetic with his views, it will seem
sad to reflect that ideas may be realistic and even hard-headed
at an economic level and at the same time almost Utopian at a
social level.

The seeming remoteness of Professor Galbraith's goals
will tempt many readers, especially in the spring of 1958, to
regard his book primarily as a treatise on the difficulty of
avoiding depressions and inflation in our present society.
But at a more basic level it ranks as a work which whether
Utopian or not, ought to contribute in the long run to the re-
shaping of some of our basic social ideas.

Saturday Review, (June 7, 1958): 31-32

REVIEW: *Time Magazine* (1958)*

Harvard's John Kenneth Galbraith, 49, is an economist who
has always found a wider audience than his less articulate
colleagues. His *American Capitalism; the Concept of Countervailing Power* was a bestseller in 1952; some of its ideas went
into the 1956 campaign speeches of Adlai Stevenson, which Galbraith helped write. This week, in *The Affluent Society*
(Houghton Mifflin; $4), Galbraith published what he obviously
intended to be a searching inquiry into the U.S. economy. Instead, it is a well-written but vague essay with the air of
worried dinner-table conversation.

What worries Galbraith is "the myth that production is
the central problem of our lives." This concept of social efficiency, says Galbraith, originated in the days of Adam Smith
in an era of scarcity. The classic economists have repeated
it; the public has echoed them. Now it is obsolete: the
present-day economy not only turns out all the goods needed
but spends much of its energy whetting the consumers' appetites
for things they do not need. The consequence of this lack of
"social balance" is that production, largely in private hands,
has far outdistanced services, which Galbraith seems to think
are the responsibility of government. Thus there are plenty

of vacuum cleaners but few street cleaners, a plethora of automobiles but no place to park. "The more goods people procure, the more trash must be carried away . . . the greater the wealth the thicker the dirt."

What Galbraith says about the lack of parking places will hardly be news to Americans. Nor will anyone argue with the need for better schools, parks, sanitation systems, traffic control. But having pointed his bat at the bleachers, Galbraith steps away from the plate. He never takes a full swing at drafting the program that he implies: that the state, local and federal governments must take a larger role in society. What Galbraith suggests concretely is much more conservative. He believes that the economy can absorb up to 4,000,000 unemployed proposes a sliding scale for unemployment compensation. He feels that use of the sales tax should be expanded to provide better communities, and takes to task liberals who resist city and state sales taxes.

When the national frenzy for production has abated, Galbraith says, the Government can devote itself to the frontiers of education, science, world development. But these sonorous generalizations are left in the air. Galbraith has found it easier to sketch the problem than provide the answers.

Time Magazine, (June 21, 1958):78-80

"The Affluent Society After Twenty-Five Years," J. R. Stanfield (1983)*

The Affluent Society was published in May, 1958. It is quite possibly the most important book published in the postwar period, with enduring significance for the 1980s and beyond. Few words need be spent justifying a retrospective and prospective look at The Affluent Society. I proceed by briefly reviewing The Affluent Society, considering its impact, criticism, and relation to Galbraith's later works, and commenting on its continuing relevance.

Summary

The Affluent Society examines the continuing urgency that affluent societies attach to higher consumption and to the growth of production. The general explanation for this paradox, very familiar to students of Veblen, is that ideas are held over from one historical setting to another, where they are obsolete and ill-suited. Moreover, these ideas persist

not by inertia alone but because they are convenient to powerful vested interests. *The Affluent Society* also considers the
implications and consequences of this tenacious devotion to
economic growth. The general issue here is that the outmoded
mentality of more-is-better is obstructionist and stands in
the way of the further economic progress that would be possible
if the tremendous wealth of the democratic industrial societies
were put to reasonable use.

The main currents of the "conventional wisdom" in economic
affairs were established in the eighteenth century, refined in
the next century by the classical and neoclassical traditions,
and amended by the Keynesian Revolution in the present century.
After centuries of relatively slow permanent economic growth,
the modern discipline of economics arose concomitant to the
persistent and spectacular growth of output known as the Industrial Revolution. As an outgrowth of the long history of mass
privation and the new history of economic insecurity resulting
from industrial instability, the "tradition of despair" central
to economic thought focused on production, inequality, and
insecurity.

Inequality and insecurity have been subordinated to the
overriding objective of raising production. The miracle of
growth enables all classes to advance absolutely and defuses
the vastly more difficult and controversial problems of income
and wealth redistribution. A liberal and conservative concen-
sus on growth has supplanted the bitter controversy on inequality. Then, too, so long as income is linked to productive performance, economic security is possible only through the high
employment made possible by sustained growth. For good measure,
national security is attached to expanding output because industrial supremacy is seen as a necessary ingredient to superior military preparedness.

There are also strong vested interests behind the "paramount position of production." Those who in one way or another
enjoy their income, prestige, and power because they can contribute to, guide, or understand the process of expanding production have a vested interest in maintaining economic growth
as a top priority. Put negatively, any decline in the importance attached to expanding output would *pari passu* lead to a
decline in their income, prestige, or power. Business executives and technical professionals who run the social machinery
of production, wealthy people who have accumulated purchasing
power, politicians whose platforms and constituencies are
based on government fostering of growth, and academic economists whose central ideas are concerned with scarcity and

growth all have varying degrees of vested interests in the continuing preoccupation with expanding production.

Nothing in *The Affluent Society* so invited controversy as the discussion that deals with the maintenance of popular emphasis on consuming more--that is, with assuring that people continue to want more no matter how much they have already. In discussing the process of want creation, Galbraith utilizes the concept of the *dependence effect,* by which wants arise from what one sees others consuming, especially as portrayed in advertising. Emulation is the passive aspect of the process of want creation. People emulate one another in an attempt to curry favor, display their modernity or good taste, or keep up with the Joneses and ahead of the Smiths. But the active and crucial elements of the process are advertising and the related salesmanship activities that drone on in modern culture, always with the incessant message, BUY. Given that so much effort and expense goes into contriving wants, Galbraith finds dubious the case for the continuing urgency of expanding output to satisfy them. This doubt is all the stronger because the powerful groups whose interests are vested in expanding production constitute the most active forces in contriving wants.

Galbraith foresaw grave consequences flowing from this preoccupation with consumption and growth. He felt it imperiled economic security.[2] Economic security is threatened by the runaway growth in consumer debt that is part of the salesmanship activities. Easier credit checks, lower down payments, longer repayment terms, and other inducements for people to go further into debt are permanent and necessary fixtures of the consumer society described in *The Affluent Society*. This increases uncertainty and economic instability, thereby threatening economic security.

The paramount position of production also makes persistent inflation inevitable. The economy must operate near full capacity, where excess demand and the market power of organized economic agents make inflation *normal* rather than exceptional. Policies that would contain inflation, most especially policy founded on the crude instruments of monetary and fiscal policy, would also damage production and are therefore inadmissable because of the production's paramount position. More effective policy measures, such as wage-price controls, an incomes policy, national economic planning, and similar structural policies, cannot be applied effectively until policy formulation is freed from the restrictive grip of the conventional wisdom.

Some of the most interesting and controversial discussion

in *The Affluent Society* is that dealing with the theory of
social (im)balance. Galbraith argued that the preoccupation
with production and the process of consumer want creation that
sustains it would contribute to a penurious public sector.
Added to the traditional antigovernment bias of market capitalist ideology, the incessant attention to private consumption
obscures the need for collective action in areas critically
important to the quality of life in contemporary society.
Nothing so strong as the dependence effect, especially its active ingredient, advertising, operates to draw attention to
these collective wants.

Yet a moment's reflection establishes that private and
collective wants are complimentary: more cars require more
roads and traffic control, more packaged goods require more
trash removal, and so on. The principle of social balance
states that for a given level of private consumption there exists a corresponding optimal level of public consumption. The
contemporary consumer society contains a debilitating social
imbalance and the contrast between private opulence and public
squalor is one of Galbraith's major themes.

There are other serious consequences of the preoccupation
with production. Personal or human capital is neglected, as
is the serious poverty that remains and the continuing but du-
biously necessary agony of toil. Insecurity, inflation, social
imbalance, and the failure to affirm personal development,
eradicate poverty, and reduce the burden of toil are the legacy
of the obsolete mentality described in *The Affluent Society*.
Galbraith insisted that a reasonable society would make far
better use of its affluence.

Impact, Criticism, and Later Works

Very little space is required to establish the impact of
The Affluent Society, so long as we keep in mind that its basic
message has yet to wield the influence that it should (on which,
more below). The book has enjoyed remarkable sales success and
been given tremendous attention, both critical and favorable,
in popular and academic literature. The phrases it coined,
especially the title and the epithet hurled at intellectual
complacency--the conventional wisdom--have been widely adopted
and paraphrased. The book catapulted Galbraith from the position of a well-known if eccentric economist into that of an
intellectual celebrity, serving to renew his varied career in
public service and to guarantee attention to his subsequent
work.[3] The book played a considerable role in his ascension
to the presidency of the American Economic Association of Evo-

lutionary Economics, and was directly responsible for his receiving the Sidney Hillman Award.

The influence of *The Affluent Society* on a generation and more of university students has been immense. I trust I can be permitted a personal note. I remember vividly my encounter as an undergraduate economics major with *The Affluent Society* and *The New Industrial State*. I was instantaneously emancipated from the elegant calculus of the irrelevant that quite possibly would have been my lot otherwise. The same experience must have been repeated for myriad others. *The Affluent Society* and its author influenced the student movements of the 1960s and, especially, the counter-culture of that period. Similar influence can be detected on the politics of the 1960s in which a liberal revival set out to deploy more of the affluence in question toward collective goals of social justice, environmental protection, improved working conditions, urban renewal, and cultural development. Although Galbraith would be the first to cite fact and circumstance as causative historical forces over the musings of an academic scribbler, his ideas played no small part in these and other areas.

Galbraith's ideas have been met by vociferous criticism and outright disdain, especially in conservative philosophical quarters and among the neoclassical faithful. His analysis of the process of want creation was severely criticized. F. A. Hayek charged that the dependence effect is a *non sequitur* because of the assertion that learned wants are relatively unimportant compared to those that are innate. Hayek rightly pointed out that all human tastes are acquired by socialization, but he missed an essential point of *The Affluent Society,* that there is an important difference between the general acquisition of tastes through acculturation and the systematic imposition of tastes to fit the needs of powerful vested interests. Hayek also charged Galbraith with ambiguity in only implying and not making explicit the argument that the wants of consumers are dictated by producers. Finally, Hayek contended that the want-creating activities of producers are only a part of the cultural milieu and that they compete with one another.

Galbraith met Hayek's criticisms head on in his later works, especially *The New Industrial State,* in which he formulated the "revised sequence" concept.[5] The argument is that producers and not consumers are sovereign in the new industrial state and that the accepted notion of consumer sovereignty serves to obscure the reality of corporate power. Galbraith also argued in this later book that although individual advertisements are competitive--buy product A rather than B--their aggregate message is Buy, period. Moreover, in such a society, the messages and control of powerful producers exert a disproportionate influence on cultural programming and social attitudes.

Galbraith's later works also went a long way toward meeting the more sympathetic criticism leveled at *The Affluent Society* by C. A. Zebot.[6] Zebot argued that merely describing emulation and advertising as media of social learning is not enough to challenge the validity of the wants created in the process. A necessary further step is analyzing the content of these wants and constructively criticizing the learning process so as to indicate how it can be improved. Galbraith's formulation, in *The New Industrial State,* of tastes cultivated to fit the interests of the technocracy in the large corporations answers many of Zebot's questions. The wants that serve the interests of the corporate system do not advance quality of life in general. A new departure, led by the scientific-intellectual estate, and a revitalized liberal political force are necessary to emancipate the popular mind and redirect the use of social resources.

It is interesting to note at this point how well Galbraith's argument in this regard epitomizes institutional economics. The intellectual establishment's emphasis on political involvement rekindles the incipient force of institutionalism as a political movement toward the conscious collective governance of the economy in the service of social values. It also brings to mind the formative influence of John Dewey's frequent insistence on the role of creative intelligence and inquiry in social process and progress.

There is also the basic framework of analysis in which the purpose of inquiry is to adjust institutions, in light of the advance in tools and knowledge, to more perfectly serve human ends and needs. *Institutions* here means both organizations and structures of power and culture or contexts of meanings. The powerful--and everyone has some power notwithstanding its obvious stratification--attempt to imbue culture with meanings that legitimate, preserve, and extend their power.

In his later works, Galbraith identifies the corporate technostructure as the primary source of power in the democratic industrial societies. He also identifies, most emphatically in *Economics and the Public Purpose,* the interests of this technostructure and the means by which it attempts to imbue culture with meanings that serve these interests.[7] Culture is the telling of stories, and the technostructure seeks the tell-

ing of stories that elevate to the highest social purpose the
maximization of income and consumption. The technostructure
uses its considerable instruments of persuasion to maintain
the pecuniary culture of commodity festishism, invidious distinction, and competitive emulation. Income-earning, income-
spending automatons are the desired populace of the society
committed solely to the expansion of commodity production, and
such an expansion is the vested interest of the technostructure.
In his works, Galbraith outlines the negative consequences for
the quality of life in a society whose culture is wedded to a
value system of more-is-better. He also attacks the power
structure that promulgates this intellectual confusion or false
consciousness.

The complicity of economists in this intellectual confusion
is another theme that Galbraith develops often and forcefully.
The fixation on the expansion of commodity production as the
basic indicator of social achievement owes much to vested interests and to the hold on the popular mind of a long human history
of scarcity, but it is as well "a product of the elaborate ob-
scurantism of the modern theory of consumer need" (p. 349). The
conventional economic theory of the consumer provides a defense
of the present value system, "a defense which makes the urgency
of production largely independent of the volume of production"
(p. 140). The economists' doctrine of insatiable consumer wants
provides the intellectual bedrock of the continuing importance
of more output (p. 143). For the conventional economist, human
wants are *datum* (p. 144); neither their formation nor their
quality is appropriate subject matter for economic investigation
(p. 147). Instead, the extent of wants is simply *assumed* to ex-
ceed the extent of the resources available to satisfy them.
This effectively prohibits practitioners of the economics art
from examining, *by any standard,* such questions as the influence
exercised on popular wants by powerful economic agents, or the
legitimacy of these wants.

Indeed, the spirit of the conventional wisdom, and the example of most economists serving under its thrall, is that such
a critical theory of human wants and needs, grounded in objective analysis of historical context, is neither possible nor
desirable. Conventional economists deride any effort toward
such a theory--notably Galbraith's--as the mere substitution of
one set of preferences for alternative sets. Their argument
quickly becomes ad hominem; the scholar who puts forward such a
critical theory is condemned as a power-thirsty totalitarian who
aspires to impose his or her preferences on everyone else.

Of course, economists do not dictate popular consciousness,

but they are an important voice in public opinion and their
failure to critically examine popular consciousness and its
formation is significant. In *Economics and the Public Purpose*,
Galbraith clarified this by arguing that economists practice
the "convenient social virtue" of retaining a theory of consumer
choice based on the notion of consumer sovereignty. The "imag-
ery of choice," by preserving the comfortable conception that
consumers dictate the use of resources, obscures the reality of
power and forestalls critical analysis of the process of want
creation by powerful vested interests. The convenient stance
of economists, then, is to look the other way and refuse to examine the source and implications of a popular consciousness
that embodies an ideology of consumption, that is, "the proposition that the production and consumption of goods, notably
those produced by the planning system, are coordinate with happiness and virtuous behavior."[8]

To employ the notion of culture as the telling of stories
with significant meanings, conventional economics tells a story
of scarcity and consumer sovereignty that buttresses or at
least deflects attention from the power of the technostructure.
In this story, environmental protection, cultural development,
the alleviation of poverty and injustice, and the improvement
of worklife are but so many competing ends. They compete with
one another and with the expansion of other collective ends,
and especially with private ends as expressed in the effective
demand for commodities. No hierarchy of needs or critical
evaluation of wants, individual or social, is seen as possible,
other than that which takes place within the inscrutable mind
of the sovereign individual who votes with dollars and ballots
for an allocation of resources that he expects will maximize
his utility, all things considered. But none of these things
are considered concretely by the neoclassical conventional wisdom, whose elegant formalism strongly suggests that social values rank Pet Rocks above environmental preservation and anything of pecuniary value above anything merely useful, just, or
beautiful.

The theory of social balance has drawn its share of criticism. Henry C. Wallich argued that Galbraith was guilty of a
non sequitur in arguing that poor taste in the purchase of
goods in the private sector supported a conclusion "that the
only alternative to foolish private spending is public spending. Better private spending is just as much of a possibility."[9] This is logically unassailable but is not addressed to
the actual argument of *The Affluent Society*. Galbraith cited
many examples of penurious public sector spending and their
deleterious effects, such as insufficient resources devoted to

education, playgrounds, municipal services, and delivery of
medical care. He then contrasts these incontrovertible limitations on the quality of life with the plethora of gadgets
and ostentation in the private sector, not to prove the need
to expand collective consumption, but only to argue that the
opportunity cost of such an expansion is not as great as people think because the importance of the private consumption
that would have to be foregone is not as much as people believe.

Paul Baran and Paul Sweezy leveled criticism at *The Affluent Society* from another angle.[10] They argued that Galbraith's
contrast between private affluence and public squalor does not
capture the pivotal forces at work in modern capitalist society
because the state does do a lot, especially in the areas of defense, roads and highways, traffic control, and parking. What
the state does, however, is constrained and shaped by powerful
private interests so that there are definite limits on social
spending for health, education, housing, and the like that conflict with the class structure and business hegemony of capitalist society. In his later works, Galbraith expands his
analysis of social imbalance, recognizing that some public sector spending is favored because it fits the interests of the
powerful corporate system. Other collective and, indeed, private wants, not only in conventional social welfare areas, but
also in the cultural sphere, fare badly because there is no
strong voice for them amongst the powers that be.

In *The New Industrial State,* Galbraith strongly develops
the theme that a symbiotic if one-sided relationship exists
between the state and the technostructure.[11] In its management
of aggregate demand, support of certain kinds of technical and
scientific research and education, and waging of the cold war,
the state serves the interests of the technostructure. But
that which is of little or no use, or is contradictory to the
interests of the technostructure, fares badly within such a
state.[12] Public health clinics, public parks and recreation
areas, environmental protection, and aesthetic development fit
into these categories as do public planning for transportation
and housing. Galbraith is even more emphatic on these points
in *Economics and the Public Purpose.*[13]

In the final analysis, although Galbraith is not explicit
on the point, social imbalance becomes less a matter of the
public sector versus the private sector than of that which
serves the purpose of expanding commodity production versus
that which does not. Stated thusly, the theory of social balance is more obviously related to the obsolete commitment to
the value system of a pecuniary culture. This formulation of

social imbalance has the added advantage of being consistent
with Galbraith's frequent point that the public versus private
sector dichotomy is declining in relevance to the point of obsolescence. It should also render Galbraith's work more acces-
sible and more acceptable to those social critics steeped in
the Marxist tradition. Finally, it links the present section
to the following discussion of Galbraith's continuing relevance.

Continuing Relevance

The vociferous criticism levelled at *The Affluent Society*
is a mark of its significance, much of which remains unrealized.
The fundamental themes of *The Affluent Society* continue to
threaten conservative puffery and neoclassical complacency.
In part this continuing relevance reflects the work's uncanny
anticipation of matters of detail that have since emerged as
problems or issues. Among these it is sufficient to mention
consumer credit (p. 200); the independence of the Federal Reserve Board (p. 227); the importance of human capital to economic growth (p. 271); the need for revenue sharing (p. 263);
the rising participation of women in the labor force (p. 258);
the degradation of the environment (p. 355); the other, poverty-
stricken, America (pp. 97 and 327-28); the obsolescence of the
link between work and income (pp. 289-91); and the many issues
in the area of quality of worklife (p. 334).

On a deeper level, this power of anticipation and the continuing relevance of *The Affluent Society* results from Galbraith's superior method of inquiry and its power to uncover
the fundamental social trends and problems of an affluent society. The three unsolved problems noted in *The Affluent Society*
remain so and continue to serve as the major impediments to advancing human development and quality of life. These are the
process of consumer demand creation and financing, persistent
inflation, and social imbalance between the public and private
sectors (pp. 250-51). These problems are interrelated. The
invidiousness encouraged by the process of manipulating consumer demand reinforces an incomes race and consumer treadmill
(see pp. 154 and 159) that virtually guarantees inflation, social imbalance, and environmental deterioration. Financing
this invidious consumer demand and the investment to service
it makes it difficult to finance much needed and highly beneficial collective action. This invidious pecuniary calculus
is blind to non-commodity, non-income needs. Power wielded by
those illuded by this mentality will be used to secure more
income to sustain purchases of more commodities. Prices and
incomes spiral upward, and social and environmental consideration lying outside the scorer's reach in this game of competi-

tive emulation are neglected. The culture of competitive emulation places such emphasis on individual pecuniary success
that the degree of solidarity and social responsibility necessary for the welfare state to function smoothly is not present.[14] Programs designed to remedy social imbalance and social
injustice tend to be exploited by greedy manipulators and their
failure written off to some original sin in human nature rather
than to a defective culture.

The complicity of much of the economics profession in the
ideological lacuna that inhibits society's ability to squarely
face these problems is also a major theme of *The Affluent Society*. The obsolescence of the conventional wisdom in economics
is now woefully apparent as is its rootedness in an ahistorical
approach to an essentially historical subject matter.[15] Galbraith forcefully raised the spectre of the obsolescence of
economic thought in the face of social change at a time of general complacency in the economics profession: "There are . . .
grave drawbacks and even dangers in a system of thought which
by its very nature and design avoids accommodation to circumstances until change is dramatically forced upon it. In large
areas of economic affairs the march of events . . . has again
left the conventional wisdom sadly obsolete" (p. 29).

This obsolescence is apparent not only in the general refusal to accommodate the reality of an affluent society but
also specifically in the area of macroeconomic stabilization
policy. An insistent theme of Galbraith's works, not only in
The Affluent Society but also in *A Theory of Price Control* and
American Capitalism before it and in *The New Industrial State*
and *Economics and the Public Purpose* after it, is the need for
a direct intervention mechanism to deal with the wage-price
spiral. Such a policy is, however, effectively prohibited by
the conventional wisdom because of the bureaucracy necessary
to maintain it and the distortion of relative prices and resource allocation it would cause (pp. 224, 246-47). The logic
of scarcity and the paramount position of commodity production
underlies this handwringing about resource allocation. The
prohibition of direct controls necessarily links economic security to inflation. Those who would be damaged by the requisite slack in aggregate demand to restrain wages and prices
are likely to be the least able to bear such a burden. Their
voices and those of sympathetic observers are raised in support of maximum aggregate demand, along with those that simply
want maximum output because of the paramount position of production.

However, neither inflation nor its control is free. The

relevant comparison involves the costs of uncontrolled inflation versus the costs of various methods for controlling it. The insecurity and suffering caused by restraining solely by aggregate demand policy needs no elaboration in light of recent experience. The costs of controlling inflation by more direct means, such as misallocation of resources because of relative price distortions and the provision of an administrative bureaucracy, must be qualified by recognition of the artificial nature of insatiable wants and scarcity in the affluent society.

These costs must also be net of any increased efficiency because of *improved* relative prices by direct controls. There are at least two grounds for expecting some improvement in this regard. One is the familiar phenomenon of external benefits and costs. Direct control of wages and prices would facilitate the adjustment of relative prices to more accurately reflect social costs and benefits. More important, perhaps, is the fact of power that enables private economic interests to administer wages or prices. Such power abrogates the preconception of optimality that surrounds relative prices established without public intervention, and probably at the same time reduces the administrative cost of public control. Direct intervention may very well improve the correspondence of the pattern of relative prices to that of social values in relation to real costs. It may also compel the public to reflect on the relation between social values and resource allocation and income distribution.

A particularly important example of the reality of power versus the market myth is found in the area of nominal and hidden remuneration of corporate executives. The notion of competitive markets leads one to write off as the necessary supply price of executive talent such things as high executive salaries and bonuses, luxurious built environments in the corporate suites, private jets and helicopter shuttles, and a host of expense account benefits. Yet the executives themselves control the purse strings and it is their word alone by which society holds such lavish expenditures necessary. Consumers may well be paying, in the prices of the products they buy, not the necessary supply prices for scarce talent but the economic rents of sheer economic power.

This limited example is of interest not just for reasons of obscene inequity alone. It may point as well to the real roots of a decade or more of stagnant economic performance. The conventional wisdom ascribes the outmoded real capital structure and lagging productivity of the U.S. economy to public regulations and anemic capital formation. Leaving aside the regulation issue for the moment, it is noteworthy that in the

U.S. the ratio of gross investment to gross national product in the 1970s was actually a bit above the postwar average. This coupled with the aged condition of plant and equipment suggests something besides anemic capital formation as an explanation for economic stagnation: the funds were available for investment but those with administrative power over this flow of purchasing power misallocated it. Rather than invest in product development and line research, corporate executives engage in financial manipulation for short-run profit and feather their own nests by playing a high stakes game of competitive emulation in their office suites. In this regard, it is interesting to note that the office-building boom persisted well into the recent great recession. Financial manipulation for short-run gains is also more in the interest of staff executives than of the corporation as a going concern. The reputation earned by quick results can secure a lucrative move to another corporation. Such a game is particularly inviting when the executive is personally protected against failure by a golden parachute clause, no matter the damage imposed on the corporation as a going concern.

The danger of the obsolete economic wisdom to which Galbraith referred has been rendered patently clear by the Reagan Administration. Nineteenth-century economic wisdom is the vision underlying increasing inequality to stimulate capital formation, reducing labor's bargaining strength, and pursuing a viciously restrictive monetary policy. Keynesian economists who should have been able to block the rise of the supply-side charlatans and monetarist sycophants were silenced by their embarrassment at their own policy failures. Had they long ago coupled the wisdom of Keynes with that of a direct intervention strategy, they probably could have prevailed the mayhem wrought by Reagan's old-time economic religion. One is tempted to hypothesize that a mode of economic inquiry that does not move forward with history is destined to give way to a backward movement that dredges up ideas long since thought outmoded and duly abandoned. For those who find merit in this notion, I humbly suggest that it be called Stanfield's Law of Progressive Anachronism of Ahistorical Economic Thought.

The rise of President Reagan and his nativistic nostrums is part of a counter-revolt against the twentieth century that includes the considerable handwringing in the 1970s about a capital shortage, inadequate saving, declining productivity, excessive capital fund commitments to the housing stock, excessive government regulation, and the impossibility of achieving the goals of the welfare state. The gullibility of the so-called neo-conservatives of the 1970s in all of this is exceeded only by that of the so-called neo-liberals of the early 1980s.

In *The Affluent Society,* Galbraith anticipated this counter-revolt. He noted the possible harbingers of "an incipient revolt against goods or at least a refusal to allow competitive emulation to be the source of wants" (p. 193). Such a revolt definitely arose and exerted considerable influence in the 1960s counter-cultural, student, and environmental movements and in the growing general concern for quality of life. Galbraith also argues, however, that any such revolt against production would be met by a counter-revolt of the vested interests. Those so interested can be expected to "battle vigorously for a value system which emphasizes the importance of production" (p. 183). This ideological battle over the relation between quality of life and quantity of output now rages. The regulatory programs introduced to secure social and environmental objectives are under severe attack largely on the basis of their negative effects on productivity and economic growth. Social imbalance is involved here also because many of the programs that moved society toward a better sectoral balance are imperiled by the current attack on the welfare state in the name of scarcity, productivity, and growth.

The clamor about crowding out is indicative of the counter-revolt. The concern is focused on public deficit-spending crowding out private deficit-spending by households and businesses. The conventional wisdom, battered but still standing, upholds as a self-evident truth the superiority of the latter. But the argument of *The Affluent Society* insists upon asking the unsettling question, *What is being crowded out?* How seriously can a reasonable person fret about foregoing the creation of the consumer debt necessary to satisfy wants derived from the corporate-sponsored game of competitive emulation? And, other than its connection to employment security, a connection that could be linked instead to expansion of the public sector, how much concern is warranted about denying borrowed funds to corporate executives to invest in meeting such consumer wants or, perhaps worse, to be devoted to financial manipulation or intensified ostentation in the executive suites? Is it not more distressing that funds are denied public education, parks, income maintenance, and support of the arts in order to service such dubious priorities?

The problem in question is not, of course, limited to the public sector versus the private sector. Within the public sector itself, the counter-revolt is taking its toll. The guns-over-butter budget policies begun by President Carter, the neoconservative, have been intensified by President Reagan, the old-style conservative.[16] The neo-liberals accept this scheme of social priorities in general, though they quibble about the

rate of the military build-up. The neo-liberals are also in
unison with the neo-conservatives and old-style conservatives
in calling for a build-up in scientific and technical education
to spur economic growth and restore the economy's competitive
edge. Although there is perhaps nothing wrong per se with a
policy of encouraging technical training and advance, in this
case it is evidence of a deep-seated neglect of the more fundamental crisis facing the affluent society, one which cannot be
resolved by technical manipulation.

The affluent society's more fundamental problems relate to
the spirit or ideology of the age and have more to do with the
folly of continuing the game of competitive emulation than with
who succeeds at it. As someone once said, "The trouble with
joining the rat race is that even if you win, you're still a
rat." Sadly, in a government operated as an adjunct to corporate capitalism, education for the sake of human development as
a goal in and of itself remains an external economy (p. 275),
without compensable pecuniary benefits and therefore subject to
pathological neglect in a pecuniary culture. Still, one shares
Galbraith's "hope that investment in the things that differen-
tiate man from his animals requires no further justification"
(p. 278).

On the whole, the major lesson of Galbraith's work is that
realization of this hope will require that the conventional wisdom be discarded. As an evolutionary positivist,[17] Galbraith
frequently notes that intellectual obsolescence will ultimately
yield only to the force of hard fact and circumstance (pp. 13
and 20). He does not, however, neglect the need for an ideological struggle that strategically makes use of historical circumstance in its quest to overturn the conventional wisdom.

Indeed, one of his most important themes is the need for
some more or less organized *cultural resistance* to the ideological hegemony exercised by the corporate elite and the com-
plicitous neoclassical mainstream. The myth that expanding
production is the central social problem can be debunked only
through sustained effort devoted to the "emancipation of the
mind" (p. 281). In *The New Indistrial State,* published in the
same year that Clarence Ayres argued that the intellectual's
responsibility includes the "responsibility to understand something of the nature and functioning of the ideology of our own
society, and to convey this knowledge to the intellectually
less advantaged community," Galbraith urged the "educational
and scientific estate" to take the "political lead" in breaking
"the monopoly of the industrial system on social purpose."[18]
In *Economics and the Public Purpose,* Galbraith devotes a chap-

ter to "The Emancipation of Belief," which is usefully read in
conjunction with his 1969 address to the American Economic Association.[19] The belief from which we must emancipate ourselves
is, of course, the ideology that subordinates all other social
concerns to the maximization of income and consumption. Galbraith identifies the four instruments for perpetuating this
ideology as the present pedagogy in economics, the "resigned
acceptance" of the overt persuasion contained in advertising
messages, the process of public policy formation, and the present orientation of the educational system. His comments on the
last named are particularly revealing in light of the recent
consensus on increasing scientific and technical education:

> The implicit assumptions of the modern educational
> system. . . , broadly speaking, make income and con-
> sumption coordinate with achievement. They hold sci-
> entific, engineering, business, and legal instruction
> to be useful; instruction in the arts, notably if it
> is creative in character, to be decorative or recrea-
> tional. What serves the planning system is standard
> fare; the rest is justified negatively in academic
> oratory as something the civilized man does not ne-
> glect. Educators have a particular responsibility to
> see that education is not social conditioning. This
> means the elimination of all distinction between use-
> ful and unuseful fields of learning, all suggestion
> that there is an economic standard of social achieve-
> ment.[20]

A large part of this cultural resistance must necessarily
be aimed at the economics profession. In this area, Galbraith
shares with other institutionalists the unwarranted if somewhat
self-inflicted reputation of being a purely negative critic of
the mainstream's epistemology. In fact, however, Galbraith and
other institutionalists do offer an alternative. Consider the
critical theme reviewed in this paper that the formal, maximi-
zation-oriented theory of the mainstream, with its simplistic-
ally individualistic, utility-oriented theory of consumer behavior, buttresses the dominant pecuniary ideology that holds
human welfare to be a function of commodity production and consumption. Since this theory is essentially logical and deductive rather than historical or empirical, any attack on it is
taken by its adherents to be a logical attack.

However, there is nothing logically wrong with the theory
of consumer behavior; indeed, in a sense, it cannot be wrong
because it is tautologically true. The criticism to be made
is rather that it is not very useful for practical personal

philosophy, social criticism, or policy advice because it rests satisfied with logical theorems and omits the concrete aspects of the choices in question. The quality of life is determined precisely by that in which the mainstream economist *qua* economist is so little interested; the values and judgments, ends and means of concrete historical situations. Institutionalism counters this neglect with a more concrete approach that has enabled its scholars to emphasize the many non-pecuniary, non-indivious, and non-commodity determinants of the quality of human life.

Similarly, there is no logical contradiction of the notion that, *ceteris paribus,* more is better. The criticism to be made is rather that the mainstream method has no basis for ascertaining if, *in fact, ceteris peribus* applies. This empirical question necessitates a holistic, concrete approach capable of coming to grips with the effects on society, culture, and polity of an economy geared to maximizing commodity production via an invidious incomes race. The critical astigmatism of the mainstream is, in contrast, the central question of institutional or social economics: how is the economy instituted in society and what are the implications of alternative institutional arrangements?

I think institutionalists rather generally share a value system superior to that implicit or explicit in conventional economics. This is the instrumental or substantive value system that places the economy in a subordinate position to the reproduction and fuller unfolding of the human life process as a whole.[22] With his classic concept of the *test of anxiety,* Galbraith very well captures this methodical conviction.[23] Economics should be relevant to popular concerns. To be so, it must have a concrete focus and be in touch with the culture or set of meanings that exists in society. Through this method, Galbraith and other institutionalists have undertaken the task of telling an economic story that is an alternative to the mainstream's rococo elegance, and that challenges rather than reinforces the invidious, pecuniary culture of market capitalism.

Conclusion

In short, I take the enduring message of *The Affluent Society* to be that pernicious effects on the quality of life flow from the fact that democratic industrial society is wedded to an ideology of consumption and economic growth. The ideology of consumption means that the affluent society's central cultural context, the core of its idea and value systems, is more-is-better (pp. 281 and 349). People are socialized to judge

the system and its leaders by the economic cornucopia, to seek
happiness via consumption, to solve problems by buying, and to
relate to one another through possessions. Advertising converts any and every human need to commodity terms; any feeling
of impotency, lack of belonging, purposelessness, or unhappiness
is portrayed as a consumption problem. If one is not happy, one
is systematically taught that the problem must rest with the
selection of a deodorant, toothpaste, hairstyle, automobile,
diet soft drink, or other consumer commodity. All needs are
reduced to needs for consumer commodities, all problems are to
be resolved through consumption and any perceived deficiency in
one's life stems from inadequate consumption. The only answer
is to consume more, no matter the problem.

In such a society, human time and resources are very poorly
allocated (p. 346). Time for reflection and contemplation is
usurped by the incessant quest to earn and buy. Education for
human development takes a back seat to that which serves to expand commodity production. All of this is reminiscent of John
Dewey's argument that the twentieth-century crisis of liberalism
is caused by its fixation with one historically specific *means*
for human progress to the neglect of the enduring *ends* of that
progress. The result is that liberal society utilizes the character and initiative of its people in their least significant
realm--expanding economic output--and largely neglects the application of these means to the development of culture and human
relations.[24]

Severely pernicious cultural effects and foregone opportunities for human liberation and self-realization are the costs
we bear in order to expand the production of commodities that
have a highly tenuous and ambiguous relation to human needs and
development. Clearly, the issues of values and public policy
raised in *The Affluent Society* are very relevant to the 1980s
and beyond. No less clearly, *The Affluent Society* remains,
after twenty-five years, not merely remarkably fresh but absolutely indispensable reading.

[2]I choose to ignore the less ingenious notion that Galbraith
put forth concerning the consumer society's threat to national
defense. I trust that Galbraith would not take exception to
this benign neglect.

[3]The substantial secondary literature on Galbraith includes
several monographs and books: Charles H. Hession, *John Kenneth
Galbraith and His Critics* (New York: New American Library,
1972); Myron E. Sharpe, *John Kenneth Galbraith and the Lower*

Economics (White Plains, N.Y.: International Arts and Sciences Press, 1973), now in a second edition; John S. Gambs, *John Kenneth Galbraith* (Boston: Twayne, 1975); C. Lynn Munro, *The Galbraithian Vision* (Washington, D.C.: University Press of America, 1977); and David Reisman, *Galbraith and Market Capitalism* (New York: New York University Press, 1980). In addition, considerable emphasis on Galbraith is found in Allen M. Sievers, *Revolution, Evolution, and the Economic Order* (Englewood Cliffs, N.J.: Prentice-Hall, 1962); and Edmund S. Phelps, ed., *Private Wants and Public Needs,* rev. ed. (New York: W. W. Norton, 1965).

[5] J. K. Galbraith, *The New Industrial State* (Boston: Houghton Mifflin, 1967), esp. chapter 19.

[6] C. A. Zebot, "Economics of Affluence," *Review of Social Economy* 17 (September 1959): 112-25.

[7] J. K. Galbraith, *Economics and the Public Purpose* (Boston: Houghton Mifflin, 1973), esp. chapter 22.

[8] Ibid., p. 223.

[9] Henry C. Wallich, "Public versus Private: Could Galbraith Be Wrong?" in Phelps, *Private Wants,* p. 45.

[10] Paul Baran and Paul Sweezy, *Monopoly Capital* (New York: Monthly Review Press, 1966), esp. chapter 6.

[11] Galbraith, *The New Industrial State,* chapter 26-29.

[12] Ibid., chapters 30-31 and 35.

[13] Galbraith, *Economics and the Public Purpose,* esp. chapter 16 and Part Five.

[14] See the author's *Economic Thought and Social Change* (Carbondate, Ill.: Southern Illinois University Press, 1979), esp. chapter 6.

[15] This is the theme of *Economic Thought and Social Change,* in which note is taken of the literature that swelled during

the 1970s on the crisis of economic thought.

[16] It is interesting to note that the buildup under President Reagan has been most spectacular in the purchase of weapons systems and less pronounced in personnel or maintenance expenditures. The commodity production needs of corporate defense contractors may be more significant in the Reagan rearmament scheme than purely military considerations. The response, or more accurately the lack thereof, to Senator John Tower's March 1983 questionnaire to fellow senators concerning possible defense expenditure reductions in their states suggests that what I once called *peace-war* is still very much alive. See "Limited Capitalism, Institutionalism and Marxism," *Journal of Economic Issues* 11 (March 1977); 61-71.

[17] So far as I know, this useful term to characterize the methodology of institutionalism was coined by Norman D. Markowitz, *The Rise and Fall of the People's Century* (New York: Free Press, 1973), p. 14.

[18] C. E. Ayres, "Ideological Responsibility," *Journal of Economic Issues* 1 (June 1967): 3-11; Galbraith, *New Industrial State,* p. 387.

[19] J. K. Galbraith, "Economics as a System of Belief," *American Economic Review* 60 (May 1970): 469-78.

[20] Galbraith, *Economics and the Public Purpose,* p. 227.

[22] See Galbraith, *Economics and the Public Purpose,* chapter 20.

[23] John Dewey, *Liberalism and Social Action* (New York: Capricorn, 1963), pp. 38-39.

Journal of Economic Issues, Vol. XVII, No. 3, (September, 1983): 589-607

Business Cycles
by
Wesley Clair Mitchell

REVIEW: O. M. W. Sprague (1913)*

Readers of the *Journal of Political Economy* have doubtless
long since become well acquainted with this important work.
In this much-belated review I shall therefore limit myself to
a discussion of the nature and extent of the very considerable
addition which it makes to our understanding of the business
cycle.

Somewhat more than half the volume is devoted to the presentation of statistical data relating to business cycles
between 1890 and 1910, in the United States, England, France,
and Germany. An imposing mass of statistical material on the
prices of commodities, labor, securities, and loans, on the
volume of trade, and on banking operations in these countries
is brought together and made available for comparison by means
of index numbers. No sources of information on these subjects
have been overlooked, so far as I am aware, with the exception
of the five abstracts of the condition of the national banks
published in pamphlet form by the Comptroller of the Currency.
Professor Mitchell has used only the single abstract for each
year which appears in the annual reports of that official.

In the construction of his index numbers Professor
Mitchell has taken the period 1890-1900 as a basis. A shifting base would perhaps have yielded slightly more exact
results, but it is doubtful whether the gain would have been
sufficient to warrant the additional labor involved. A more
serious matter is the use of the calendar year in the measurement of changes in business conditions. When the investigator
is concerned with broad general tendencies over a long period
of time, annual figures serve the purpose. But, in the case
of the business cycle, it is a series of changes which follow
one another in rather quick succession that are to be measured.
Here figures showing changes by months would seem to be required. The statistical data as presented, for example, do
not show in comparable fashion the effects of the crisis in

1893, which began in the spring, and that of 1907, which began in the early autumn. They are still less serviceable for the determination of the relative severity of the business reactions which followed these crises.

For those particular aspects of the business cycle, however, which are subjected to detailed analysis by Professor Mitchell, the method of presenting the statistical data which he has adopted seems to be entirely adequate. He does not much concern himself with the quantitative analysis of business cycles. Differences in degree and duration are held to be of minor significance. He is rather seeking to discover and determine the causes of uniformities among business cycles. That all business cycles have features in common, the statistical data as presented afford ample proof, and it is not probable that on these aspects of the business cycle monthly figures would have yielded important additional information.

Nearly a third of Professor Mitchell's treatise is devoted to an analytical explanation of the uniformities among business cycles. During each business cycle there are decided but uneven fluctuations in the prices of particular commodities and kinds of labor, marked variations in the physical volume of trade, in rates for loans, in the yield of securities, and in the efficiency of labor. As a consequence of all of these variations there are wide fluctuations in money costs of production and in business profits. All these variations, it is argued, are an inevitable consequence of the existing organization of economic activities upon a pecuniary basis, in which the principal directing influence is exercised by business men in the quest of profits. During a period of prosperity, for example, industry becomes subject to numerous stresses and strains of increasing intensity owing to the business undertakings which are occasioned by, and which in turn occasion, the various fluctuations mentioned above. Finally, a reaction becomes inevitable, and during the subsequent period of depression changes in the opposite direction pave the way for another period of activity for the beginning of a new cycle.

It is not possible, within the limits of a review, to give any adequate idea of the clearness and convincingness of this brilliant example of economic analysis. But precisely because the analysis is so convincing and well documented, there is a danger that the reader may draw the conclusion that a complete analysis of the business cycle has been accomplished. To the reviewer, at any rate, it would seem clear that only a part of the complex phenomena of the business

cycle has been explained. The uniformities among business
cycles arising out of the organization of industry upon a
pecuniary basis have to do with factors which by themselves
would occasion merely slight temporary oscillations in the
condition of trade. A short period of depression is sufficient to correct maladjustments directly due to such factors
as tension in the money markets, the uneven movement of
prices, and the inefficiency of labor which develops during a
period of superabundant employment. The difference in duration and intensity of the depression following the crisis of
1873, compared with that accompanying the reaction in 1903,
is not explained by differences in price movements or other
distinctly pecuniary matters. It is noteworthy in this connection that Professor Mitchell distinguishes four complete
cycles in the United States between 1890 and 1910, a period
during which, if pronounced changes only are taken into
account, there were not quite two complete cycles.

For the quantitative analysis of business cycles, it is
necessary to dig beneath the pecuniary surface of economic
activities. The general character of the agriculture, industry, and commerce of a country, and the particular undertakings
which are in process of most rapid development during the
period of expansion must be treated in order to understand the
business cycles. Variations in prices and interest rates, as
well as other financial developments, will manifest the same
general characteristics in all cycles, but even here the extent of such fluctuations will be largely determined by the
opportunities for development in agriculture, industry, and
commerce.

In conclusion let me repeat that although much still remains to be done in the field of the business cycle, the very
great value of Professor Mitchell's contribution to our knowledge of the subject can hardly be overestimated. On the
pecuniary side he has laid a broad foundation of fact, presented in comparable form, coupled with an adequate analysis.
Other aspects of business cycles require equally comprehensive
collection and analysis of material, and it is much to be hoped
that future investigators in this field will follow Professor
Mitchell's example, avoiding the all too frequent error of
assuming that a high degree of correlation between two or more
kinds of phenomena affords an explanation of any of the complicated problems of the business cycle.

*Journal of Political Economy, Volume 24, Number 6, (June
1916): 609-11*

"Mitchell's Business Cycles," Joseph Schumpeter (1930)*

As far as it is the primary function of a review to draw
to a book the attention of the scientific community and to
tell by summary or critique what readers are to expect from
it, this review is superfluous. Every economist knows Professor Mitchell's great book of 1913 and also the present installment of the new monumental work. It does not want any introduction to the public, and is beyond any critic's power to
help or to hurt. The only task left, it would seem, would be
to enter into a discussion of the vast mass of important
points of detail raised—a task to the fulfillment of which
this book is fairly entitled both by its merits and by the
eminence of its author, but which it is impossible to carry
out within the compass of a review.

Yet every book of weight tells us something beyond what
it has to say about its particular subject. It conveys necessarily a general message from author to readers about methods,
horizons, aims and views, of which the treatment of the subject in hand is but an application or paradigma. If this be
true of any book of stature, it is, in the economic field,
especially true of books on the problem of business cycles,
which by its very nature calls for a display of practically
all the powers and acquirements of the author and unavoidably
bears, by implication at least, upon every other department of
our science. One of the best things said in the volume before
us, is the suggestion (p. 452), "that ideas developed in the
study of business fluctuations may lead to reformulations of
economic theory." It is indeed obvious that in dealing with
business cycles we are dealing with all the most fundamental
elements of the economic life of capitalist society, and are
sure to meet practically all our great problems on our way.
Rarely, if ever, has any worker in this field made so full a
use of the possibilities thus offering themselves as Professor
Mitchell has, and it is this aspect of his work on which primarily I shall undertake to comment.

First, we cannot be too grateful to the eminent author for
rigorously brushing from his path idle controversy on fundamental principles of "method," which lingers in this field
longer than in any other. The reader has but to look at pp.
469-474, where there is a resume of Professor Mitchell's views
on this point, in order to be assured that he will be able to
follow the argument without feeling in duty bound to turn from
relevant discussion and to send in some grand remonstrance on
such topics as the respective merits of collecting facts, of
statistical treatment of facts, and of handling them by that

kind of refined and systematized common sense, which we have
come to call "economic theory." Professor Mitchell's every
line is, needless to say, well nourished with every kind of
available fact, including his "own store of experiences and
observations;" he is "ready to apply the mathematical technique
of statisticians;" and he proposes "to guide our statistical
investigations by rational hypotheses," repudiating the "error
to think that free use of factual materials reduces the need
for careful reasoning." Guarded and judicial as these utter-
ances are, they cover in their admirable brevity and simplicity
a great deal of ground. They are infinitely valuable, when
said ex cathedra by a prominent leader in a field in which
they are as yet less universally accepted than in others and
which still suffers from a belief, harbored by many ardent
workers, that explanation can ever come to us as a by-product
of mere collection of facts and that it spells scientific sin
to use, in dealing with these facts, any logical tools not at
the command of the "man in the street." Nor is this all.
Via facti, by starting in his first chapter with a survey of
the work done since the discovery of the problem as well as
of the solutions now current, he testifies to his belief in
the continuity of science, thereby condemning implicitly any
program of "starting anew" and that attitude which takes a
pride in mere lack of scientific training. His teaching on
this point may be summed up, I believe, saying that any "New
Economics" can come about not by program but only by achievement.

True, Professor Mitchell does not take kindly to what
savors of "theoretical construction," and his preferences,
while toned down both by scrupulous fairness and by his invariable courtesy and generosity, are yet clear enough. He can
hardly help associating the work of theorists with insufficient
command over facts and with ways of thinking which seem to him
backward. Even in cases in which an author's command of facts
was no more backward than his analytic apparatus, he would
stress the former and underrate, as it seems to me, the importance of the latter point; just as, on those few and well-timed
occasions when he is looking for formal analogy to the procedure of physical science, he seems to overstate the importance
of the experimental, and to understate the importance of the
theoretic side of their work. In places he forgets or denies
that there is such a thing as theoretic proof or disproof of
a proposition, and seems to consider "theories" as so many
suggestions of which one is really as good as any other before
being put to the decisive judgment of statistics. I confess
to some doubt, whether every one of the authors considered in
the first chapter will recognize themselves in the pictures

drawn of them. But this matters little. In spite of it he
is leading up to common ground, on which we may hope to work
harmoniously towards the common goal, even tho the task being
a complex one and calling for very different mentalities,
aptitudes, and likings, we may never be able fully to appreciate each other. To quote a colleague of mine, professor of
Experimental Physics at the University of Bonn: "If I call in
a theorist to hear what he has to say about the results of my
experiments, and if my man shows so much experimental aptitude
as is implied in being able to switch off the light, I begin
to doubt his competence as a theorist." Yet he calls him in.

There is another comment I should like to make upon the
work as a whole or its "general message," which extends the
importance of the book far beyond the precincts of the mere
problem of business cycles. Professor Mitchell, as he has told
us somewhere, is no friend to systematic treatises--which most
of us will probably agree to be in some respects necessary
evils. But as a matter of fact, he has written one or, at all
events, sketched out the fundamental contours of one, with
such unmistakeable clearness, that any competent economist
could supply most of the rest without risk of serious error.
I think it safe to say that no more than one fifth of the book
before us bears specifically on business cycles in the sense
that it has not just as much to do with any other group of the
great problems of our science--distribution, or pricing, or
monopoly. Now, inasmuch as we have before us the work of one
of the leading figures of the scientific world of economics
and of a leader who has, in former years, often betrayed some
displeasure at the state of our science and our ways of dealing
with its problems, both in toto and on a number of well-defined
headings, it seems but natural, and hardly unfair, to ask what
the outstanding features are, which could be pointed to as constituting or implying fundamental differences in results or
horizons, and whether the presence of such differences spells
revolution or evolution. It is natural, in trying to answer
this question, to think of that mighty structure which, tho
battered in places by the impact of newer methods and results,
still stands broadly in the background of much, if not most,
of the best work of our day--Marshall's great treatise.

There is undoubtedly a difference in aim and character.
Marshall's fame and influence rest on his mastership in constructing tools of analysis, on his having built, out of the
material of the theoretic ideas of his time, an engine of
analysis. It is the fifth book of the Principles (and matter
placed elsewhere in the treatise which really belongs in that
book) which is immortal in the sense in which scientific

achievement can ever be called immortal. Now Professor Mitchell, being of the experimental type, would never undertake a
similar task; he would consider it, as all experimentalists
do, of secondary importance; he thinks of theory not as an
analytical engine, but primarily either as a store of rational
hypotheses, or as a body of doctrine or as an arsenal of generalizations gleaned from arrays of well-digested facts. He
even would never, I presume, preface factual analysis by an
elaborate theory as, to quote another instance, Professor
Taussig has done in his International Trade. He would think
theory in the Marshallian or Walrasian sense just as little
worthwhile for its own sake as he would refinements on statistical methods which have no immediate bearing on problems in
hand. But, again, just as he is not prepared to forego the
use of the tools put at his command by modern statistical
methods or to condemn the use of all of them except the elementary ones, so he would not and could not deny--he would in
fact have no logical standing ground to do so--that science
cannot progress, after a certain stage has been reached, without the construction of tools of thought different from those
of every day life, growing up as the result of conscious effort: *id est,* without a theory, which has as little to do with
metaphysical speculation or political doctrine as the discussion by the pure theory of mechanics of "possible" forms of
movement, and which is not an unscientific or provisional substitute for facts, but an instrument--spectacles, so to speak--
needed in order to discern the facts.

This being the case there is a great difference in emphasis, and yet no epistemological gulf between Mitchell and
Marshall; not even between Mitchell and Marshall's fifth book
(appendix included). If difference there be, it can only be
found under one of the following headings, in none of which
it spells break or revolution.

(1) It can be held, that, while theoretical tools are a
necessary evil, yet all the tools so far devised are vitiated
at their root by some initial error, *e.g.* a fundamentally
false psychology. To which I should reply, that, however
faulty we may think the psychology of economists to be in
dealing with such problems as property, taxation, motives of
enterprise or saving and so on, our tools of analysis such as
quasi-rent, equilibrium, coefficients of production, *even* marginal utility can be interpreted so as to tally with *every*
kind of psychology. The psychological background is, so far
as any point of this kind is concerned, little more than a
facon de parler and hence cannot be the logical--as distinct
from historical--derivate of any particular one.

(2) Without attacking fundamentals there is, of course, plenty of room for difference as to the usefulness or otherwise of any single tool or method--that is, any way of handling a given set of facts for given purposes. For myself, I confess to a strong belief, for example, in the future role, both within theory itself and in the practical problems of "Welfare Economics," of the tool called "sum total of consumers' surpluses." Perhaps Professor Mitchell does not share this belief. But if we were to discuss the question, we could not but discuss it as a question of theory and by means of theoretical arguments. Epistemology and methodological creeds would not enter. Such differences, necessarily incident to scientific work, are no cleavages between "schools."

(3) But must the tools of theory not prove useless for the book before us, being constructed without reference to its task--a *numerical* treatment of our problems? But have they been thus constructed? Have those who went before us not all theorized with an eye to quantitative[2] treatment, present or future? In Marshall's case especially, Mitchell, the fairest of critics, surely would not deny that he both saw and worked for, this task. We need not read between the lines in Marshall or dwell on the explicit statement in that great manifesto of his, "The old generation of economists and the new." We need only look at the text, at the treatment of demand or of cost, at the distinction between external and internal economies, the theory of monopoly, the dealing with the element of time, the formula of point elasticity--all opening their arms, as it were, to future masses of statistics. Nor need we speak of his reiterated hints at the stores of statistics of all kinds already available. It is true that, to take the simplest instance, his demand curve has repeatedly been denied the aptitude to serve as the demand curve of statistics. Yet it has been the beacon to all work in the field, and whether it will or will not prove useful in the end is still *sub judice*.

(4) Finally, our analytic engine, it is held, is bound to undergo continuous change, fully as much as mere "hypotheses" are, under the influence of the results of "factual" study. It can never stand by the side of them as if an immovable organon of hyperempirical canons. Not only must the stream of new fact present to us ever new problems necessitating, to use a phrase of Pigou's, the attaching of new arms to our engine; but also, and much more important, increasing insight into facts necessarily makes some instruments of theory obsolete and creates the need for new ones. As Mitchell says apropos of a special case (p. 54): "But as our knowledge grows wider and more intimate, our attitude toward the discussion of causes

undergoes a subtle change." Of course it does. The theoretical part of every science always refers to, and acquires its
meaning from, a given state of factual knowledge. The instruments of theory which have been useful, and theorems which, in
the sense of pragmatism, have been "true" in one state, may
very well, and often *do*, prove bars to progress and even downright wrong in another. New theories and new criteria for the
acceptance of theories become inevitable as time and work go
on. They would be necessary even if the old ones had been
perfect for their day. A single fact a la Michelson may change
the face of theory. But *quis negavit*? Difference on this head
can arise only if "factual" students deny that the influence
of factual study on the apparatus of theory is no greater than
the influence of theory on factual study; if they overlook the
necessity of continuously directing part of our collective
effort toward improving our theoretic tools as such, independently of the impulse of new facts or problems; if they refuse
on general grounds to acquire a working knowledge of them; and
if they reject particular instruments in cases in which it is
doubtful whether they have fully mastered their meaning.

[1]Business Cycles; The Problem and Its Setting, by Wesley C.
Mitchell, with a foreword by Edwin F. Gay, New York, National
Bureau of Economic Research, Inc., 1928.

[2]"Quantitative" and numerical" are synonymous in Mitchell's
book.

*Quarterly Journal of Economics, (November 1930): 150-58

"Wesley Mitchell in Retrospect," Geoffrey H. Moore (1978)*

One of the marks of a great economist is that his works
live after him. Wesley Mitchell's works had this enduring
quality. I should like to recall to mind some of the concepts,
ideas, methods of analysis, and, indeed, institutions that
Mitchell initiated and developed which are still very much
alive.

Some ten years ago quite a few economists were pronounc-
ing a benediction upon the business cycle. Not only could
recession be avoided, but also booms could be turned off before they got out of hand. The business cycle was dead. It
is interesting to recall that the government's compendium of

economic indicators, which started publication in 1961 with the title *Business Cycle Developments*, had its name changed in 1968 to *Business Conditions Digest*. The initials BCD remained, and the content stayed much the same, but in 1968 the term "business cycle" was deemed obsolete. One of the arguments for dropping the term was that the government did not want to be in the position of seeming to perpetuate the phenomenon it had disposed of.

It is now obvious that the interment was premature. BCD turned out to mean not Business Cycle Dead, but Boom Control Deficient. The boom did get out of hand, producing the inflation with which we are still struggling. It led to the world wide recession of 1973-1975, proving to everyone that the business cycle was still a formidable beast. Mitchell would have been disappointed. He had devoted most of his life to studying business cycles in order to find ways of taming them.

It is ironic that Mitchell did not live to see that his hopes had been at least partly fulfilled. Between 1948, when he died, and 1973, the United States experienced five recessions, and they proved to be briefer and milder than most of those that Mitchell had studied. The sixth recession, 1973-1975, was indeed a setback, but not enough to reverse the trend. Few people seem to be aware, in rating 1973-1975 as the worst recession since the 1930s, that in terms of the decline in employment it was one of the briefest and mildest since World War II. Furthermore, the major reason for this, the rapid growth of the more stable service-type industries, is destined to continue. This is just the kind of observation that Mitchell himself would have made, in view of his interest in the secular changes that business cycles undergo. So, while the severity and scope of the 1973-1975 recession would have been a disappointment to him, he would also have noticed the hopeful signs emanating from the changing structure of the job market. For if jobs are becoming more recession-proof, this will be a powerful force making for milder recessions. It will be one of the factors, as Mitchell's colleague Arthur Burns pointed out in 1959, enabling us to continue to make "progress toward economic stability," a goal very close to Mitchell's heart Burns [1960]. Unfortunately, we make such progress gradually, and not by revising the titles of government publications.

The concern for human welfare that was at the root of Mitchell's interest in business cycles has continued to motivate his followers. Much of what he had to say on the losses

due to depressions has a modern ring. In 1923 he wrote: "The
amount of energy it is wise to spend on efforts to control
the business cycle depends on the gains in national welfare
which can be secured. The most definite of these prospective
gains consists in diminishing the economic losses we now suffer
from the wastes of booms, the forced liquidations of crises,
and the involuntary idleness of depressions" [President's Conference on Unemployment 1923, p. 32].

In the ensuing analysis Mitchell developed probably the
first estimate of what is now known as the "GNP gap," the difference between actual and potential output. It covers the
years 1909 to 1918, shows an aggregate loss of real income of
2.4 percent during the ten years, and a maximum loss of 9.4
percent in the depressed year 1914. Some interesting questions
are posed, such as how to estimate the deleterious effects on
efficiency from "the haste, worry and strain to which workers
on overtime and harried business men are subject" in boom
years, and how to allow for the fact that "men unemployed in
years of depression turn out many goods not represented in
statistics of production—garden products, home improvements,
and the like." Mitchell also noted the longer run effects
not captured by a simple comparison of good years with bad.
"Are not many adults made permanently less capable workers by
the distress suffered and bad psychological or bad mental habits formed when out of their jobs for months at a time? And
are not many children prevented from becoming as useful citizens as they might have become, had family incomes been regular" [ibid., p. 34]?

Mitchell took the business cycle as a unit of observation
to be studied. He did this as early as 1913, when he published
Business Cycles, the book that made him famous. The cycle
could be divided into phases, which he then labeled revival,
prosperity, crisis, depression, and revival again. Each phase
had its characteristic pattern of development, related to the
developments of the preceding phase. Each phase and cycle
also was unique, differing from its predecessors even though
family resemblances could be traced. It was this similarity
with a difference that intrigued Mitchell and formed the basis
for his researches. In it he found the main challenge to
business cycle theory.

"A theory of business cycles," he wrote, "must therefore
be a descriptive analysis of the cumulative changes by which
one set of business conditions transforms itself into another
set" [Mitchell 1913, p. 449]. Because the process is cumulative, he regarded a thoroughly adequate theory applicable to

all cycles, past and future, as unattainable. There will always be antecedents and consequences that we do not know about.
But if the ideal is unattainable, this does not mean that useful approximations cannot be made. It was to this end that
Mitchell sought uniformities among the cyclical observations
available to him and tried to explain both the uniformities
and the differences.

This approach led him to establish, with the help of
others such as William Thorp, Simon Kuznets, and Arthur Burns,
a business cycle chronology. It defined the unit of observation. During the 1920s and 1930s the chronology underwent
several modifications in concept and definition before emerg-
ing, in the 1940s, in the form that is known and used today.
The dates of business cycle peaks and troughs, and the corresponding durations of expansion and contraction, have been
among the most widely used products of the studies conducted
by the National Bureau of Economic Research during the past
thirty years. If a chart is constructed with "shaded areas"
representing periods of recession, the dates delineating those
areas are almost certain to be the National Bureau's dates.
Mitchell's unit of observation is still serving a useful purpose.

It is curious, also, that two of the more recent developments in work on business cycle chronologies were foreshadowed
by Mitchell's studies. One is their spread to countries other
than the United States. Chronologies are currently established
either by governmental or private agencies in Canada, Japan,
the United Kingdom, West Germany, Italy, Australia, and elsewhere. But as early as 1913 Mitchell based his study of business cycles on experience in four countries--the United States,
Great Britain, France, and Germany--and later made extensive
use of Thorp's *Business Annals*, which covered business cycles
in seventeen countries [Thorp 1926]. For Mitchell, the cycle
was an international phenomenon.

The second recent development is what we have come to call
growth cycle chronologies. These are swings in rates of economic growth or, alternatively, in economic data adjusted for
long-term trend. In the 1920s many studies of business cycles
were conducted in terms of data adjusted for long-term trend,
and in Mitchell's 1927 book, *Business Cycles: The Problem and
Its Setting*, five U.S. indexes of business activity are analyzed in this way. The average length of the thirteen periods
of business expansion between 1878 and 1923, as delineated by
these five trend-adjusted indexes, was 23 months. The average
for the twelve intervening periods of contraction was 20 months

[Mitchell 1927, p. 338]. These averages compare closely with those recently reported by Victor Zarnowitz for the eight U.S. growth cycles from 1948 to 1975: 20 months for expansions, 18 months for contractions [National Bureau 1977, p. 35].

Growth cycles since 1948, therefore, seem to be made from the same mold, so far as average duration and frequency of occurrence are concerned, as those observed by Mitchell before 1923. He did not, however, believe these durations were of much value in forecasting how long the next cycle would last. For this purpose, he wrote, "neither modal length, nor the duration of the preceding cycle is a safe guide" [Mitchell 1927, p. 417]. They have been, however, a rather good guide to the *average* duration of the growth cycles experienced during the 29 years following Mitchell's death. The frequency of cycles has not changed as much as their amplitude.

The business cycle chronologies that Mitchell developed enabled him to make systematic obeservations on the sequences in which cyclical changes in different economic processes occurred. He had found, in his early work, a large number of hypotheses about this but very little factual information. He believed that by comparing the peaks and troughs in specific series with the peaks and troughs in the business cycle, one could obtain useful information on the sequences among the processes represented by the series. Individual business cycle turns could be studied closely, and one could also see which sequences were repetitive and which were not, whether they changed over time, whether they were different at high points than at low points, and so forth. When put together with knowledge about how different parts of the economic system work—what motivates the holding of inventories of different kinds; how making goods to order and making them to stock affect the relations between orders, shipments, and production; how prices affect costs and costs affect prices—Mitchell and his colleagues would be able to weave a logical account of how business cycles came about.

Mitchell himself did not live to write all that he intended to about this—he contemplated a final work of synthesis. In that work I believe he would have developed what would have become known as a general theory of business cycles. For Mitchell realized the value of theory and always had a theoretical, motivational framework in mind as he pursued his own research and evaluated that of others. Milton Friedman [1950] believed that Mitchell's theoretical framework could be put in the form of a mathematical model, and when he tried it he found that Mitchell had included most of the basic ideas upon

which modern models are based. As do present-day model builders, Mitchell insisted that the theory fit the facts. But the
realm of facts that Mitchell thought the theory should fit
covered a wider historic and geographic range, and more aspects of economic life, than most model builders nowadays en-
visage. Ultimately, the difficulties of finding what the
facts were and how they could be accounted for in a coherent,
understandable theory of the business cycles of experience
proved to be more than Mitchell could surmount in his life-
time. The "general theory" remains to be written.

Nevertheless, one of the advantages of the plan of study
that Mitchell organized was that it did not depend upon the
output or the intellectual capacity of any single individual.
He did not believe that he alone had the requisite capacity,
and so he organized a group, most of whose members would spe-
cialize in particular fields of research, such as inventories,
consumption, construction, prices, employment, or finance.
The group not only would broaden the scope of what could be
thoroughly investigated, but also could carry on over a longer
span of time. That is what happened. Three works in the National Bureau's Studies of Business Cycles series, which began with Mitchell's 1927 book, were published before he died,
but 20 have been published since. And this does not count the
large number of articles published by the bureau or elsewhere,
such as Arthur Burns's basic article on business cycles for
the *International Encyclopedia of the Social Sciences* [Burns
1968].

Mitchell's work has lived on in these studies, and it has
also lived on in the statistical data they have helped to generate. The leading indicators issued each month by the Department of Commerce make front-page news and are reported on
television and radio. Yet, few who hear about them are aware
that they are directly descended from the work that Mitchell
and Burns did in 1937, utilizing what was already a substantial body of knowledge about business cycle processes and a
voluminous collection of statistical time series pertaining
to those processes. That work was the progenitor of a series
of studies of leading, coincident, and lagging indicators issued in 1950, 1960, 1967, and 1975. Each of these examined
what had previously been done in the light of subsequent experience, showing whether and in what respects the previous
work had been deficient or misleading and could now be improved upon. I like to think of this series of studies, together with the monographic reports that account for and document the behavior of particular types of indicators, including
the file of current data that is constantly accumulating and

providing fresh evidence, as one of the longest continued scientific experiments in the field of economics. For many years
few but specialists in business cycle research paid any attention to it. Only in the 1950s and 1960s did the "leading indicator approach" become widely used by government and business economists. Mitchell would not, of course, have predicted that this would happen, but his plan of work did make
it possible. That is a measure of his genius as an organizer
and director of research.

The idea of the business cycle as a unit of analysis has
become popular in recent years in another connection. During
the present recovery, following the recession of 1973-1975, I
have been impressed by the widespread use of the device of
comparing the current recovery with previous ones to see whether we are keeping pace or falling behind, or in what respects
the current recovery is unusual, is developing imbalances, requires stimulation, and so forth. Indeed, I have kept a little
collection of these published comparisons, and the sources now
include news magazines and newspapers, business periodicals,
and reports by government agencies and congressional commit-
tees. All of them use the business cycle as the unit of analysis, and all of them are, whether they know it or not, copying
the procedure that Mitchell devised for studying the cyclical
behavior of different economic processes. For historical work,
Mitchell used a nine-point pattern, constructed by dividing a
complete cycle into nine stages. From these patterns rates
of changes, amplitudes, timing differences, and measures of
conformity could be computed on a comparable basis. The nine-
point pattern is not well adapted to current analysis, since
the current cycle is always incomplete, but a simple modification of the scheme makes it possible to compare a current recession or recovery with its historical counterparts. The
observations can be used not only for simple comparisons of
this sort, but also for analyses of why some recessions are
severe and some are not, why some recoveries are more inflationary than others, and which policies have had a clearly
visible effect and which have not.

Throughout his studies of business cycles Mitchell emphasized the central importance of the pursuit of profits.
We read in his 1913 volume: "Since the quest of money profits
by business enterprises is the controlling factor among the
economic activities of men who live in a money economy, the
whole discussion [of how business cycles come about] must center about the prospects of profits" [Mitchell 1913, p. 450].
In his 1927 volume he wrote: "In our analysis of business cycles, then, we must recognize that profit making is the cen-

tral process among the congeries that constitute the activities of a business economy" [Mitchell 1927, p. 183; see also p. 107]. Although Mitchell did not live to complete his final descriptive analysis of business cycles, it seems likely that he would have accorded much attention to the relationship of profits to the course of the business cycle. He would have shown how costs rise relative to prices during a business cycle expansion, squeezing profit margins, reducing incentives to invest, and often reducing the wherewithal to invest. He sould have shown how this situation is reversed during a recession, with costs falling relative to prices, profit margins beginning to pick up, and the prospects for an adequate return on investment reviving. This was a leading argument in Mitchell's 1913 volume, which he developed on the basis of very sketchy statistical evidence coupled with careful observation of the way business enterprises function. One of the ironies of fate is that it was not until 1972, nearly a quarter-century after Mitchell died, that the definitive data were published that showed the essential validity of his hypothesis.

What happened in 1972 was that the Bureau of Labor Statistics began publishing quarterly figures on prices, costs, and profits per unit of output for all nonfinancial corporations. The data begin in 1948, the year Mitchell died, and now cover six business cycles. In every one of these cycles, unit costs, prices, and unit profits follow essentially the course that Mitchell had described [Moore 1975; 1977]. In the early stages of each expansion, prices rose faster than costs, reversing the previous downward trend in profits per unit of output. In the later stages of each expansion, costs rose faster than prices, causing a downward trend in unit profits to emerge, a trend that continued until the next recession began. These cyclical changes in the price/cost situation appear to me to be very closely related to changes in investment commitments by business enterprises, such as contracts for the construction of new plants and orders for new equipment. Favorable shifts in prices relative to costs have had a stimulating effect on investment, unfavorable shifts a retarding effect. Mitchell would have been pleased, of course, to see his hypothesis supported by evidence, and even more pleased to see that the evidence to support or contradict was now so much more abundant than when he formulated the hypothesis.

On this point one of the most telling sections of his 1913 volume contains his recommendations for improvement of statistics on business activity. He supported, for example, the idea of obtaining reports on contracts let for construc-

tion work and the percentage of work performed on old contracts, saying that "few sets of figures would give more insight into business conditions when prosperity was verging
toward a crisis or when depression was engendering prosperity" [Mitchell 1913, p. 593]. He goes on to say: "Most to be
desired of all are statistics depicting the relative fluctuations of costs and profits. Unhappily, the difficulties both
theoretical and practical in the way of obtaining such figures
are particularly great. But certainly every extension of public authority over corporate activity should be utilized to
require such uniform methods of accounting as have been imposed upon the interstate railways, and the reports obtained
by the government should be made available in some significant form for the information of the business public" [Mitchell
1913, p. 594].

The "extension of public authority over corporate activity" that Mitchell referred to came promptly with the enact-
ment of the corporate income tax in 1913, and the annual data
from this source were for many years the only comprehensive
data available. But their annual form and long publication
lag made them of limited use for business cycle analysis. The
quarterly survey data now available, published about two months
after the end of the quarter to which they refer, come much
closer to fulfilling Mitchell's prescription. It is strange
that nearly sixty years elapsed before this important step was
taken. In the meantime, virtually all the other statistical
recommendations that Mitchell made in 1913--including comprehensive data on unemployment, an index of the physical volume
of trade, an index of bond prices and yields, and a general
recommendation that data be published more promptly--have long
since become part of our statistical intelligence system.

To conclude these remarks upon the intellectual legacy of
Wesley Clair Mitchell, let me note that, as befitted an economist who liked to consider how the institutions man creates or
inherits shape his economic destiny, Mitchell himself created
an enduring institution. For many years it was unique in the
economic world. It was peculiarly Mitchellian in design and
operation. It was organized in 1920 "in response to a growing demand for objective determination of the facts bearing
upon economic problems, and for their interpretation in an
impartial manner." It was to "concentrate upon topics of national importance that are susceptible of scientific treatment." And it was to do so "under such auspices and with such
safeguards as should make its finding carry conviction to all
sections of the nation." By "issuing its findings in the form
of scientific reports, entirely divorced from recommendations

on policy, it was to aid all thoughtful men, however divergent their views of public safety, to base their discussions
upon objective knowledge as distinguished from subjective
opinion" [National Bureau 1977].

This institution was, and is, the National Bureau of
Economic Research. Directed by Mitchell during its first
twenty-five years, and imbued then and thereafter with his
instinct for workmanship and his scholarly yet practical interests, it multiplied his own capacities manyfold. It is
today a living monument to his creative energy.

*Journal of Economic Issues, Vol. XII, No. 2, (June 1978):
277-286

A *Monetary History of the United States, 1867-1960*
by
Milton Friedman and Anna Jacobson Schwartz

REVIEW: Robert M. Solow (November, 1964)*

Provessor Milton Friedman, the senior author of the massive
"analytical history" of the monetary mechanism in the United
States, occupies a special place in contemporary American economic thought. He is the intellectual leader of the "Chicago
School"--with branch offices as widely scattered as Charlottes-
ville, Virginia and Los Angeles, California--whose guiding principles are that "money [and little else] matters," that the way
it matters is best analysed with the help of a more or less
jazzed-up version of the Quantity Theory, and that the correct
approach to social and economic policy is a new Manchester liberalism no less shallow than the old. He is famous as a sharp
and pertinacious thinker and as a formidable debater, a subtle
theorist and a resourceful statistician. He has been an active
adviser to Senator Goldwater during the Presidential campaign--
and is said to have found him a little too moderate for his economic taste. Although only a small minority of the profession
is persuaded by his opinions, around any academic lunch table
on any given day, the talk is more likely to be about Milton
Friedman than about any other economist. As one would expect
from such a lively and dedicated man, and as the epigraph from
Marshall--about the treacherousness of pretending to let the
facts speak for themselves--suggests, this *Monetary History**
is a work simultaneously of scholarship and special pleading.
One ought not to be misled by either aspect into forgetting
about the other.

The history begins in 1867 with the United States on an
inconvertible fiat-money standard--with gold and greenbacks
circulating side by side and foreign exchange rates freely
floating--and ends 93 years and 700 pages later in rather different circumstances. One of the authors' contributions is
the production of a continuous time series of the stock of
money, annually or semi-annually from 1867 to 1906 and monthly

from May, 1907, to the end of 1960. In their running discussion
they use a hybrid definition of the money supply: currency held
by the public plus demand deposits (adjusted for inter-bank and
U.S. government deposits and for items in collection) plus time
deposits in commercial banks. But the appendix tables provide
also the more usual totals; one less inclusive (without any time
deposits), one more inclusive (with deposits in mutual savings
banks and the postal savings system, but without saving and loan
shares which became important only after 1945). All this attention to the stock of money is no accident; in Professor Friedman's strict-construction view of the Quantity Theory it is
Money that matters, not "credit," not "liquidity," not interest
rates.

Ruthless Concentration

The evolution of the stock of money and its arithmetic determinants is the thread around which the narrative is organized. There is also much penetrating discussion of the development of monetary institutions, monetary policies and monetary
ideas. Nothing could be more natural than that a Monetary History should be primarily about the (narrowly) monetary side of
economic events, all the more so when prevailing economic doctrine has only recently--prodded by Professor Friedman, among
others--swung around from the view that monetary phenomena are
not very important to the view that perhaps they are. Yet monetary history, like political history, can indoctrinate through
its choice of what to emphasize and what not to say. Here, for
instance, is the Friedman-Schwartz discussion of the recession
in 1953-54:

> At the outset of 1953 the monetary authorities became con-
> cerned about inflationary pressures and initiated a series
> of restrictive actions, further described below, which pro-
> duced a drastic tightening of money markets and the closest
> thing to a money market crisis since 1933. The restrictive
> actions, the changed general expectations about monetary
> policy that accompanied them, and the final bond market
> crisis may well have played an important role in determin-
> ing the timing of a peak in general business--in July 1953,
> rather than later. If so, the bond market crisis itself
> was probably only the final straw since, as we have seen,
> such events take time to produce their effect. Yet the
> bond market crisis came only two months before the peak in
> general business. It is also possible that the monetary
> events were not decisive but that other underlying forces
> were making for the culmination of the expansion in any
> event; and that those forces enhanced the tightening effect

of the monetary measures taken.

There is hardly a word in this paragraph to which one could take exception. And yet, a reader of this book ten years from now--when it will still be read--may not remember that the Korean War came to an end in 1953, and that the decline of $8,000 millions in the annual rate of inventory accumulation between the second and fourth quarters of 1953 may conceivably have been related to the expectation of falling defense expenditures, that the annual rate of defense spending did fall from $53,000 millions in the second quarter of 1953 to $40,000 millions in the fourth quarter of 1954, that other federal spending fell during the same interval, and that these events may even have had something to do with the behaviour of the monetary totals.

The pages of narrative are peppered with bits of incisive analysis, often devastating refutations of traditional views. When there is no ideology showing, the book is a pleasure to read, even on events now so remote as the resumption of specie payments in 1879 and the silver agitation of the next 20 years. British readers will naturally be more interested in the authors' interpretation of more recent monetary history. I mention only two examples: the depression of the 1930s and the postwar rise in the velocity of money.

The Great Depression: Blaming the Fed

The long 120-page chapter "The Great Contraction, 1929-33" makes fascinating reading. The discussion is almost exclusively about the monetary facets of the depression; we are reminded only in a few lines and in one chart that money income fell by 53 percent, real income by 36 percent, and industrial production by about 50 percent, during those four years. With all the distortion that ruthless compression of subtle argument entails, the Friedman-Schwartz view may be summarized as follows: the depression began as a more or less standard business-cycle contraction; it may have been destined--for "real" or monetary reasons--to be a severe contraction as contractions go; but what turned it into catastrophe and trauma was the collapse of the monetary system, beginning with the banking crises of October, 1930, and March, 1931, and culminating in the panic and bank holiday of March, 1933. From 1929 to 1933 the stock of money fell by a third (most of that took place after 1930) and velocity by nearly as much. Precisely the kind of liquidity crisis took place that the Federal Reserve System had been invented to prevent. Why?

The authors' answer to this question is implied in the further question they put as title to the last section of the chapter: "Why was monetary policy so inept?" The liquidity crisis occurred because the central bank did not do what was necessary to stop it, namely to provide reserves, and more reserves, through open-market purchases. The contraction in 1929-30 was sharper than the mild recessions of 1923-24 and 1926-27; but the Reserve System added less to its holdings of government securities than it had in the second of those recessions--and most of its purchases had come in 1929 in reaction to the stock market crash. Well, why *was* monetary policy so inept? Friedman and Schwartz conclude that the explanation is the shift of power within the System, from the New York Bank to an enlarged Open Market Committee in Washington, and the ignorance and inexperience of those to whom the power shifted. They argue convincingly that Benjamin Strong, had he not died in 1928, would have carried the System into action or have acted alone with the New York Bank. George L. Harrison, Strong's successor, favoured an active policy but had neither the force of character nor the prestige to ram it through.

I think one must grant the substantial truth of this account. There is a common half-formulated notion that the great depression was the inevitable culmination of deep-lying forces that could not have been reversed by any instrumentality on earth--or at least by none in a capitalist economy. This would be a more attractive hypothesis if its proponents could specify just what those mysterious forces were. It seems nearer the truth to say that a determined provision of reserves by the Federal Reserve early in the game could have lessened the likelihood and the magnitude of the financial collapse, that the financial crisis was responsible for a good part of the length and depth of the depression, and that therefore the worst of the depression could have been avoided. I suspect--and I think Friedman would agree--that such capital salvage operations as the Reconstruction Finance Corporation and the Federal Deposit Insurance Corporation might have been as useful as conventional open-market operations in preventing the worst of the slump.

Granted that, one can ask what would have happened if the Reserve System had bought in the open market in 1929 and 1930 as generously as Strong, or Bagehot for that matter, would have recommended. The short answer is that no one can possibly know. The doctrine of this book, part unspoken, is that significant industrial fluctuations are primarily a reflex of changes in the stock of money, and that changes in the stock of money--though influenced, of course, by volatile elements in the public's desire to hold cash--can be reliably engineered by the central bank. From this it would follow that correct monetary policy could have turned the 1929 contraction into something in the same league as 1923-24 and 1926-27. Someone like myself, with no confidence in the first of the underlying propositions and less than perfect confidence in the second, would prefer a weaker statement. I see no good reason to doubt, however, that the *combination* of sensible monetary policy, capital-salvage operations, and appropriate tax-and-expenditure policy could, then as now, have controlled the level of output and employment.

Prosperity Through Bigger Reserves?

The authors would presumably go much further and argue that at any time during the 1929-33 contraction or during the incomplete 1933-37 recovery, the monetary authorities could have restored prosperity simply by generating the right amount of reserves. The conventional argument to the contrary rests on the emergence after 1929 of substantial excess reserves. (Cash assets of member banks in excess of required reserves almost tripled between 1929 and 1940 as a percentage of total assets in excess of required reserves, despite the doubling of the required reserve ratio in 1936-37.) Officials of the Federal Reserve convinced themselves that they were pursuing an easy-enough monetary policy by pointing to the vast unused lending capacity of the banking system. Friedman and Schwartz argue to the contrary that those reserves were excess only in name. The shock of the successive bank crises and the failure of the Federal Reserve to defend them had intensified the bank's desire for liquidity to the point where it could not be satisfied by the required volume of reserves. The formal excess reserves thus represented desired liquidity for the commercial banks.

There is some evidence for this view in the fact that the banks reacted to the (unfortunate) doubling of reserve requirements in 1936-37 by moving sharply to restore their excess reserves, the consequent tightness no doubt contributing to the substantial recession in 1937-38. But Friedman and Schwartz fail to make a convincing case for the rest of their argument. In the first place, continuity may suggest, but cannot prove, that because banks moved in 1936 to restore excess reserves that were taken from them they would not willingly have absorbed substantial additions to their excess reserves. In the second place, 1936 was not 1933 (nor was it 1938); only the most simple-minded theory would extrapolate back to the worst years of the depression the reaction observed after three or four years of substantial, if incomplete, recovery. In the third place, the authors make no serious attempt to consider the borrower's side of the deposit-creation mechanism. In 1932, as they might have reminded the reader, corporations lost in the aggregate $3,400 millions (the national income was $42,500 millions). For many a businessman in that year, a deposit in a liquid bank must have seemed like a better earning asset than any real investment he could have undertaken.

To assert the importance of monetary policy, it should be enough that at almost all times an engineered increase in the quantity of money will not itself induce a completely-offsetting decline in velocity. Why should one try to argue the more questionable hypothesis that the potency of an increase in the money supply in a year like 1938 (when the Treasury bill rate is infinitesimal) is likely to be of the same magnitude as in a tight-money era like 1920 or the first years of the 1930-35 slump? Of course, if the authors took this sensible eclectic view, their theory would degenerate into anybody's modern Keynesian theory of money and interest, which does say that engineered changes in the quantity of money will move business activity in the same direction. By overstating their case, the authors fail to make convincingly the point that readers of the Radcliffe Report need to have brought home to them—that mere refutation of constant-velocity assumptions does not deny to the stock of money a role as an active determinant of total liquidity and of business activity.

Rising Velocity and Interest Rates

It is characteristic of the Friedman version of the Quantity Theory that in principle it is admitted that velocity is an economic variable like any other and open to influence from many sides, but in practice velocity is always treated like Old Reliable. In discussing the might-have-beens, they pay little attention to the possibility mentioned above that engineered increases in the quantity of money might themselves induce at least partially-offsetting reductions in velocity. When I say that velocity is taken to be reliable I do not mean it is treated as constant. It is recognized that velocity exhibits typical trend and cycle movements. In particular, there is a marked downward trend, which Friedman explains by the hypothesis that consumers of the services of cash balances—and restaurant meals and education—tend to increase their consumption more than proportionally with increases in income. Thus the period since the end of the war presents the authors with a major difficulty, for from the (artificial) low point of 1.16 in 1946, the velocity of money rose to 1.69 in 1960, a value not surpassed since 1930. It does not seem to me that they meet the difficulty well; indeed at times the quality of the

empirical argument falls embarrassingly low. I am perhaps
reading more into this than I ought; but it seems to me that
the authors have created a convoluted sort of dilemma for themselves. In principle the Quantity Theory could do what comes
naturally: explain the postwar rise in velocity as the natural
response to the postwar rise in interest rates. But in practice
the New Quantity Theory professes not to be able to find any
influence of interest rates on velocity. I cannot suppress the
feeling that this is because once interest rates enter, the New
Quantity Theory becomes almost indistinguishable from Keynesian
liquidity preference.

In any case, Friedman and Schwartz feel obliged to deny
the interest-rate explanation. To do so they have to explain
away the work of Latané (*Review of Economics and Statistics*,
November, 1954, and November, 1960) which relies heavily on
the relation between velocity and interest rates. They make
something of differences in monetary definitions, more of differences in the time-period covered by Latané's analysis and
their own, and conclude finally that "there is no irreconcilable
conflict between Latané's results and our own." But this
leaves us precisely nowhere, since Latané believes the postwar
rise in velocity to be explicable in terms of interest rates
and Friedman-Schwartz believe it is not.

As Friedman and Schwartz justly point out, the initial
rise in velocity after 1945 must to some extent have been simply a correction of the artificially high accumulation of cash
balances during the war. They go on to make much of a comparison of velocity curves for 1929-42 and 1942-60. There is a
certain similarity between the two curves; the fall in velocity
from 1929 to 1932 parallels the fall from 1942 to 1946; the
rise from 1932 to 1937 matches the rise from 1946 to 1951. But
interest rates were generally falling during the earlier period,
not rising. Ergo, movements of interest rates can not explain
the postwar behaviour of velocity, since the same velocity pattern appears prewar with a different movement of interest rates.
One does not know what to make of the spectacle of Professor
Friedman--who could produce, and no doubt has produced, a with-
eringly sophisticated critique of any Chicago student's attempt
to estimate the demand curve for peanut butter--relying on so
weak a form of argument. For one thing, the two velocity curves
are not so parallel: velocity fell fairly sharply from 1937 to
1940 and the rise from 1940 to 1942 is presumably fully accounted for by the coming of the war; but velocity moved roughly sideways from 1951 to 1954 and then resumed a fairly steady
rise. And secondly, by no stretch of the imagination can this
kind of selective comparison of two historical episodes be

treated as if it were a controlled experiment. There is presumably more than one causal factor operating on velocity: if
interest rates by themselves do not explain 1929-37 they may
yet explain a lot about 1946-60.

No Substitutes for Money?

In a similar spirit, the authors reject the hypothesis
that the postwar rise in velocity (i.e. fall in money balances
per unit of income) might be accounted for in part by the development and ready availability of new and closer substitutes
for what they happen to be calling money. The usual candidates
are mutual savings bank deposits, savings and loan shares, and
short-term government securities. Their main ground for this
conclusion is a fairly casual discussion of the years 1954-58.
"The noticeable slackening off in the growth of commercial bank
time deposits [which do count as money] from the end of 1954 to
the end of 1956 and subsequent rapid rise from early 1957 to
mid-1958 leave no detectable imprint on either mutual savings
deposits or savings and loan shares." As a result of this reading of the facts, the authors conclude that "neither mutual savings bank deposits nor savings and loan shares are very close
substitutes for commercial bank time deposits, at least for
short periods." One is tempted to respond to that conclusion
as the Duke of Wellington responded to the man who mistook him
for Mr. Smith.

In the end, Friedman and Schwartz propose a hypothesis of
their own: that the postwar fall in cash balances per unit of
income reflects the public's improved expectations about economic stability. A more tranquil and confident world calls for
less liquidity. But since this is a once-for-all change, once
velocity has found the higher level appropriate to the new expectations one would expect the downward trend to re-assert
itself. It is not clear that this suggestion is meant to be
taken seriously. I am so eclectic I am prepared to believe
that it may actually represent one among several factors. But
many of those who think the Radcliffe Committee went too far
in the "velocity can be any old thing" direction may find the
Friedman view even less attractive.

The Banker, Vol. CXIV, No. 465, (November, 1964): 710-717

REVIEW: Harry G. Johnson (June, 1965)*

I. Introduction

The long-awaited monetary history of the United States by
Friedman and Schwartz is in every sense of the term a monumental scholarly accomplishment--monumental in its sheer bulk,
monumental in the definitiveness of its treatment of innumerable
issues, large and small, in U.S. monetary history, monumental in
the consistency and coherence of its analysis of nearly a century of drastic institutional change, monumental, above all, in
the theoretical and statistical effort and ingenuity that have
been brought to bear on the solution of complex and subtle economic issues. The volume sets, if not a new style, a new standard for the writing of monetary history, one that requires the
explanation of historical developments in terms of monetary
theory and the application to them of the techniques of quantitative style--apart from some brief arid stretches of statistical description of monetary changes over and within particular
time-periods--and its readability is enhanced by the dramatic
character of several of the episodes it chronicles, notably the
tragic demoralisation of the Federal Reserve System after 1929.
One can safely predict that it will be the classic reference on
its subject for many years to come--and this despite the fact
that the theoretical foundations of the work are currently the
subject of acute controversy.

The book is actually the first to be published of a series
of three, in which the other two will be statistical studies of
the cyclical and secular behavior of the stock of money (by the
same authors) and of the determinants and effects of changes in
the supply of money (by Phillip Cagan). Preliminary versions,
sections, progress reports and partial summaries of the statistical studies have been published. The present volume originated as and is intended to provide a narrative introduction to
the statistical studies, and in turn relies heavily on their
results. The interdependence between the book and the statisti-

cal studies, which are not yet available but whose broad outlines are known, imposes a serious handicap on the reader and
reviewer--the inability to make an independent evaluation of
the reported findings--a handicap that familiarity with Professor Friedman's style of operation leads one to suspect is not
entirely unintentional. The origins of the book in a much
larger research endeavor also account in part for a characteristic that many readers are likely to find exasperating, namely a
strong propensity not to spell out the theoretical model explicitly, but instead to leave it implicit in the concrete analytical use made of it. Thus, for example, the concept of money
employed (currency plus deposits in commercial banks) is not defended against its popular rival (currency plus demand deposits)
until a footnote on p. 649, and the formal model for analysis of
the proximate determinants of the money stock is presented in an
Appendix inserted at the insistence of Clark Warburton. This
propensity, however, is also characteristic of Professor Friedman, as is the book's general theoretical approach, which entails the use of extremely simple naive models--specifically,
the quantity equation, the simple mechanical money supply model
just mentioned and the purchasing-power parity theory--supple-
mented by more elaborate theoretical and statistical analysis to
the extent required by the concrete problem at hand.

Given the interdependence of the book with the related statistical research, and the relevance of its contents to contemporary issues of economic policy, monetary theory and empirical
monetary research, not to mention the role of the senior author
as the foremost modern proponent of the quantity theory and pioneer in its post-war revival, a reviewer is obliged to strike
some balance between approaching the book as a history and approaching it as a contribution to current controversy. The former approach is fairer to the conception of the book, while the
latter is more interesting, though riskier for the reasons
given. In this review I shall first consider the book as a history, then comment on the contemporary issues it raises. Fortunately, these subjects correspond closely to the structure of
the book itself, the last two chapters of which are directed at
contemporary issues.

II. The Monetary History of the United States

As already implied, the book is intended as a monetary
history in a special sense, which the authors define as "a
prologue and background for a statistical analysis of the secular and cyclical behavior of money in the United States" (p.
xxii). It is concerned with tracing changes in the stock of
money, examining the factors responsible for them and analysing

the influence of these changes on the course of events. This concern presupposes that the stock of money is the dominant monetary variable in the economy, a presupposition that the narrative seeks to document, and in my judgment does document quite conclusively. Its consequence for the history is to concentrate attention on those institutional developments that have changed the supply of money or the system of supplying it, to the neglect of developments that might be considered important for other reasons; but in fact the authors deal exhaustively, either in the text or in lengthy footnotes, with virtually everything of conceivable interest to a monetary economist. It also determines the starting-point of the period studied, since 1867 is the first year from which a consistent continuous series of the money stock can be compiled.

Analytically, the period under review can be divided up in various ways (in the first half of it there was no central monetary authority, in the first eighth of it the country was on a floating exchange rate); the authors have chosen to divide it into nine "episodes," periods marked by some major policy debate, crisis or institutional change. These are the greenback period (1867-79) culminating in the resumption of specie payments at the pre-Civil War parity; the period of secularly declining prices (1879-97) and agitation for a silver standard; the period of inflation in response to new gold discoveries (1897-1914), the banking panic and restriction of payments of 1907, and the reform of the banking system; the first period (1914-21) of the Federal Reserve System, culminating in the sharp deflation of 1920-21; the golden age of the Federal Reserve System (1921-29), ending in the stalemate of policy over stock market speculation; the great contraction of 1929-33 and the demoralisation of the Federal Reserve (a separate chapter is devoted to New Deal changes in the banking system and the monetary standard); the period 1933-41, marked by Treasury management of monetary policy and the disastrous increase in reserve requirements in 1936-37; the inflation of the Second World War (1939-48) during which the Federal Reserve supported interest rates on government debt; and the revival of monetary policy, 1948-60.

For each period, the authors present statistical analyses of changes in the money stock, velocity, prices and real income, and of what they term the "arithmetical" or "proximate" sources of change in the money stock. The latter involves an accounting of the change in the stock of money in terms of changes in "high-powered money," $i.e.$, types of money eligible for holding as bank reserves, and changes in the ratios of deposits to currency held by the public and deposits to reserves held by the banks. These factors are proximate determinants because under a gold standard high-powered money is a variable ultimately determined by the balance of payments, and under a bond-support programme high-powered money is passively determined by the public's demand for money; also, the two deposit ratios are themselves behavioural variables, and much of the analysis is concerned with the exploration of changes in them. On this common foundation, the authors investigate the special monetary puzzles of each period, the institutional changes, and the policy problems and developments.

The treatment of the puzzles of particular periods is frequently an intellectual delight. Examples from the earlier periods are the demonstration that government actions made only a minor contribution to the success of resumption, the main factor being the growth of the economy relative to its money supply (pp. 79-85); and the argument that the threat of silver purchases to the gold standard was the precise opposite of what it was thought to be at the time (pp. 130-2). (Two unsolved puzzles are the failure of the national banks to issue as many national bank notes as they apparently could have done with profit (p. 23) and the development of capital exports in 1897-1906 [pp. 142-8].) Examples from later periods are the discussions of the effects of U.S. gold purchases under the Act of 1934, which are treated as a commodity price-support policy (pp. 462-83), and the definitive analysis of the "bills only" policy of the late 1950s, which is shown to have been essentially a device for making the legal ceiling for interest rates on government borrowing effective (pp. 632-6).

Space limitations preclude a detailed commentary on the historical analysis presented. In broad terms, the story is dominated by the failure of the Federal Reserve, after it had pursued what was generally agreed to be an enlightened policy in the 1920s, to stem the monetary collapse of 1929-33, and its subsequent passivity (with the exception of the 1936-37 increase in reserve requirements) until the revival of monetary policy in the 1950s. The failure of the System is documented and explained in a magnificent chapter (Chapter 7) of 121 pages. The explanation offered is essentially one of personal weaknesses and an intra-institutional struggle for power. The commendable performance of the 1920s (about the excellence of which the authors clearly have some doubts) was attributable to the personal force and wisdom of Governor Benjamin Strong of the New York Bank, and to the dominance of the New York Bank in the Federal Open Market Investment Committee. Strong's death in 1928, and the succession to the Governorship of the less forceful George L. Harrison, were responsible for the deadlock between New York

and the other banks over the appropriate policy to deal with
stock market speculation in 1928-29; the enlargement of the Open
Market Committee in March 1930 to include all twelve Governors,
with the New York Bank reduced to an executive agent, permitted
the jealousy of the other Banks--notably Chicago and Boston--
towards the more sophisticated New York group to express itself
in resistance to positive remedial action, which hardened into
the conviction that the System was powerless to act, and indeed
ought not to act.

The description of the process by which the Federal Reserve
System became deadlocked and gradually abdicated its responsibility is remarkably perceptive and convincing. It does, however, raise some questions. One concerns the extent to which
the System really had a consistent and well-thought-out theory
of policy in the twenties, from which internal rivalries diverted it in the thirties; Friedman and Schwartz note the contradiction in its policy statements of the 1920s between the
"real bills" doctrine and an inchoate inventory theory of the
cycle. Another concerns the notion of a "struggle for power"
of which the authors make so much; the struggle was one between
those who believed in the capacity and responsibility of the
System to exercise monetary control and those who denied both;
and the unexplored question--perhaps too broad for a monetary
history--is how the latter acquired the positions from which to
seize power and why they were permitted to exercise it so fatal-
ly. The answer obviously lies in the social psychology and popular understanding of economics at the time; while the authors
are frequently scornful of the Keynesian Revolution, that Revolution probably guarantees that the disaster of 1929-33 will not
be repeated.

The failure of the Federal Reserve in 1929-33 dominates the
story in another and different sense: it has led the authors to
reinterpret the historical experience that led to the establishment of the Federal Reserve System. In their view, the problem
of inelasticity of the currency under the National Banking System was essentially the problem that efforts by the public to
convert deposits into currency automatically produced a multiple
contraction of the money supply; the restrictions of cash payments that normally accompanied banking panics, therefore, far
from being a serious source of disturbance, had the thereputic
effect of preventing such multiple contractions, while permit-
ting continued use of deposit money for most commercial purposes. The problem could have been solved in several other ways
than by establishing the Federal Reserve System--the authors
favour the Aldrich-Vreeland Act of 1908--and the Federal Reserve
Act embodied a fatal confusion between elasticity in the afore-

mentioned sense and elasticity in the sense of the "real bills" doctrine. In the event, the Federal Reserve System not only failed to provide elasticity but also produced a far worse banking crisis than had ever occurred under the National Banking Act, in waves of bank failures that ended in the Banking Holiday of 1933 and, in combination with other developments, wiped out one-third of the U.S. money supply. This interpretation of the record also leads the authors to conclude that what finally removed the instability of the U.S. monetary system was not the Federal Reserve but the system of Federal Deposit Insurance, adopted in 1934; that system both directly removed the incentive for runs on weak banks and indirectly fostered improvements in bank management.

The authors' treatment of this subject exemplifies one of the strengths of the book, which also raises one of the major questions about it. The strong point referred to is the consistent treatment of the monetary experience surveyed as a unity, with its various component episodes used to illuminate and explore others. This approach expresses itself in two major ways. One is through the placarding and examination of parallels between different historical periods--for example, between 1873-93 and 1893-1913 (pp. 183-8) and between 1929-42 and 1942-60 (Chapter 12). The other is through the frequent resort to what the authors term "conjectural history" (and defend on p. 168)--which consists of asking whether the outcome would have been better had some particular historical decision been made differently. This technique, a favourite of Professor Friedman's, is a treacherous one unless used with disciplined care. In the present work it is on the whole employed in an acceptable and extremely illuminating fashion: the authors discuss such interesting questions as whether it would have been better for the United States to adopt a silver instead of a gold standard (p. 134), whether there would have been less inflation during and after the First World War had the Federal Reserve Act not been passed (p. 238) and what might have happened had different policies been followed at three key points in the 1929-33 debacle (p. 391). There are, however, some points at which conjectural history strains the bounds of credibility, notably in connection with the discussion on the consequences of Strong's death; such points are signalled to the alert reader by the use of such phrases as "almost surely." The question raised by this treatment of the 97-year period as a homogeneous entity from the viewpoint of the influence of the money stock is, of course, whether economic behaviour is sufficiently impervious to historical change to justify it, a question that derives its point from the extremely simple theory of demand for money employed in the analysis, as well as the arithmetic treatment of money supply.

As already mentioned, one of the impressive features of
the detailed analysis is the ingenuity of the statistical and
theoretical work. Two technical devices are particularly noteworthy: the use of Canadian experience as a control for checking
propositions about the effects of various American policy developments and the use of the difference between corporate bond and
equity yields as a measure of price expectations. A third technique, of more dubious reliability, is the use of the purchasing-power parity theory to deal with international monetary relationships throughout the book (except, surprisingly, for the
period since 1948, where the subject is scarcely mentioned,
though the authors might have developed some useful background
analysis of the chronic U.S. deficit). According to the theory
used by the authors, purchasing-power parity should hold unless
disturbed by capital movements, changes in tariff barriers or
controls on trade; and this simple notion is used among other
things to determine whether exchange controls were an important
influence on international commerce in the First World War, to
decide how far the golden avalanche of the 1930s was due to the
gold purchase policy as contrasted with capital flight from
Europe, and to argue that price controls in the United Kingdom
prevented "true" prices from being reflected in the price indexes during and after the war. The authors' faith in purchasing-power parity, given the observed range of variation in it,
raises the question of how much of a departure from parity it
would take to refute the theory. They also ignore the point,
recently formalised by Samuelson and Balassa, that price indexes
that include services will show high-productivity countries to
have over-valued currencies, since service prices will vary with
wage-rates. This factor, rather than the question-begging notion of a "growing comparative advantage of the United States
relative to Britain" presented in a footnote on p. 588, probably
accounts for the fact, puzzling to the authors, that the ratio
of U.S. to British prices consistent with a given ratio of U.S.
capital exports to national income has been rising over time.

III. Theoretical and Policy Issues

While the *Monetary History* is a narrative or chronicle of
the past 93 years of U.S. monetary experience, its ultimate purpose is to draw lessons from that experience for contemporary
theory and policy. In addition, parts of its analysis have a
direct bearing on technical issues in monetary theory and empirical research in the field.

To take the more general issues first, the prime and frequently reiterated theme of the book is that the stock of money and changes in it exercise an important influence on the economy, in sharp contradiction to the interpretation placed by majority opinion at the time on the failure of the Federal Reserve to halt the Great Depression in the United States. That failure, the book demonstrates conclusively, was a failure of the policy-makers to prevent monetary contraction, not of monetary expansion to influence the economy (on the contrary, it was the power of monetary policy that made the policy failure so costly). More specifically, a major conclusion is that money plays a determining role in the business cycle; over the longer run, monetary variations do not appear to be so decisive, in the sense that historically the U.S. economy has been capable of growing at similar rates whether the money stock was growing slowly with prices falling or rapidly with prices rising. Nor can the stock of money be regarded as a passively dependent variable--an old-fashioned criticism of the quantity theory to which the authors devote excessive attention--since historical cases of autonomous monetary change can readily be found.

This conclusion is, of course, in opposition to the general tenor or much contemporary monetary analysis, especially that concerned with monetary policy, which emphasises interest rates and credit conditions rather than the quantity of money. The authors devote considerable space to illustrating, convincingly in my judgment, the pitfalls of the alternative approach to monetary policy; it is perhaps worth remarking that their criticisms of the alternate approach do not exclude interest rate changes from the mechanism by which monetary policy influences the economy, though characteristically they do not present an explicit account of how money governs economic activity. In this connection, however, they may have been premature in acclaiming as a radical innovation the adoption by the Federal Reserve in the early 1950s of the two principles of providing for growth of the money supply *pari passu* with the growth of the economy, and varying the money supply contracyclically (pp. 627-32), since the older credit-oriented habits of thought seem to be remarkably tenacious. Nevertheless, the performance of the System in controlling the money supply in the past decade or so has been notably superior to both its own previous performance and monetary experience before 1914.

To turn to the more technical issues, two in particular are worthy of comment; both relate to fundamental cleavages between the quantity theorists and the Keynesians over theoretically crucial empirical issues in U.S. monetary experience. The first, and less far-reaching, is whether there existed a "liq-

uidity trap" in the 1930s banking system, a question important
both for the Federal Reserve's justification of the increase in
required reserves in 1936-37 and for the strictest versions of
Keynesian theory. The authors argue instead that the growth of
excess reserves reflected shifts in the preferences of the
banks, prompted first by the failure of the Reserve System to
come to their rescue in the early thirties and later by the increase in reserve requirements. Their argument on this score,
while broadly plausible, involves a very dubious attempt to reconcile the hypothesis with the facts by some intricate infer-
ences about the lags involved.

The second, and more important, issue concerns the validity
of Professor Friedman's "permanent income" formulation of the
demand for money. According to this hypothesis, which makes demand for money depend only on expected income and prices and not
on interest rates, velocity should have fallen during the postwar period. Instead, it has risen. Other students of money
have generally associated this increase with the increase in interest rates, though one school has attributed it to the improved availability of money substitutes. Professor Friedman
has instead suggested an extension of the permanent income hypothesis to make the demand for money depend on confidence in
economic stability, and attributed the post-war behaviour of
velocity to increased economic stability.

Chapter 12 of the book is devoted to this issue. It is an
instructive example of the art of winning an argument by establishing the form the debate must take. The authors begin by establishing a parallel between the period 1929-42 and the period
1942-60, and insisting that the explanation advanced for the
latter must also hold for the former; they also assert that the
first stage of the post-war rise in velocity was a natural rebound from abnormally low war-time levels. This strategy enables them to argue that the interest rate explanation is superfluous for the rebound phase, and does not explain the rise in
velocity from 1932 to 1942; further, they calculate that the
rise in interest rates could not have accounted for very much of
the increase in velocity. Similar analysis disposes of the
money substitutes and the hypothesis of expected inflation, the
authors calculating that all these factors together could only
explain a minor part of the increase in velocity. They are,
however, unable to explain it statistically by their own hypothesis; nevertheless, the implication is that the superiority of
their hypothesis over alternatives has been maintained. This
could, of course, be true only on the assumption that the analyst is necessarily restricted to simple hypotheses that must
fit the whole historical period, an *a priori* requirement that

has no obvious merits over allowing more complex hypotheses that
would allow different variables to dominate at different times
and the magnitude of their influence to vary. Occam's Razor is
a useful principle, but there is no need to cut the throat of
empirical research with it.

Professor Friedman's attachment to the permanent income
formulation of the demand for money, and his resistance to allowing interest rates any important influence on velocity, in
spite of good theoretical reasons and a great deal of empirical
evidence attesting to such an influence, is itself a rather
perplexing puzzle in the monetary history of the United States.
Contemplation of this book suggests two mutually sustaining hypotheses to explain it. One relates to the methodological position just discussed, which reflects the more fundamental position that U.S. monetary behaviour must be treated as homogeneous
over the century on record. The other involves recognition of
the enormous simplification permitted by a velocity function independent of interest rates. If interest rates do not affect
velocity monetary analysis can be divorced from analysis of the
real sector, since the quantity of money will affect money income in the short run and prices in the long run without interference from the real forces. If, on the other hand, interest
rates do affect velocity, monetary analysis must incorporate the
real sector in a general equilibrium model simultaneously explaining interest rates, velocity, real income and prices.
Moreover, this need for a general equilibrium model comprising
the real and monetary sectors is what the Keynesian Revolution
was about; hence to admit interest rates into the demand function for money is to accept the Keynesian Revolution and Keynes'
attack on the quantity theory. And finally, in the absence of a
velocity function independent of interest rates, the case for
replacing discretionary monetary management by a fixed rule of
monetary increase related to the normal growth of the economy,
advocated elsewhere by Professor Friedman, loses its attractiveness, because variations in interest rates generated by the real
sector would make such a policy rule automatically destabilis-
ing.

IV. Concluding Remarks

This review has sought to convey both something of the
flavour of the Friedman-Schwartz *Monetary History of the United
States* and the bearing of the book on current issues in monetary
theory, monetary research and monetary policy. No review could,
however, hope to do justice to the full range, depth and sophistication of the monetary analysis presented in its pages. The
authors have made a major contribution to monetary history and

monetary theory; and they have conclusively demonstrated that money matters to the general welfare. The book is open to serious criticism on the score of the demand function for money on which it relies, a function that lacks empirical validation and whose validity or failure is associated, as explained in the previous section, with fundamental issues in monetary theory. Nevertheless, it is a most impressive work of painstaking and intelligent scholarship.

*Economic Journal, Volume 75, (June, 1965): 388-396

"The New Economic Faith," Robert B. Zevin (1981)*

...

The initial heyday of conservative conviction and practice lasted for a century and a half. It was decisively terminated by the ubiquitous Great Depression, which began around 1929 and failed to end as promptly and meekly as everyone anticipated. The Depression affected conservatives like a thunderbolt hurled by a wronged god. Here were apparently free and competitive markets, in which desperate producers and workers continually reduced the prices at which they offered their goods and labor, and yet goods could not be sold nor labor employed. To all appearances, governments had done relatively little to intrude on economic activity before or after the Depression's onset. Where were the technical efficiency, the moral justice, the elementary common sense of such a hopelessly fouled system?

Conservatives were routed by these events. Into the abandoned field stepped John Maynard Keynes to expose the fallacies of the orthodox and expound the validity of what had been heresy. There was some confusion in Keynes, as well as among his followers and critics, about whether he had disproved the logic of the conservative argument that showed how free markets led to full employment or whether he had simply revealed that the emperor had no clothes by remarking on the absence of perfect competition to begin with. Keynes's view is expressed in *The General Theory of Employment, Interest and Money.* "Our criticism of the accepted classical theory of economics has consisted not so much in finding logical flaws in its analysis as in pointing out that its tacit assumptions are seldom or never satisfied, with the result that it cannot solve the economic problems of the actual world."

For better or worse, Keynes occupied himself with observed economic behavior more than with the axioms from which behavior could be deduced. *The General Theory's* message is something like this: Relatively small departures from perfect competition make it possible and probable that modern industrial economies will experience some unemployment, as they did for most of their histories even before the Depression. The operational sequel is that modern states have the capacity to ensure full employment by generating a sufficient level of demand, and they ought to do so since unemployment is a waste that serves no valid social or economic purpose.

Most people did not care very much whether the Depression was proof of the absence of competition or of the failure of economists' theories to comprehend the consequences of competition. What it did prove, as Keynes rather unnecessarily argued, was that deep and prolonged unemployment was quite possible in modern economies. The Age of Keynes was the age of commitment by central governments of the industrial democracies to eliminate unemployment, using techniques that had seemed more obvious to laymen than they had to economists. For all his eloquence, acumen, and compassion, Keynes only codified a trend that had been growing longer than his lifetime.

For a long time the Depression loomed over economics. The hapless conservatives could not get out from under its shadow. No matter how many errors of thought they uncovered in the works of Keynes and his followers—and there were plenty of them—the plain truth for economists, plainer still for those less troubled with logical complexities, was that governments had the ability to overcome the Depression's unemployment by acting as employers of ultimate resort. The idea that there were limits to the efficiency of free markets—and that their very existence was in doubt—became central to the new wisdom in all the industrial democracies.

Redemption

The first serious intellectual breach of the Keynesian consensus was achieved in 1963 with the publication of *A Monetary History of the United States, 1867-1960*, by Milton Friedman and Anna Schwartz. Milton Friedman had already led stunning changes of conservative Rough Riders against liberal barricades, and he has led more since, but none has had such penetrating effect as this one.

For nearly three decades conservatives had been attacking the usurpers with little reward, elegantly but vainly presenting the virtues of freedom in economic and political life. A number of theoretically impeccable dissections were performed on the structure of Keynesian thought. These were accorded due respect in graduate economics courses, but had little impact on political economy. The essential weakness of the conservative opposition was its failure to offer an explanation of the Great Depression that was consistent with unqualified faith in the existence and efficacy of free markets.

This defect was remedied by Friedman and Schwartz. They argued that the length and depth of the Depression was not a natural outcome of free-market behavior but a direct result of the perverse misbehavior of the Federal Reserve System. The

nation's central bank, created by the federal government for
the purpose of overriding perceived defects in a competitive
private-bank market, had instead compounded those defects to
a disastrous degree. Hence blame for the Depression was put
on meddlers with the free market rather than on the market
itself.

If such a thesis could be supported, the free market would
be restored to grace and there would be a basis for the restoration of conservative rule. Friedman and Schwartz had constructed the platform from which other conservative ideas could be
broadcast. The necessity of the platform was appreciated by
the conservative faithful, all of whom promptly adopted it and
all of whom continue to pay their respects to *monetarism*.

Money Matters

Modern monetarism is a crisp set of propositions. It begins with the fundamental conservative faith: Left to its own
devices, the free market will provide optimal solutions to the
problems of achieving full employment, deciding what to produce,
producing it at least cost, and balancing investment for the
future against consumption for the present. This is accomplished by the singly insignificant responses of selfish individuals to a system of prices that is determined by their
aggregate behavior.

As everyone understands, if an economic system is to
achieve advanced levels of diversity, specialization, and abundance, money is essential. It enables each specialized worker
or producer to be paid in a common form. It reduces a staggering complexity of relative prices (how many bushels of wheat
equal an hour of a welder's time?) to a manageable comparison
of money prices ($11.00 divided by $4.50). Money changes hands
as goods and services change hands and productive activity is
measured by the flow of money.

For some time political institutions have had the capacity
to produce or destroy what passes for money. The abuse of this
capacity is the source of most economic evil, in the monetarist
view. If the supply of money is reduced, the monetary value of
economic activity will be reduced proportionately. The reduction may take place in the volume of production, in the prices
of things, or in a combination of the two. When the quantity
of money is excessively increased there will be a proportionate
increase in the value of total economic activity. As the increased money is supplied to an economy that is already at the
perfection of free-market full employment, the total increment

in value will be through inflationary price increases, since it is not possible to induce further additions to employment and production.

If prices rise or fall as a result of monetary distur-bances, it becomes more difficult to distinguish changes in the relative prices of things from changes in the general money level of prices. This has a negative effect on efficiency and well-being. Monetarists concede that the Keynesian remedies for depression work. They believe monetary stimulus also works, and that proper monetary policy would prevent depression from occurring.

A proper policy, in the view of most monetarists, would be to keep a steady hand at the monetary throttle. A strong minority among monetarists would eliminate direct control of money as a government function. They would have the government merely enunciate and uphold a gold-for-money exchange standard and permit an otherwise unregulated, competitive, private bank-ing system to determine the supply of money.

The monetarist hypothesis is a good deal flashier than the evidence warrants. Friedman and Schwartz in 1963 had shown a general tendency for the supply of money to fluctuate in the same direction as the dollar value of economic activity and for the monetary movements to occur before the changes in output and prices. At the same time, the relationship was imprecise, the division of movements between prices and employment was un-certain, and the observable measures of these relationships changed in inexplicable ways. Friedman and his followers ar-gued that there was a cause-and-effect mechanism between changes in the money supplied and changes in prices and employ-ment. But neither they nor anyone else has been able to pro-vide a convincing description during the past eighteen years.

Nevertheless, during this time, the liberals came to admit that money did matter in our economy, that monetary policy could abet or abate depression and inflation under many circum-stances. A compromise interpretation of the Great Depression has emerged in academic circles. The initial sharp decline from 1929 to 1931 was caused by an unusual confluence of ill winds of the sort that are always breezing about in our economy. Neither unwarranted changes in money nor other types of inept government meddling were significant among them. The further collapse from 1931 to 1933 is largely attributable to the fail-ure of the Federal Reserve to perform the basic function for which it was created: preserving the integrity of banks and money.

While monetarism has made modest progress among academic economists on the strength of modestly appealing arguments and evidence, it has achieved overwhelming dominance in the realm of public policy on a record of repeated failures. Obviously, the source of its success must be elsewhere. Monetarism enables conservatives to escape the Depression bogey. The rise of monetarism is thus in part ancillary to the rise of conservatism. Indeed, recent conservative strength springs from many phenomena of a noneconomic or tangentially economic character, phenomena that have been skillfully described by Christopher Lasch in *The Culture of Narcissism*.

Three years after Friedman and Schwartz revived monetarism, economic developments began to make the thesis look better still. The economic difficulties of the past fifteen years, without exception, have readily been perceived as causes or consequences of an ever-present and widely resented inflation. Inflation is a surefire prescription for a conservative resurgence. It proves they were right, since they are always predicting it as the consequence of liberal excesses. It seems intuitively obvious that almost any schemes to ensure full employment and transfer income to the disadvantaged will contribute to inflation. Inflation also adds directly to the popularity of monetarism. It appears only tautological to assert that inflation is the consequence of a disregard for sound money. Too many dollars are being created to "chase" the finite quantity of goods we can produce. The solution, obviously, is to stop "printing" so many of those troublesome dollars. The technique that conservatives choose out of necessity becomes the technique that easily generates popular conviction.

In the English-speaking Atlantic triangle, monetarism has been a major element of economic policy in Canada for about five years, in Britain since May of 1979, and in the United States since October of 1979. Not surprisingly, the Canadians have found that their interest rates, unemployment, and inflation tend to move in concert with counterpart statistics for the United States. For the roughly three years that Canadians observed monetarist canons of good behavior and Americans did not, the Canadian dollar became perversely more abundant relative to ours, at least as measured by its rapidly falling exchange rate during this period.

Britain was next under Mrs. Thatcher. A front-page headline in a recent New York *Times* charitably described the results: BRITISH UNEMPLOYMENT INCREASES DESPITE MRS. THATCHER'S POLICIES. The same story notes that "Inflation, which stood at 8 percent when the Conservatives came to power in May, 1979, is now nearly double that--15½ percent on an annual basis in 1980."

Finally came Mr. Volcker's triumphant introduction of orthodox monetarism to the United States. In the year and a half since, interest rates have been higher and more volatile than ever before in our history. But that, after all, was an anticipated consequence of the new policy direction. The various measures of the money supply and its components, which the Federal Reserve announced it was going to control closely *instead* of interest rates, have also been considerably more volatile than they were when nobody was trying so hard to control them. From October of 1979 until now, the Federal Reserve has succeeded in making most of the money measures grow at rates approximately equal to its policy targets. Even though this accomplishment means that all the versions of money have been growing at rates below their averages for the past ten years, the rate of inflation is the second or third highest for a comparable period since 1920. And, as a diabolic bonus, our national income is down and an additional 2 million people are unemployed. The conservative doctor has powerful medicine; but workers who lose their jobs and politicians who run for re-election cannot survive the side effects long enough to enjoy the promised cure.

Money Muddles

Why doesn't monetarism work? Or, better yet, how does it work? When the Federal Reserve, or any central bank, endeavors to reduce the growth of money, it utilizes a handful of well-known standard techniques. It can sell securities it owns (U.S. government bonds and bills) for money that then "disappears" from the private economy. It can be more parsimonious about money it lends to banks, or it can charge more interest for such loans. If it wants to move more forcefully, it can alter for member banks the maximum permissible ratio of deposits to reserves. Finally, with presidential authorization, it can move precipitously by directly regulating the quantity of new loans made by banks, through which the banks create money (credit controls).

It doesn't take a Ph.D. in economics to see that the common effect of these techniques is to make it more difficult and more expensive for individuals and businesses to borrow money from banks. It is a little less obvious that this is the *only* channel through which monetary policy affects the economy. Our system of money and credit has ramified into an enormous, tenuously balanced structure. Its stability depends on our confidence in its stability. The maintenance of this confidence and stability is the primary task of the Federal Reserve. It used to be that the holders of bank notes (paper money) and bank deposits (book-keeping money) worried about whether or not they would be able, as promised, to convert these into gold (real money). That problem has now been solved by declaring that paper money *is* real money. But an identical problem remains. Can the holders of bank deposits, savings accounts, dollar deposits in London, money-market funds, and Treasury bills convert them with confidence into each other or into currency? The total of such claims on dollars in the world exceeds 3 trillion, while the total of actual U.S. paper money and coins is about 130 *billion*, or about one dollar for every twenty-five potential claims.

If the depositors at the First National Bank of Anytown decide that they want to hold dollar bills instead of bank deposits, it is the responsibility of the Federal Reserve to make the dollar bills available. It will convert into currency the deposits the First of Anytown has at the Federal Reserve. Then it will lend the Anytown bank additional currency against the collateral of loans made and securities purchased by Anytown with its depositors' money. This is precisely what was *not* done during the chaotic slide into the depths of the Great Depression. This mistake is not likely to be repeated.

Now consider an example from the other end of the economic spectrum. The great multinational corporations, such as IBM, hold huge deposits denominated in dollars in banks outside the United States. The banks may be German or British or overseas subsidiaries of American banks. The deposits may have been created by borrowing dollars abroad, by earning dollars abroad, or by converting some other currency into dollars. Collectively these deposits are referred to as "Eurodollars"--a somewhat misleading name since the deposits may reside in Hong Kong or in Nassau. The Federal Reserve does not count Eurodollars in the money supply that it is now trying to control. Suppose that IBM decides to move $10 million from Chase Manhattan in London to Chase Manhattan in New York. This appears to have been a frequent enough occurrence over the past five years, as the American economy has grown faster than the economies of many major countries, and multinationals have found more needs to use money in the United States. As far as IBM is concerned, one account has been debited and another credited by the same amount. However, as far as the Federal Reserve is concerned, a net $10 million has been added to U.S. bank deposits and therefore to the money supply. Under the rules that maintain the system's stability, a new deposit must be secured by new reserves. Only the Federal Reserve can create the assets necessary to support the new deposit. If it fails to do so, it may provoke a crisis by creating a situation in which its own rules are not satisfied, thus forcing a sudden liquidation of bank credits, a loss of confidence in banks, or both. Thus, one way or another, the Federal Reserve supplies the cash and reserves necessary to support fully whatever liquidity has been created. It doesn't matter if the claim on dollars was created years ago or yesterday, in New York or in the Bahamas. These claims are so extensively fungible that the integrity of all depends on the integrity of each.

Most students are taught that the Federal Reserve can directly expand or contract the currency and deposit reserves that it supplies to the economy and thus determine the total supply of money. This proposition is correct from a legal or an algebraic point of view; but it is a woeful guide to policy in the world today. If Mr. Volcker and his colleagues, in a fit of anti-inflation zeal, were to supply less currency and reserves than are demanded by the people and required by the banks, they would cause banks to fail. This is the cardinal sin committed by their predecessors fifty years ago. Monetarism is built on the exposure of this transgression. Hence, its fundamental fallacy is apparent. A central bank that is true to its primary responsibility cannot control the supply of money. Rather, it can only influence the demand for money by changing the level of interest rates.

This may seem like a small distinction until we return to the question of how the application of monetarist principles actually affects the economy. If the Federal Reserve attacks price inflation and a ballooning money supply with monetarist policies, the immediate effect will be to make borrowing more difficult and expensive. Obviously, the proximate effect will be to curtail the quantity of borrowing. If banks lend less money, they will create fewer new deposits for the accounts of borrowers. Thus the growth of money will be successfully curtailed.

To see the next link in the chain, we must ask what most people and businesses borrow money for. The answer is usually to buy things that cost a lot of money and last a long time: automobiles and factories, machines and television sets, college educations and airplanes, houses and inventories. If less is borrowed to finance these sorts of purchases, less will be purchased. If less is purchased, less will be produced. Unemployment will increase. For reasons that were extensively analyzed by the Keynesians and are disputed by no one, the original drop in purchases and the increase in unemployment will be multiplied into further declines in economic activity.

It is time to pause and count up the victories of orthodox
monetarism against the inflationary dragon. Thus far, monetaris
has increased interest rates while also increasing unemployment
and decreasing national income. What about inflation? Higher
interest rates will make a modest but perceptible contribution t
increasing the cost of everything from houses to asparagus, and
thus to increasing the rate of inflation. For some considerable
period of time, higher unemployment and lower production will
also increase the rate of inflation. If General Motors makes
fewer Chevrolets, it can lay off production workers and some su-
pervisors. But it will still have the same complement of executives, research-and-development personnel, and administrative
employees; the same interest on its debt; the same property
taxes to pay; the same rent; the same pensions for retired employees; and so on. Hence, many fixed costs will be spread over
fewer units, increasing the cost per unit. Also, because total
employment will not be cut back as fast as production, the number of automobiles produced for each hour worked will also decline. Both effects will increase the cost of each car. The
pressure on General Motors to increase the price of its cars
will thus be intensified, and inflation will again be exacer-
bated by the application of orthodox monetarism.

This is essentially what has happened in Britain under
Mrs. Thatcher and in the United States under Paul Volcker. Proponents of this approach can still argue that persistance will
ultimately produce rewarding results. If unemployment is increased and production reduced far enough and long enough, workers will accept lower wages in order to keep or obtain employment, while corporations might cut prices in order to keep or
expand their market share. Something like this did happen as a
result of the deep recession from 1973 to 1975, during which the
rate of inflation was finally cut in half, from about 10 percent
to about 5 percent. Implicitly, a reliance on monetarism is a
reliance on prolonged unemployment and decreased profits to beat
inflation out of the economy.

Again, the central issue is the degree to which the actual
economy satisfies the assumptions of perfect competition inherent in all conservative economics. Because the United Auto
Workers and other unions benefit from closed shops, three-year
contracts, and quasi-monopoly power; because General Motors and
other large corporations also possess some amount of monopoly
power in their markets; because the government administers or
supports the prices of everything from wheat to telephone calls,
minimum wages to fighter planes; because of all such protections
against the effects of inflation, it takes a longer, deeper,
more nearly lethal dose of economic decline to have any impact
on inflation.

*Atlantic Monthly Review, (April, 1981): 26-36

The Principles of Scientific Management
by
Frederick Winslow Taylor

REVIEW: Engineering Record (1911)*

The author of this book was among the first works managers in this country to introduce what has come to be known
as scientific management. The general system of management
is to rely on particularly competent foremen; scientific management not only does this but aims furthermore to increase
the efficiency of the workingmen by making a thorough study
of every detail of their work and of the physical and mental
exertion really required to do the tasks most efficiently.
Scientific management aims to be equally helpful to everybody
connected with the work, and the exposition of it in this
book, which is admirably written, deserves to be read by all
who wish to see the same unity of good feeling and mutual
helpfulness in great organizations which is too often considered possible only in small groups of well-educated men.
The author's views will not be accepted in every detail by
every superintendent, but they are certainly well worth careful consideration.

There has been a tendency to confuse the methods employed
in effecting efficiency in some cases with those general principles which are really the essence of scientific management,
and so Mr. Taylor devotes his first chapter to pointing out
just what such management is really intended to accomplish.
In the second chapter he shows what the general principles
referred to are. He describes what he considers the finest
type of ordinary management and points out wherein it fails
to develop the full working usefulness of the men, and then
shows how the scientific method overcomes these defects. This
is illustrated by the author's now famous achievement in getting ordinary laborers to load pig iron more comfortably at
the rate of 47 tons a day per man than they had formerly loaded
it at the rate of 12½ tons. The details of this story are
well worth reading and still more interesting is the account
of the way in which scientific management was introduced at
the shops of the Midvale Steel Company. Still another case

that contractors will be particularly interested in is the account of an investigation to determine the best methods of shoveling different materials, which resulted in reducing one kind of work from 7.2 cents to 3.3 cents per ton.

There is another feature of scientific management which is brought out forcefully in several places in this book. There seems to be an impression, not very well defined but still quite prevalent, that it is an easy matter for a specialist in such work to tell what should be done; that all he has to do is to look at the machinery, count the men, examine the product and then try to collect his fee. Now this is all wrong and one of the best things about Mr. Taylor's book is the insight given into the long study and tedious experiment which are sometimes needed to effect a satisfactory improvement of some conditions. Perhaps the best illustration of this is the account of the different steps taken to develop high speed metal cutting, a work requiring 26 years and resulting in the development of special slide-rules which enable a mechanic to apply in less than half a minute the information which it took this long period to collect and arrange in a form for ready use.

Finally the book will prove useful for the encouraging statements of the author regarding the opposition of workmen to any change in their methods which will increase their efficiency. We cannot shut our eyes to the existence of such opposition, but we can obtain a good deal of help from his account of what has been done, and of the better condition of the men as well as the employer where scientific management is tactfully introduced and maintained. As has been said before, the author has his critics among those who make a specialty of work of this nature, but no one can truthfully deny that such a book as this is helpful in every sense.

Engineering Record, Vol. 64, No. 6, (August 5, 1911)

"Frederick Winslow Taylor Revisited," J. Boddewyn (1961)*

A well-known remark of John Maynard Keynes says that "practical men, who believe themselves to be quite exempt from any intellectual influences, are usually the slaves of some defunct economist."[1] It is safe to assume that similar spirits are haunting the managers and administrators of our factories, offices and bureaus.

Since Keynes noted in the same passage that few are influenced by new theories after they are twenty-five or thirty
years of age, it would seem that the ghost of Elton Mayo must
presently reign supreme among the postwar generation of managers.

And yet, the phantom of Frederick Winslow Taylor is not
quite dead. Born more than one hundred years ago (1856), departed for more than two-score years (1915), and father of
scientific management for over three-quarters of a century
(1882), the consulting engineer from Chestnut Hill, Philadelphia has been subjected to many second thoughts--particularly
since the 1930's. Now that the heat is on Mayo *et al.*,[2]
another look at and some further thoughts about Taylor appear
indicated.

CHARGES AND COUNTERCHARGES

The value of a good part of Taylor's work is hardly questioned nowadays. His fundamental insight that control rests
on measurement was simplicity itself but, as the French say,
il fallait y penser, i.e., someone had to think it out first.
A few years back, Peter F. Drucker undertook a reappraisal of
scientific management which he credited for being all but a
systematic philosophy of workers and work:

> Altogether it may well be the most powerful as well as
> the most lasting contribution America has made to Western
> thought since the Federalist Papers. As long as indus-
> trial society endures, we shall never lose again the in-
> sight that human work can be studied systematically, can
> be analyzed, can be improved by work on its elementary
> parts.[3]

On the other hand, added Drucker, scientific management
had two big blind spots: (1) the replacement of meaningful
"jobs" by poorly integrated "motions," and (2) the separation
of planning from doing.[4]

Unfortunately, few authors have managed to share Drucker's
insight into Taylor's works. A garden variety of critics,
generally to be encountered in the introductory chapters of
books or the opening remarks of articles on human relations,
have commonly given Taylor the once-over lightly. The most
charitable thing to be said about such synopses is that they
are dutiful copies of what someone else said on the subject.
Hence, an endless echoing of statements to the effect that
Taylor:

1. Emphasized the individual worker and ignored the group.
2. Sacrificed the worker to the system.
3. Stressed the use of financial incentives to induce workers to produce more.

The purpose of this paper will be to set the record straighter on this count. Since clichés become anonymous anyway, no particular author need be refuted.

SOME OF THE FACTS

A. *Individuals*

Quoting out of context is an old trick of polemists, and Taylor was taken to task more than once for some of his pronouncements. As far as stressing the individual worker is concerned, however, there can be little doubt that Taylor did just that. Examples can be multiplied.

In dealing with workmen under [scientific management], it is an inflexible rule to talk to and deal with only one man at a time, since each workman has his own special abilities and limitations, and since we are not dealing with men in masses, but are trying to develop each individual man to his highest state of efficiency and prosperity.[5]

Throughout the early stages of organization each change made should affect one workman only, and after the single man affected has become used to the new order of things, than change one man after another from the old system to the new ...[6]

We are individualizing every man.[7]

B. *Groups*

It is common to read that Taylor ignored groups and overlooked their influence. If anything, such statements prove that their authors never bothered to read Taylor, who related in every book and testimony how he was "indoctrinated" by his co-workers at the Midvale Steel Works, and how he "soldiered" along with them.

Whatever the workingmen of this country are or are not, they are not damned fools. That is straight.... It just takes one cut [in piece rate] like this--just one--to make

them soldier for life.... I did not even have to have
it before I started soldiering. I never got my cut. I
was too keen. The$_8$boys informed me beforehand, when I
was an apprentice.

It evidently becomes for each man's interest, then, to see
that no job is done faster than it has been done in the
past. The younger and less experienced men are taught
this by their elders, and all possible persuasion and
social pressure$_9$is brought to bear upon the greedy and
selfish men....

The workmen together had carefully planned just how fast
each job should be done, and they had set a pace for each
machine throughout the shop, which was limited to about
one-third of a good day's work. Every new workman who
came into the shop was told at once by the other men exactly how much of each kind of work he has to do, and unless he obeyed these instructions he was sure before long [10]
to be driven out of the place by the men.

Such statements make one wonder about the people who
"discovered" the group's influence after reading the Bank Wir-
ing Room part of the Hawthorne Studies.

C. *The System*

Speaking of the bitter fight he waged as a gang boss
against his subordinates' soldiering, Taylor commented:

My anger and hard feeling were stirred up against the [11]
system; not against the men.

The system in case was the piecework plan. Describing
the restrictions of output which he practiced with other workers, Taylor added:

We felt justified in doing this, owing to the piecework
system--that is, owing to the necessity for soldiering [12]
under the piecework system....

Under the finest type of ordinary management where workmen give their best *initiative* and, in return, receive some
special incentive from their employers, soldiering is bound
to take place because workers fear rate cuts--whether or not,
they ever experienced one. [13] Hence, mutual suspicion and deceit. From this first-hand experience Taylor concluded that
commonly used systems were bad. Thus, when in the preface of

his main book he stated: "In the past the man has been first;[14] in the future the system must be first,"[14] he was clearly[15] thinking of a new system--scientific management.[15]

D. *Financial Incentives*

There is little doubt that Taylor considered money an essential adjunct of the new order:

> The one element which the Towne-Halsey system and task management have in common is that both recognize the all-important fact that workmen cannot be induced to work extra-hard without receiving extra pay.[16]

Throughout Taylor's Testimonies the magic words "from 33 to 100 percent higher wages" keep popping all the time--clearly reflecting his concern for financial rewards.

E. *Preliminary Conclusion*

Thus far then, it appears correct to say that Taylor:

1. Stressed the individual worker.
2. Was aware of the "small face-to-face group."
3. Visualized a new system that would replace the Old Régime.
4. Considered financial rewards essential to the success of scientific management.

So far so good. It remains, however, to study the context in which these statements were made, and to interpret them in terms of Taylor's philosophy.

MORE FACTS AND THEIR INTERPRETATION

A. *The Moral Viewpoint*

Hardly a word of blame is to be found in the Hawthorne Studies on matters such as restriction of output or falsification of records. Not so in Taylor's works where a moral viewpoint clearly underlies pronouncements on individuals, troups and systems.

This is readily apparent in Taylor's vocabulary which abounds in terms such as right and wrong, reward and punishment, virtues and defects, example and conscience, etc. The only visible slip is in the matter of swearing which Taylor practiced profusely. This habit even led one of the examiners to ask him:

> Mr. Redfield: Does not scientific management take the
> third commandment into account?
>
> Mr. Taylor: I am sorry to say that it does not take it
> into account as it ought to. I was brought
> up wrong--[17]

In general, Taylor considered that conventional management led to waste, injustice and character deterioration:

> This paper has been written:
>
> *First.* To point out, through a series of simple illustrations, the great loss [of human effort] which the country is suffering through inefficiency in almost all of our daily acts.[18]

> It is a curious fact that with the people to whom the writer has described this system, the first feeling, particularly among those more philanthropically inclined, is one of pity for the inferior workmen who lost their jobs in order to make way for the first-class men. This sympathy is entirely misplaced.... The feeling, instead of being one of pity for the inferior workmen, should be one of congratulation and rejoicing that many first-class men--who through unfortunate circumstances had never had the opportunity of proving their worth--at last were given the chance to earn high wages and become prosperous.[19]

> Unfortunately for the character of the workman, soldiering involves a deliberate attempt to mislead and deceive his employer, and thus upright and straightforward workmen are compelled to become more or less hypocritical.[20]

> The loss of ambition and initiative will be cited, which takes place in workmen when they are herded into gangs instead of being treated as separate individuals.[21]

On the other hand, under scientific management, workers "live rather better, begin to save money, become more sober and work more steadily.... This certainly forms one of the strongest reasons for advocating this type of management."[22]

The editor called the Philadelphian's last and main book "Mr. Taylor's Philosophy of Human Labor."[23] This name was quite apt since all systems ultimately rest on a vision of man and society--and Elton Mayo certainly had his. It is well known that the Protestant Ethic stressed *continuous, systematic, methodic* effort--not just plain hard work.[24] Such emphasis is reflected in the first two "new duties assumed by management" in Taylor's new system:

> *First.* [The management] develop a science for each element of a man's work, which replaces the old-rule-of-thumb method.

> *Second.* [The management] scientifically selected and then train, teach, and develop the workman, whereas in the past he chose his own work and trained himself as best he could.[25]

Another tenet of the Protestant Ethic considers salvation as a strictly personal affair between God and man. A parallel vision is found in Taylor's attempts to substitute the superior-subordinate collaboration for the relationships between workers.[26] The last two principles of scientific management emphasize this viewpoint:

> *Third.* Bringing the first-class [workman] and the science of [work] together, through the constant help and watchfulness of the management, and through paying each man a large daily bonus for working fast and doing what he is told to do.

> *Fourth.* An almost equal division of the work and responsibility between the workman and the management. All day long the management work almost side by side with the men, helping, encouraging, and smoothing the way for them, while in the past they stood at one side, gave the men but little help, and threw on to them almost the entire responsibility as to methods, implements, speed, and harmonious co-operation.[27]

Taylor's Puritan frame of reference--compounded with a touch of Quaker concern for responsible service and Unitarian rationalism[28]--thus goes a long way toward explaining his attitudes towards individuals, groups and systems. It also takes care of the first two clichés listed in the Introduction. Now to the third.

B. *The "Task-and-Bonus" Concept*

There is one part of Frederick Winslow Taylor's work which appears to be as dead as a doornail, and that is his "Differential Rate Piece Work."

This wage system provided for two rates: one low rate to be applied to all workers who did not attain standard, and a high rate for those who attained or exceeded standard--in short, a task-and-bonus plan.[29] Commonly viewed as a piece-rate plan that failed in competition with systems such as the 100% Premium or the Halsey, this plan is presently relegated to the Museum of Industrial Management--if such a place exists.

Yet, a careful reading of Taylor places the task-and-bonus plan in a completely different light.

It is well known that, in this system, the daily *task* (= standard) was set for a *first class* (= superior) worker who was expected to perform the task most of the time and to better it once in a while. In either case, the first-class worker was to receive "from 33 to 100 per cent higher wages" (= *bonus*) than the average for his trade.[30]

The reward, however, was not for *producing more*--in a spirit of "the more you produce, the more you earn"--but for *carrying out orders*. Taylor is quite vocal on this point, and his pronouncements still bear a lesson for managers burdened with wage incentive grievances:

> The mistake which is usually made in dealing with union men, lies in giving an order which affects a number of workmen at the same time and in laying stress upon the increase in the output which is demanded instead of emphasizing one by one the details which the workman is to carry out in order to attain the desired result. In the first case a clear issue is raised: say that the man must turn out fifty per cent more pieces than he has in the past, and therefore it will be assumed by most people that he must work fifty per cent harder. In this issue the union is more than likely to have the sympathy of the general public, and they can logically take it up and fight upon it. If, however, the workman is given a series of plain, simple, and reasonable orders, and is offered a premium for carrying them out, the union will have a much more difficult task in defending the man who disobeys them.[31]

> The greatest incentive to bring [the science and the trained man] together is this, that you show the man that if he does the new way in the first place he will get from 33 to 100 per cent higher wages.... Every time he carries our the new set of laws, he increases his output and his wages from 33 to 100 per cent.[32]

Answering a question regarding tasks simplified through mechanization or motion-study, Taylor clearly emphasized the *task* rather than the *piece*.

> I want to make the fact perfectly clear that there is no implied bargain under scientific management that the pay of the man shall be proportional to the number of pieces turned out. There is no bargain of that sort. There is a new type of bargain, however, and that is this: Under scientific management we propose at all times to give the workman a perfectly fair and just task, a task which we would not on our side hesitate to do ourselves, one which will never overwork a competent man. But that the moment we find a new and improved or a better way of doing the work everyone will fall into line and work at once according to the new method. It is not a question of how much work the man turned out before with another method.[33]

This view bears striking resemblance to Barnard's "zone of indifference" or Simon's "area of acceptance" within which the subordinate is willing to accept the decisions made for him by his superior, in return for "inducements."

> To an employee of a non-volunteer organization the most obvious personal incentive that the organization offers is a salary or wage. It is a peculiar and important characteristic of his relation with the organization that, in return for this inducement, he offers the organization not a specific service but his undifferentiated time and effort. He places this time and effort at the disposal of those directing the organization, to be used as they see fit.[34]

Taylor a forerunner of Barnard and Simon! This should automatically guarantee him a revival, and it permits us in all decency to exhume the task-and-bonus system from its museum showcase.

Actually, such view should have been expected from a man wedded to the idea of "the one best way" and its implication of continuous improvement in methods. Taylor knew from experience that any cut in piece rates—even because of simplified tasks—made workers resort or revert to deceit.

Now that it has been exhumed, Taylor's plan may prove to be quite fitting for the Age of Automation and the premium it puts on keeping machines in constant operation. On the basis of engineering reports or of work studies, high operating rates could be determined, with high "bonus" for attaining or bettering the "task." But not, as Taylor warned, for producing more.

CONCLUSION

This review of several of Frederick Winslow Taylor Winslow's thoughts has pointed to (1) the coherence of his "Philosophy of Human Labor" which parallels the main tenets of the Protestant Ethic, and (2) the superficiality of some of the notions held about parts of his system.

Charles Péguy, the French poet and philosopher, once observed that "*tout commence en mystique, tout se termine en politique.*" Freely translated, it means that great ideas have a way of degenerating into petty techniques. It is to Taylor's credit that he urged administrators not to mistake the mechanism of management for its essence or underlying philosophy.[35] True to Péguy's prophecy, however, scientific management has stopped far short of the lofty objectives of its father:

Science, not rule of thumb.
Harmony, not discord.
Cooperation, not individualism.
Maximum output, in place of restricted output.
The development of each man to his greatest efficiency and prosperity.[36]

Part of the failure of scientific management must be blamed on hasty misapplications against which Taylor warned. Drucker, however, has pointed to some basic defects in the system itself. Besides, Taylor's vision of man and society fitted his time and his person. Since both are gone, it is useless to try to resuscitate scientific management.

The German philosopher Hegel used the concepts of thesis, antithesis and systhesis to picture the development of conflicting philosophies that finally become reconciled on a higher plane. The time may well have come for a similar integration of the best of two worlds: scientific management and human relations. "Revisionists" such as Drucker and McGregor are already doing just that. And the "ethical viewpoint," after a lengthy eclipse, is now re-appearing in a wealth of articles.

Clearly, Frederick Winslow Taylor, our defunct managerialist twice-removed, remains good for a few great insights.

[1] John Maynard Keynes, *The General Theory of Employment, Interest and Money* (New York: Harcourt, Brace and Company, 1936), p. 383.

[2] See the section on "Human Relations in Perspective" in *Human Relations in Managements*, eds. I. L. Heckmann and S. G. Huneryager (Cincinnati: South-Western Publishing Company, 1960).

[3] Peter F. Drucker, *The Practice of Management* (New York: Harper and Brothers, 1954), p. 280.

[4] *Ibid.*, pp. 282-87. Taylor, who had his own qualms about specialization, should properly be pronounced guilty on the second count only.

[5] Frederick Winslow Taylor, *Scientific Management* (New York: Harper and Brothers, 1947). This book contains *Shop Management, The Principles of Scientific Management,* and the *Testimony Before the Special House Committee.* There is also a *Testimony Before the Senate Commission on Industrial Relations*(1914) which is included in U.S. Senate, Commission on Industrial Relations, *Industrial Relations*, 64th Cong. 1st Sess., 1916. This quotation is from *Principles*, p. 43.

[6] *Shop Management*, p. 135.

[7] *Senate Testimony*, p. 780.

[8] *Ibid.*, p. 771.

[9] *Shop Management*, p. 34.

[10] *Principles*, p. 49.

[11] *House Testimony*, p. 83.

[12] *Ibid.*, p. 79.

[13] *Principles*, pp. 23-24, 34.

[14] *Ibid.*, p. 7.

[15] Taylor preferred to call it "task management" (*Principles*, p. 120) or "systematic management" (*Principles*, pp. 6-7).

[16] *Shop Management*, p. 43.

[17] *House Testimony*, p. 219.

[18] *Principles*, p. 7.

[19] *Shop Management*, pp. 57-58.

[20] *Ibid.*, p. 35.

[21] *House Testimony*, p. 219.

[22] *Shop Management*, p. 27

[23] Preface of the Harper edition, p. 14.

[24] Max Weber, *The Protestant Ethic and the Spirit of Capitalism* (New York: Charles Scribner's Sons, 1958), p. 235 and *passim*.

[25] *Principles*, pp. 36-37. These "new duties" are commonly called the "Principles of Scientific Management." See *House Testimony*, p. 40.

[26] *Principles*, pp. 39, 115, 143.

[27] *House Testimony*, p. 77.

[28] All three denominations were present in Taylor's background. Frank Barkley Copley, *Frederick W. Taylor, Father of Scientific Management*, Vol. I (New York: Harper and Brothers, 1923), *passim*.

[29] Actually, this is the official title of Gantt's Plan which shares with Taylor's Differential (a) a large daily task, (b) high pay for success, and (c) loss in case of failure.

Shop Management, pp. 73-80.

[30]Workers paid under a wage incentive system generally earn
from 15 to 20% more per hour than they would under a time
wage system. William B. Wolf, *Wage Incentives as a Managerial Tool* (New York: Columbia University Press, 1957), p. 21.

[31]*Shop Management*, pp. 192-3. This is also quite evident in
the double wage paid to workers being time-studied, in exchange for a full effort: *Senate Testimony*, p. 778.

[32]*Senate Testimony*, p. 776.

[33]*House Testimony*, pp. 232-33.

[34]Herbert A. Simon, *Administrative Behavior* (2nd ed. rev.; New
York: The Macmillan Company, 1957), pp. 115-16, 133 ff. See
Also Chester I. Barnard, *The Functions of the Executive* (Cam-
bridge: Harvard University Press, 1938), 169.

[35]*Principles*, p. 128.

[36]*Ibid.*, p. 140.

*The Journal of the Academy of Management 4, (August 1961): 100-1

"Frederick Winslow Taylor, The Messiah of Time and Motion,"
Spencer Klaw (1979)*

Toward the end of the last century an idea took form in
the mind of a Philadelphia factory engineer that was destined
to change, in profound and troubling ways, the nature of work
in the modern world. The engineer was Frederick Winslow Taylor, a brash and eccentric young man whose most notable prior
accomplishment had been the invention of a crook-handled tennis
racquet, shaped like a giant teaspoon, with which he had taken
the measure of a number of the leading players of the day. The
idea that came to Taylor was that just as there was a science
of metals (metallurgy) and a science of machines (mechanics),
there must be a science and technology of work, whose laws could
be discovered by observation and experiment. He was soon con-
vinced--and he was to spend the rest of his life trying to con-

vince others--that only by requiring workers to submit to the
authority of those laws, and thereby to surrender all claims
to autonomy or discretion in their work, could the full potential of the industrial revolution at last be realized.

The key element in Taylor's new technology of work, to
which he later gave the name of "scientific management," was
the time-and-motion study. This was, and is, a technique for
determining how fast a job can reasonably be performed, and
for identifying, and eliminating, inefficient and time-wasting
practices. Its symbol and principal tool is the stop watch,
and its end product is an instruction sheet specifying the
exact sequence of operations to be followed in doing a given
job, and the exact time, to the second, in which each operation is to be completed. Workers, Taylor wrote, "must do what
they are told promptly and without asking questions or making
suggestions.... It is absolutely necessary for every man in
an organization to become one of a train of gear wheels."

In factories where Taylor's ideas were put into effect,
output doubled or even tripled, and profits soared. Wages
went up too, for it was a fixed principle with Taylor that
workmen meeting the new production standards were entitled to
bonuses of 30 to 60 per cent or more. Such striking demonstrations of what scientific management could do eventually
caught the public fancy, and in the last years of Taylor's
life--he died in 1915--magazines and newspapers competed in
praising him. The popular journalist Will Irwin, writing in
The Century, observed, for example, that efficiency was "a
kind of religion" for Taylor and his disciples. Their object,
he added, "is not only the increase of production, but the ultimate happiness of the world--satisfied stomachs, shod feet,
light hearts, untroubled souls." Taylor's admirers included
a number of the leading reformers of the day, among them Louis
D. Brandeis and Herbert Croly, the founder of the New Republic,
who saw scientific management as a magical device for enrich-
ing labor without impoverishing capital.

Capital and labor, however, were slower than the general
public and the reformers to embrace Taylor's ideas. For many
years, factory managers, with a few notable exceptions, refused to make the sweeping changes in the way they ran their
plants that Taylor insisted were just as important as time-
and-motion studies if the full benefits of scientific management were to be reaped. Union leaders, for their part, denounced Taylorism as a new form of the speed-up, and as a
scheme for turning men into machines.

But the principles of factory management laid down by Taylor--principles whose most spectacular application was the modern assembly line, with its meticulously planned flow of parts and materials, and its complete subordination of man to machine--were too potent to be resisted very long. Within a few years of Taylor's death, the unions largely had ceased to oppose his ideas--who could oppose efficiency?--demanding only that they be given say in determining what was to constitute a fair day's work. A new generation of managers, many of whom had been trained, like Taylor, as engineers, impatiently rooted out the wasteful practices and the permissive attitudes toward work that Taylor had deplored, and took pride in transforming their factories into huge, intricately articulated production machines. Scientific management soon took root in other countries besides the United States, notably in France, where, in 1918, Premier Georges Clemenceau ordered all factories under control of the Ministry of War to begin at once to put Taylor's ideas into operation. In the same year Lenin took note of "the refined brutality of bourgeois exploitation" that he said was a mark of scientific management, but went on to say that Russians must nevertheless "systematically try it out and adapt it to our own ends." By the 1930's Taylor's ideas were regarded by practical men everywhere as revealed truth.

Recently, to be sure, those ideas have come under increasing attack. The attackers include, for example, the Marxist writer Harry Braverman, whose influential *Labor and Monopoly Capital*, subtitled *The Degradation of Work in the Twentieth Century*, is taken up largely with a bitter critique of the Taylorian gospel. Scientific management is also out of favor with many business school professors. Some corporate executives have even become disenchanged to the point of supporting heretical experiments in the organization of work on non-Taylorian lines. In the United States and Europe, notably in Norway and Sweden, workers have been grouped into teams whose members are freed from the tyranny of time-and-motion studies and are permitted to arrange among themselves how best, for example to put together an automatic transmission.

But most factory managers and industrial engineers, in Russia and the socialist countries of Eastern Europe as well as in the noncommunist world, are inclined to look on such experiments as softheaded so-goodism. By and large, Taylor's truth is still mighty and prevails. Indeed, as Peter Drucker, a leading student of business management, has suggested, scientific management "may well be the most powerful as well as the most lasting contribution America has made to Western thought since the Federalist Papers."

Frederick Taylor was born in Germantown, on the outskirts of Philadelphia, in 1856, and very early in life displayed two closely related traits that were strongly to mark his career. According to his admiring biographer, Frank Barkley Copley, these were "a passion for improving and reforming things," and "a divine discontent with anything short of the *one best way*." "Even a game of croquet was a source of study and careful analysis with Fred," a boyhood friend recalled years later, adding that, on cross-country tramps, Taylor "was constantly experimenting with his legs" to discover the most efficient method of walking.

Taylor grew up in easy circumstances, his father having come into enough money as a young man so that he could give up the practice of law and devote himself to reading poetry and the classics, and performing good works. In his teens young Fred Taylor traveled in Europe with his family for three years, during which he briefly attended schools in Germany and France. Later he went to Exeter, where he captained the baseball team and, in his senior year, ranked first in his class. He had planned to go to Harvard and, eventually, to become a lawyer. Instead, for reasons that are obscure--Taylor himself used to speak unconvincingly of a need to rest his eyes after too much night study at Exeter--he went to work as an apprentice pattern-maker and machinist in a small Philadelphia pump factory. He stayed there four years, leading a double life as machine-shop hand by day and a proper Philadelphian by night. He belonged to the Young America Cricket Club, sang in a choral society, acted in amateur theatricals--he was particularly admired for his skill in impersonating young women-- and went to dances where he discharged his debt to Philadelphia society by choosing half (but no more) of his partners from a group of wallflowers whose names he had listed for himself in advance.

In 1878, having completed his apprenticeship, he took a job with another Philadelphia firm, the Midvale Steel Company, where he rose, over the next six years, from lathe-hand to machine-shop foreman, master mechanic, and chief works engineer. He had not been at Midvale long before he was seized with an urge to improve and reform things there. To fit himself better for the task he persuaded Stevens Institute, in Hoboken, New Jersey, to let him take its regular course in mechanical engineering on a home-study basis. Since he was working six and sometimes seven days a week at Midvale, he had to do most of his studying at night or early in the morning.

For a while he got up at 2:00 A.M., studied until 5:00, and
then napped for half an hour to freshen himself for his day
at Midvale, which began at six-thirty. But for most of the
astonishingly short time that it took him to earn his engineering degree—he got it in two and a half years—he studied
each evening from nine until midnight, and then cooled himself mentally by taking a half hour's run through the streets
of Germantown. "Sometimes," Copley writes, "he would be seen
stopping under a street lamp to consult a paper or a blank-
book; apparently even he who runs may study."

Taylor got his degree from Stevens in 1883, and it was
around this time that he began timing jobs with a stop watch.
His aim was to get a fair day's work out of the men in Midvale's machine shop, who he was convinced could easily double
or triple their daily output but chose instead to "soldier" on
the job—thereby, in Taylor's view, sinning not only against
their bosses, but against themselves and society at large.
Taylor recognized, however, that it was not easy to persuade
men to produce more when experience had taught them that, if
they did, the piece rates governing the amount of their wages
would sooner or later be cut, and they would end up doing more
work for the same pay.

The first requirement, Taylor decided, was to end the
wrangling over what constituted a fair day's work by determining how each job could be done most efficiently, and by
establishing daily output standards from which there would be
no appeal because they would be, as he saw it, completely scientific. But as he went about analyzing how the machinists
did their jobs, he was impressed by the amount of time wasted
because of improper (or improperly sharpened) tools, or because
spare parts or materials were not at hand and had to be hunted
up. He concluded that if Midvale were to get the most out of
its machinists, there would have to be changes in the way the
shop was run. Work would have to be planned, for instance,
so that the right tools and materials would be available when
and where they were needed. In short, management as well as
labor would have to learn to go about its work in a scientific
way. The problem remained of persuading the machinists to
accept the new order. His solution was to offer them a big
raise, along with assurances that since the new arrangement
was "scientific," and since it was profitable to employer as
well as to employees, there would be no reason for management
ever to alter it.

Taylor's fellow managers viewed his stop-watch experiments as symptoms of mild insanity. He was permitted to carry

them out, his biographer suggests, mainly because Midvale's owners were ready to indulge the whims of a man who had been able to get more work out of the company's machine-shop hands even without a stop watch—and who, moreover, was contributing to Midvale's profits by his talents as an inventor of new and more efficient metal-working machinery. But gradually Taylor was able to show that his work with the stop watch was paying off. "Eventually," Copley writes, "they all had to concede that in the madness of a man who gets two forgings turned where only one had been turned before, there must be a gleam of method, and that it might be a good thing for the works in general to go crazy to this extent."

Word of what Taylor had accomplished at Midvale had begun to get around by 1893, and he decided to set himself up as a new kind of consulting engineer, offering to install his management system in any plant whose owners were prepared to pay him thirty-five dollars a day and to do exactly as he told them. Among the clients who agreed to this arrangement was Bethlehem Steel, which retained Taylor at the urging of Joseph Wharton, the Philadelphia financier and philanthropist, who was one of the company's major stockholders. Taylor spent three years in Bethlehem, Pennsylvania, where he rode a bicycle to work and was known as "Speedy."

Bethlehem's huge plant was the scene of two feats of scientific management of which Taylor was particularly proud. One was his success in boosting, in some instances by 300 percent, the tonnage handled each day by the laborers whom the company employed to load pig iron onto railroad cars. He also saved Bethlehem large sums of money by introducing science into shoveling. In 1898, when Taylor went to work for Bethlehem, some five hundred men were employed by the company to shovel coal, iron ore, coke, and other materials. With a view to increasing their efficiency, Taylor set out to discover, by experiment, exactly how much a shoveler should pick up each time he stuck his shovel into a pile of iron ore or coal. It turned out that the shovelers worked most efficiently, moving the greatest amount of material in the course of a day, when each shovel-load weighed no more and no less than twenty-one and a half pounds. To make sure that a shoveler picked up exactly twenty-one and a half pounds, no matter what he happened to be shoveling, Taylor had the company lay in various sizes and shapes of shovels, ranging from a very small flat shovel for shoveling ore, to an immense scoop for lightweight rice coal. He also worked out rules for shoveling. Shovelers were shown, for instance, exactly how to use their body weight, instead of just their arm muscles, when pushing a shovel into

a pile of iron ore, and they were required to develop, and
stick to, the proper shoveling form.

At the end of three years one hundred and forty shovelers
were doing the work formerly done by five hundred. Even after
taking into account a 60 per cent pay increase for the shovelers, and a sharp rise in overhead costs--the payroll now included shoveling instructors, as well as work planners whose
jobs included seeing to it that the right shovels were on hand
at the right places--Taylor had succeeded in reducing by 50
per cent Bethlehem's cost of handling materials.

Despite such achievements, Taylor was far from popular
at Bethlehem. Some resistance to his ideas was to be expected,
since he was bent not only on shaking up comfortable old rou-
tines, but on transferring authority from old-line department
heads and foremen to a new hierarchy of production planners,
specification writers, and other technical specialists. But
Taylor made things much harder for himself by the tongue-
lashings he administered to anyone at Bethlehem who had the
gall to question his orders. A visitor to his office later
recalled the terms in which Taylor, at the time of his arrival,
was bawling out a hapless works manager. "Now look here,"
Taylor told his victim, "I don't want to hear anything more
from you. You haven't got any brains, you haven't got any
ability--you don't know anything. You owe your position to
your family pull, and you know it. Go on and work your pull
if you want to, but keep out of my way, that's all." Taylor
made little effort to hide his scorn for Bethlehem's president, Robert Linderman. Once when he was scheduled to meet
with Linderman and other company officials he allegedly showed
up half an hour late, swinging a golf club, and insisted on
talking about golf. Linderman, for his part, complained to
Taylor's patron, Joseph Wharton, that Taylor's bullheadedness
was disrupting operations. Eventually Wharton gave in. One
day in April, 1901, Taylor found a note on his desk, signed
by Linderman, which read, in full: "I beg to advise you that
your services will not be required by this Company after May
1st, 1901."

Over the years Taylor had made money in successful business deals as well as from his inventions, and he had invested
his money shrewdly. As a result, by the time he was fired by
Bethlehem he was in a position to support himself, his wife,
and three young adopted children in a more than comfortable
style even if he never earned another dollar. He therefore
decided, at the age of forty-five, to get out of the consulting business and to spend the rest of his life as an unpaid

proselytizer for scientific management, ready to offer free
counsel to anyone genuinely interested in his ideas. The task
of putting those ideas into effect, for which Taylor must now
have recognized that he was temperamentally unsuited, was to
be left to disciples who had worked with him at Bethlehem and
other companies.

This decision enabled Taylor to end the peripatetic life
he and his wife had been leading, and to move back to Philadelphia to stay. Buying an eleven-acre estate in Chestnut
Hill, to which he gave the name "Boxly" after the century-old
box hedges that were one of its most striking features, he
flung himself into the job of improving his new property.
Large sections of the hedgerows were relocated by means of a
gigantic transplanting machine of Taylor's devising, and a
hill was leveled to improve the view from the newly built
Southern Colonial mansion into which the Taylors moved in 1904.
Taylor took personal charge of the leveling, applying his customary methods not only to the twenty-odd laborers employed
on the job, but to the horses that pulled the excavating
scoops. "We found out," he used to tell visitors, "just what
a horse will endure, what percentage of the day he must haul
with such a load, how much he can pull, and how much he should
rest." The house itself contained special features designed
by Taylor. The circular conservatory, for example, was equipped with a moving platform that ran on a high circular track,
so that the man charged with caring for the flowers could
stand above them and pull himself around the room.

After settling at Boxly, Taylor had more time for golf,
which he had taken up as therapy but had come to love. He
played the game well—he once shot an impressive seventy-six
on the championship Ekwanok course in Manchester, Vermont—
but in a thoroughly unorthodox fashion, using clubs of his
own design. When teeing off he customarily employed a driver
nearly a foot longer than other people's, and started his
swing with his back turned to the ball. His boldest innovation was a two-handled putter, which he swung between his
legs, like a croquet mallet, and which he used with excellent
results until it was outlawed by the U.S. Golf Association.
Taylor was as dissatisfied with conventional putting greens
as he was with conventional putters, and at Boxly he conducted
elaborate, and ultimately successful, experiments aimed at
shortening by five years the time needed to produce a first-
class putting surface.

But Taylor permitted neither hedge-moving nor golf to
interfere seriously with his missionary work for scientific

management. In 1903 he presented to the American Society of
Mechanical Engineers a paper called *Shop Management*, later
published as a monograph, in which he set forth systematically
the ideas he had been working out for twenty years. It gradually gained him a number of converts, and elicited a stream
of letters from manufacturers, military officers, government
officials, and others eager to learn more about his theories
and their application. Many of these inquiries drew from
Taylor an invitation to visit him in Chestnut Hill. Singly
and in groups those so favored would be shown into the great
living room at Boxly, with its two huge Taylor-designed picture windows, where Taylor would lecture them for two hours.
Interruptions were frowned on, visitors being provided with
scratch-pads on which to jot down, for later asking, questions
that might occur to them along the way. Later the visitors
were sent off to tour two Philadelphia factories that had been
Taylorized under the watchful eye of the master. Taylor's
ideas also began to attract attention at universities. Dean
Edwin F. Gay of Harvard's new Graduate School of Business
Administration, who had been a visitor to Boxly, decided to
make scientific management the keystone of the first-year
curriculum, and invited Taylor to give a series of lectures
at the school. Yet despite such recognition Taylor remained
a rather obscure figure, unknown to the general public and
thought of by most manufacturers, if they had heard of him
and bothered to think of him at all, as just the sort of crank
one would expect to find lecturing at Harvard.

Then, quite suddenly, he became a national hero. The
agent of his transformation was Louis D. Brandeis. The railroads of the eastern half of the country had asked the Interstate Commerce Commission for permission to raise their freight
rates, and Brandeis had agreed to represent, without charge, a
group of shippers who were protesting the increase. It occurred to Brandeis that it might impress the ICC if he could
show that the railroad owners would not need higher rates if
they would only manage their properties more efficiently. He
had read *Shop Management*, and he now went to Boxly, where Taylor gave him the standard two-hour lecture, holding up a warning finger whenever Brandeis tried to break in with a question. "I quickly recognized," Brandeis said later, "that in
Mr. Taylor I had met a great man--great not only in mental
capacity, but in character."

After further meetings with Taylor, and talks with several
of his followers, Brandeis was convinced that he had found the
right weapon with which to batter down the railroads' defenses.
The ICC had begun hearings on the proposed increases, and in

November, 1910, Brandeis fired his first salvo. He announced
that he had witnesses who would prove that scientific management could save American railroads at least a million dollars
a day. This statement, and the testimony of the engineers
and industrialists whom Brandeis put on the stand, were promi-
nently featured in the newspapers and--the railroads' sour
demurrals notwithstanding--warmly hailed by editorial writers.
Although Taylor did not himself testify before the ICC (which
eventually ruled against the railroads), most of Brandeis'
witnesses generously acknowledged him as their guide and
teacher.

Soon pilgrims were showing up at Boxly in bands of twenty-
five or more, and the press was filled with accounts of Taylor
and his work. The Philadelphia *North American*, swelling with
local pride, printed an appreciation, headed "A Great Philadelphian." In it, Taylor was praised as "the economic...
revolutionist whose gospel may prove to be the hitherto un-
discovered means of remedying all the industrial wrongs
against which socialism is a protest." The *Outlook*, more restrained, allowed that he had organized "a new and important
force in American industrial and social life." The March,
1911, issue of *The American Magazine* carried an editorial ti-
tled "The Gospel of Efficiency," followed by a laudatory sketch
of Taylor written by the one-time muck-raker Ray Stannard
Baker. The sketch was followed by the first installment of
a book by Taylor, *The Principles of Scientific Management*,
which he had been working on for years, and which turned out
to be perhaps the most influential work on management ever
published.

Public fascination with scientific management was height-
ened by its association with a new religion of efficiency.
While Taylor himself was concerned almost exclusively with
efficiency in industry, bookstores were soon filled with books
explaining how to apply the principles of scientific management
to one's personal life. Some of these inspirational works
were written by ex-ministers, and some by established producers of success literature, like Elbert Hubbard and Orison
Swett Marden, who knew a good thing in the success line when
they saw it. Churchmen spoke of making worship more efficient. "People," one minister explained, "like to be tied up
to progressive, wide awake, and going concerns." A proposal
was made to introduce efficiency into higher education by encouraging professors to establish central banks of standardized lecture notes. Books appeared with titles like *The New
Housekeeping* and *Household Engineering: Scientific Management
in the Home*. One writer suggested setting up a chain of house-

keeping experiment stations to develop and test "principles of domestic engineering."

Meanwhile, demand was rising for the services of engineers trained by Taylor. By 1914, scientific management, while it could not be described as widespread, was being practiced to some degree in eighty industries, including naval construction, printing, and mining, and the manufacture of typewriters, locomotives, clothing, glass, shoes, soap, and textiles. To Taylor's gratification, moreover, his belief that scientific management was as good for the workers as it was for their bosses was shared by many progressives like Brandeis and the young socialist writer Walter Lippmann. In their eyes, scientific management beautifully exemplified the kind of benevolent expertise with which they hoped to bring about social harmony and material progress without overthrowing the capitalist order.

Yet for all the attention his ideas were finally receiving, Taylor's last years were not happy ones. More and more often he fell prey to the conviction that he was being martyred on the altar of ingratitude and greed. The perpetrators of his martyrdom, as he saw it, included false prophets of scientific management--"a crowd of industrial patent medicine men," as they were described by Professor Robert F. Hoxie of the University of Chicago--who promised instant salvation to manufacturers afflicted by low output and low profits.

Taylor was less hurt, however, by the corruption of his ideas, and by the eagerness with which business men were buying worthless nostrums instead of the genuine article, than he was by the hostility of organized labor. Addressing his fellow workers in 1911 on the evils of scientific management, President Samuel Gompers of the American Federation of Labor wrote sarcastically, "So there you are, wage-workers in general, mere machines.... Hence, why should you not be standardized and your motion-power brought up to the highest possible perfection in all respects, including speed? Not only your length, breadth, and thickness as a machine, but your grade of hardness, malleability, tractability . . . can be ascertained, registered, and then employed as desirable. Science would thus get the most out of you before you are sent to the junkpile."

Taylor publicly denounced Gompers as one of the country's "most blatant demagogues." But he could not so scornfully dismiss objections of intelligent workmen like A. J. Portenar, a union printer (and the author of a book about labor) who had

visited Boxly, and who thoughtfully set forth his criticism
of scientific management in a letter to Taylor that he composed directly on a linotype. In reply, Taylor noted plain-
tively that the time and money he had devoted to the cause
had been spent "entirely with the idea of getting better wages
for the workmen--of developing the workmen coming under our
system to make them all higher class men--to better educate
them--to help them live better lives, and, above all, to be
more happy and contented."

Such protestations of good intentions did not disarm
Taylor's labor critics. They not only shared Gompers' revulsion at the prospect of men being turned into robots by the
Circe's wand of Taylorism, but attacked scientific management
on other grounds as well. They scoffed at the claim that work
standards derived from stop-watch studies were scientific. In
practice, they argued, such standards reflected the time-study
man's entirely subjective estimate--or his boss's estimate--
of how hard a man should be expected to work. Time-and-motion
studies could thus be used as justification for driving workers to exhaustion, and there was little comfort to be had from
Taylor's protests that any manager who improperly speeded up
his workers was a traitor to scientific management. Skilled
workers, who made up the bulk of union members at the time,
were further alarmed by the prospect that, as jobs became
Taylorized--that is, split up among several workers, each performing a relatively simple and rigidly specified task--tra-
ditional skills would lose their market value. Taylor himself
conceded the truth of this argument. No machine-shop boss
should be satisfied, he wrote, "until almost all of the machines in the shop are run by men who are of smaller calibre
and attainments, and who are therefore cheaper than those required under the old system."

Union men also derided Taylor's assertion that the bonuses offered to workers for meeting the new goals set by their
scientific managers were scientifically determined. The only
fixed rule governing the size of such bonuses, they suggested,
was that however much a worker might benefit from scientific
management, his employer should benefit even more. This point
was neatly made by the socialist Upton Sinclair in a letter
to The American Magazine, which had carried Taylor's account
of the prodigies performed under his tutelage by Bethlehem's
pig-iron handlers. "[Taylor] tells how workingmen were load-
ing twelve and a half tons ... and he induced them to load
forty-seven tons instead," Sinclair wrote. "They had formerly
been getting $1.15; he paid them $1.85.... I shall not soon
forget the picture which he gave us of the poor old laborer

who was trying to build his pitiful little home after hours,
and who was induced to give 362 [sic] per cent more service
for 61 per cent more pay." Taylor was provoked into answering
in words that betrayed--indeed, proclaimed--the condescension,
often tinged with contempt, that underlay his attitude toward
workingmen. Citing "a long series of experiments," about which
he gave no details, he wrote that it had been established that
when men of the caliber of pig-iron loaders were given much
more than a 60 per cent bonus "many of them will work irregu-
larly and tend to become more or less shiftless, extravagant
and dissipated. Our experiments showed, in other words, that
for their own best interest it does not do for most men to get
rich too fast."

     In 1912 Taylor testified at length before a congressional
committee looking into scientific management. The investigation had been authorized after a group of molders employed at
the army's arsenal at Watertown, Massachusetts, had walked off
the job rather than submit to the "humiliating" and "un-Ameri-
can" ordeal of being timed with a stop watch. The committee
chairman, a former miners' union official, allowed union representatives to question all witnesses, and when it came Taylor's
turn to face them, he blew up. "At the close of his testimony,"
his biographer, Copley, writes, "he was deliberately baited
by his labor-leader opponents. Two of them went at him at the
same time with insults and sneers. Insofar as the plan was
to make him lose his temper, to destroy his self-control, it
was a success. With flushed face, he hurled denunciations
at his opponents and made accusations which in the nature of
things he could not prove. For a time it appeared as if blows
would be struck." Exactly what was said is unknown, since the
interchange was stricken from the record. According to Copley's account, "Taylor's friends who were there present viewed
the scene with emotions such as one might experience upon seeing a magnificent stag worried and brought low by a pack of
wolves."

     Over the next three years Taylor's friends had more and
more reason to worry about his state of mind. "While he gave
many signs of a mellowing nature," Copley writes, "there at
the same time were symptoms of increasing nervous instability.
Men who had business relations with him could not be sure in
what mood they would find him. He who all along had been an
inspiration now sometimes depressed people, giving them a sense
of fearful strain." For comfort Taylor turned repeatedly to
an uplifting essay called "The Dreamers," by a writer named
Herbert Kaufman, which read, in part, "They are the architects
of greatness.... They are the chosen few--the Blazers of the

Way--who never wear Doubt's bandage on their eyes--who starve
and chill and hurt, but hold to courage and to hope."

In one way time has vindicated Taylor. His ideas are
now taken as much for granted, by most planners and organizers
of factory and office work, as the idea of the division of
labor that so powerfully influenced the Industrial Revolution.
If Taylor had not invented scientific management, it would
have been invented by someone else. The engineering principles
that had been applied with such success to the design of industrial machines were certain to be applied, sooner or later,
to the men who operated them.

But Taylor's vision of an era in which managers and the
managed would work together in harmony and mutual respect was
not to be fulfilled. Nor could it have been fulfilled, since
Taylor, for all his obviously genuine protestations of concern for the workingman, looked at the world of work through
the eyes of the employer. As Braverman argues convincingly
in *Labor and Monopoly Capital*, Taylor did not develop a science of work, but something quite different: a science of
management that would enable employers to get the most possible work out of their employees.

It is true that factory workers, partly through the power
of the unions that Taylor so hated and mistrusted, have secured
a share of the fruits of their increased productivity. But
there have been unmistakable signs-absenteeism, carelessness,
sabotage, wildcat strikes--of a mounting conviction that the
price exacted from them for their relative prosperity has been
much too steep. The recent experiments in job enlargement,
offering workers more variety and autonomy on the job, mark
a recognition that applying Taylorism in its undiluted form
may not, after all, be the best way to maximize profits.

But such palliatives seem inadequate to restore significantly the reliance on individual knowledge and skill that
Taylor taught employers to regard as an impediment to higher
profits. That these profits were to be achieved by condemning
industrial workers to a spiritual and psychological hell was
clear to, among others, Taylor's printer correspondent, A. J.
Portenar. "It depresses me horribly," Portenar wrote after
reading Taylor's *Shop Management*. "The whole thing looms up
vaguely before me ·as an inhuman inexorable machine, gliding
smoothly on its way, but crushing not only all in its way,
but sapping the vitality of all connected with it." The years
have confirmed the validity of Portenar's fears, and exposed
the naiveté of the 1912 progressives who so warmly embraced

Taylor and Taylorism. For today it is hard to take seriously any general scheme for human betterment that does not seek to revive the pride in craftsmanship, and the sense of control over one's work, that Taylor was at such pains to do away with in the name of progress.

American Heritage 39(5), (1979): 26-39

The Practice Of Management

by

Peter F. Drucker

REVIEW: Leo Teplow (1955)*

Those management specialists whose horizon is limited to
their particular area of specialization will avoid this book,
for it deals with the broad problems of management as the "Most
Important Function in American Society," in the words of its
subtitle. But those whose interest in management is broader
than the task or assignment of the moment cannot help but
gain valuable insights and a better understanding of their
own role in their company and in society by a careful
reading of this book.

In undertaking this study of *The Practice of Management,*
Peter Drucker has made a searching review and analysis of
management as it is practiced today in order to distill the
necessary general concepts, develop the right principles,
and show the basic patterns for the management task of tomorrow.

That is a large order. Few are equipped to undertake
it. Professor Drucker is one of those few. His back-ground
includes international banking economics, economic consultation
for banks and insurance companies, and intimate probing
of corporate policies and management structures as a management consultant to various large companies. What is more
important, he is the possessor of a keen intellect, an
original turn of mind, and a healthy disregard for the
accepted truisms and shibboleths underlying the basic assumptions concerning management that many of its practitioners
hold dear.

Peter Drucker attacks standard assumptions with intellectual vigor and enthusiasm, Building on the basis of
his earlier works, *Concept of the Corporation,* and *The New
Society,* he displays a remarkable ability to accept and
develop the logical conclusions that flow from his analysis.

His iconoclasm is that of the logician rather than the sensationalist, the scientific researcher rather than the seeker of headlines.

Professor Drucker regards management as an economic organ which determines how well or ill an enterprise fulfills its essential function: economic performance, His basic assumption is that in determining the economic performance of an enterprise, the manager can improve his performance through the systematic study of principles, the acquisition of organized knowledge, and the systematic analysis of his own performance, This impact of the manager on modern society is so great "as to require of him the self-discipline and the high standards of public service of a true professional."

Within the economic realm, Drucker's view of management requires more than mere passive adaptation to changing conditions. "It is management's specific job," he says, "to make what is desirable first possible and then actual. Management is not just a creature of the economy; it is a creator as well."

Since management's job is to make a productive enterprise out of men and materials, it accomplishes its mission by managing managers, who will be effective in fulfilling the two major functions of any business enterprise: to create customers and to innovate. These, according to Drucker are the two entrepreneurial functions.

Management must know the function of the enterprise it is managing- a matter that is not so obvious of a telephone company. Is the function of the telephone company to sell telephones or to render a communication service? The answer may well determine the survival of the company as a private enterprise.

Every business, according to Drucker, should set objectives in every area where performance and results directly and vitally affect the surivival and prosperity of the business. The eight areas in which objectives of performance and results have to be set in every business are: market standing; innovation; productivity; physical and financial resources; profitability; manager performance and development, worker performance and attitude; public responsibility. The last three areas constitue the major consideration of *The Practice of Management.*

Managers, says Professor Drucker, are the basic resource

of the business enterprise, and its scarcest resource. This
resouce is also the most expensive, has the fastest rate of
depreciation, and needs the most constant replenishment.
Managers, in short, should be the top executives' most vital
concern in insuring the present and future success of the
enterprise. Drucker finds it a serious mistake for "personnel
management" to concern itself primarily with the rank-and-file
employee, while the company's major resource - its management -
is largely left out of consideration.

The manager's job should be so structured as to permit
management by objectives and self-control. This requires that
the manager's job - every manager's job - be so organized that
his department's contribution to the over-all objectives of
the business is carefully defined. He himself should be
asked to define it, and also to set forth his department's
responsibility to other departments and what assistance he
can rightfully expect from them in turn. Then he must be
given authority commensurate with his responsibility for the
outlined objectives and the tools by which to measure his
performance and prepare toward the objectivs. Once objectives
are set, management by self-control becomes possible, in
place of management by domination.

Drucker makes short shrift of the theory of delegation
of authority. In his view, the jobs of higher management
are derivatve and should be designed to help "the firing-
line manager do his job." It is the latter in whom all
responsibility and authority center (in theory).

When he turns to consideration of the chief executive's
job, Drucker goes all out in favor of a team rather than a
one-man operation: "There is only one conclusion: the
chief-exective job in every business (except perhaps the
very smallest cannot properly be organized as the job of
one man. It must be the job of a team of several men acting
together."

Nor is the board of directors beyond Drucker's analytical
scalpel. Despite the broad authority to act vested in it
by law, Drucker concludes that, except in case of emergency.
the board's function should be that of an organ of review, of
appraisal, and of appeal.

In discussing management development, Drucker steers
away from the static concept of mechanical rotation or mere
provision for replacement of managers. Development must be
self-development (just as the most effective control is

self-control), and must focus on performance and challenge to growth. The most important function of any manager is the review of the performance of his subordinate managers, and determination of the manner in which he can best contribute to their self-development.

Drucker also tilts his lance at the pervailing concept of line and staff organization. Believing as he does that a manager should be fully responsible for results in his departmant, he holds that all service functions must report to him, and that the headquarters staff should consist of a very few people who should; (1) spell out what a manager can expect from the service people he selects as has service specialists; (2) train such service specialists; and (3) engage in research in the service area. The headquarters staff should *not* provide the service, however.

Perhaps the most controversial - and the most provocative- phases of Drucker's philosophy are presented in the chapters entitled "Employing the Whole Man" and "Is Personnel Management Bankrupt?" In the first of these, Drucker insists that employee motivation and voluntary cooperation are to be obtained, not through work simplification and the theory of "a fair day's pay for a fair day's work" but rather through job enlargement and a challenge to the employee's sense of responsibility. In fact, Drucker goes so far as to demand of the employee the kind of responsibility usually reserved for managers.

In the second of these chapters, the author concludes that the major problems of managing worker and work under the new technology will be to enable the worker to do a complete and integrated job and to do responsoble planning. (Which to do this reviwer, seems a goal not possible of attainment in our time.) Personnel management may not be bankrupt, Drucker concludes but it is cerainly insolvent. However, there is hope for the future.

The use of scientific management to analyze work and its requirements is good. But once analyzed, work should be *integrated* in actual operation in such a way as to make it interesting and challenging to the individual or small group of individuals who will perform the work. What is mechanically efficient amd productive may be humanly stultifying and inefficient in end results.

The highly responsible worker Drucker visalizes can be developed by careful placement, high standards of performance, provision of information by which the worker may control himself, and opportunities for such participation as will give the worker managerial vision.

In order that the employee may identify his interests with those of the company, Drucker insists that it is essential that management commit itself to maintain jobs (without going to the extreme of the guaranteed annual wage). While some companies have done so successfully, it seems clear to this reviewer that the practicability of such a commitment depends largely on the nature of the industry. There can, of course, be no cavil with the position that concern about continuity of employment and employee income should rank high in the list of management problems requiring urgent attention.

Drucker's solution for the ambivalent position of the supervisor goes to the root of the problem. Instead of telling the manager he is a member of management, says Drucker, make him a manager. Give him wider scope, enlarge his department, provide him with specialized clerks and assistants *who report to him* (rather than dilute his responsibilities by assigning functions to staff members reporting elsewhere). Make his job big enough to warrant the kind of assistance a manager should have, large enough to make his department subject to definite objectives and tests of achievement. Then let the manager manage. Such an organization would offer a real challenge to the incumbent, and yet give him the help he needs without robbing his job of significance. And, as a desirable byproduct, the number of levels in the management hierarchy will be greatly reduced, bringing the rank and file employees closer to the top management group.

Drucker's analysis of the work of the manager results in the conclusion that because the manager deals with people, it is not enough that he know how to set objectives, to organize work, to motivate, to measure results, and to help people develop themselves; he must also have personal intergrity. "It is vision and moral responsibility that, in the last analysis, define the manager."

Finally, in the area of public responsibility, Drucker believes that modern management must succeed in harmonizing public and private interest "by making what is the common good coincide with its own self-interest." The American Revolution of the Twentieth Century, he says, was to develop a form of capitalism in which the objective of management has increasingly become so to manage the private enterprise

as to make the public good become the private good of the
enterprise.

Professor Drucker writes as brilliantly as he thinks,
interpersing his thesis with dozens of case histories which
include historical sketches of paragraphs beg to be quoted.
Here is just one. explaining profit in the modern context
of an age of automation:

Indeed. profit is a beautiful example of what today's
scientists and engineers mean when they talk of the
feed-back that underlies all systems of automatic
production: the self-regulation of a process by its
own product.

Not the least valuable part of the book is a highly
selective, concise bibliography of the literatire of modern
management.

Most managers and students of management will find in
The Practice of Management what is probably the most stimulating
and thoughtful book in the over-all management field.
It will be particularly valuable to practicing managers,
as management experience is an excellent vantage point from
which to evaluate the author's conclusions and consider
their practicability.

*The Management Review, Vol. 44, (February 1955): 131-134

REVIEW: Asa Briggs (1955)*

Managerial Manifesto

In his powerful and influential analysis of totalitarianism, *The End of Economic Man,* published in 1939, Peter
Drucker claimed that for the western democracies to exorcise
the fear of Fascism "economic progress has to be relegated
to a secondary place." His mood in 1955 is very different.
In his brand-new managerial survey, he chooses as his slogan
"Human Organisation for Peak Performance" and claims the
"management, which is the organ of society specifically
charged with making resources productive, that is, with the
responsibility for organised economic advance, therefore
reflects the basic spirit of modern age." The change in
mood does not merely reflect a switch from depression
psychosis to inflationary optimism; it records the fact that

that between 1939 and 1955 Drucker discovered America.
The result has been books like *Big Business* and *The New
Society*. His latest product is a manifesto, rather long as
manifestos go (355 pages) but a rousing call to universal
action, which makes existing text-books of business administration even more dull and archaic than vulgar political economy
before Marx.

The manifesto is designed for managers the whole world
over, including the Soviet Union: it has the practical purpose
of narrowing the gap between what they are doing now and
what the could do if only they were sufficiently enlightened.
It is particulary eloquent when Drucker is dismissing the
three sets of people for whom he has an abiding contempt.
The first are those muddle-headed businessmen who misdirect
subordinates rather than turn their businesses into growing
concerns. The second are those professional dispensers of
industrial advice who do not trouble to analyse the outmoded
premises of "personnel administration," "scientific management"
and "human relation." The third are the economists who,
with a few exceptions like Schumpeter, are either casuists
of dupes. The people Drucker really likes are those "friends
in American management" who have provided him with an ample
supply of fact and folklore concerning American business.
The manifesto smells of a factory and not of a museum. It is
doubtful, however, whether any British friend would have
been of much use to him. British business reticence does
not greatly encourage the writer of manifestos of this kind.

Nonetheless this is a book for the British market.
There is just enough of Machiavelli in it to make managers
diagnose their weaknesses and improve their efficiency.
"If the top executive in a company gets a salary several times
as large as the salaries paid to the Number Two, Three and
Four men, you can be pretty sure that the firm is badly
managed." "The most common source of mistakes in management
decisions is the emphasis on finding the right answer rather
than the right question." The Machiavellian pill is coated
with the sugar of Samuel Smiles. There are the same moral
tales, the same insistence on character and intrgrity,
the same ultimate dependence on the Bible, Aeschylus and
Shakespeare- with St. Thomas Aquinas added. The only big
difference is what Smiles talked about the road to success,
Drucker, as a true believer in the American Revolution of
the Twentieth Century, assumes success and talks most about
what to do when you have got it. "Problems of success are
always the hardest-if only because the human mind tends to
believe that everything is easy once success has been attained."

Yet neither Machiavelli for managers nor Smiles for
students of automation are the magnets which should draw
British readers to the book. The biggest magnet is Drucker
himself. He has three outstanding gifts as a writer on
business-acute perception, brilliant skill as a reporter
and unlimited self-confidence. His sharp insights into
organisation theory and decision-making within the firm
reveal exceptional intelligence and save him from unlimited
belief in the dogmas of American capitalism. His penetrating
accounts of the Ford Company, the retail enterprise of Sears,
Roebuck, and, most interesting of all, the International
Business Machines concern, are worth a library of formal
business histories. His unlimited self-confidence permits
him to judge where other men would be content to observe
and report, and he is equally shrewd in dissecting the
weakness of the "human relations" approach to industry,
of which he admits himself to be a disciple, and the failures
of the business practice of nominally successful ventures.

It is only his underlying philosophy which can be challenge
He is uninspired by the "socialist dream" and maintains
stoutly in face of critics of the profit motive that "management must, therefore find some way to get the worker to
accept profit as necessary, if not as beneficial and in his
own interest." While rejecting as primitive the slogan
"what is good for General Motors is good for the country"
he warmly commends the slogan, "what is good for the country
must be made good for Sears, Roebuck." In consequence his conclusions have only manipulative implications for European
economics: they cannot in themselves clarify some of the
most important issues on this side of the Atlantic. It
is at this strategic point-to use his own terminology- that
the managerial manifesto loses force as a basic document,
and we are left wondering whether Drucker himself is not
more interested in the right answers than the right questions.

*The New Statesman and Nation, Vol. 50, (October 29, 1955):
547-548*

"An Evaluation of the Practice of Management," Ronald Ritchie,
(1970)*

In the popular view, the role of a prophet is to prophesy,
to foretell the future. In fact, his task is less mysterious
and more important. It is to understand the men and the

society around him and to use that understanding to help
create the furture Drucker's role as analyst, interpreter,
and adviser in management practice is inseparable from his
role as prophet for his day and age.

The great prophets of history have looked through veils
of complexity and controversy to discover the true nature of
the society of their day, the directions in which it was
moving, the fundamental forces which were at work. The
fiery prophets of the Old Testament warned the children of
Israel that the supreme threat was not the yoke of foreign
oppression but a spiritual poverty of their own making.
They called for repentance, for a new purpose, and for a
new dedication. In the last century, de Tocqueville's insights
revealed the essential foundations of popular democracy
and laid bare its inherent tendencies, both desirable and
undesirable. His intended audience was his own countrymen,
who did not have the experience of popular democracy in their
bones. His actual audience has been very much wider, and his
work has influenced the development of modern democracy in its
original homes.

Drucker is more in the style and tone of Alexis de Tocqueville than of the highly charged Old Testament prophet, but
he is very much a social analyst, critic, and prophet of his
day. Hard as it is to be confident about judgements on men
and events of one's own time, it seems assured that Drucker's
major insights will stand the test of a century, as well as
they have stood the test of thirty years.

Drucker is also an expert reporter, researcher, consultant,
adviser, analyst, synthesizer, innovator, and above all,
interpreter of the practice of management. This is not a
separate, nor even a subordinate, career. Everything he
has to say about management is an integral part, a specific
elaboration, of what he has been saying about the nature
of our modern society and of the forces at work in it. His
books on social analysis have been regularly followed by
books on management: *The Future of Industrial Man* in 1942 by
Concept of the Corporation in 1946; *The New Society* in 1950 by
Practice of Management in 1954; *The Landmarks of Tomorrow*
in the late 1950s by *Managing for Results* and *The Effective
Executive* in the mid 1960s. If this pattern continues,
The Age of Discontinuity of 1969 will be followed in due
course by another direct contribution to the advancement
of thinking about management.

Each of these works focuses on or takes as its essential

framework, our evolving industrial society, the forces at
work in it, and the demands it makes. The theory and practice
of managements emerge, not as abstract, intellectual concepts,
but as revelations of both practical and intellectually
stimulating wisdom derived from a concentration on the nature
of the task, the nature of man, and the nature of group
effort in the kind of society in which we live. The management
knowledge is a part of the social knowledge. Its application
is important to the future of our society.

Shortly after *Concept of the Corporation* appeared, a
reviewer wrote: " It is to be hoped that the author's talent
will soon be devoted to more respectable topics." That
reviewer recognized the quality of what he had read but
filed to grasp the central message about the large-scale
corporation as the representative institution of our day.
It would be harder to make the same error twenty-five years
later. Drucker has had much to do with the change.

THE TASK OF MANAGEMENT

The insights Drucker has contributed to our understanding
of managment and the managment process come, to a great
extent, from his insistence on the task as the basic determinant
Results are required. They shape the role and define the
required performance of the corporation itself, its management
workers, its knowledge workers, and the best of its work
force. Neither the task itself nor the setting in which it
must be performed are the product of individual whim or
predilection. Both are socially determined. The need is
to identify the results to be achieved and to understand
their requirements will enough to make an adequate contribution.
Although he does not use the phrase, Drucker's analysis has
always to do with the "authority of the situation," with the
requirements which it imposes and the opportunities for
contribution which it offers.

Thus, he begins with the corportation as the specific
organ through which a modern society discharges its basic
economic functions. The corporation, then, is intimately,
involved in the social and economic development of a modern
society. But, like all good definitions and descriptions.
these statements exclude as well as include. Economic
activity is related to many of society's other concerns and
is influenced by many of them, but it does not encompass
them. The primary role of the corporation does not, therefore,
bring responsibility for these other social concerns,
except to the extent that society demands their performance

in the economic process. The shape, the size, and the processes
of the corporation as an organ of the economic task are
determined by the time span of modern production and business
decisions, the kind of permanence required for combining
material and human resources into a productive organization,
and the scale of aggregation required for performance.

The task of managers is, in turn, determined by the
task of corporations. Their focus must be on the requirements
of the enterprise, both internal and external. In fact,
this is true for all participants in the organization, whether
managerial, professional, clerical, or labor. For managers,
it means accepting the objective requirements of the enterprise as the guide for managing the business itself, for
managing the managers, and for managing work and workers.

Managing a business requires an understanding of the
needs of economic performance and a commitment to it. A first
step is to determine what the business really is. For this,
one looks not internally but externally, for it is the customer
who determines whether there is a business and who determines
what the business is by his perception, conscious or unconscious,
of the need it meets and the values it offers. Well before
"market orientation" and "marketing myopia" had become
common terms, Drucker was telling managers that the heart
of the business was marketing and market innovation, not the
production processes. He was describing how business leaders
such as Alfred P. Sloan, Jr., and Julius Rosenwald had created
hugely successful business organizations on just this premise.
Equally, well before any wide-spread application of a systems
approach to business and other social processes, he was
emphasizing the need to view the activities of the particular
enterprise in the relation to the total process from initial
resource to final consumption, citing the success stories of
Sears, Roebuck and American Telephone and Telegraph.

While many management theorists have been implicitly
assuming that management is concerned with known and defined
tasks, Drucker has been proclaiming that the entrepreneurial
language is central to the task of managing the business.
To adopt language from another context, the manager is engaged
in "creating futures." The manager's business today is to
make decisions which can have their results only in the future.
His business also includes sloughing off activities from the
past which either should never begun or which, successful
as they have been, have now had their day. The economic
performance task of management is not achieved by adapting
or reacting but by creating and changing. Hence, the necessity

for management of the conventional wisdom about the methods
of management since Drucker introduced it in *Practice of
Managment* in 1954.

The discipline of task orientation is central also to
what Drucker has to say about managing managers. Each
managerial job must be real, that is, it must be grounded
in the needs of the enterprise, and the authority and the
responsibility which it carries must be task focused. Where
the task is too big for one man, a team is required. This
is increasingly true of the chief executive role. Management
should be by objectives and self-control, and it should be
measured by the contribution made to the performance of the
business. The task orientation and the contribution test
determine the nature of relationship upward, horizontally,
and downward. In this perspective, the essential contribution of
the superior is to assist rather than to direct and control.

A major need of the enterprise is a continuing flow of
leaders for tomorrow, In the 1940s, Drucker was stressing
that managers develop only by being given something to manage
and that such opportunities should come early enough in their
careers and at such level in the enterprise that they can
make mistakes without too serious consequences. In the
decentralization of General Motors, he described a system
of organization which offers such opportunities on a large
enough scale to provide for the increasing requirement of
managers in modern enterprise. Consistent with the results
orientation, there is an emphasis on self-development,
concentration on building strengths, and discouragement
of long-range promotion planning or potential rating.

Management structure plays a key role both in managing
managers and in managing the enterprise. Here again, task
orientation and the objective requirements of the enterprise
are the key determinants. Periodic analysis of required
activities, decisions and relations is necessary to keep
the structure of management appropriate to the needs. The
aims must form a structure which permits, and demands, business
performance from all managers, has the least number of
managers, has the least number of management levels, and
facilitates training tomorrow's managers.

The third part of the task of management is managing
work and workers. Here, the stress is on employing the
whole man, that is, recognizing the distinctive productive
potential of the human being and so organizing the work and
the work place, that the strengths, initiative, responsibility,

and competence of each individual become a source of strength
and performance for the enterprise as a whole. This requires
organizing jobs so that each constitutes a distinct stage or
complete step, dependent for its speed and rhythm on the
performance of the individual rather than on what comes before or after, and embodying challenge or thought. What
must be sought is a sense of responsibility which can be
induced and encouraged but not bought. The worker needs the
kind of information which will allow him to measure his
contribution and his performance. He needs to share in the
managerial vision. He can do so only if he can, to come
degree, participate in planning the job or in the organization
and administration of the enterprise's community and information services. Most of what is required psychologically
is now widely known, but the hard task of converting such
knowledge has been tackled by very few.

Managing work and worker includes today managing the
knowledge worker, the professional. Knowledge has become the
central factor of production in a modern economy, and the
knowledge worker is the successor to the manual worker,
skilled or unskilled, of yesterday. The emergence of the
knowledge worker as a major element in the enterprise brings
home even more forcibly the absolute need for the organization
to focus on task and results. Only with such a focus can
the efforts of the knowledge worker to made productive,
Drucker has contributed more than most to an understanding
of the management implications of the advent of the knowledge worker. In his view, "to make knowledge work productive will be the great management task of this century,
just as to make manual work productive was the great managment
task of the last century." The knowledge worker, the professional, is not a manager, but he is responsible for
ensuring his own contribution to the task of the enterprise
and to a major degree for setting his own standards of perfor-
ance. In him, even more readily than in the nonprofessional
employee, it should be possible to approach more closely
the ultimate goal of realization of the managerial vision
for all members of the enterprise, an acceptance of significant
responsibility and decision-making power by every worker.

Decision-making is a primary activity of management,
It is, in fact, the specific exective activity. Again,
analysis in terms of the objective requirements of the
enterprise tells much about the requirements of the decision-
making responsibility and about effective approaches to it.
This kind of analysis tells which decisions can be reduced
to routine and handled at lower levels of the organization,

and which are the few that are strategic. It helps to find the right questions and reveals the need for identifying and evaluating alternative answers. It makes it clear that decisions have to do with an uncertain future, that the objective is not to minimize or even to reduce risks but to find the right risks to take in light of relevant expectations. Finally, it shows who are the right people to involve in each decision and what implementation and follow-up components must be built in to assure results.

It is of the essence of the corporation that it is a social, that is, a human organization. Society determines the task demands on the corporation and, therefore, on management. At the same time, it imposes other demands and constraints which are not inherent in the economic tasks. In our society, where the individual has a paramount place, the requirements and atmosphere of corporate life must not be in conflict with basic beliefs and promises of our society for the individual. This raises questions about the dignity of the individual in the work place and about equality of opportunity. It introduces ethical considerations into the internal organizational relationships and structures of the corporation.

Such aspects of the management task and of the performance of the corporation enter frequently into Drucker's treatment of the subject. He stresses integrity as a key attribute of the manager, as an essential underpinning for acceptable and effective human relationships within the corporation. He emphasizes the life-and-death power involved in promotion and management-development decisions and labels them as too critical to be left to a single superior. In all these areas, the immediate functional needs of the enterprise are interwined with society's expectation that the enterprise will discharge its function on ways compatible with, and reinforcing, society's views about the place and objectives of the individual.

THEORY OF CORPORATE BEHAVIOR

Management's responsibility is to the enterprise, but through the enterprise it has a functional and clearly delineated responsibility to society. Its functional role is economic and gives it no authority in other areas of social concern except that which stems directly from its economic responsibility. Even authority exercised over those members of society in the employ of the enterprise is illegitimate if it goes beyond the objective needs of the

enterprise., Managemnt and the enterprise share with other
institutions the objective of fulfilling basic social
values, especially fulfillment of the individual, but they
work toward this objective through the creation of business
opportunities rather than by the assumption of social
responsibility that restrains or lies outside their primary
functions.

Management's obligation to the enterprise calls for
continuing care that its present actions and decisions do
not create future public-opinion threats to the enterprise
or to its function. In other words, as part of its primary
function, management must be always alert to trends in public
thinking and to their significance for the ways in which
it performs its tasks.

Drucker's analysis of management philosophy and practice
has the odor of the real world about it. Unlike many others
who have written about management, it is not his practice
to construct intellectual scaffolding upon which to hang
suitably chosen or contrived examples from corporate experience.
Instead, he has studied in depth, both corporate experiences
and the forces at work in the societies in which management
performs. On this basis he arrives at conclusions and
interpretations which carry the conviction of reality de-
ciphered.

In *Concept of the Corporation,* he set out to study
corporation as the representative social institution of the
United States, not by focusing on abstract principle, but
by focusing on the analysis of one corporation, General
Motors, which could fairly be considered as respresentatioce
of the possibilities, problems, perils, and achievements
of the large corporation. Twenty years before, Alfred P.
Sloan, Jr. had worked out the marketing approaches and the
managerial organization and climate which made possible
a corporation of the size, diversity, and effectiveness of
General Motors. It was left to Drucker to put before the
world both a report on what had been done and an interpretation and analysis which suggested its generic importance.

In the early 1950s with *Practice of Management,* Drucker
sought "to narrow the gap between what can be done and what
is being done, between the leaders in management and the
average." It is, he said, " a practical book,..written
fully as much for the citizen without direct management
experience" as for men in management. The book, like others
he has written, shows the detailed knowlege of actual

business-managment situations and problems acquired in years
of working with business as a consultant. Its major principles
are based upon historically significant experiences of
Sear, Ford, IBM, and others. Their relevance is apparent,
the insights and perspectives associated with them often as
refreshingly new on rehearing as they are compellingly
persuasive.

This continued relevance of Drucker's writings is startling.
In an age of change as rapid as that of the last few decades,
it has been difficult to avoid being dated by the passage
of twenty-five years, or even of ten. The likelihood is
great in literature and in art, in science and in technology.
The past quarter of a century has certainly demagnetized
much of the earlier writing about management. The threat appears
scarely to have touched the works of Drucker. One reads
Concept of the Corporation with perhaps more appreciation of
its full meaning and pertinence today than would have been
likely for most readers twenty-five years ago.

Since that time, for instance, there have been many
arguments, political and professional, about size in business
orgainzation, but Drucker's 1946 view of the large corporation
as the prototpye organization of a modern industrial society
is even more persuasive today. The advantage of bigness,
he said, is that it enables the enterprise to have a policy
and to have a special policy-making body sufficiently far
removed from day-to-day problems to take the long view and
to take into acount the relationship between the organization
and society. Eight years later, in *Practice of Management*
he pointed out that size does not affect the nature of the
enterprise, the principles, for managing it, or the basic
problems of managing managers, work and workers. What size,
does affect is the structure of management. "A company
is as large as the management structure it requires."
The business which is too small suffers from limitation of the
size of management structure it can support. The business
which is unmanageably large is the one which has come to
require too many management layers between the managers of
the actual operating business of which it is composed and
the chief executive team. What he has to say on this score
goes to the heart of organizational theory, of the management-
structure requirements of large enterprises and of the
management hazards which encompass a variety of unrelated
businesses. It has much to contribute to the current
controversy about conglomerates.

Over the past several decades, discussion has swayed back

and forth on the merits and the requirements of decentralization, of delegation, and of staff, line, and functional relationships. Decentralization has been seen as the essential
pattern for large and geographically extensive organization;
delegation, as almost an end in itself. The appropriate dimensions of span of control have worked out with scholastic
precision. As the first waves of computers washed over
the management scene, second thoughts about decentralization
and delegation came to the fore. It was argued by some that
in the computer age decision-making must once more be centralized. Later, the decentralizers were able to bring the computer
in as an ally, establishing that it can strengthen the ability
of decentralized management to cope with decision-making.

The Drucker analysis of these questions in *Concept of the
Corporation* seems just as pertinent in 1970 as it did in 1946.
What he had to say then was based on the actual working experience and achievements of General Motors. He saw that decentralization in General Motors sought to combine the greatest
corporate unity with the greatest divisional autonomy and
responsibility, that like every true federation it aimed at
realizing unity through local self-government and vice versa.
He saw that it was not confined to the relations between divisional managers and central managers but that it extended in
theory to all managerial positions and to the relations with
General Motors' partners in business, particularly the automobile dealers. The analysis of the aims and the requirements
of decentralization as a managerial principle is as valid today
as when it was written and as it was even earlier when Sloan
devised it. Equally valid is the insight that centralization
cannot develop tomorrow's leaders. In other words, centralization works against the achievement of one management's primary responsibilities.

Practice of Management also deals extensively with federal
decentralization, building on the initial analysis and insights
of *Concept of the Corporation*. Everything which is said in
both treatments is based on demonstrated experience and is
subjected to the tests of the needs of the enterprise for
performance and of the needs of managers for developmental
opportunities. Federal decentralization requires, among other
things, management by objectives, the approach which focuses
the vision and efforts of managers directly on business performance and business results. Decentralization and management by objective between them destroy the relevance of the
whole idea of "span of control." The relevant concept in
Drucker's words becomes "span of managerial responsibility,"
the number of people whom one superior can assist, teach,
and help to reach the objectives of their own jobs. The

Sears experience is cited to show that one vice-president
may have a hundred stores under him, each an autonomous unit
responsible for marketing and for profit. Each store manager may, in turn, have thirty section managers under him.

Concept of the Corporation puts forward yet another
basic idea which has been developed and elaborated in
Drucker's subsequent works. Today, after twenty-five years,
it still represents profoundly important prophecy rather
than an accepted guideline to current managerial practice.
At that time, he stressed the need for individual dignity
and fulfillment in an industrial society to be found in and
through work. He related individual fulfillment to a sense
of importance. He pointed to the links between uncon-
structive and negative worker emphasis on seniority and
economic improvement on one hand; and, on the other, the
frustrations, lack of status, lack of equal opportunity
for promotion, and lack of understanding of the enterprise
as a whole.

Practice of Management carries the analysis much further.
The analysis starts from the basic assumption that people
want to work. It focuses on the objective needs of the
enterprise, as well as on the needs of the human beings
involved. In the process, it lays bare in reasonably
sympathetic fashion the partial irrelevancy and bankruptcy
of many of the major fashions in personnel management. It
stresses organizing the job so that it constitutes a distinct
stage or complete step and provides motivation for peak
performance, for which an essential element is a feeling
of individual responsibility. This feeling of responsibility
cannot be bought, but it is ready to spring into existence
in the right atmosphere. It accompanies emergence of the
managerial vision. The suggestions for stimulating this
managerial vision, detailed in both books, still sound like
productive approaches. Some element of the managerial
vision is needed for all members of the enterprise. It
is absolutely essential for the growing number of professional
and knowledge workers whose inherent autonomy can be enlisted
in the needs of the enterprise only if they do catch at
least some of the managerial vision. The insights which
Drucker described in 1946, in 1954, and later, are as relevant
now, and much needed as they were at the time of their
first exposition, perhaps much more. We can no longer in
our industrial society maintain even the fiction of a
hierarchical organization directed by edict from the center.

CONCLUSION

Had Drucker written nothing but *Practice of Management*, his major contribution to understanding of the management task and its inherent requirements would have been largely complete. His subsequent books, *Managing for Results* and *The Effectice Executive,* are rich in productive and stimulating insights, but they do more to show the relevance and practical application of the 1954 analysis than to enlarge it. To read them is to have one's sights lifted, one's understanding improved, one's competence enchanced. Both are "how-to-do-it" books and "why-to-do-it"books. They bear the essential trademark of all of Drucker's work in the field of management, the sense of relevancy and immediacy which they have, as much for the manager who practices the art as for the layman who simply seeks to understand an important sector of his society. That this relevancy and immediacy are as compelling today in the works he produced twenty-five years and fifteen years ago, as those he is now producing, fully justifies the assertion at the beginning of this essay that Peter Drucker is truly a prophet of his age.

The literature of management is seldom laced with references which span the course of human history and range through philosophy, religion, military science, biology, and government. Perhaps because he was a teacher of philosophy and a student of history and international finance before he ever thought of being a student of management, Drucker's work are laced with such references. There is no affectation in them, Rather, they add immensely to the meaning he seeks to convey, and in their frequency and their aptness to much to explain the quality of mind which has succeeded so well in piercing surface appearances and conventional wisdom to the real essence of process and social requirements.

In a discussion of the size of the corporation, we are reminded of the biological law that the larger an organism grows the greater is the ratio between its mass and its surface and the less exposure to the outside there is for the cells on the inside. As living organisms grow, they have, therefore, to develop special organs of breathing, circulation, and excretion. It is this law that sets a limit to the size of living organisms. Thus, we gain new dimensions of understanding of certain characteristics, particular needs, and particular dangers inherent in the very large organization.

In a discussion of decision-making, there is telling
emphasis on the need for forcing consideration of alternatives
as a key to effectiveness. The point is made by reference
to Franklin Delano Roosevelt's habit of creating dissension
and disagreement among his advisers, to President Kennedy's
reaction to the Bay of Pigs fiasco, and to the inability
of the Tsar of All the Russians in 1914 to halt the mobilization
which had been started because, as his chief of staff reported,
"Your Majesty, this is impossible; there is no plan for
calling off the mobilization once it has started."

The effect of such a wide-ranging perspective is to
bring the practice of management into the mainstream of human
experience, to emphasize the essentials upon which it
rests, and, in some measure, to give it the status and the
wider understanding which it deserves and needs.

Peter Drucker, Contributions to Business Enterprise, eds.
T. Bonaparte and J. Flaherty (1970): 82-95

"The Other Half of the Message," Tom Peters (1985)*

Clearly there was management before 1950, when Peter
Drucker's first widely read book, *Concept of the Corporation*,
began to have impact, and before 1954, when *The Practice
of Management* arrived (burst) on the scene as a landmark
treatise taking on the entire scope of managing. Great
managerial taks (particularly in the political and military
spheres, though in city building and engineering as well)
obviously had been accomplished for centuries. Superb
writers on "management" (such as Machiavelli) had taught
kings, princes, and would-be princes for ages. Yet a true
"discipline of management" really didn't exist before Drucker.

Drucker arrived exactly when we needed him. Seat-
of-the-pants, input-based, shoebox-controlled management
was pretty much adequate to pre-war tasks. But coming out
of World War II- with demand booming and enterprises reaching
epic size- we were finally ready for, and in need of, the
professionalization and systemization of management.

There is no doubt that Drucker changed the face of
industrial America. He brought us decentralization, management

by objectives, and the idea of customer-first business
strategies. All are sound, garden variety practices in 1984
(even if not always used effectively.) But all three were
truly novel when Drucker began writing about them. GM
and DuPont were models of decentralization, starting in
the 1920s, but Drucker was the first to label the phenomenon,
and he deserves a huge share of the credit for moving
some 75% or 80% of the *Fortune* 500 to radical decentralization.

Drucker brought us MBO. I dislike MBO as a technique-
as typically practiced. I do like management by objectives
as Drucker put forth in *The Practice of Management*. Peter
Drucker never capitalized in letters "m" or "b" or "o."
He was not talking about a technique, but a way of life-
focused on outcomes and results, not on inputs (the previous
obsession of management).

Surprisingly, from today's perspective, Drucker's
output-oriented notion was a *radical* one at the time.
Unfortunately, the most important part of his output-based
message, the self-control part (he usually referred to the
concept as "management by objectives and self-control"),
never really did blossom; the mbo portion became MBO and
often deteriorated into a rote bureaucratic technique.
Nonetheless, parts of "mbo" did significantly and usefully
change the face of managerial America. To fail to measure
a manager by output today would be rare. To do so when
Drucker started to write was equally rare.

Drucker also invented "customers." At first blush,
that's an absurd statement, but I contend it's not. Prior
to World War II, most business activity was factory-driven
(and, of course, this tendency was accentuated during the
war). In contrast, Drucker talked aobut the vital importance
of a coherent management pholosophy, stressing that profit
and profit maximization were not enough (in fact he
said the focusing on these two ends was downright dangerous
and misleading). The only reason for being in business,
he argued, was to create and satisfy customers. Again, that
was a radical message.

I'm not a well-versed historian of marketing literature,
but I am inclined to say that he also invented marketing.
I remember reading *Managing for Results* and learning for the
first time about segmentation, product profitabilty calculation,
and the like.

I focus on these three points-- decentralization,

management (and measurement) by objectives (and self-control), and the customer/marketing/external focus -- because: (1) Each was truly revolutionary at the time; (2) despite excesses of various sorts, each will survive for all time, I am sure; and (3) they are, in my view, Drucker's most lasting and significant contributions-- along with the overall "invention of (modern) management."

Lack of Scholarly Recognition

I racked my brain before making the following bold statement, and after substantial thought, I can only say that it is true to the best of my memory: In the course of my two years of MBA study and 18 months of in-depth Ph.D. exam reading, never once was a book by Peter Drucker assigned, and, I am quite certain, never once was Peter Drucker's name mentioned within the halls of Stanford.

I suppose the reason is obvious: Drucker's writing is not scholarly in the traditional sense. It is impressionistic, anecdotal, and borders on the dogmatic (and occasionally slides over the border). At Stanford, we went back as far as Max Weber in out systematic, historical reading. We plumbed the depths of the pioneers of sociology, psychology, economics, statistics, and operations research, and never once so much as glanced at Drucker. I don't necessarily fault graduate school training for not focusing on practitioners like Drucker, although scholars should consider that if eight out of ten practicing managers swear by Drucker (as they do in my experience), then "the Drucker phenomenon" is of unparalleled importance to students of managing. But I do fault graduate training severely for not focusing on management--and I don't think it does. Drucker made an exceptional effort to integrate purpose-setting, controlling, managing people, managing managers, and managing strategically for customers in one book - *The Practice of Management*. That is what most manager (and all senior managers) do, and it desperately needs to be studied in such a holistic sense. The characteristic reductionist approach is a sound candidate for the number one sin in business schools--and Drucker simply doesn't fit the compartmentalized approach dictated by the departmental and course structures of higher education.

Drucker Said Everything

I had considered at least a little of what Bob Waterman and I had written in *In Search of Excellence* to be new--

but I had not read *The Practice of Management* until given
the assignment to write this piece. To my amazement (perhaps
dismay is a better word), I found everything we had written-
in some corner or other- in *The Practice of Management*! We
are told ceaselessly that we "invented" the idea of business
culture (which of course we didn't): Drucker has a chapter
on the spirit of the organization. We are told that we
"invented" the notion of the "value driven organization"'
Drucker has a chapter forcefully arguing that the prime
task of top management is the development of a simple
statement of purpose derived from asking the all-too-often-
question, "What business are we in?" We surely felt that we
were making a useful step forward in talking about "ownership
of the job." Drucker's major focus, it turns out, is *not*
on MBO, but, as noted before, "management by objectives
and self-control." In other words, a prime reason for MBO
is to provide the autonomy for a person, in any job, to
fully develop. Drucker talks about employing the whole
person. He talks about the inadequacy of financial rewards
alone. He talks of the inappropriateness of profit maximization and profit orientation as a superordinate objective,
arguing instead that a focus on the customer is the only
legitimate aspiration for business.

Drucker also talks about the negative aspects of bureaucraccy,
so many of them unintentional. He argues, even in the ''50s
for fewer managerial layers. He rails against spans of
control that are invariably too narrow. He dislikes even
the word staff; he doesn't think it should exist. To Drucker,
every person (manager) in an organization should be directly
contributing to the overall results; there's no room for
side-line kibitzers. And on it goes. He said it all.

Radical Reform, Druckerian Base

Pendulums swing back and forth, and always will. In
1950, Drucker was bound and determined to wipe out the
intuitive manager (*"intuitive managers, a luxury few companies,
small or large, can afford"*..."*we cannot depend on the intuitive
manager"*..."*The intuitive manager cannot do the chief
executive's job, no matter how brilliant, how quick, how
perceptive. The job has to be planned and the work has to
be performed in accordance to plan"*). And that *was* the
right message for the shoebox era of 1950. However, those
who listened only to his attack on intuition and to his
advocacy of MBO, strategy formulation, and plan-plan-plan
were led to a new set of failures.

It has become clear to me that the managerial pendulum
has swung too far toward Druckerian rationality. A marketing
manager gave me a big bear hug the other day-and he'd never
met me before. He said he loved my chapter on "close to the
customer", after reading it, he'd immediately phoned a few
customers to ask them if they actually liked his product.
By over-listening to Drucker (and-more significantly- his
army of simplistic interpretors), we've arrived at a world
in which cold-phoning a few customers is almost unheard of.
And yet the same Drucker invented the customer-driven
organization. What irony: America's greatest failing of
the 1970s and 1980s may be our failure to really listen to
customers and provide the service and quality which are
required in newly competitive world markets. At the same
meeting at which I was accosted by the marketing manager,
I was also cornered by a hospital administrator, who said,
"But they never taught us to wander around in school."
What a sad world! Not the world Drucker intended. but the
world that has evolved. An MBA student of mine; queried by
a reporter as to the value of my course, replied: *"Tom
teaches all those* intangibles-customers. quality, service,
innovation, people--that don't show up on the P&L statement."
That's a hearty condemnation of American management in the
'80s, in my view, and nothing that Drucker would ever have
contemplated. So it goes with excessive swings of pendulums
in either direction.

Had Drucker's readers also listened to his comments about
spirit, purpose, living for the customer, self-control,
single-mindedness of focus (such a marvelous part of *The
Effective Executive)*, American management might not be in
much of the trouble it is in today. But Drucker was only
partially listened to, and the pendulum swung much too far.
For the next 20 years, we will have to swing back toward
the side of spirit and intuition and, yes, some (or many)
will overdo that, too.

Thomas Kuhn says that science, in the long run, is not
cumulative. Instead, there is a complete shift from one
paradign to the next at times of great stress, and the radically
new model seldom (he says never)builds on the old. There is
an element of that process in today's new managment revolution
(the word is carefully chosen). No doubt about it, we *are*
in the process the throwing the baby (financial controls and
strategic plans) out with the bathwater (dehumanization,
bureaucracy, mechanical responses to customers). On the
other hand, I believe there is an exceptional difference
between progress in the field of management and scientific

progress as Kuhn describes it. The true objective of the
new management is not to throw out the old (except for some
excessive middle-level staff- and Peter Drucker would agree
with that), but to build upon it. We need strategic planning.
But we also need to induce, in large doses, somewhat less
planned internal entrepreneurship. We need systematic
assessment of customers, but we also need an executive out
wandering around in customer locations, paying attention
to the intangibles of customer perception of product, service,
and quality. We need management by objectives, but we
definitely need to increase substantially the self-control
part and the availability of information for all hands
(which Drucker begs for as well, in a part of his message
that went virually unheeded until very recently). We need
senior managers to think through how they spend their time.
and we also need managers who pay attention to words like
spirit, pride, enthusiasm, and fun. And, like it or not,
a lot of this is intuitive (though the tummy can be somewhat
schooled), and it always will be. It can be learned, but
much of it has to come from the heart.

So a sea change in managing is underway. But it's a
sea change that will be built upon the solid base of Peter
Drucker's professionalization and systemization of the
management of enterprises. Enterprises, even tiny ones,
will not survive if they attempt to run themselves out of
shoeboxes. Peter Drucker we needed you desperately. You
served the nation exceptionally well. And I hope you won't
take offense at some of the upstarts who are nudging into
your turf today. What we're doing, in the main, is paying
attention to the second half of the message that you articulated
30 years ago, which perhaps, people are just becoming ready
to hear today. The most important part of your message,
I'd argue, was 30 years ahead of its time. Now people like me
are getting credit for what you (and others) said 30 years
ago. But then you got credit for some things that people
like Mary Parker Follett and Chester Barnard had said 30
years before. So it goes. When it comes to management,
I think Dr. Kuhn is more than a bit wrong. Knowledge is
cumulative. Our debt to Peter Drucker knows no limit.

New Management, Vol. 2, No. 3, (Winter 1985),: 14-17

NAME INDEX

Acton, Lord 280
Addams, Jane 31
Aeschylus 401
Alavi, Hanza 178, 179
Alchain, A.A. 79
Aldrich Vreeland Act 351
Alexander, Charles C. 292
Allen J. 201
Antionette, Marie, 259
Aristotle 214
Arrow, Kenneth J. 154, 155,
  156, 157, 158, 159, 160,
  161, 162, 163, 164, 165
Ayres, Clarence E. 88, 99,
  102

Bain, Joe S. 90, 101
Baker, John C. 231
Baker, Ray Stannard 389
Baran, Paul 171
Barker, Charles Albro 16, 17,
  22
Barker, W.S. 231, 238
Barlowe, Raleigh 22
Barnard, Chester I. 380, 420
Barralt-Brown, Michael 178,
  182
Baver, Otto 264
Baumd, William 235, 240
Beard, Charles 235, 236
Beard, Mary R. 236
Becker, Gary 90, 101
Bell, Daniel 291
Beroff, Max 23
Bemis, Edward W. 54
Bendiner, Robert 296
Berle, Adolf A. 92, 103, 205

206, 210, 214, 215, 216, 217,
218, 219, 220, 221, 224, 225,
226, 229, 230, 231, 232, 233,
234, 235, 236, 237, 238, 239,
240
Blum, F.H. 82
Bogart, E.L. 236
Branch, Mary Sydney 294
Brandelis, Louis D. 381, 388
Bravermanm Harry 382, 393
Brown, Elizabeth Read 24
Brown, Professor Harry
  Gumison 21, 22, 24
Brewer, Anthony 194
Bright, J. 201
Buch, N.S. 236
Burlehead, Jesse 135
Burns, Arthur 330, 332, 334
Butler, Nicholas Murray 22

Cagan, Phillip 347
Cain, P.J. 201, 202
Cairncross, J. 176, 177,
  180, 182
Calhorn 214
Cannan, Edwin 134
Cardozo, Judge 205
Catlin, Mr. George 6
Chamberlain, John 279, 280
  292
Chamberlain, Joseph 178, 201
Chamberlain, William Henry
  292
Chamberlin, Edward 65, 66,
  67, 68, 69, 70, 71, 72, 73,
  74, 75, 76, 77, 78, 79, 80,

Chamberlin, Edward (cont'd)
  81, 82, 83, 84, 85, 86, 87,
  88, 89, 90, 91, 92, 93, 94,
  95, 96, 97, 98, 99, 100,
  101, 102, 103, 104
Chase, Stuart 215, 292, 294,
  295
Chesterton, Mr. Gilbert 7
Clark, John Bates 46
Clark, John Maurice 88, 100
Clay, Henry 136
Clemenceau, Georges 382
Clements, R.V. 201
Cobb-Douglass Production
  Function 255
Cobden, Richard 198, 201, 202
Cole, G.D.H. 201
Cole, M. 201
Coleman, McAlister 296
Commons, John R. 92, 98, 102,
  107
Copeland, Morris A. 88, 89,
  99, 100
Copley, Frank B. 379, 383
Corey, Lewis 286, 295
Cournot 255
Cowlen Commission 254
Croley, Herbert 381
Crum, W.L. 227, 236, 237

Davenport, H.J. 58
Davenport, John 287, 290,
  292, 296, 297
Davis 158
Depew, Chauncey 59, 60
Dewey, Dr. John 31, 32, 33,
  41
ewing, A.S. 236
de Tocqueville, Alexis 463
Dillard, Dudley 193, 194
Dobb 175, 181
Dodd, E.M. 225, 236
Douglas, Paul 125, 132, 133
Douglas, McDonnell 218
Dove, Patrick 22
Dorfman, Joseph 49, 57
Drucker, Peter F. 369, 378,
  382

Durbin, E.F.M. 288, 297

Eastman, Max 279, 293
Edwards, Corwin d. 88, 99,
  235, 240
Elsinger, Chester E. 291
Ekirch Jr., Arthur A. 291,
  292
Ely, R.T. 236
Etherington, Norman 187, 194,
  195, 200

Fairchild, F.R. 236
Faulkner, H.U. 236
Fieldhouse, D.K. 181, 182
Finer, Herman 293, 295, 296
Fisher, Irving 254
Fitch, R. 237
Flamm, Irving H. 294
Florence, P. Sargant 86
Follett, Mary Parker 420
Ford, Henry 218
Frank, Jerome 224, 235, 236
Frank, Laurence R. 292, 294,
  296
Friedland, Claire 220
Friedman, Milton 89, 101,
  136, 144, 345
Frieldrich, Carl J. 293
Furniss, S. 236

Gailbraith, John Kenneth 61,
  64, 92, 103, 216, 235, 240
Gallagher 175, 177, 178
Gambs, John S. 87, 91, 98, 102
Gay, Edwin F. 388
George, Henry 44, 199
Gesell, Silvio 109, 132
Gide, Charles 19, 20, 23
Gilbert, James Burkhart 291
Gillman, Joseph 171
Gold, August 296
Goldman, Eric F. 292
Goldsmith, Raymond W. 238
Gompers, Samuel 390
Gordon, R.A. 82, 87, 227, 223,
  230, 233, 237

Gordon, R.S. 98
Gordon, Wendell 102
Gottschalk, Louis 294
Grattan C. Hartley 296
Gruenung, Ernest 215
Gruchy, Allan 91, 100, 102

Haberler, Professor 124
Hacker, Louis M. 292, 296
Hamby, Alonzo L. 296
Hamilton, David 102, 214
Hansen, Alvin H. 147, 293, 294
Harris, Seymour E. 134, 135, 295
Harrison, George L. 342, 350
Harrod, R.F. 296
Hartz, Louis 292
Hawley, Ellis W. 291
Hayek, Friedrich A. 291, 297
Hazlitt, Henry 279, 292, 297
Herberg, Will 295, 296
Herbert, Will 286
Hermans, F.A. 294
Hess, R.H. 236
Hicks, John R. 155, 158, 159
Himmelfarb, Gertrude 295
Hitler, Adolf 280
Hobson, John A. 109, 115, 171, 172, 173, 174, 175, 176, 177, 178, 180, 194, 195, 196, 197, 198, 199, 200, 201, 202
Hook, Sidney 294
Hopkins, Harry 58
Hoxie, Robert F. 390
Howe, Truing 296
Howells, William Dean 57
Hubbard, Elbert 389

Insull, Samuel 210
Irwin, Will 381

James, Dr. William 31, 32, 41
James, Louis 34
Jefferson, Thomas 16
Johnpoll, Bernard K. 291

Johnson, Alvin 23
Johnson, V. Webster 22
Johnson, President 217, 218
Jordon, David Starr 57
Josephson, Matthew 291

Kaldor 155, 158, 159
Kaufman, Herbert 392
Kazin, Alfred 291
Kemp, Alexander 175, 181, 182
Kemp, Stephen Bailey 297
Kempton, Murray 291
Kennedy, President 217
Keynes, J.M. 88, 109, 110, 111, 112, 113, 114, 115, 116, 117, 118, 119, 120, 121, 122, 123, 124, 125, 126, 127, 128, 129, 130, 131, 132, 133, 134, 135, 136, 137, 138, 139, 140, 141, 142, 143, 144, 145, 146, 147, 148, 149, 150, 151, 152, 153, 216, 380, 390
Khomeini, Ayotolla 144
King, J.E. 201
Kingsley, J. Donald 295
King, Willford I. 137
Kline, Joseph 225, 236
Koebner, Richard 175, 181, 182
Kohn, Hans 179
Kolko, Gabriel 182
Kuhn, Thomas 419
Kuznets, Simon 61, 118, 332
Kwakiutl Indians 259

Lancaster, Kelvin 90, 101
Larner, Robert J. 238, 239
Lasch, Christopher 362
Laughlin, J. Laurence 49, 50
Lawson, Alan 291
Leftwich, Richard H. 101
Lenin, V.I. 169, 170, 171, 172, 173, 174, 175, 176, 177, 178, 180, 181, 183, 184, 185, 186, 187, 188, 190, 191, 192, 193, 194, 214
Lerner, Abba P. 145, 292, 294
Lester, R.A. 81

Lewis, Ben 216, 226, 227, 236
Lincoln, Abraham 301
Lindsey, Charles 183, 184,
  185, 186, 187, 188, 189,
  190, 191, 192, 193, 194
Lippmann, Walter 390
Linderman, Robert 386
Locke, John 22, 91, 102, 280
Long, Huey 274
Lubin, Isador 58
Lutz, Harley L. 292
Luxemburg, Rosa 171, 180, 181

Machiavelli 214, 401, 402,
  414
Machlup, Fritz 81
Madison, Hamilton 211, 214
Magdoff, Harry 192, 194
Marden, Orison Swett 389
Marshall, Alfred 23, 60, 85
Marx Brothers 260
Marx, Karl 10, 43, 54, 169,
  171, 180, 183, 188, 192,
  193, 194, 210, 211, 214,
  229, 280
Mason, Edward 85, 98
Masse, Benjamin L. 296
Matthews, Brander 58
Mayer, Joseph 293
Mayo, Elton 373
McDonald, Dwight 297
Means, Gardiner 92, 102, 203,
  206, 211, 214, 215, 216,
  217, 218, 219, 220, 221,
  222, 223, 224, 225, 226,
  227, 229, 230, 231, 232,
  233, 234, 235, 236, 237,
  238, 239, 240
Mendelsohn 169, 170
Meyers, Norman L. 236
Mill, John Stuart 19, 265,
  273, 280
Mishan, E.J. 160, 161
Mitchell, Wesley Clair
  50, 59, 61, 321, 322, 323,
  324, 325, 326, 327, 328,
  329, 330, 331, 332, 333,
  334, 335, 336, 337, 338,
  339, 340, 341, 342, 343,
  344, 345, 346, 347, 348,
  349, 350
Mogigliani, Franco 134
Moses 290
Mussolini, Benito 214, 280

Nearing, Dr. Scott 32
Niebuhr, Reinhold 295
Nourse, Edwin G. 294
Norkse, Ragnar 176, 177

Ogilvie, William 22
Oliver, H.M. 82
Oppenheimer, M. 237
Orbinson 178
Orwell, George 286, 289
Orwell, Sonia 295

Paine, Thomas 22, 201, 202
Palme, Dutt 182
Palyi, Melchior 294
Pares, Richard 182
Parmalee, Rexford C. 238
Peguy, Charles 377
Pells, Richard H. 291
Perham, Margery 179
Pigou, A.C. 117, 121, 126,
  131, 133, 134, 136
Platt, D.C.M. 182
Portenar, A.J. 390, 393
Porter, B. 200
Porter, Noah 48
Porter, Sylvia 296
Post, Louis F. 19, 20, 23,
  24
Radcliffe Report 342
Rayburn, Samuel 226
Reuther, Victor G. 296
Reynolds, L.G. 82
Ricci, D.M. 201
Richmond, W.H. 201
Rideout, Walter B. 291
Ripley, William Z. 203, 224
Rist, Charles 19, 20, 23
Robertson, Dennis 117, 118,
  119, 129, 135

Robinson, E.A.G.   80, 86
Robinson, Joan   71, 72, 74,
    75, 77, 79, 86, 88, 99,
    145
Robinson, Romney   96, 107,
    175, 177, 181, 182
Rogers, J.E. Thorold   201
Roll, Eric   180, 293, 294
Röpke, Wilhelm   125, 132,
    133, 137
Roosevelt, Franklin Delano
    58, 314
Roosevelt, Theodore   178,
    226
Rosenof, Theodore   291, 296
Rosenwald, Julius   405
Ross, Irwin   296
Rubenstein, W.D.   201

Samuelson, Paul A.   20, 21,
    23, 103, 118, 148, 154,
    158, 159
Schlesinger, Arthur M., Jr.
    236, 286, 291, 296
Schumpeter, Joseph   136, 137,
    179, 255, 256, 293
Scott, Robert Haney   90, 101
Seckler, David   102
Seidler, Murray B.   291
Seligman, Ben B.   295, 296
Seligman, Edwin R.A.   23
Shannon, F.A.   236
Simon, Herbert A.   380
Sinclair, Upton   391
Slichter, Sommer   131, 137
Sloan, Alfred P., Jr.   405
Smiles, Samuel   401, 402
Smith, Adam   17, 122, 207,
    213, 214, 223, 224, 235,
    255
Smithies, Arthur   128, 135,
    137
Spence, Thomas   22
Spencer, Herbert   48
Spengler, Joseph J.   294
Skotheim, Robert Allen   292
Sraffa, Piero   92, 103
Stewart, Maxwell S.   293, 295

Stigler, George J.   79, 81,
    89, 100, 220
Stokes, Eric   193, 194, 195
Strachey, John   109, 174, 181
Strong, Benjamin   342, 350
St. Thomas Aquinas   401
Sumner, William Graham   48
Sweezy, A.R.   295
Sweezy, Paul M.   237, 253
Sznamski, Albert   192

Taussig, Frank W.   57, 231,
    238, 327
Thomas, Norman   278, 279,
    291, 292, 293, 294, 295
Thorp, William   332
Tobin, James   135
Tolstoy, Leo   14, 41
Triffin, Robert   79
Trilling, Diana   296
Trilling, Lionel   256
Trotsky, Leon   276
Tucker, Rufus S.   293
Tugwell, Rexford G.   61, 291

Veblen, Thorstein   30, 33, 34,
    35, 36, 37, 38, 39, 40, 41,
    42, 43, 44, 45, 46, 47, 48,
    49, 50, 51, 52, 53, 54, 55,
    56, 57, 58, 59, 60, 61, 62,
    63, 64, 88, 91, 97, 98, 99,
    102, 187, 189, 224
vonMises, Ludwig   278
Von Neumann-Morgenstein Theory
    of Games   154, 247
vonWeizsäcker, Carl Christian
    161

Wade, John   198, 201
Walker, E.R.   131, 137
Wallace, Henry A.   296
Walras, Leon   254
Warburton, Clark   348
Ward, Lester   57
Warren, Frank A., III   291
Warshaw, Robert   260, 261
Waterman, Bob   416
Watson, Donald S.   101

Weber, Max   379, 416
Wharton, Joseph   386
White, Morton   291
Wicksell, Kurt   255
Wilshire   195, 196, 197, 200
Wilson, Charles   180
Webster   214
Wolf, William B.   380
Wormser   225
Wouk, Herman   259
Wright, C.S.   236
Wright, David McCord   116, 253

Yarros, Victor S.   293, 294,
  295
Zarnawitz, Victor   323
Zeitlin, M.   237